Neural Smithing

Neural Smithing
Supervised Learning in Feedforward Artificial Neural Networks

Russell D. Reed and Robert J. Marks, II

A Bradford Book
The MIT Press
Cambridge, Massachusetts
London, England

This book was set in Times Roman by Windfall Software using ZzTEX.

Library of Congress Cataloging-in-Publication Data

Reed, Russell D.
 Neural smithing: supervised learning in feedforward artificial neural networks /
 Russell D. Reed and Robert J. Marks II.
   p.   cm.
 "A Bradford book."
 Includes bibliographical references and index.
  ISBN 978-0-262-18190-7(hc. : alk. paper)— 978-0-262-52701-9 (pb.)
  1. Neural networks (Computer science). I. Marks, Robert J. II. Title.
QA76.87.R44   1998
006.3′2—dc21   98-13416
                                                                      CIP

The MIT Press is pleased to keep this title available in print by manufacturing single copies, on demand, via digital printing technology.

Contents

Preface

This book considers supervised learning in a class of artificial neural networks called multilayer perceptrons (MLP). This covers just a small part of the field of neural networks, but it is a significant part worth considering in detail. Interested readers are, of course, encouraged to consult other sources for information on the broader field.

The book is oriented to the practical reader whose goal is to train neural networks for a specific task. This may include students and practitioners in many fields. The typical reader may already have some familiarity with neural networks. This is a multidisciplinary field though and readers are likely to have a variety of backgrounds so we start with basic properties of single-layer networks and build from there. A mathematical background including college calculus and basic statistics is assumed.

The book surveys MLP training algorithms and includes practical hints for obtaining networks that train in reasonable amounts of time and generalize well. It is not a high-level debate about the fundamental capabilities of neural networks or their possible role as models of human intelligence. The goal is to describe selected techniques in enough detail to allow implementation by the motivated reader. Where possible, we attempt to explain how and why methods work (or don't) and the conditions that affect their success.

Part of our intent is to suggest ideas and give pointers for further study. We attempt to summarize theory where it is available and point out the major implications without going into rigorous derivations. In most cases the reader is referred to other sources for more detailed development. A warning: Some of the ideas are rather speculative and have been criticized as ad hoc. Exploration often precedes theoretical explanation, but ideas must be tested. Where possible, we try to provide references to empirical evaluations.

Neural Smithing

1 Introduction

Artificial neural networks are nonlinear mapping systems whose structure is loosely based on principles observed in the nervous systems of humans and animals. The major parts of a real neuron include (see figure 1.1) a branching dendritic tree that contacts and collects signals from other neurons, a cell body that integrates the signals and generates a response, and a branching axon that distributes the response to other neurons. The response of each neuron is a nonlinear function of its inputs and internal state. It is thought to be largely determined by the input connection strengths. Real neurons are more complex than this, of course, but still simple in comparison to the entire brain. The interesting idea is that massive systems of simple units linked together in appropriate ways can generate many complex and interesting behaviors.

Artificial neural networks are loosely based on these ideas. In general terms, an artificial neural network consists of a large number of simple processors linked by weighted connections. By analogy, the processing units may be called neurons. Each unit receives inputs from many other nodes and generates a single scalar output that depends only on locally available information, either stored internally or arriving via the weighted connections. The output is distributed to and acts as an input to other processing nodes.

By itself, a single processing element is not very powerful; the power of the system emerges from the combination of many units in a network. A network is specialized to implement different functions by varying the connection topology and values of the connecting weights. Depending on the connections, many complex functions can be realized. In fact, it has been shown that a sufficiently large network with an appropriate structure and properly chosen weights can approximate with arbitrary accuracy any function satisfying certain broad constraints.

In many networks, the processing units have responses like (see figure 1.1b)

$$y = f\left(\sum_k w_k x_k\right) \tag{1.1}$$

where x_k are the output signals of other nodes or external system inputs, w_k are the weights of the connecting links, and $f(\cdot)$ is a simple nonlinear function. Here, the unit computes a weighted linear combination of its inputs and passes this through the nonlinearity f to produce a scalar output. In general, f is a bounded nondecreasing nonlinear function such as the *sigmoid* function (figure 1.2)

$$f(\mu) = \frac{1}{1 + e^{-\mu}}. \quad \text{(the sigmoid)}$$

The tanh and step functions are other common choices. f is sometimes called the *squashing function* because it limits very large positive or negative values. The term *perceptron*

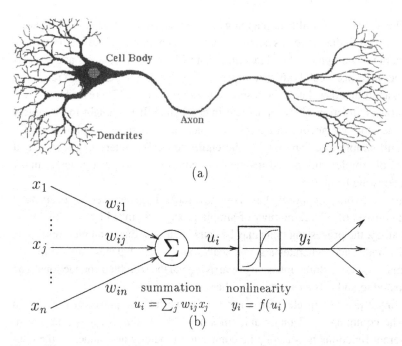

Figure 1.1
(a) A real neuron collects input signals from other neurons through a dendritic tree, integrates the information, and distributes its response to other neurons via the axon. (b) An artificial neuron model.

is commonly used to refer to any feedforward network of nodes with responses like equation 1.1.

A network can have arbitrary structure, but layered architectures are very popular. The multilayer perceptron (figure 1.3) is widely used. In this structure, units are arranged in layers and connected so that units in layer L receive inputs from the preceding layer $L - 1$ and send outputs to the following layer $L + 1$. External inputs are applied at the first layer and system outputs are taken at the last layer. Internal layers not observable from the inputs or outputs are called *hidden* layers. The simplest networks have just one active layer, the output units. (By convention, inputs are not counted as an active layer since they do no processing.) Single-layer networks are less powerful than multilayer circuits so applications are relatively limited.

The network in figure 1.3 has a *feedforward* structure, meaning there are no connection loops that would allow outputs to feed back to their inputs (perhaps indirectly) and change the output at a later time. The network implements a static mapping that depends only on its present inputs and is independent of previous system states. Although recurrent networks

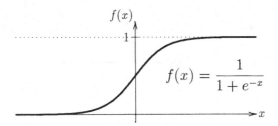

Figure 1.2
The sigmoid is a continuous, bounded, monotonic function of its input x. It saturates at 0 for large negative inputs and at 1 for large positive inputs. Near zero, it is approximately linear.

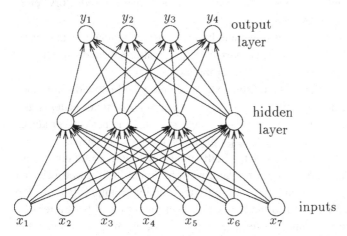

Figure 1.3
A layered feedforward network.

with feedback have a wider range of possible behaviors, analysis and training are more difficult. This book focuses on feedforward models, which form an important subclass in themselves.

The network in figure 1.3 is also *fully connected*. That is, every node in layer L receives inputs from every node in the preceding layer $L - 1$ and projects outputs to every node in the following layer $L + 1$.

This model is, of course, a drastically simplified approximation of real nervous systems. This isn't the place to dwell on its limitations; the model captures certain major characteristics which are thought to be important and undoubtedly ignores others. A few differences between multilayer perceptrons and real nervous systems are listed in table 1.1. More

Table 1.1
Artificial Neural Networks versus Real Nervous Systems.

MLP ANN	Real nervous system
feedforward	recurrent
fully-connected	mostly local connections
uniform structure	functional modules
a few node types	hundreds of neuron types
10–1000 nodes	human brain: $O(10^{11})$ neurons, $O(10^{15})$ synapses
mostly static	dynamic: spike trains, facilitation, fatigue, synchronization

details can be found in Kandel and Schwartz [206], a comprehensive introductory reference on the structure of the human nervous system.

In spite of its limitations, the model is rich enough to have useful computational properties. It can also be argued that its simplicity is a virtue because it allows theoretical analysis, which may lead to further understanding and better models.

Like real nervous systems, one of the reasons why artificial neural networks are interesting is that they "learn from examples." That is, given examples of input patterns and desired outputs, algorithms exist for changing the weights so that the network produces the correct output for each training input. Back-propagation, discussed in chapter 5, is one of the most popular methods. There are practical difficulties, of course, so training is not always successful, but in principle a network can always be found to fit a well-behaved data set. If things go well, the system learns not only the training examples but also the underlying relationship that allows it to produce the correct output (or at least a reasonable output) in response to new inputs. Useful learning may occur in spite of noisy and sometimes misleading data, incomplete patterns, and other defects in the training set.

Because it is adaptive, the system is potentially self-repairing. In physical implementations, small manufacturing defects may be tolerated because the weights can be adjusted to 'train around' defective elements. Periodic retraining might also compensate for minor damage or parameter drift due to wear and aging. This is attractive because it could lead to lower manufacturing costs.

The system also derives some fault tolerance from its redundant parallel structure. Many inputs contribute to the output of each node and many nodes interact to produce the overall output so the system is relatively insensitive to minor damage. Functions are spread over many elements rather than isolated in a single location, so loss of a few elements degrades overall performance somewhat but generally does not cause a complete breakdown. This property has been called *graceful degradation*.

Another potential benefit of the parallel structure is very fast computation. A unit's output at time t depends only on its inputs at time $t - 1$ (and maybe some stored parameters).

Units in a layer are independent so they can all be evaluated simultaneously. The layers have a serial dependency so a feedforward network with L layers would respond to a change in the input after L time steps. A network with 2000 nodes in two layers, say, could produce an output in just two time steps instead of the 2000 steps that would be required if each node were evaluated serially.

At the present time, most networks are simulated on serial computers so not all of the potential advantages are realized. Even so, artificial neural networks are still very useful because of their functional mapping properties and the ability to learn from examples. Multilayer networks have been shown to have a certain "universal approximation" property. As noted, a sufficiently large network with the appropriate structure can, theoretically, approximate almost any desired function. Networks have been compared with many other functional approximation systems and found competitive in terms of accuracy. (Learning speed is sometimes a problem, however.) This and the ability to learn from examples allow modeling of complex systems whose behavioral rules are not known in detail or are difficult to analyze correctly. This includes the common case where a good theoretical model exists but depends on physical parameters that are difficult or expensive to measure. Networks offer the possibility of modeling the actual system behavior based on its observed input-output response instead of using a simplified and necessarily imperfect parametric model. By learning from real data, an adaptive system may be able to include nonlinear effects (e.g., friction and backlash in mechanical systems) that might be ignored in simplified theoretical models.

This book focuses on practical aspects of designing and training feedforward multilayer networks. It should be noted, however, that aside from possible technological applications, artificial neural networks are important as simplified models of real nervous systems and have been used to test theories about brain function, cognition, and learning. Indeed, much of the original work has been done, and continues, in fields such as psychology, neuroscience, and cognitive science. Even among many of those interested only in technological applications, the biological connection is part of the model's appeal since there is undoubtedly more that can be learned which may lead to more powerful models and better applications.

The preceding lists some of the promise of artificial neural networks. Unfortunately, difficulties do arise and learning is not always successful. This book focuses on practical aspects of multilayered perceptron networks—how to develop and use them in practical applications.

Chapter 2 describes the general idea of supervised learning, the process of training a system to perform a desired function. Chapter 3 describes the simplest possible systems, single-layer networks, and properties that result from this structure. Chapter 4 considers multilayered networks and additional properties that result from the layered structure.

Chapter 5 introduces the back-propagation algorithm, the most popular method for training layered networks. The next several chapters consider how training parameters affect learning and describe some variations of the basic algorithm. Chapter 6 discusses effects of the learning rate and momentum parameters on learning time. Chapter 7 considers various methods for initializing the network structure and weights prior to training. Chapter 8 describes some properties of the error surface and how they affect the training process. Chapter 9 describes some variations of the basic back-propagation algorithm. Chapter 10 describes classical optimization methods that may perform better than back-propagation in some cases. Chapter 11 describes the genetic algorithm.

Chapters 12 and 13 consider methods for adapting the structure of the network to the problem. Chapter 12 considers constructive training methods, which start with a small network and add elements as required. Chapter 13 considers pruning methods, which take the opposite strategy and start with a large network and then remove elements as needed.

Learning from examples is a sampling process. Once a network learns the training data, it is reasonable to ask how well it generalizes to patterns outside the training set. Chapter 14 discusses factors influencing generalization. Chapter 15 continues by examining some theoretical methods for assessing and predicting generalization performance. Chapter 16 describes a number of heuristics for obtaining better generalization. Chapter 17 focuses on one particular heuristic and considers the effects of training with noisy input data.

2 Supervised Learning

In machine learning, *supervised learning* has come to mean the process of adjusting a system so it produces specified outputs in response to specified inputs. It is often posed as a function approximation problem (figure 2.1). Given training data consisting of pairs of input patterns, $\mathbf{x}$, and corresponding desired outputs or *targets*, t, the goal is to find a function $y(\mathbf{x})$ that matches the desired response for each training input. The functional relationship between the input patterns and target outputs is usually unknown (otherwise different methods would be used) so the idea is to start with a system flexible enough to implement many functions and adjust it to fit the given data.

"Training" refers to the adaptation process by which the system "learns" the relationship between the inputs and targets. This is often a repetitive incremental process guided by an optimization algorithm (figure 2.2). The process is "supervised" in the sense that an external "teacher" must specify the correct output for each and every input pattern. In some cases, the teacher is a person who specifies the correct class for each pattern. In other cases, it may be a physical system whose behavior we want to model.

In this book, the learning system is an artificial neural network. During training, each input pattern is presented and propagated through the network to produce an output. Unless the network is perfectly trained, there will be differences between the actual and desired outputs. The real-world significance of these deviations depend on the application and is measured by an *objective function* whose output rates the quality of the network's response. (The terms "cost function" and "error function" are also used.) The overall goal is then to find a system that minimizes the total error for the given training data.

When defined in this way, training becomes a statistical optimization problem and there are a number of interacting factors to be considered:

- Variable selection and representation. What information should be presented to the network and in what form?

- Selection and preparation of training data.

- Model selection. What structure should the network have?

- Choice of error function. How is network performance graded?

- Choice of optimization method. The network output is a function of its parameters (weights). How should parameters be adjusted to minimize the error?

- Prior knowledge and heuristics. If we know useful rules or heuristics (which may not be learnable from available data) can we somehow insert them into the system? Can we make the system favor particular sorts of solutions?

- Generalization. How well does the network *really* work? Did it learn what we intended or did it simply memorize the training set or find a set of tricks that work on this data but not on others?

These issues are discussed at length in following chapters.

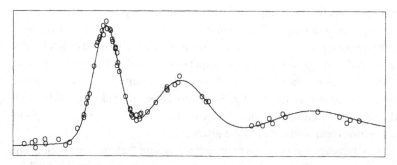

Figure 2.1
Supervised learning is often viewed as function approximation problem. Given a set $\{(\mathbf{x}_i, t_i)\}$, $i = 1 \ldots M$, of training pairs with inputs $\mathbf{x}_i$ and target outputs t_i, the goal is to find a function $f(\mathbf{x})$ that captures the input-output relationships illustrated in the training examples, $f(\mathbf{x}_i) \approx t_i$. If the search is successful, the new function can then be used to estimate the correct output for new points not in the original training set. Ideally, the functional form may also be more compact and faster to evaluate.

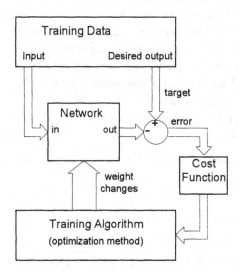

Figure 2.2
Supervised learning model. In supervised learning, a desired output is specified for every pattern encountered during training. Differences between the network output and training target are treated as errors to be minimized by the training algorithm.

2.1   Objective Functions

As noted, the role of the objective function is to measure how well the network performs the intended task. The function defines the difference between good or bad performance and thus guides the search for a solution. It has a fundamental effect on the outcome so it is important to choose a function that accurately reflects our design goals.

A few standard error functions are commonly used. The most common is the sum of squared errors (SSE),

$$E_{SSE} = \sum_p \sum_i (t_{pi} - y_{pi})^2 \tag{2.1}$$

where p indexes the patterns in the training set, i indexes the output nodes, and t_{pi} and y_{pi} are, respectively, the target and actual network output for the ith output node on the pth pattern. This is the sum of the squared errors on each training pattern. The mean-squared-error (MSE)

$$E_{MSE} = \frac{1}{PN} E_{SSE} \tag{2.2}$$

normalizes E_{SSE} for the number of training patterns P and the number of network outputs N. The logarithmic or cross-entropy error function

$$E_{log} = \sum_p \sum_i t_{pi} \ln y_{pi} + (1 - t_{pi}) \ln(1 - y_{pi}) \tag{2.3}$$

is often used for classification problems where the network output is interpreted as the probability that the input pattern belongs to a certain class. Here y_{pi} is the estimated probability that pattern p belongs to class i and $t_{pi} \in \{0, 1\}$ is the target. Other functions have been developed for various applications.

Each of these functions carries assumptions including, among others, assumptions about the distribution of fitting errors that arise given the model and the data. In a statistical setting the mean squared error function, for example, corresponds to a maximum likelihood model with the assumption that errors have a Gaussian distribution (see section 15.2). The logarithmic error function corresponds to a classification model and the assumption of a binomial error distribution. Reasonable performance can be expected if these assumptions match reality but poor performance may result if the assumptions are not met. More details can be found in [328], as well as numerous statistics texts.

These standard functions are convenient to use and are well-understood. Advantages include easy differentiability and independence. (All numerical deviations of equal magni-

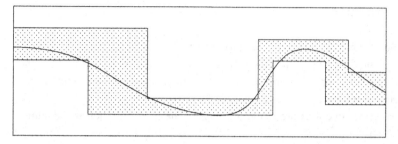

Figure 2.3
Supervised learning can be applied to many different error functions. The figure illustrates a piecewise linear error function with upper and lower tolerance limits; the error is zero when $f(x)$ is within the limits. Functions like this are sometimes useful in engineering applications.

tude have equal costs which do not depend on the input pattern, the sizes of other errors, the trend of previous errors, and so on.) These properties simplify analysis considerably and allow valuable theoretical study that would not be possible otherwise. In spite of this, more idiosyncratic functions may be useful in applications where errors of similar numerical magnitude may have quite different costs depending on the input pattern and other factors. These considerations are completely application dependent, however, so the standard error functions are used for most discussions.

Figure 2.3 illustrates an error function that falls a bit outside the range of standard models but is still included in the supervised learning model. In this case, the target function has piecewise constant upper and lower tolerance limits; the error is zero when $y(x)$ is within the limits and increases quadratically otherwise. Functions like this are sometimes useful in engineering applications. An application-specific error evaluation function is required and the mathematical analysis is not as clean, but the training procedure is basically the same otherwise.

Penalty Terms   In addition to the primary terms that measure fitting errors, the cost function is often augmented with terms reflecting goals or preferences, which are not directly measurable in terms of differences between outputs and targets on a set of patterns. "Penalty terms" may be added to steer the solution in preferred directions or enforce constraints. Some common biases include:

• a preference for simple solutions over complex ones (Occam's razor),

• a preference for smooth continuous solutions over wildly varying or discontinuous solutions, and

• beliefs about the relative probabilities of various solutions (corresponding to prior probabilities in Bayesian methods).

Many of the heuristics discussed later can be viewed as modifications of the basic error function which introduce these types of biases. These hints can be especially useful when training data is limited.

2.2 Alternatives and Extensions

An advantage of the supervised learning model is that it is well-defined. It is detailed enough to be useful but simple enough to be analyzed. Details of specific applications are abstracted away. The model has been criticized as an artificial and limited model of learning, however, amounting to nothing more than nonlinear regression—a way to fit a function to a set of data points. Indeed, in many practical applications neural networks are used mainly for function approximation and nothing more is asked. Perhaps the major limitation is the requirement for a teacher to specify in detail the correct output for each and every input. This is not how people learn to walk, for example.

Obviously, there is much more to learning than function approximation so researchers interested in more realistic learning systems must consider additional factors. The model can be extended in many ways, however, and simplified abstract models like this are likely to be useful as core components in a larger system. Some proposals, for example, surround a supervised learning module with key subsystems designed to translate available information into the detailed signals required by the simplified model. Extensions such as this are fascinating, but beyond the scope of this book. Other abstract models at similar levels of complexity include unsupervised learning and reinforcement learning.

Unsupervised Learning   A requirement for supervised learning is presence of a teacher to specify the target output for every input. In unsupervised learning, there is no teacher. The training data is unlabeled and there are no targets. Instead, the system adapts to regularities in the data according to rules implicit in its design. The nature of the regularities found by the system depend on details of its design so the teacher is, in a sense, built into the system. Unsupervised learning is useful because unlabeled data is often more readily available than labeled data.

Some systems extract a set of prototype patterns from the training set; given an input, the most similar prototype is recalled. Parameters of the system determine how similarity is defined. In statistics, unsupervised learning often refers to clustering algorithms or probability density approximation. The k-means algorithm and vector quantization are examples.

Unsupervised learning modules are sometimes used as a component of a supervised learning system. To be useful, the unsupervised model must partition the data in a way that preserves the information needed for supervised learning.

Autoassociative networks are on the borderline between supervised and unsupervised learning. Given an input, the network is trained to reproduce the identical pattern at the output. The network acts as autoencoder, mapping an input pattern to itself. This may seem pointless but if the system is constrained by a bottleneck in a small middle layer, the network is forced to find an efficient internal representation of the pattern that preserves as much information as possible. Ideally, it will strip away nonessentials and reproduce only the significant features of the pattern, perhaps making it more useful for other purposes. Alternatively, the output of the bottleneck layer may be useful in itself as a compressed representation of the input pattern. This is related to principal components analysis (see appendix section B.1).

Reinforcement Learning   Reinforcement learning (e.g., [25, 364, 24]) is a more realistic model of low-level learning in humans and animals. Reinforcement learning resembles supervised learning in that there is a defined goal, but the objective is defined more abstractly. Instead of a teacher providing detailed targets for each and every output, the only feedback is a sparse reinforcement signal which grades the system response as "good" or "bad" without providing further details. The reinforcement may be sparse in time as well as space. Game playing is a commonly mentioned example: the outcome of a game of chess is a single win-lose signal rather than a detailed list of which moves should have been made at each step in the game. In general, the system produces outputs that act on an external environment and affect the reinforcement eventually received. The training objective is to maximize the amount of positive reinforcement received over time.

In many reinforcement learning models, the key element is a subsystem which learns to predict the future reinforcement expected given the current network inputs and outputs. If this prediction can be learned accurately, then target signals for supervised training of the action selection module can be derived from changes in the predicted reinforcement.

Supervised Learning with a Distal Teacher   As noted, the supervised learning model has been criticized because it puts a heavy burden on the teacher to specify detailed, low-level, target signals for every possible input. The model is not completely unrealistic, however, because there may be higher level targets available from which the low level targets needed for network training can be derived. Supervised learning with a distal teacher [200, 201, 199] is intermediate between regular supervised learning and reinforcement learning (figure 2.4). The system output targets are more informative than in reinforce-

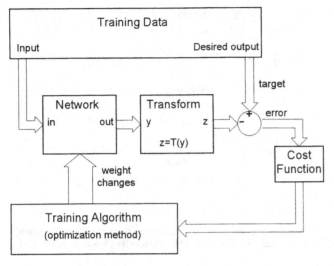

Figure 2.4
In supervised learning with a distal teacher the network output drives another system, T, which produces the final output. This makes the teacher's job easier because targets can be specified at a higher, less detailed, level. When T is a known function, the low-level signals needed for network training can be derived from the high-level errors.

ment learning, but less informative than in regular supervised learning. As in reinforcement learning, the network outputs act as inputs to another system, T, which transforms the network outputs into the final output. When T is well-defined or can be accurately modeled, errors in the overall system-output can be translated backwards to the low level network-output error signals needed for network training. When the overall targets can be specified simply, the teacher's job is simpler.

Using the task of throwing a ball as an analogy, the network outputs are the numerous coordinated muscular actions needed to toss the ball and T is the physics that transform these actions into a result. If the overall goal is to land a basketball in a hoop, the sight of it bouncing off the rim may be a high-level error signal. No coach can tell you exactly when and how to move each individual muscle, but they can provide high-level suggestions in terms you already know how to implement, for example, "put more spin on it." Knowledge of the situation then allows you to translate the high-level suggestion back to individual low-level actions.

Simulation results for a simple robot arm controller are described in [200, 201, 199]. Given inputs representing a position (x, y), the desired network outputs are the joint angles that put the manipulator in this position (figure 2.5). Physical properties of the arm determine the relationship T between the network outputs (joint angle commands) and the

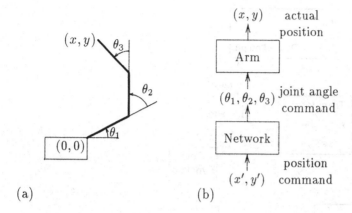

Figure 2.5
Learning with a distal teacher, robot arm example: (a) a robot arm, (b) a neural network translates input commands to joint angles that put the manipulator in the desired position after transformation by the physics of the robot arm.

system output where position errors are measured. The physics of the arm are well-known so the position errors can be translated back to joint-angle error signals needed for training.

Referring ahead a few chapters, it is interesting to note that this model covers the problem of training internal layers of a multilayer network if the first layer is viewed as the network and following layers are viewed as the transform T.

3 Single-Layer Networks

Single-layer networks (figure 3.1) have just one layer of active units. Inputs connect directly to the outputs through a single layer of weights. The outputs do not interact so a network with N_{out} outputs can be treated as N_{out} separate single-output networks. Each unit (figure 3.2) produces its output by forming a weighted linear combination of its inputs which it then passes through a saturating nonlinear function

$$u = \sum_j w_j x_j \tag{3.1}$$

$$y = f(u). \tag{3.2}$$

This can be expressed more compactly in vector notation as

$$y(\mathbf{x}) = f\left(\mathbf{w}^T \mathbf{x}\right) \tag{3.3}$$

where $\mathbf{x}$ and $\mathbf{w}$ are column vectors with elements x_j and w_j, and the superscript T denotes the vector transpose. In general, f is chosen to be a bounded monotonic function. Common choices include the sigmoid function $f(u) = 1/(1 + e^{-u})$ and the tanh functions. When f is a discontinuous step function, the nodes are often called *linear threshold units* (LTU). Appendix D mentions other possibilities.

3.1 Hyperplane Geometry

Equations 3.1 and 3.2 are fundamental to most of the networks considered later so it is useful to examine them more closely. The locus of points $\mathbf{x}$ with a constant sum $\sum_j w_j x_j$ defines a hyperplane perpendicular to the vector $\mathbf{w}$. The Euclidean vector norm $\|\mathbf{x}\| = \sqrt{\sum_i x_i^2}$ measures vector length. Because $\mathbf{w}^T \mathbf{x} = \|\mathbf{w}\| \|\mathbf{x}\| \cos \phi$, where ϕ is the angle between $\mathbf{w}$ and $\mathbf{x}$, u is proportional to the projection $\|\mathbf{x}\| \cos \phi$ of $\mathbf{x}$ onto $\mathbf{w}$ and all points with equivalent projections produce equivalent outputs (figure 3.3). The locus of points with equivalent projections on $\mathbf{w}$ are hyperplanes orthogonal to $\mathbf{w}$, so the output y is a function of the distance from $\mathbf{x}$ to the hyperplane defined by $\mathbf{w}$. The constant-output surfaces of (3.2) are hyperplanes perpendicular to $\mathbf{w}$.

Orientation The orientation of the node hyperplane is determined by the direction of $\mathbf{w}$. This depends on the relative sizes of the weights w_i but not on the overall magnitude of $\mathbf{w}$. Let $\mathbf{e}_i$ be the unit vector aligned with the ith coordinate axis, for example, $\mathbf{e}_1 = (1, 0, 0, \ldots, 0)$ (w_i will still be used to refer to the ith component of a vector, however). The angle ϕ_1 between the hyperplane normal and the ith coordinate axis is then

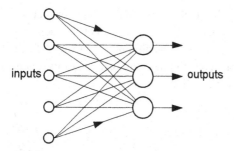

Figure 3.1
A single-layer perceptron has no hidden layers. One layer of weights connects the inputs directly to the outputs.
The outputs are independent so this network can be treated as three separate networks.

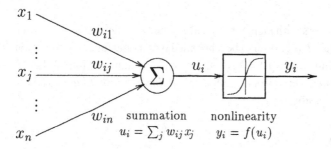

Figure 3.2
Node function. Each node i computes a weighted sum of its inputs and passes the result through a nonlinearity,
typically a bounded monotonic function such as the sigmoid.

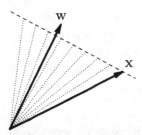

Figure 3.3
Projection of $\mathbf{x}$ onto $\mathbf{w}$. The output of a single unit is determined by the inner product of the input vector $\mathbf{x}$ and
the weight vector $\mathbf{w}$: $u = \mathbf{w}^T \mathbf{x} = \|\mathbf{w}\| \, \|\mathbf{x}\| \cos \phi$. All inputs $\mathbf{x}$ with the same projection onto $\mathbf{w}$ produce the same
output. The locus of points with equivalent projections onto $\mathbf{w}$ defines a hyperplane perpendicular to $\mathbf{w}$.

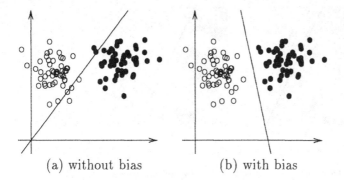

(a) without bias   (b) with bias

Figure 3.4
Effect of bias weights. A linear threshold unit divides its input space into two half-spaces: (a) without bias, the dividing surface must pass through the origin and certain data sets will not be separable; (b) with bias, the dividing surface can be offset from the origin to obtain better classification.

$$\mathbf{w}^T \mathbf{e}_i = \|\mathbf{w}\| \, \|\mathbf{e}_i\| \, \cos \phi_i$$
$$w_i = \|\mathbf{w}\| \cos \phi_i \qquad (\|\mathbf{e}_i\| = 1)$$
$$\cos \phi_i = w_i / \|\mathbf{w}\|. \tag{3.4}$$

The orientation of the plane is independent of the magnitude of $\mathbf{w}$ because the ratios $w_i / \|\mathbf{w}\|$ remain constant when $\mathbf{w}$ is multiplied by a constant.

Distance from the Origin   As noted previously, the constant-output surfaces of (3.2) are hyperplanes perpendicular to $\mathbf{w}$. More specifically, the weighted sum $\sum_j w_j x_j = 0$ defines a hyperplane *through the origin*. Inclusion of a *threshold*, or *bias*, term θ

$$u = \mathbf{w}^T \mathbf{x} - \theta \tag{3.5}$$

shifts the hyperplane along $\mathbf{w}$ to a distance $d = \theta / \|\mathbf{w}\|$ from the origin. To see this, let $\mathbf{v}$ be the vector from the origin to the closest point on the plane. It must be normal to the plane, and thus parallel to $\mathbf{w}$, so $\mathbf{v} = d\mathbf{w}/\|\mathbf{w}\|$. The node hyperplane is the locus of points where $\mathbf{w}^T \mathbf{x} - \theta = 0$ so we have

$$\mathbf{w}^T \mathbf{v} - \theta = 0$$
$$d\mathbf{w}^T \mathbf{w}/\|\mathbf{w}\| - \theta = 0$$
$$d = \theta / \|\mathbf{w}\|. \tag{3.6}$$

Figure 3.4 illustrates the utility of the bias term. Without bias, the decision surface must pass through the origin and so will be unable to separate some data sets. Addition of a bias allows the surface to be shifted from the origin to obtain better classification. To simplify

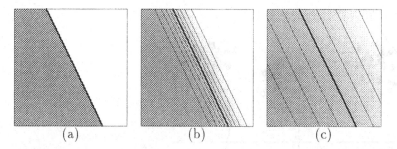

Figure 3.5
Graded responses: (a) a hard-limiter divides the input space with a hyperplane, (b) a sigmoid gives a similar response, but has a smoother transition at the boundary, and (c) a sigmoid with small weights gives an almost linear response for a wide range of inputs.

analyses, the threshold is usually absorbed into the weight vector by assuming that one of the inputs is constant, $x_{bias} = 1$. The constant input is called the *bias node*.

Gradation   The node nonlinearity f in (3.2) controls how the output varies as the distance from $\mathbf{x}$ to the node hyperplane changes. As noted, f is usually chosen to be a bounded monotonic function. When f is a binary hard-limiting function as in a linear threshold unit, the node divides the input space with a hyperplane, producing 0 for inputs on one side of the plane and 1 for inputs on the other side. With a softer nonlinearity such as the sigmoid, the transition from 0 to 1 is smoother but other properties are similar.

The magnitude of $\mathbf{w}$ in equation 3.3 plays the role of a scaling parameter that can be varied to obtain transitions of varying steepness. The slope of the transition is $\|\partial y / \partial \mathbf{x}\| = f'(u) \|\mathbf{w}\|$, which is proportional to $\|\mathbf{w}\|$, the magnitude of the weight vector. For large $\|\mathbf{w}\|$, the slope is steep and the sigmoid approximates a step function. For small $\|\mathbf{w}\|$, the slope is small and $y(\mathbf{x})$ is nearly linear over a wide range of inputs. Figure 3.5 illustrates functions with various degrees of gradation. In any case, the output is solely a function of the distance of the input from the hyperplane.

3.2   Linear Separability

An important limitation of single-layer perceptrons was pointed out by Minsky and Papert [268]: a single-layer perceptron can correctly classify only data sets which are *linearly separable*. Classes A and B are linearly separable if they can be separated by a hyperplane, i.e., if a plane exists such that classes A and B lie on opposite sides (figure 3.6). In two dimensions, the hyperplane reduces to a line and classes are linearly separable if a line can be drawn between them. Section 3.3 discusses the probability that a random set of patterns is linearly separable. The exclusive-OR function (figure 3.7) is a well-known example of

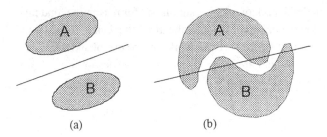

Figure 3.6
(a) Linearly separable classes can be separated by a hyperplane. In two dimensions, the hyperplane is a line. (b) Classes that are not linearly separable cannot be separated by a hyperplane.

a	b	XOR(a,b)
0	0	0
0	1	1
1	0	1
1	1	0

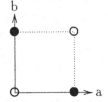

Figure 3.7
The two-input exclusive-OR function is a simple binary function that is not linearly separable and thus not learnable by a single-layer perceptron. In more than two dimensions, it generalizes to the parity function, which is 1 when the number of active inputs is odd and 0 when it is even.

a simple function that is not linearly separable and thus not computable by single-layer perceptrons.

This result is significant because many classification problems are not linearly separable. There are 2^{2^d} Boolean functions of d Boolean input variables, for example, only $O(2^{d^2})$ of which are linearly separable [278]. When d is large, the fraction of Boolean functions that are linearly separable and thus computable by a single-layer net becomes very small. For $d = 2$, a total of 14 of the 16 Boolean functions are linearly separable. (Exclusive-OR and its complement are the exceptions.) But for $d = 4$, only 1,882 out of 65536 are linearly separable [278; 273].

A large part of the appeal of neural networks is that they "learn" from examples, apparently imitating human abilities. The letdown when it was demonstrated that single-layer networks could not compute functions even as simple as exclusive-OR is said to have nearly stopped research in neural networks. Although it was known that multilayer nets are more powerful than single-layer nets, effective multilayer learning procedures were not well known at the time. In the 1980s, learning algorithms for multilayer networks became widely known and research interest revived.

In spite of their limitations, single-layer networks are significant for reasons beyond historical interest. There are significant signal processing applications that can be handled by single-layer networks. Understanding of single-layer networks is also useful and necessary for insight into multilayer networks, which are, after all, simply cascades of single-layer networks.

3.3 Hyperplane Capacity

What is the probability that a random set of points with random binary labels is linearly separable? Cover [87] provided the following result. Given N points in a d-dimensional input space, there are 2^N possible ways of labeling the points 0 or 1. Each of these forms a *dichotomy*—a division of the N points into two classes. A dichotomy is linearly separable if all the 0s can be separated from all the 1s by a hyperplane. It is *homogeneously linearly separable* if the points can be separated by a hyperplane passing through the origin. A linear separation of N points in d dimensions is a homogeneous linear separation in $d + 1$ dimensions because the offset of a hyperplane that does not pass through the origin can be absorbed into an extra bias weight.

Cover [87] defines the capacity of a hyperplane as the number of dichotomies it can separate. For N points in general position (defined below) in a Euclidean space of dimension d, the number $C(N, d)$ of homogeneously linearly separable dichotomies is

$$C(N, d) = \begin{cases} 2^N & N \le d + 1 \\ 2 \sum_{k=0}^{d} \binom{N-1}{k} & N > d + 1. \end{cases} \tag{3.7}$$

This result is for N points in *general position*. If the N points are not in general position, the number of linearly separable dichotomies may be much lower. A set of d-dimensional vectors is in general position if all possible subsets of $d + 1$ or fewer vectors are linearly independent. For $N > d$, this requires that no set of $d + 1$ points lie on a $(d - 1)$-dimensional hyperplane. In $d = 3$ dimensions, for example, no set of 4 points may be coplanar. For $N \le d$, N points are in general position if no $(d - 2)$-dimensional hyperplane contains them all.

$C(N, d)$ can be computed recursively with the following relations.

$$C(1, d) = 2 \qquad (d \ge 1) \tag{3.8}$$
$$C(N, 1) = 2N$$
$$C(N + 1, d) = C(N, d) + C(N, d - 1)$$

The first relation says a single point can be classified in two ways. The second relation says N points on a line can be classified by a linear separator in $2N$ ways: the separator can fall in any of the $N - 1$ intervals between points and it can be oriented in 2 ways so the zeros fall on one side or the other. Adding the two cases where all points are either zero or one gives the total $2N$.

The recurrence relation is obtained as follows. Suppose N points in d dimensions form $C(N, d)$ dichotomies and we add another point p. This divides the existing dichotomies into two classes:

• Some of the existing dichotomies cannot be obtained by a hyperplane through p. When p is added, each of these continues to be a single dichotomy in the new system with p taking whichever value the existing dichotomy dictates.

• The rest of the existing dichotomies could have been obtained by a hyperplane passing through p. Each of these gives rise to two new dichotomies where p is either 0 or 1 because the hyperplane can be shifted infinitesimally to either side of p without changing the classification of the remaining points.

If M_1 and M_2 are the number of dichotomies in the two classes, then the number of dichotomies in the new system is $C(N + 1, d) = M_1 + 2M_2$. But $M_1 + M_2 = C(N, d)$ so $C(N + 1, d) = C(N, d) + M_2$. However, $M_2 = C(N, d - 1)$ because constraining a hyperplane to pass through p (as well as the origin) is equivalent to reducing the dimension d to $d - 1$. Substitution gives the recurrence relation $C(N + 1, d) = C(N, d) + C(N, d - 1)$.

Repeated application of the recurrence to the terms on the right yields

$$C(N, d) = \sum_{k=0}^{N-1} \binom{N-1}{k} C(1, d - k), \tag{3.9}$$

and (3.7) follows on noting that [87]

$$C(1, m) = \begin{cases} 2, & m \geq 1 \\ 0, & m < 1. \end{cases} \tag{3.10}$$

Returning to Equation 3.7, all dichotomies on $N \leq d + 1$ points in general position are linearly separable in d dimensions. (All possible labelings of 3 points in 2 dimensions are linearly separable, for example.) For $N > d + 1$, only $C(N, d)$ of the 2^N possible dichotomies are linearly separable. The probability that a randomly chosen dichotomy is linearly separable is then

$$f(N, d) = \begin{cases} 1 & N \leq d + 1 \\ \frac{2}{2^N} \sum_{k=0}^{d} \binom{N-1}{k} & N > d + 1. \end{cases} \tag{3.11}$$

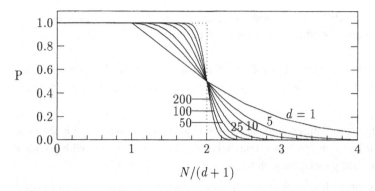

Figure 3.8
Capacity of a hyperplane. Shown is the probability that a random dichotomy on N points in d-dimensions is linearly separable, for various values of d. The probability is greater than $1/2$ for $N < 2(d+1)$, and less than $1/2$ for $N > 2(d+1)$. As d increases, the transition from high to low probability becomes steeper and approaches a step function.

This probability is plotted as a function of $N/(d+1)$ in figure 3.8 for a few values of d. It can be shown that $C(N, d) = 2^{N-1}$ and so $f(N, d) = 1/2$ at $N = 2(d+1)$. When d is large, $f(N, d)$ is greater than $1/2$ as long as $N < 2(d+1)$ and less than $1/2$ for $N > 2(d+1)$. As d becomes large, the transition becomes steeper and almost all dichotomies of $N < 2(d+1)$ points are linearly separable while almost all dichotomies of more points are not. At $N = 2(d+1)$, one-half of the dichotomies are linearly separable, which suggests $N = 2(d+1)$ points as the separating capacity of the hyperplane.

On the average, a single linear threshold unit with d weights and a threshold can be made to correctly classify up to $2(d+1)$ random binary patterns before the probability of error falls to $1/2$ [87]. For large N, only a tiny fraction of the possible mappings are linearly separable. In terms of generalization, this means that a d-input linear threshold unit can implement any dichotomy on $d+1$ or fewer patterns (in general position) and, when d is large, has a high probability of being able to learn a random dichotomy on up to $2d$ patterns. When $N < 2d$, generalization may be poor because there is a high probability that the training points will be linearly separable even if the function generating the labels is not; the network is underconstrained and the solution is unlikely to generalize well to new patterns. In linear regression, a common heuristic is to require $N \geq 3d$ or more training patterns to avoid overfitting.

The assumptions behind this result should be noted: the points are presumed to be in general position with randomly chosen target labels. In real problems, the points will not necessarily be in general position and if the labels are determined by a physical process there is an assumption that the label of a point can be inferred from its position. Obviously there are sets of $N \gg 2d$ points which are linearly separable (two well separated clusters, for example) and there are sets of as few as 4 points, not in general position, which are not linearly separable (e.g., four coplanar points in an exclusive-OR configuration).

3.4   Learning Rules for Single-Layer Networks

A single-layer network can be trained by many methods. Almost every optimization technique has been applied to neural network training at some time or another. In addition to the general purpose optimization algorithms (some are reviewed in chapter 10) there are methods specialized for single-layer classifiers.

Rosenblatt's original perceptron learning algorithm (described in section 3.4.1) can be used for binary input-output problems that are known to be linearly separable. Statistical procedures can be applied in many cases. Linear discriminant analysis may be used for classification problems where the data form Gaussian clusters. The mathematics of single-layer perceptrons are similar to linear regression. Indeed, when f is linear, the output is a simple linear combination of the inputs and optimal weights can be calculated directly. Logistic regression (e.g., [178]) is very similar to learning binary functions with a single-layer network of sigmoid units using a cross-entropy error function.

When the node nonlinearity is smooth and the error function is differentiable, various gradient-based optimization methods including back-propagation can be used. More sophisticated gradient based techniques such as Newton's method, Levenberg-Marquardt, or conjugate gradient descent may be especially effective for single-layer networks because their error surface does not depart too much from the basic quadratic error function for which these methods are specialized.

3.4.1   The Perceptron Learning Algorithm

The perceptron learning algorithm is suitable for learning linearly separable binary functions of binary inputs and is guaranteed to find a solution if the classes are linearly separable. Unfortunately, if the classes are not linearly separable, the algorithm may not even converge and is unlikely to produce the best solution when it does. (Section 3.4.3 describes a possible way of handling this problem.) Because of these problems and the general limitations of single-layer networks, the method is rarely used except in special circumstances.

Because the outputs are binary, linear threshold units are used. Each unit computes the weighted sum u of its N inputs x_j, $j = 1 \ldots N$, and generates a binary output y

$$u = \sum_{j=0}^{N} w_j x_j \quad = \mathbf{w}^T \mathbf{x} \tag{3.12}$$

$$y = \begin{cases} -1 & u \leq 0 \\ +1 & u > 0. \end{cases} \tag{3.13}$$

A node threshold is absorbed into the weight vector by assuming the presence of a constant value bias unit, $x_{bias} = 1$. Input, output, and target values are assumed to be ± 1.

The weights can be updated by a number of simple learning rules [166]. During training, input patterns $\mathbf{x}$ are presented and the outputs $y(\mathbf{x})$ are compared to the targets $t(\mathbf{x})$. Weights are adapted by

$$\Delta \mathbf{w} = \begin{cases} 2\eta t\mathbf{x} & \text{if } t \neq y \\ 0 & \text{otherwise}, \end{cases} \tag{3.14}$$

where η is a small positive constant controlling the learning rate. Typically $0 < \eta < 1$. Because $t, y \in \{-1, +1\}$, the following are equivalent:

$$\Delta \mathbf{w} = \eta(1 - ty)t\mathbf{x} \tag{3.15}$$

and

$$\Delta \mathbf{w} = \eta(t - y)\mathbf{x}. \tag{3.16}$$

In both cases, no change occurs when the output classification is correct. Otherwise, each element of the weight vector is incremented by 2η when the output is less than the target or decremented by 2η when the output is greater.

For improved reliability, it may be desirable that a unit activates only when the weighted sum $u = \mathbf{w}^T \mathbf{x}$ is greater than a threshold $N\kappa$, where $0 \leq \kappa < 1$. The following rule may be used [325]:

$$\Delta \mathbf{w} = \eta \, \Theta(N\kappa - tu) \, t\mathbf{x}, \tag{3.17}$$

where $\Theta(u)$ is the unit step function

$$\Theta(u) = \begin{cases} 1 & u \geq 0 \\ 0 & u < 0. \end{cases}$$

Note that as the classification accuracy improves, the system makes fewer errors so weight changes become less and less frequent. The effective learning rate therefore slows down so convergence to perfect classification may take a long time.

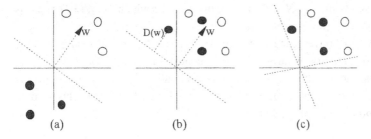

Figure 3.9
The separation problem. (a) A weight vector must be found that separates the positive samples (open circles) from the negative samples (filled circles). (b) The transformation $\mathbf{z} = t\mathbf{x}$ reflects the negative examples across the origin and changes the problem to one of finding a weight vector such that $\mathbf{w} \cdot \mathbf{z} > 0$ for each transformed pattern $\mathbf{z}$. $D(\mathbf{w})$ is the minimum distance from any point $\mathbf{z}$ to the separating hyperplane defined by $\mathbf{w}$. (c) The difficulty of a problem is determined by how much $\mathbf{w}$ can be varied and still meet the separating criterion. Easy problems can be satisfied by many $\mathbf{w}$ vectors.

3.4.2   Perceptron Convergence Proof

With input, output, and target values of ± 1, and using learning rule (3.17), a test of correct classification is that [166]

$$t\mathbf{w} \cdot \mathbf{x} > N\kappa \tag{3.18}$$

($\mathbf{w} \cdot \mathbf{x} \equiv \sum_i w_i x_i$ denotes the inner product of $\mathbf{w}$ and $\mathbf{x}$). As shown in figure 3.9(b), the transformation $\mathbf{z} = t\mathbf{x}$ reflects the negative examples across the origin and changes the problem to one of finding a weight vector such that $\mathbf{w} \cdot \mathbf{z} > 0$ for every pattern $\mathbf{z}$. The points $\mathbf{z}$ will be classified correctly if

$$\mathbf{w} \cdot \mathbf{z} > N\kappa. \tag{3.19}$$

The $N\kappa$ term adds the additional requirement that all $\mathbf{z}$ must be at least a distance $N\kappa/\|\mathbf{w}\|$ from the origin and provides a margin for noise- and fault-tolerance.

The difficulty of a problem is determined by how much $\mathbf{w}$ can be varied and still meet the separating criterion. Easy problems can be satisfied by many hyperplanes while hard problems require very precise placement of the separator (figure 3.9(c)). Let $D(\mathbf{w})$ be the minimum distance from any point $\mathbf{z}$ to the separating hyperplane defined by $\mathbf{w}$

$$D(\mathbf{w}) = \frac{1}{\|\mathbf{w}\|} \min_\mu \mathbf{w} \cdot \mathbf{z}^\mu, \tag{3.20}$$

where the superscript μ indexes the points. $D(\mathbf{w})$ is positive when all the points are on the positive side of the hyperplane, in which case (3.19) can be satisfied by making $\|\mathbf{w}\|$ large enough to ensure the safety margin $N\kappa$. There is some $\mathbf{w}_{opt}$ for which $D_{max} = D(\mathbf{w}_{opt})$ is maximized; this defines the *optimal perceptron*.

The following proof of convergence is provided in [166]. Additional results may be found in [284], a good summary of early work in perceptron-like networks. At each step, a pattern is chosen and the weights are updated only if equation 3.19 is not satisfied. Let M^μ denote the number of times that pattern μ has been used to update the weights at some point in the learning process. Then at that time

$$\mathbf{w} = \eta \sum_\mu M^\mu \mathbf{z}^\mu \tag{3.21}$$

if the initial weights are 0.

Assume that a solution vector $\mathbf{w}^*$ exists. Because $\mathbf{w}^*$ is a solution, $D(\mathbf{w}^*) > 0$. The proof computes bounds on $\|\mathbf{w}\|$ and on the overlap $\mathbf{w} \cdot \mathbf{w}^*$. These are used to show that $\mathbf{w} \cdot \mathbf{w}^*/\|\mathbf{w}\|$ would get arbitrarily large if $M = \sum_\mu M^\mu$ kept increasing. This is impossible, however, because $\mathbf{w}^*$ is fixed, so updating must stop after some finite M.

Using (3.20) and (3.19)

$$\mathbf{w} \cdot \mathbf{w}^* = \eta \sum_\mu M^\mu \mathbf{z}^\mu \cdot \mathbf{w}^* \tag{3.22}$$

$$\geq \eta M \min_\mu \mathbf{z}^\mu \cdot \mathbf{w}^* \tag{3.23}$$

$$= \eta M D(\mathbf{w}^*) \|\mathbf{w}^*\|. \tag{3.24}$$

$D(\mathbf{w}^*)\|\mathbf{w}^*\|$ is a constant, so $\mathbf{w} \cdot \mathbf{w}^*$ grows like M.

An upper bound on $\|\mathbf{w}\|$ is obtained by considering the change in length of $\mathbf{w}$ at a single update by pattern α

$$\Delta \|\mathbf{w}\|^2 = \|\mathbf{w} + \eta \mathbf{z}^\alpha\|^2 - \|\mathbf{w}\|^2 \tag{3.25}$$

$$= \eta^2 \|\mathbf{z}^\alpha\|^2 + 2\eta \mathbf{w} \cdot \mathbf{z}^\alpha \tag{3.26}$$

$$\leq \eta^2 N + 2\eta N \kappa \tag{3.27}$$

$$\leq N\eta(\eta + 2\kappa). \tag{3.28}$$

The inequality comes from the fact that (3.19) is not satisfied when a weight update occurs. Because $z_i^\mu = \pm 1$, $(\mathbf{z}^\alpha)^2 = N$. The upper bound results from summing the increments for M steps

$$\|\mathbf{w}\|^2 \leq M N \eta(\eta + 2\kappa). \tag{3.29}$$

Thus $\|\mathbf{w}\|$ grows no faster than $\sqrt{M}$.

Next, consider the normalized scalar product

$$\phi = \frac{(\mathbf{w} \cdot \mathbf{w}^*)^2}{\|\mathbf{w}\|^2 \|\mathbf{w}^*\|^2}, \tag{3.30}$$

which is the square of the cosine of the angle between $\mathbf{w}$ and $\mathbf{w}^*$ and cannot be greater than one. By (3.24) and (3.29),

$$M \frac{D(\mathbf{w}^*)^2 \eta}{N(\eta + 2\kappa)} \leq \phi \leq 1, \tag{3.31}$$

which gives an upper bound on the number of weight updates (using the best possible $\mathbf{w}^*$)

$$M \leq N \frac{1 + 2\kappa/\eta}{D_{max}^2}, \tag{3.32}$$

where $D_{max} \equiv \max_{\mathbf{w}} D(\mathbf{w})$ is $D(\mathbf{w})$ maximized over all possible $\mathbf{w}$. Thus M has an upper limit that is an unknown, but finite, constant. Because there can be no more than this number of updates, the weights must eventually converge to a final unchanging value.

This upper bound is proportional to N, the number of inputs, but does not depend on the number of patterns. In reality, however, in order to find the patterns that require weight updates, we have to cycle through the patterns, a process that takes time proportional to the number of patterns on the average. Also, D_{max} usually decreases as the number of patterns grows, resulting in a larger M. M also grows linearly with κ, because for larger κ, a larger $\|\mathbf{w}\|$ is needed to satisfy (3.19) along a good weight vector.

Equation 3.32 cannot be used to calculate the time required for convergence because it requires knowledge of a solution vector. Hampson and Volper [151] studied average case upper and lower bounds for M. The number of weight updates required is bounded by

$$M \leq \frac{\|\mathbf{w}^*\|^2 \|\mathbf{x}\|_{max}^2}{a^2}, \tag{3.33}$$

where $\|\mathbf{x}\|_{max}^2$ is the largest squared magnitude of any input vector ($N + 1$ for N bivalent input units), $\mathbf{w}^*$ is any solution vector, and $a \equiv \min_{\mu} \mathbf{x}^{\mu} \cdot \mathbf{w} \geq 0$. The worst case upper bound is $M \approx N^N$. An average case upper bound may be $O(4^N)$ for large N. The worst case lower bound is $M \geq 2^N$. The average case lower bound is $O(1.4^N)$ for large N [151]. It is reported that M grows linearly with the number of irrelevant inputs that are uncorrelated with the target outputs.

3.4.3   The Pocket Algorithm

Although the perceptron algorithm is guaranteed to learn pattern sets that are linearly separable, it does not converge when the training data is not linearly separable. Most of the time, the weight vector stays in regions that give small numbers of errors, but it does not always stay there. It is possible for the system to visit a near optimal set of weights and then wander away to a very bad set; the total error may be small at one moment and suddenly become large in the next so there is no guarantee that a weight vector obtained late in the training process will be near optimal.

Gallant's "pocket algorithm" [133] keeps a copy of the best weight vector obtained so far. Two sets of weights are maintained, a working set and the pocket set. Training examples are chosen randomly and whenever the current weights have a run of consecutive correct classifications longer than the best run by the pocket weights, they replace them. The quality of the pocket weights thus tends to improve over time and converge to an optimum set.

3.4.4   Rosenblatt's Perceptron

Single-layer sigmoidal networks are often called perceptrons even though this isn't strictly accurate. The original perceptron described by Rosenblatt [324, 325, 46] actually consisted of a family of networks, most having more than one layer and some having recurrent connections. In most cases, however, only the final layer of weights to the output units were modifiable. Connections in preceding layers had fixed values, either randomly chosen or set by some systematic procedure. The output nodes were often connected in a winner-take-all fashion. The label probably stuck because Minsky and Papert [268] reduced the structure to a single layer for the purpose of analyzing what could be learned by the modifiable units. The well-known result was to show that single-layer networks were adequate only for linearly separable functions.

Unlike a single-layer network, Rosenblatt's perceptron was capable of correctly classifying patterns that were not linearly separable if the preceding units had appropriate responses. But because only the final layer of weights was modifiable, it could not learn certain functions if this required adjustment of the responses of the preceding units.

Rosenblatt's perceptron is historically significant because it was one of the first biologically plausible models specified precisely enough to simulate and complex enough to show interesting behavior [46]. It was responsible for much of the initial interest in neural networks during the 1960s.

Now the term "perceptron" is commonly used to refer to any feedforward network of nodes with responses like $f(\mathbf{w}^T\mathbf{x})$ where f is a sigmoid-like "squashing function." Single-layer networks are often simply called perceptrons and networks with more than one layer are typically called multilayer perceptrons.

3.5   Adalines and the Widrow-Hoff Learning Rule

Adaline networks (short for *adaptive linear neuron*) were described by Widrow et al. in the 1960s [402, 399, 404, 401, 400, 357]. The structure is a single-layer network with a step function as the nonlinearity. Although the perceptron was analyzed assuming binary inputs, Adaline inputs may be continuous. Weights are adjusted with the Widrow-Hoff learning rule to minimize the difference between the output and an externally supplied target.

The Widrow-Hoff learning rule, also called the LMS algorithm or the delta rule, is basically an iterative implementation of linear regression (see appendix A). Both minimize the mean squared error of a linear fit. Ideally, the solutions are the same so it shares many properties with linear regression and succeeds or fails in similar situations.

An input pattern $\mathbf{x}$ is selected at random from the training set, applied to the input, and the output is calculated by equations 3.12 and 3.13. The weights are then updated by

$$\Delta \mathbf{w} = \eta(t - u)\frac{\mathbf{x}}{\|\mathbf{x}\|^2}, \tag{3.34}$$

where η is a small positive constant learning rate. Note that this minimizes the difference between the target and the weighted input sum u, not the output $y = f(u)$. Weight adjustments are repeated with new patterns until the total error (summed over all training patterns) is minimized.

The error is reduced by a factor of η each time the weights are updated with the input pattern fixed. Stability [406] requires that $0 < \eta < 2$ and generally $0.1 < \eta < 1.0$. For $\eta = 1$ the error on the present pattern is completely corrected in one cycle; for $\eta > 1$, it is overcorrected. Because of the linearity of the rule, the error function is quadratic and has only one global minimum; there are no local minima.

If the input patterns are linearly independent, the weights will converge to unique values. If not, the corrections will be oscillatory and η should decrease over time to allow the weights to settle. One possible schedule is $\eta = k^{-1}$, where k indexes the iterations [212].

Vectors $\mathbf{a}$ and $\mathbf{b}$ are *orthogonal* if $\mathbf{a}^T \mathbf{b} = 0$. A set of vectors $\{\mathbf{v}_i\}_{i=1}^n$ are *orthonormal* if any two distinct vectors are orthogonal and each has unit length. For orthonormal input patterns, the optimal weights to which the rule converges iteratively can be computed directly [359]

$$\mathbf{w} = \sum_{p=1}^{P} t_p \mathbf{x}_p. \tag{3.35}$$

Here p indexes training patterns, not vector elements; $\mathbf{x}_p$ is the p-th input pattern, a column vector, and t_p is the p-th output target. This is essentially Hebbian learning. Because the patterns are orthogonal, stored patterns don't interfere with each other so recall is perfect

$$t_p = \mathbf{w}^T \mathbf{x}_p. \tag{3.36}$$

Orthonormality is not, however, a requirement for perfect recall of the stored patterns. The correct output will be produced in response to every stored pattern as long as the patterns are merely linearly independent. Unlike the perceptron algorithm that does not converge when the patterns are not linearly separable, the delta rule converges to the optimal mean-squared-error solution. When the patterns are linearly separable, the minimum MSE solution may separate the classes, but this is not guaranteed. There are linearly separable data sets that a MSE solution does not separate correctly.

3.5.1 Adaline Capacity

An Adaline can store and recall perfectly up to N linearly independent patterns. This is limited by the dimension of the input since N patterns can be linearly independent only if $N \leq d$, where d is the dimension of the patterns (the number of inputs including the bias unit).

For random input patterns and targets, the capacity approaches $2d$ [401]. This is an average capacity for random inputs and targets and is determined by the results discussed in section 3.3. But as few as four patterns can create a not-linearly-separable set that is unlearnable by the Adaline. In a sense, random data is the hardest to learn. In most real problems, however, patterns and targets are not random; the target usually depends on the inputs in a systematic way. When the patterns are linearly separable (or nearly so), the system is able to correctly classify many more than $2d$ patterns [401]. The case of two well-separated clusters is a simple example.

In simulations, it is reported that approximately $5d$ training passes are required to achieve a 20% error level [402], where d is the number of bits per pattern. This generalizes to approximately d/ϵ where ϵ is the acceptable error level. For linearly separable problems, it is sufficient to train only on the border patterns since all patterns farther from the border will be classified correctly if the border patterns are [401].

4 MLP Representational Capabilities

The standard multilayer perceptron (MLP) is a cascade of single-layer perceptrons (figure 4.1). There is a layer of input nodes, a layer of output nodes, and one or more intermediate layers. The interior layers are sometimes called "hidden layers" because they are not directly observable from the system inputs and outputs. Each node has a response $f(\mathbf{w}^T\mathbf{x})$ where $\mathbf{x}$ is the vector of output activations from the preceding layer, $\mathbf{w}$ is a vector of weights, and f is a bounded nondecreasing nonlinear function such as the sigmoid. Normally, one of the weights acts as a bias by virtue of connection to a constant input. Nodes in each layer are fully connected to nodes in the preceding and following layers. There are no connections between units in the same layer, connections from one layer back to a previous layer, or "shortcut" connections that skip over intermediate layers. Although back-propagation can be applied to more general networks, this is the most commonly used structure.

The following sections summarize some properties and limitations that result from this structure, independent of methods used to set the weights.

How to Count Layers? A minor digression: there is some disagreement about how to count layers in a network. Some say a network with one hidden layer is a three-layer network because there are three layers of nodes: the inputs, the hidden units, and the outputs. Others say this is a two-layer network because there are only two layers of active nodes, the hidden units and outputs. Inputs are excluded because they do no computation. We tend to follow this convention and say that an L-layer network has L active layers; that is, $L - 1$ hidden layers and an output layer. Conveniently, this is also the number of weight layers. Not everyone uses the same convention, however, so it is often simplest to explicitly specify the number of hidden layers. The network in figure 4.1, for example, would be called a two-hidden-layer network. In spite of the convention, it is natural to refer to the input layer at times; we did so in the first paragraph of this chapter.

The notation $N_1/N_2/\cdots/N_L$ is sometimes used to describe the structure of a layered network. This is simply a list of the number of nodes in each layer. A 10/3/2 network, for example, has 10 inputs, 3 nodes in a hidden layer, and 2 outputs. A 16/10/5/1 network would have 16 inputs, 10 nodes in the first hidden layer, 5 nodes in the second hidden layer, and 1 output. Unless otherwise specified, each layer is presumed to be fully connected to the preceding and following layers with no short-cut or feedback connections. Figure 4.1 illustrates a 5/5/3/4 structure.

4.1 Representational Capability

The representational capability of a network can be defined as the range of mappings it can implement when the weights are varied. A particular mapping is within the representational

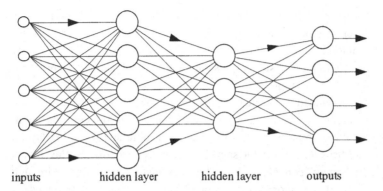

Figure 4.1
MLP structure. A multilayer perceptron is a cascade of single-layer perceptrons. There is a layer of input nodes and a layer of output nodes with one or more hidden layers in between.

capability of a net if there is a set of weights for which the net performs the mapping. Theories about representational capability answer questions like: Given a set of inputs and associated target outputs, is there a set of weights that allow the network to perform the desired mapping? Is the network capable of generating the desired outputs from the given inputs? In some cases, an exact solution may be required while in others, an approximation may be allowed. Results say whether a particular problem might be solvable by a particular network without necessarily producing the weights that generate the solution. If the answer is negative, we know the network cannot solve the problem and this saves us the expense of a futile search. If the answer is positive, we know a solution exists but these results don't guarantee that it will be easy to find or that a chosen optimization method will be able to find it. Results of this kind provide broad guidelines in selecting an architecture for a problem. One well-known representational result, for example, is that single-layer networks are capable of representing only linearly separable functions.

Two Hidden Layers Are Sufficient   When designing a layered network, an obvious first question is how many layers to use. Lippmann [247] shows that two hidden layers are sufficient to create classification regions of any desired shape. In figure 4.2, linear threshold units in the first hidden layer divide the input space into half-spaces with hyperplanes, units in the second hidden layer AND (form intersections of) these half-spaces to produce convex regions, and the output units OR (form unions of) the convex regions into arbitrary, possibly unconnected, shapes. Given a sufficient number of units, a network can be formed that divides the input space in any way desired, producing 0 when the input is in one region and 1 when it is in the other. The boundaries are piecewise linear, but any smooth boundary can be approximated with enough units.

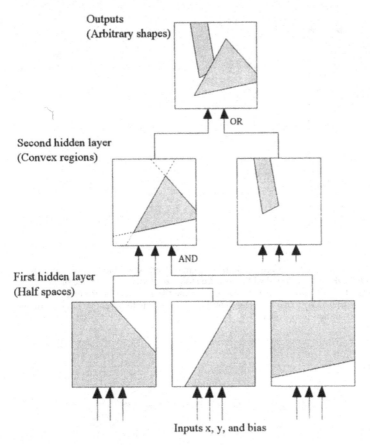

Figure 4.2
Three layers of linear threshold units are sufficient to define arbitrary regions. Units in the first hidden layer divide the input space with hyperplanes, units in the second hidden layer can form convex regions bounded by these hyperplanes, and output units can combine the regions defined by the second layer into arbitrarily shaped, possibly unconnected, regions. Here, the boundaries are piecewise linear, but any smooth boundary can be approximated with enough units (based on [247].)

   To approximate continuous functions, one can add and subtract (rather than logically OR) convex regions with appropriate weighting factors so two hidden layers are also sufficient to approximate any desired bounded continuous function [234].

One-hidden-layer Nets Can Represent Nonconvex, Disjoint Regions   Units in the second hidden layer of figure 4.2 respond to convex regions in the input space. Because these would be the outputs in a single-hidden-layer network, it is sometimes mistakenly assumed that single-hidden-layer networks can recognize only convex decision regions.

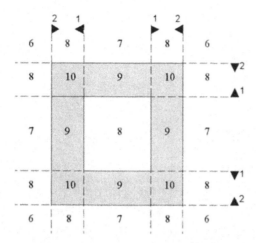

Figure 4.3
Single-hidden-layer networks can recognize nonconvex decision regions. Here, eight hidden units in a single layer create a nonconvex "square donut." Each dashed line is the decision boundary of one of the hidden units. The hidden unit is active (1) on the side of the line indicated by the pointer and connects to the output unit with the weight indicated next to the pointer. The other numbers show the summed input to the output unit in different regions. Thresholding at 8.5 creates the square donut.

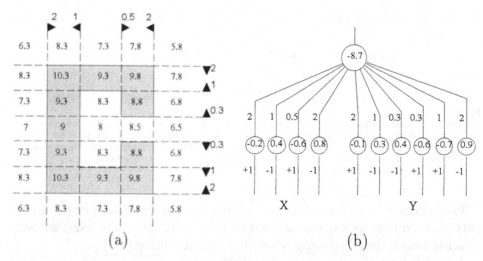

Figure 4.4
Weiland and Leighton [407] provide this example of a nonconvex region recognized by a single-hidden-layer network. Thresholding at 8.7 creates the 'C' shaped region: (a) a nonconvex decision region, and (b) the network. There are 10 hidden nodes. Each has one connection with weight $w = \pm 1$ from either the x or y input. Numbers inside the circles are the node thresholds.

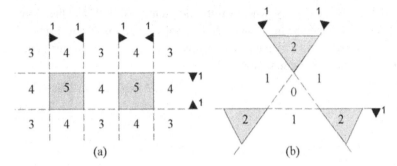

Figure 4.5
Disjoint regions recognized by single-hidden-layer networks. In addition to nonconvex regions, single-hidden-layer networks can also recognize disjoint (unconnected) regions.

Counter-examples are shown in figures 4.3 through 4.5. Figures 4.3 and 4.4 illustrate nonconvex regions recognized by three-layer nets. (Figure 4.4 is derived from Weiland and Leighton [407].) Figure 4.5 shows examples of disjoint (unconnected) regions recognizable by three-layer networks. Other examples can be found in [180, 255, 249].

4.2 Universal Approximation Capabilities

The examples above suggest that any bounded function can be approximated with arbitrary accuracy if enough hidden units are available. These ideas have been extended theoretically to show that multilayer perceptrons are *universal approximators*. That is, they are capable of arbitrarily accurate approximation of essentially arbitrary continuous mappings from the $[-1, +1]^n$ hypercube to the $(-1, 1)$ interval. This is an important result because it says neural networks, as a class, are powerful enough to implement essentially any function we require.

4.2.1 Kolmogorov's Theorem, One Hidden Layer Is Sufficient

A somewhat surprising result is that two hidden layers are not necessary for universal approximation; one hidden layer is sufficient. Kolmogorov [219, 220] showed that a continuous function of several variables can be represented *exactly* by the superposition of continuous one-dimensional functions of the original input variables. A refined proof by Sprecher [355] is often cited. Hecht-Nielsen [161] introduced the result to the neural network community and showed an implementation in the form of a single-hidden-layer network. Briefly, the result is that any continuous function mapping an n-dimensional input, $n \geq 2$, to an m-dimensional output can be implemented exactly by a network with one hidden layer. For $\phi : \mathbf{I}^n \to \mathbf{R}^m$, $\phi(\mathbf{x}) = \mathbf{y}$, where $\mathbf{I}$ is the closed interval $[0, 1]$ and therefore $\mathbf{I}^n$ is an n-dimensional hypercube, the function ϕ can be implemented *exactly* by a single-hidden-layer neural network having n elements in the input layer, $(2n + 1)$ elements in the middle layer, and m elements in the output layer. That is,

$$z_k = \sum_{j=1}^{n} \lambda^k \psi(x_j + \epsilon k) + k \tag{4.1}$$

$$y_i = \sum_{k=1}^{2n+1} g_i(z_k), \tag{4.2}$$

where λ is a real constant, ψ is a continuous real monotonic increasing function independent of ϕ but dependent on n, and ϵ is a rational number, $0 < \epsilon \leq \delta$, where δ is an arbitrarily chosen positive constant. The output node functions g_i are real and continuous and depend on ϕ and ϵ. Unfortunately, the proof is not constructive; it does not say how weights should be chosen to implement a particular mapping or specify the functions g_i (different for each i), which have unknown and often extremely nonlinear shapes.

Girosi and Poggio [139] point out that the theorem might not be relevant because the inner functions ψ are extremely nonsmooth. (The theorem fails when restricted to smooth functions.) The functions are very unlike the sigmoids normally used in neural networks and not likely to be learnable because of their extreme roughness. Further, the functions g_k depend on ϕ, are all different, and do not form a parameterized family. They are likely to be at least as complex as ϕ, if not more so, and therefore no easier to learn than ϕ itself. In effect, the complexity of approximating the original function is shifted into the task of finding the internal node functions.

In more recent work, Sprecher [356] describes a stronger version of the theorem using translates of a single function in place of the multiple internal functions g_k. The replacement function remains nonsmooth, however, so the objections remain.

Kurkova [231] notes that although exact representation is not possible with smooth internal functions, approximation is, and goes on to show universal approximation properties of sigmoidal networks with two hidden layers. But other work [244] suggests that approximation of the internal functions does not yield approximation of the target function.

4.2.2   Other Proofs of Universal Approximation Capability

Several proofs are based on showing that single-hidden-layer networks can implement Fourier transforms and thus have the same approximation capabilities. The idea is that a sinusoid can be implemented by sums and differences of many shifted sigmoids, one for each half cycle. Irie and Miyake [186] give a proof based on Fourier integrals where the number of nodes required for exact approximation is infinite. Gallant and White [132] give another Fourier transform proof using monotone "cosine-squasher" sigmoids. Funahashi [131] approximates the integral representation of Irie and Miyake with a discrete sum and shows that networks with at least one hidden layer of sigmoid units are universal approximators.

Cybenko [95, 96] provided one of the first rigorous proofs of universal approximation capability, showing that a network with linear output units and a single hidden layer of sigmoid units is sufficient for uniform approximation of any continuous function in the unit hypercube. Hornik, Stinchcombe, and White [177] and Stinchcombe and White [358] show that standard multilayer networks using arbitrary squashing functions are universal approximators; single-hidden-layer nets are included as a special case. Approximation of a function and its derivatives using arbitrary bounded nonconstant squashing functions is discussed by Hornik [175]. Other work on approximation includes [162, 48, 188, 226, 176].

In most cases, these are existence proofs rather than constructive recipes for finding a solution to a particular problem. These results do not guarantee that a chosen optimization method will find the necessary weights or that the solution found will be efficient. A constructive proof based on the Radon transform is given by Carroll and Dickson [64].

It should be noted that universal approximation is not a rare property. Many other systems have similar capabilities: polynomials, trigonometric polynomials (e.g., Fourier series), kernel regression systems, wavelets, and so on. By itself, this property does not make neural networks special. The results are important because they show that neural networks are powerful enough to approximate most functions that people find interesting. The lack of a universal approximation capability, on the other hand, would be bad news; neural networks would then be too weak for many problems and therefore much less appealing.

Given that there are many universal approximation systems, the choice of one over another depends on other factors such as efficiency, robustness, and so on. Barron [21, 22, 23] addresses the problem of how the MLP approximation error scales with the number of training samples and the number of parameters. One important result is that the error decreases like $O(1/\sqrt{N})$ as the number of training samples N increases. Another result is that the error decreases like $O(1/M)$ as a function of M, the number of hidden nodes. Unlike other systems (e.g., polynomials), this is independent of the input dimension and appears to avoid the "curse of dimensionality" (see [317: 178] for a skeptical view, however). These results can be used to put bounds on the necessary number of hidden nodes (in one hidden layer) and provide another justification for the rule of thumb that the number of training samples should be larger than the number of parameters divided by the desired approximation error, $N > O(Mp/\epsilon)$. Here N is the number of samples, M is the number of hidden nodes, p is the input dimension (so Mp is approximately the number of parameters), and ϵ is the desired approximation error.

One Hidden Layer Is Not Always Enough   The limits of these proofs are sometimes forgotten. They say that a sufficiently large one-hidden-layer network is capable of essentially arbitrarily accurate approximation of continuous functions over compact regions. Although this covers most functions we would like to approximate, it may not include them all. Sontag [350, 351] points out that there are certain functions, important in inverse control, which cannot be approximated by single-hidden-layer nets with any number of units but which can be implemented rather simply with two hidden layers. That is, there are control systems that can be stabilized by a two-hidden-layer network but not by a one-hidden-layer net. The difference depends not on the number of units needed to achieve a certain numerical accuracy but rather on the need to approximate discontinuous functions that may arise as one-sided inverses of continuous functions.

4.3   Size versus Depth

Since a single sufficiently large hidden layer is adequate for approximation of most functions, why would anyone ever use more? One reason hangs on the words "sufficiently large." Although a single hidden layer is optimal for some functions, there are others for which a single-hidden-layer solution is very inefficient compared to solutions with more layers.

Certain functions containing disjoint decision regions cannot be realized exactly with only a single hidden layer of threshold units [255]. Certain functions can be implemented exactly by small networks with two hidden layers but require an infinite number of nodes to approximate with a single hidden layer network [255, 254]. Figure 4.6 shows an example from [255]. Gibson and Cowan [137] provide another example. Chester [80] describes a "pinnacle" function (1 at the origin and 0 elsewhere) for which a single-hidden-layer network needs $O(1/\epsilon)$ nodes to achieve $O(\epsilon)$ maximum error where a two-hidden-layer network needs only 4 nodes. This uses a maximum error criteria, however, rather than mean squared error. For certain functions, single-hidden-layer networks may require very large weights or extreme precision [180].

Although these results suggest that two-hidden-layer networks are more powerful, one-hidden-layer networks may be adequate for many functions encountered in practice. One- and two-hidden-layer networks are compared empirically by de Villiers and Barnard [104]. For fair comparison, the networks are configured to have approximately the same number of weights. Using conjugate gradient training and artificial clustered 2-dimensional data (mixtures of Gaussians), no significant difference was found in the best solution found by either architecture. The one-hidden-layer nets were reported to have lower average error and perhaps generalized better. For two-hidden-layer nets, the same authors report that

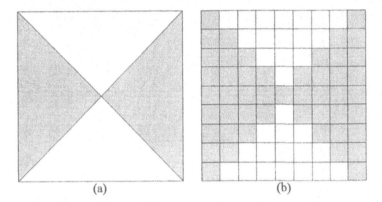

(a)   (b)

Figure 4.6
Certain functions can be implemented exactly by small networks with two hidden layers but require an infinite
number of nodes to approximate if constrained to a single hidden layer [255, 254]: (a) a simple function that can
be implemented with two hidden layers each containing two threshold units, (b) an approximation by a network
with just one hidden layer, (from [255]).

training is easier if the hidden layers have approximately equal sizes. Similar results are
reported by Huang and Lippmann [180]; no significant difference was seen in error rate or
convergence time.

4.3.1 Size versus Depth for Boolean Functions

Many results exist for Boolean logic functions, e.g., [347]. (See figure 4.7 for the elementary gates.) It is obvious that a net with one hidden layer of 2^n threshold units can compute
any Boolean function of n binary inputs since any Boolean function can be expressed in
conjunctive (or disjunctive) normal form. Each hidden unit computes one of the 2^n product terms and the output unit ORs selected product terms to produce the desired result. An
AND-OR array has this structure. This amounts to exhaustive enumeration of all positive
cases and becomes impractical for large n.

More economical solutions can often be obtained by adding more layers. The number of
nodes needed can be reduced by a factor of $O(\sqrt{n})$ because any Boolean function of n variables can be computed by a network with two hidden layers and $O(2^{n/2})$ threshold gates
[347]. This is nearly optimal as an unbounded depth circuit must have size $O(2^{n/2}/\sqrt{n})$
[347: 125]. Notice that this is an exponential reduction in size.

Because a one-hidden-layer solution may be inefficient, there may be functions that
cannot be implemented by a network of limited size using just one hidden layer. It is known
that there are Boolean functions which cannot be computed by threshold networks with

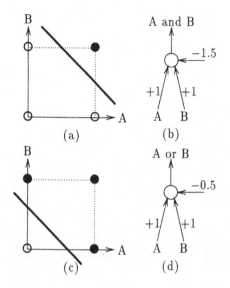

Figure 4.7
AND and OR logic functions. Any logic function can be implemented by a circuit of AND, OR, and NOT gates.
Threshold units are at least as powerful as logic circuits because they can implement all the necessary elementary
functions, as well as others: (a) the AND function, (b) linear threshold unit implementation of AND, (c) the OR
function, and (d) linear threshold unit implementation of OR. The NOT function can be obtained from a single-
input unit with a large negative weight and a zero threshold.

one hidden layer and a constant number of nodes, but which can be computed by threshold
networks with two hidden layers and a constant number of nodes ([250]; cited in [99]).

"Symmetric" functions depend only on the sum of the inputs, $\sum_i x_i$; parity is one
example. For arbitrary symmetric Boolean functions of n inputs, $O(n)$ units are needed in
depth-2 (one hidden layer) networks of linear threshold units (LTU), but only $O(\sqrt{n})$ units
are needed in depth-3 (two hidden layers) networks [348, 347]. For periodic symmetric
functions such as parity, a depth/size tradeoff can be obtained at all depths. For parity(n),
there is a depth($d + 1$) LTU circuit of size $O(dn^{1/d})$ [347]. But increasing the depth
beyond 3 does not decrease size much; $O(\sqrt{n/\log n})$ LTU gates are needed to compute
general symmetric functions if there is no restriction on depth [347].

Another reason to use more than one hidden layer is to decrease the weight magnitudes.
A one-hidden-layer implementation may require arbitrarily large weights. If permissible
weight values are bounded (e.g., by hardware limitations), networks with more hidden
layers may be more efficient. A depth-d circuit with exponential weights can be simulated
by a depth-($d + 1$) circuit with polynomially bounded weights at the cost of a polynomial
increase in network size [347: 40]. A single linear threshold unit with exponential weights

can be exchanged for a depth-3 polynomial size circuit with polynomial weights [347: 41]. Anything computable by a depth-2 threshold circuit of polynomial size can be computed by depth-3 *small weight* threshold circuits of polynomial size ([143]; cited in [142]). Thus if the range of weights is limited, networks with more than one hidden layer may be able to realize functions that cannot be realized by single-hidden-layer networks.

Caveats The results just stated say there are functions for which single-hidden-layer networks are less efficient than networks with more hidden layers. Of course, there are still functions where small single-hidden-layer networks are optimal and additional hidden layers are not useful. Single-hidden-layer networks may need large numbers of nodes to compute arbitrary functions, but small networks may suffice for particular functions.

Many of these results are statements about the power of a class of networks rather than guarantees that a particular network will be able to learn a particular set of data and generalize accurately. Many are based on asymptotic analyses valid only for large data sets or large input dimensions. Many are statements about the existence of a solution rather than constructive statements about how to find the necessary set of weights. Most depend on particular assumptions that may be violated in a given problem.

In real problems, training sets may be rather small and nonrandomly sampled, data distributions may have arbitrary forms, and the target function is unknown. It may be problematic just to determine if the data fits the assumptions. Although representational capability results can be helpful in putting bounds on the size and configuration of a network, they do not guarantee that a particular network and training algorithm will be able to learn a particular set of samples of a given function. Even if it is guaranteed that a particular network can exactly classify N training points (using some set of weights), this does not necessarily imply that the system will generalize well to new points. Finally, many of the results for Boolean functions are for exact implementation and may not hold when approximation is allowed.

4.4 Capacity versus Size

Another big question in designing a network is how many nodes to place in each layer. Universal approximation results say that a sufficiently large network can fit almost any function we are likely to want to approximate, but they do not deal with the problem of training a network to fit a finite set of discrete data points. Obviously, we cannot have infinite numbers of nodes in practice so it is useful to have bounds on the number that will be needed to fit a particular function. Even if arbitrarily large networks were allowed, it might not be possible to use them effectively given the limited amount of information contained in the training samples. After the network grows past a certain size, generalization criteria become the limiting factor on performance; a large network can often fit the training data exactly but is unlikely to do so in a way that fits the underlying function that generated the data.

Obviously, if we have m training points, a network with a single layer of $m-1$ hidden units can learn the data exactly, since a line can always be found onto which the points project uniquely [80]. (Set each weight vector parallel to this line, make the magnitude large so the sigmoid approaches a step function, adjust the threshold of node k, $k = 1 \ldots M-1$, so it separates points k and $k+1$, and assign the output weights based on the difference in target values for points $k+1$ and k.) Of course, this is inefficient and generalizes very badly; it uses as much storage as a nearest neighbor classifier, takes about the same time to evaluate on a serial computer, and probably generalizes worse. (Poor generalization could be expected just on the grounds that the number of weights would be much larger than the number of training samples.)

In general, more efficient solutions are sought. Most interesting functions have structure so each node should be able to account for more than just one training sample.

The sections that follow summarize some results on the number of patterns representable by multilayer networks of a given size. Results are simply listed in most cases; the reader should consult the references for details. Although these results may be used as guidelines in selecting a network, they should not be interpreted as inviolable rules. In many cases, they put bounds on the number of independent samples a given net can represent. The bounds may be loose, however, and actual data may be correlated so smaller networks may suffice for particular problems. Furthermore, we do not need the network to be able to fit *any* function on the samples, just the particular function that generated the data. We would like the network to fit the data and approximate the true target function, but the true target function is usually unknown and if we make the network powerful enough to represent any possible function on the data, it is probably too powerful. If the results say a given network can fit the m training points exactly, there is a danger of overfitting so smaller networks should probably be considered. Generalization depends on many factors so formulas based only on network size and number of samples cannot predict generalization performance.

4.4.1 Number of Cells Created by m Hyperplanes

For a layered network to realize an arbitrary dichotomy on m points in a d-dimensional space, each point must be uniquely represented in terms of the activities of the first hidden layer units.

Consider a network of linear threshold units. Each unit in the first hidden layer has an associated hyperplane that partitions the input space into two half-spaces. Two hyperplanes can divide the space into four quadrants, three hyperplanes may produce eight octants, and so on. In general, h hyperplanes could produce up to 2^h different regions, or cells (assuming $h \leq d$, the input dimension). The hyperplanes form the cell boundaries. Within each cell, the vector of hidden layer outputs is constant (since the input must cross at least one hyperplane boundary for the output to change) so two points in the same cell are indistinguishable in terms of the hidden layer outputs. Thus, to realize an arbitrary dichotomy on m points, each point must lie in a different cell. If the network does not have enough hidden units to create at least m cells, it won't be able to realize some dichotomies.

An expression for the number of cells created by intersections of hyperplanes is derived by Makhoul, El-Jaroudi, and Schwartz [255]. The results are similar to Cover's [87] formula for the number of linearly separable dichotomies (section 3.3). Let $C(h, d)$ be the number of cells formed by h planes in general position in the input space of d dimensions. (h planes are in "general position" in d space if none of them are parallel and no more than d planes intersect at a point.) A recursive formula is

$$C(h, d) = C(h - 1, d) + C(h - 1, d - 1). \tag{4.3}$$

with boundary conditions

$$C(0, d) = 1 \quad (d \geq 0) \tag{4.4}$$

$$C(h, 0) = 1 \quad (h \geq 1). \tag{4.5}$$

This gives [255]

$$C(h, d) = \begin{cases} 2^h & h \leq d \\ \sum_{i=0}^{d} \binom{h}{i} & h > d. \end{cases} \tag{4.6}$$

For $h < d$, each new hyperplane can be positioned to split all existing cells so up to 2^h cells can be created. For $h > d$, $C(h, d)$ grows more slowly because each new hyperplane cannot split every existing cell. For $h \gg d$, the last term $\binom{h}{d}$ dominates and

$$C(h, d) \approx \frac{h^d}{d!}, \quad (h \gg d). \tag{4.7}$$

The number of cells obtained by adding a new hyperplane (in terms of the number of existing cells) is

$$C(h, d) = 2C(h - 1, d) - \binom{h - 1}{d} \tag{4.8}$$

and the number of cells obtained when adding a new dimension is

$$C(h, d) = C(h, d - 1) + \binom{h}{d}. \tag{4.9}$$

Expressions for the number of open (bounded at infinity) and closed cells are also given in [255]. Two hidden layers are required to implement all the $2^{C(h,d)}$ possible binary functions on the $C(h, d)$ cells [255].

Although this puts bounds on the number of nodes (hyperplanes) needed to form an arbitrary dichotomy on m points, in practical problems we have one specific dichotomy to implement. The data are likely to have structure and large savings can often be obtained because a single cell can contain entire clusters of points belonging to the same class. Also, when the input data are highly correlated, the effective dimension d' may be less than d.

4.4.2 MLP Capacity I

Baum [33, 32] studied the number of examples needed to train a network with N nodes and W weights for a given error rate ϵ. These results are independent of the training algorithm and are based on an estimate of the VC dimension of the network—a relation between a system's complexity and the amount of information that must be provided to constrain it (see section 15.4).

If a network can be trained with

$$m \geq O\left(\frac{W}{\epsilon} \log_2 \frac{N}{\epsilon}\right)$$

random examples of the desired mapping so that at least a fraction $1 - \epsilon/2$ are correctly classified, then it will almost certainly correctly classify a fraction $1 - \epsilon$ of test examples drawn from the same distribution (for $0 < \epsilon \leq 1/8$) [33, 32]. This is an upper bound for the number of training examples needed. A lower bound for MLPs with one hidden layer is $\Omega(W/\epsilon)$. That is, a network trained on fewer than $\Omega(W/\epsilon)$ will fail (some fraction of the time) to find a set of weights that classifies a fraction $1 - \epsilon$ of future examples correctly.

This agrees with the W/ϵ rule of thumb given by Widrow for Adaline networks. Similar results are also obtained in linear regression. Roughly, if the network has W adjustable weights and an error rate ϵ is desired, it is necessary to have on the order of W/ϵ samples.

Assuming that the function can be learned, this gives an estimate of the network size necessary to learn m training patterns. For input patterns chosen randomly from the domain $\{-1, +1\}^n$, a network with one hidden layer of $2\lceil m/\lfloor n(1 - \frac{10}{\ln n})\rfloor\rceil$ linear threshold units can learn the $m \leq 2^{n/3}$ training patterns.

4.4.3   MLP Capacity II

Baum [30] makes the following points:

• A MLP with one hidden layer of $N - 1$ nodes is capable of computing an arbitrary dichotomy on N points [284].

• A network that implements $f(x)$ on N points in general position in d dimensions, must have at least N/d units in the first hidden layer [30]. If the points are in nongeneral position (structured data), many fewer units may be necessary.

• A one-hidden-layer net with $\lceil N/d \rceil$ hidden units can compute an arbitrary $f(x)$ on N points in general position [30]. Small changes in the input vector may cause large changes in the output, however, so good generalization is not guaranteed.

• The number of linearly separable dichotomies of N points in d dimensions, for $N \geq 3d$, is less than $4N^d/d!$ [30].

• No feedforward net (of the type considered) can compute an arbitrary map from N d-dimensional vectors into the e dimensional hypercube unless it has a number of connections $N_c \geq \frac{eN}{\log_2 N}$.

• For a one-hidden-layer network with d inputs, G hidden units, and e outputs, the number of connections is $N_c = G(e + d)$. Thus, a one-hidden-layer network cannot compute arbitrary functions on a set of N vectors in d-dimensions unless it has at least $G = \frac{eN}{(e+d)\log_2 N}$ hidden units.

• No MLP can compute an arbitrary function, no matter how many layers it has, unless it has $O(\sqrt{\frac{Ne}{\log_2 N}})$ units. As for all the items in this section, many fewer units may be needed if the training data is structured.

• A one-hidden-layer net with N hidden units can represent an arbitrary mapping of N points into the e hypercube.

• A one-hidden-layer net with $G = \lfloor \frac{4N}{d} \rfloor \lceil \frac{e}{\lfloor \log_2 \frac{N}{d} \rfloor} \rceil$ hidden units is capable of arbitrary binary mappings.

• There are 2^{Ne} mappings of N d-dimensional vectors into the e-dimensional hypercube.

4.4.4   MLP Capacity III

Widrow and Lehr [403] consider a fully connected feedforward network of linear threshold units with N_x inputs (excluding the bias), N_h hidden nodes in a single layer, and N_y outputs. There are N_w weights and N_p patterns in general position to be learned.

A bound on the number of weights needed is

$$\frac{N_y N_p}{1 + \log_2 N_p} \leq N_w < N_y \left(\frac{N_p}{N_x} + 1\right)(N_x + N_y + 1) + N_y. \tag{4.10}$$

A loose upper bound for the number of hidden nodes N_h required is

$$N_h \leq N_y \frac{N_p}{N_x} < N_y \left(\frac{N_p}{N_x} + 1\right). \tag{4.11}$$

When $N_x, N_h >\sim 5N_y$ (when there are more inputs and hidden nodes than outputs), the deterministic capacity (the number of patterns that can certainly be stored) is bounded below by $\sim N_w/N_y$. When $N_w \gg N_y$ (i.e. 1000×), the capacity is bounded above by

$$\sim \frac{N_w}{N_y} \log_2 \frac{N_w}{N_y}.$$

Thus

$$\frac{N_w}{N_y} - k_1 \leq C_d \leq \frac{N_w}{N_y} \log_2 \frac{N_w}{N_y} + k_2 \tag{4.12}$$

where k_1 and k_2 are small constants when $N_x + N_h \gg N_y$.

For good generalization, the number of training patterns should be at least several times larger than the capacity of the network. Otherwise, the amount of data will be insufficient to constrain the network.

4.4.5   MLP Capacity IV

The results of section 3.3 show that, on average, a single linear threshold unit with n inputs can be made to correctly classify up to $m = 2n$ random binary patterns before the probability of error falls to 1/2. In other words, a linear threshold unit has a probabilistic capacity of $m = 2n$ patterns.

Mitchison and Durbin [269] study the capacity of a MLP with one hidden layer. As above, the capacity is defined as the number of random input/output patterns that can be stored before the probability of error on recall reaches 1/2. They find that for a MLP with n inputs, one layer of h hidden units, and s output units, where $s \leq h \leq n$, the capacity m satisfies

$$2n \leq m \leq nt \log t \tag{4.13}$$

where $t = 1 + h/s$, $n \geq 2$, and $t \geq 2$ [269].

If there is a single output that is a fixed Boolean function of the hidden units, then $m \leq O(nh \log h)$. Comparing this to the case above when $s = 1$ and thus $t = 1 + h$ shows that allowing the output to be a variable function of the hidden units has an effect on the capacity equivalent to adding one hidden unit. Because a one-hidden-layer network can be connected in such a way that it has the same response as a single-layer network with the same number of inputs and outputs, the lower bound of $m \geq 2n$ still applies. For the special case $s = h = n$, they find $2n \leq m \leq 9.329n$.

Note that the capacity bounds are defined probabilistically for random functions on a randomly chosen set of points; the actual number of example pairs of a particular function that can be learned by a particular network will depend heavily on the function and how the examples are chosen. These are limiting bounds for the capacity; m certainly exceeds the lower bound and is certainly less than the upper bound. The actual capacity that can be achieved is less than the upper bound, possibly by a large amount.

5 Back-Propagation

Back-propagation is, by far, the most commonly used method for training multilayer feedforward networks. The term back-propagation refers to two different things. First, it describes a method to calculate the derivatives of the network training error with respect to the weights by a clever application of the derivative chain-rule. Second, it describes a training algorithm, basically equivalent to gradient descent optimization, for using those derivatives to adjust the weights to minimize the error.

The algorithm was popularized by Rumelhart, Hinton, and Williams [329, 330], although earlier work had been done by Werbos [390], Parker [295], and Le Cun ([89]; summarized in [90]). Together with the Hopfield network, it was responsible for much of the renewed interest in neural networks in the mid-1980s. Before back-propagation, most networks used nondifferentiable hard-limiting binary nonlinearities such as step functions and there were no well-known general methods for training multilayer networks. The breakthrough was perhaps not so much the application of the chain-rule, but the demonstration that layered networks of *differentiable* nonlinearities could perform useful nontrivial calculations and that they offer (in some implementations) attractive features such as fast response, fault tolerance, the ability to "learn" from examples, and some ability to generalize beyond the training data.

As a training algorithm, the purpose of back-propagation is to adjust the network weights so the network produces the desired output in response to every input pattern in a predetermined set of training patterns. It is a *supervised* algorithm in the sense that, for every input pattern, there is an externally specified "correct" output which acts as a target for the network to imitate. Any difference between the network output and the target is treated as an error to be minimized. A "teacher" must decide which patterns to include in the training set and specify the correct output for each. It is an *off-line* algorithm in the sense that training and normal operation occur at different times. In the usual case, training could be considered part of the "manufacturing" process wherein the network is trained once for a particular function, then frozen and put into operation. Normally, no further learning occurs after the initial training phase.

To train a network, it is necessary to have a set of input patterns and corresponding desired outputs, plus an error function (cost function) that measures the "cost" of differences between network outputs and desired values. The basic steps are these.

1. Present a training pattern and propagate it through the network to obtain the outputs.

2. Compare the outputs with the desired values and calculate the error.

3. Calculate the derivatives $\partial E/\partial w_{ij}$ of the error with respect to the weights.

4. Adjust the weights to minimize the error.

5. Repeat until the error is acceptably small or time is exhausted.

The error function measures the cost of differences between the network outputs and the desired values. The sum-of-squares function, below, is a common choice.

$$E_{SSE} = \sum_p \sum_i (d_{pi} - y_{pi})^2 \tag{5.1}$$

Here p indexes the patterns in the training set, i indexes the output nodes, and d_{pi} and y_{pi} are, respectively, the target and actual network output for the ith output node on the pth pattern. The mean-squared-error

$$E_{MSE} = \frac{1}{PN} E_{SSE} \tag{5.2}$$

normalizes E_{SSE} for the number of training patterns P and network outputs N. Advantages of the SSE and MSE functions include easy differentiability and the fact that the cost depends only on the magnitude of the error. In particular, a deviation of a given magnitude has the same cost independent of the input pattern and independent of errors on other outputs. For classification problems, logarithmic or cross-entropy error functions (section 2.1) are sometimes used. For real-world applications, the cost function may be specialized to assign different costs to different sorts of deviations; similar errors on different input patterns may have different costs and the cost of an error on one output could depend on the errors on other outputs.

5.1 Preliminaries

Back-propagation can be applied to any feedforward network with differentiable activation functions. In particular, it is not necessary that it have a layered structure. An arbitrary feedforward network will be assumed in the following.

Feedforward Indexing   For simplicity, assume the nodes are indexed so that $i > j$ implies that node i follows node j in terms of dependency. That is, the state of node i may depend, perhaps indirectly, on the state of node j, but node $j < i$ does not depend on node i. Such an index order is possible in any feedforward network, though it will not be unique in general. The advantage of this format is that it works in any feedforward network, including those with irregular structure and short-cut (layer skipping) connections. In simulations, it also lets us avoid the need to deal with each layer separately, keeping track of layer indexes. Of course, this indexing scheme is compatible with standard layered structures.

Because the dependencies are transmitted by the connection weights, connections are allowed from nodes with low indexes to nodes with higher indexes, but not vice versa. If

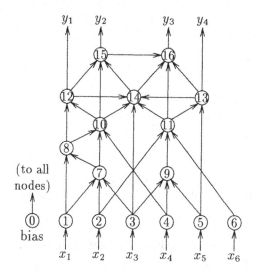

Figure 5.1
Feedforward indexing in an unlayered network. The nodes in a feedforward network can always be indexed so that $i > j$ if the state of node i depends on the state of node j (perhaps indirectly). Arbitrary connections are allowed from nodes with low indexes to nodes with higher indexes, but not vice versa; $i > j$ implies $w_{ji} \equiv 0$. This network has no particular function, but illustrates short-cut connections, apparently lateral (but still feedforward) connections, and the fact that outputs can be take from internal nodes.

w_{ij} denotes the weight *to* node i *from* node j then any forward link w_{ij}, $j < i$ is allowed, but backward links are prohibited, $w_{ji} = 0$. Figure 5.1 illustrates a possibility. Normally, the system inputs and the bias node will have low indexes since they potentially affect all other nodes and outputs will have high indexes.

5.1.1 Forward Propagation

In the forward pass, the network computes an output based on its current inputs. Each node i computes a weighted sum a_i of its inputs and passes this through a nonlinearity to obtain the node output y_i (see figure 5.2)

$$a_i = \sum_{j<i} w_{ij} y_j \tag{5.3}$$

$$y_i = f(a_i). \tag{5.4}$$

Normally f is a bounded monotonic function such as the tanh or sigmoid. Arbitrary differentiable functions can be used, but sigmoid-like "squashing" functions are standard. The index j in the sum runs over all indexes $j < i$ of nodes that could send input to node i.

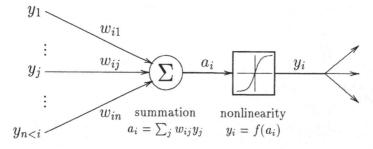

Figure 5.2
Forward propagation. In the forward pass, the input pattern is propagated through the network to obtain the output. Each node computes a weighted sum of its inputs and passes this through a nonlinearity, typically a sigmoid or tanh function.

If there is no connection from node j, weight w_{ij} is taken to be 0. As usual, it is assumed that there is a bias node with constant activation, $y_{bias} = 1$, to avoid the need for special handling of the bias weights.

Every node is evaluated in order, starting with the first hidden node and continuing to the last output node. In layered networks, the first hidden layer is updated based on the external inputs, the second hidden layer is updated based on the outputs of the first hidden layer, and so on to the output layer which is updated based on the outputs of the last hidden layer. In software simulations, it is sufficient to evaluate the nodes in order by node index. Because node i does not depend on any nodes $k > i$, all inputs to node i will be valid when it is evaluated. At the end of the sweep, the system outputs will be available at the output nodes.

5.1.2   Error Calculation

Unless the network is perfectly trained, the network outputs will differ somewhat from the desired outputs. The significance of these differences is measured by an error (or cost) function E. In the following, we use the SSE error function

$$E = \frac{1}{2} \sum_p \sum_i (d_{pi} - y_{pi})^2 \tag{5.5}$$

where p indexes the patterns in the training set, i indexes the output nodes, and d_{pi} and y_{pi} are, respectively, the desired target and actual network output for the ith output node on the pth pattern. The $\frac{1}{2}$ factor suppresses a factor of 2 later on. One of the reasons SSE is convenient is that errors on different patterns and different outputs are independent; the overall error is just the sum of the individual squared errors

$$E = \sum_p E_p \tag{5.6}$$

$$E_p = \frac{1}{2} \sum_i (d_{pi} - y_{pi})^2. \tag{5.7}$$

5.2   Back-Propagation: The Derivative Calculation

Having obtained the outputs and calculated the error, the next step is to calculate the derivative of the error with respect to the weights. First we note that $E_{SSE} = \sum_p E_p$ is just the sum of the individual pattern errors so the total derivative is just the sum of the per-pattern derivatives

$$\frac{\partial E}{\partial w_{ij}} = \sum_p \frac{\partial E_p}{\partial w_{ij}}. \tag{5.8}$$

The thing that makes back-propagation (the derivative calculation) efficient is how the operation is decomposed and the ordering of the steps. The derivative can be written

$$\frac{\partial E_p}{\partial w_{ij}} = \sum_k \frac{\partial E_p}{\partial a_k} \frac{\partial a_k}{\partial w_{ij}} \tag{5.9}$$

where the index k runs over all output nodes and a_j is the weighted-sum input for node j obtained in equation 5.3. It is convenient to first calculate a value δ_i for each node i

$$\delta_i = \frac{\partial E_p}{\partial a_i} \tag{5.10}$$

$$= \frac{\partial E_p}{\partial y_i} \frac{\partial y_i}{\partial a_i}, \tag{5.11}$$

which measures the contribution of a_i to the error on the current pattern. For simplicity, pattern indexes p are omitted on y_i, a_i, and other variables below.

For output nodes, $\partial E_p / \partial a_k$ is obtained directly

$$\delta_k = -(d_{pk} - y_{pk}) f'_k. \qquad \text{(for output nodes)} \tag{5.12}$$

The first term is obtained from equation 5.7,

$$\frac{\partial E_p}{\partial y_k} = -(d_{pk} - y_{pk}). \tag{5.13}$$

(This is the SSE result; different expressions will be obtained for other error functions.) The second term

$$\frac{\partial y_k}{\partial a_k} = f'(a_k) \tag{5.14}$$

is just the slope $f'_k \equiv f'(a_k)$ of the node nonlinearity at its current activation value. The sigmoid is convenient to use because f' is a simple function of the node output: $f'(a_k) = y(1 - y)$, where $y = f(a_k)$. The tanh function is also convenient, $f'(a_k) = 1 - y^2$.

For hidden nodes, δ_i is obtained indirectly. Hidden nodes can influence the error only through their effect on the nodes k to which they send output connections so

$$\delta_i = \frac{\partial E_p}{\partial a_i} = \sum_k \frac{\partial E_p}{\partial a_k} \frac{\partial a_k}{\partial a_i}. \tag{5.15}$$

But the first factor is just the δ_k of node k so

$$\delta_i = \sum_k \delta_k \frac{\partial a_k}{\partial a_i}. \tag{5.16}$$

The second factor is obtained by noting that if node i connects directly to node k then $\partial a_k/\partial a_i = f'_i w_{ki}$, otherwise it is zero. So we end up with

$$\delta_i = f'_i \sum_k w_{ki} \delta_k \tag{5.17}$$

(for hidden nodes). In other words, δ_i is a weighted sum of the δ_k values of nodes k to which it has connections w_{ki} (see figure 5.3).

Because δ_k must be calculated before δ_i, $i < k$, the process starts at the output nodes and works backward toward the inputs, hence the name "back-propagation." First δ values are calculated for the output nodes, then values are calculated for nodes that send connections to the outputs, then values are calculated for nodes two steps removed from the outputs, and so forth.

To summarize so far,

$$\delta_i = \begin{cases} -(d_{pi} - y_{pi})f'_i & \text{(for output nodes)} \\ f'_i \sum_k w_{ki} \delta_k & \text{(for hidden nodes)} \end{cases} \tag{5.18}$$

For output nodes, δ_i depends only on the error $d_i - y_i$ and the local slope f'_i of the node activation function. For hidden nodes, δ_i is a weighted sum of the δs of all the nodes it connects to, times its own slope f'_i. Because of the way the nodes are indexed, all delta

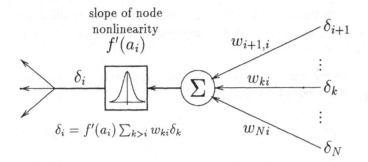

Figure 5.3
Backward propagation. Node deltas are calculated in the backward pass, starting at the output nodes and proceeding backwards. At each hidden node i, δ_i is calculated as a weighted linear combination of values δ_k, $k > i$, of the nodes k to which node i sends outputs. Note that the δ values travel backward against the normal direction of the connecting links.

values can be updated in a single sweep through the nodes in reverse order. In layered networks, delta values are first evaluated at the output nodes based on the current pattern errors, the last hidden layer is then evaluated based on the output delta values, the second-to-last hidden layer is updated based on the values of the last hidden layer, and so on backwards to the input layer. Normally it is not necessary to calculate delta values for the input layer, so the process usually stops with the first hidden layer.

Having obtained the node deltas, it is an easy step to find the partial derivatives $\partial E_p/\partial w$ with respect to the weights. The second term in (5.9) is $\partial a_k/\partial w_{ij}$. Because a_k is a simple linear sum, this is zero if $k \neq i$; otherwise

$$\frac{\partial a_i}{\partial w_{ij}} = y_j \tag{5.19}$$

where y_j is the output activation of node j. Finally, from (5.9), the derivative of pattern error E_p with respect to weight w_{ij} is then

$$\frac{\partial E_p}{\partial w_{ij}} = \delta_i y_j, \tag{5.20}$$

the product of the delta value at node i and the output of node j.

Derivatives with Respect to the Inputs   Normally, delta values are not calculated for the input nodes because they are not needed to adjust the weights. Notice, however, that for input nodes $\delta_i = \partial E/\partial a_i$ is the derivative of the error with respect to the input. Also, if the network has a single output y then setting $E = 1$ and back-propagating gives the derivative of the output with respect to the input, $\partial y / \partial x$. There are, of course, useful applications for these derivatives. They can be used, for example, in inverse problems where we seek input values that produce a particular output.

A Finite-Difference Approximation   As an alternative, the derivative can be estimated by a finite-difference approximation [44: 147]

$$\frac{\partial E_p}{\partial w_{ij}} = \frac{E_p(w_{ij} + \epsilon) - E_p(w_{ij} - \epsilon)}{2\epsilon} + O(\epsilon^2)$$

(5.21)

where $\epsilon \ll 1$ is a small offset. This is a weight perturbation technique [191, 192, 125]. Each weight must be perturbed twice and the error must be reevaluated for each perturbation. In a serial implementation, the error measurement takes $O(W)$ time so the total time required scales like $O(W^2)$, where W is the number of weights in the network. This is slower than back-propagation, which takes $O(W)$ time to find the derivative, but it is robust and simple to implement.

The method described perturbs each weight separately. A node perturbation technique is more efficient [44]. (The madeline III learning rule [403] is similar.) Recall from equation 5.10 that δ_i is the derivative of the error with respect to the node input sum, a_i. Instead of perturbing the weights, the a_i values of the hidden nodes are perturbed to obtain an approximation of the node deltas

$$\delta_i \equiv \frac{\partial E_p}{\partial a_i}$$

$$= \frac{E_p(a_i + \epsilon) - E_p(a_i - \epsilon)}{2\epsilon} + O(\epsilon^2).$$

(5.22)

Then equation 5.20 is used to calculate the gradient with respect to the weights. Each node must be perturbed twice and the error reevaluated. If there are H hidden nodes and W weights, this takes $O(2HW)$ steps. Calculation of E_p takes $O(W)$ time so the overall time scales like $O(HW)$. Depending on the relative sizes of H and W, this can be much faster than the $O(W^2)$ time of the previous method, but it is still longer than the $O(W)$ time of back-propagation. Summed weight perturbation [125] is a hybrid of weight and node perturbation methods.

Although finite-difference techniques are slower than back-propagation, they are simple to implement and useful for verify the correctness of more efficient calculations. They are also useful for training systems where analytic derivative calculation is not possible. Electronic circuit implementations, for example, may lack dedicated circuitry to do the back-propagation calculations. Finite-difference methods make it possible to estimate the derivatives using only feedforward calculations. In addition, they automatically account for nonideal circuit effects and faults that may occur in real systems.

5.3 Back-Propagation: The Weight Update Algorithm

Having obtained the derivatives, the next step is to update the weights so as to decrease the error. As noted earlier, the term back-propagation refers to (1) an efficient method to calculate the derivatives $\partial E / \partial w$ and (2) an optimization algorithm that uses those derivatives to adjust the weights to reduce the error. Having obtained the derivatives, we have the choice of continuing with back-propagation, the optimization algorithm, or using one of many alternative optimization methods that may be better adapted to the given problem.

Back-propagation (the optimization method) is basically equivalent to gradient descent. By definition, the gradient of E points in the direction that increases E the fastest. In order to minimize E, the weights are adjusted in the opposite direction. The weight update formula is

$$\Delta w_{ij} = -\eta \, \frac{\partial E}{\partial w_{ij}} \tag{5.23}$$

where the *learning rate* $\eta > 0$ is a small positive constant. Sometimes η is also called the *step size* parameter. If the derivative is positive (so increases in w causes increases in E) then the weight change is negative and vice versa. This approaches pure gradient descent when η is infinitesimal. Very small η values mean very long learning times though so larger rates are usually used. Typical values are in the range $0.05 < \eta < 0.75$. (This is just a rule of thumb, however; see section 6.1 for more discussion.)

The network is usually initialized with small random weights. Values are often selected uniformly from a range $[-a, +a]$ where $0.1 < a < 2$ typically. Random values are needed to break symmetry while small values are necessary to avoid immediate saturation of the sigmoid nonlinearities. Chapter 7 considers initialization methods in more detail.

5.3.1 Batch Learning

There are two basic weight-update variations, *batch-mode* and *on-line*. In batch-mode, every pattern p is evaluated to obtain the derivative terms $\partial E_p / \partial w$; these are summed to obtain the total derivative

$$\frac{\partial E}{\partial w} = \sum_p \frac{\partial E_p}{\partial w}. \tag{5.24}$$

and only then are the weights updated. This comes from the derivative rule for sums. The individual $\partial E_p/\partial w$ terms are obtained by application of the method of section 5.2 to each pattern p.

The basic steps are

• For every pattern p in the training set,

1. apply pattern p and forward propagate to obtain network outputs, and

2. calculate the pattern error E_p and back-propagate to obtain the single-pattern derivatives $\partial E_p/\partial w$.

• Add up all the single-pattern terms to get the total derivative.

• Update the weights

$$w(t+1) = w(t) - \eta \frac{\partial E}{\partial w}.$$

• Repeat.

Each such pass through the training set is called an *epoch*.

The gradient is calculated exactly and weight changes are proportional to the gradient so batch-mode learning approximates gradient descent when the step size η is small (figure 5.4). In general, each weight update reduces the error by only a small amount so many epochs are needed to minimize the error.

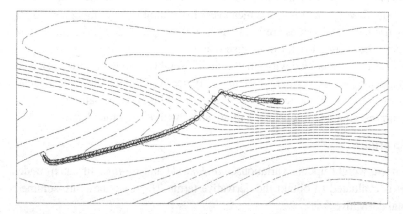

Figure 5.4
Batch-mode back-propagation is a close approximation to true gradient descent. At each step, the weights are adjusted in the direction that minimizes the error the fastest. When the learning rate is small, the weights trace a smooth trajectory down the gradient of the error surface.

5.3.2 On-Line Learning

An alternative to batch-mode is *on-line* or *pattern-mode* learning. In on-line learning, the weights are updated after each pattern presentation. Generally, a pattern p is chosen at random and presented to the network. The output is compared with the target for that pattern and the errors are back-propagated to obtain the single-pattern derivative $\partial E_p/\partial w$. The weights are then updated immediately, using the gradient of the single-pattern error. Generally, the patterns are presented in a random, constantly changing order to avoid cyclic effects.

The steps are:

- Pick a pattern p at random from the training set,

1. apply pattern p and forward propagate to obtain network outputs, and

2. calculate the pattern error E_p and back-propagate to obtain the single-pattern derivatives $\partial E_p/\partial w$.

- Update the weights immediately using the single-pattern derivative

$$w(t+1) = w(t) - \eta \frac{\partial E_p}{\partial w}.$$

- Repeat.

An advantage of this approach is that there is no need to store and sum the individual $\partial E_p/\partial w$ contributions; each pattern derivative is evaluated, used immediately, and then discarded. This may make hardware implementation easier when resources are limited. Another possible advantage is that many more weight updates occur in a given amount of time. If the training set contains M patterns, for example, on-line learning would make M weight changes in the time that batch-mode learning makes only one.

A possible disadvantage (from an analysis standpoint, at least) is that this is no longer a simple approximation to gradient descent. Figure 5.5 illustrates the relationship between the true gradient and the single-pattern terms in a typical case. The single-pattern derivatives can be viewed as noisy estimates of the true gradient. As a group, they sum to the gradient but each has a random deviation that need not be small. When the gradient is strong, the average single-pattern derivative has a positive projection on the gradient (because it is the sum of the single-pattern terms) so the error usually decreases after most weight changes. Still, there may be terms with negative projections or large orthogonal deviations which may cause the error to increase after some updates. On average though, the weight change will at least move downhill even if it doesn't take the most direct path.

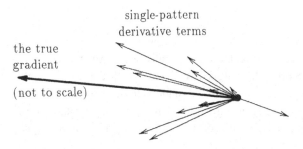

Figure 5.5
In on-line learning, weight updates occur after each pattern presentation. The single-pattern derivative terms can be viewed as noisy estimates of the gradient. They are not parallel to it in general, but on average they have a positive projection onto it (because the gradient is the sum of the single-pattern terms) so the error usually decreases after most weight changes. Some terms may have negative projections or large orthogonal deviations, however, which may cause the error to increase occasionally.

On-line learning differs from pure gradient descent in that the sum (5.24) is never evaluated exactly because the weights change after each pattern so the individual terms are evaluated at different points. The difference is minimal when η is very small; the weights won't change much between steps so the effect after all patterns have been evaluated is approximately the same as if all terms had been evaluated at a single point and summed to perform a single weight change which has the same overall result.

Very small learning rates tend to make learning very slow, however, so larger values are often used and the stochastic elements become important. Instead of following a smooth trajectory down the gradient, the weight vector tends to jitter around the $E(w)$ surface, mostly moving downhill, but occasionally jumping uphill (figure 5.6). To a first approximation, the magnitude of the jitter is proportional to the learning rate η. The randomness arises because training patterns are selected in a random, constantly changing order. Cyclic, fixed orders are generally avoided because of the possibility of convergence to a limit cycle (figure 5.7).

This randomness has advantages and disadvantages. On the plus side, it gives the algorithm some stochastic search properties. When pure gradient descent arrives at a local minimum, it is simply stuck. In on-line (per-pattern) learning, however, the weight state tends to jitter around its equilibrium value. Instead of sitting quietly at the minimum, it visits many nearby points and occasionally, if chance allows, may bounce out of a poor minimum and find a better solution. Thus, on-line learning may have a better chance of finding a global minimum than true gradient descent. On the minus side, the weight vector never settles to a stable value. Having found a good minimum, it may then wander off. Also on the minus side, when the jitter is very large, it may completely hide any deterministic gradient information so the system may be unable to follow subtle paths in the $E(w)$ surface.

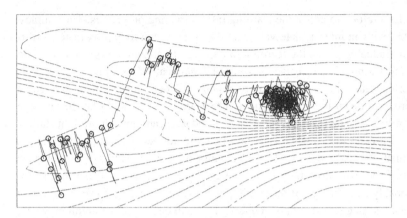

Figure 5.6
In on-line learning, patterns are generally presented in a random, changing order and weights are updated after each pattern presentation. Instead of smoothly rolling down the error gradient, the weight vector dances along a semi-random path, mostly moving downhill, but occasionally jumping uphill. Upon reaching a low spot, the weight vector jitters around the minimum but is unable to settle unless the step size is reduced. Circles show the weights at the start of each epoch and line segments show the single-pattern steps within each epoch.

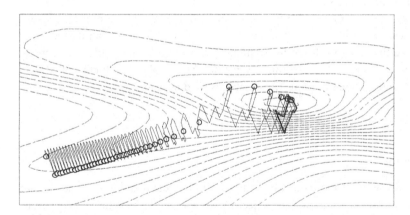

Figure 5.7
When patterns are presented in a cyclic order during on-line learning, as above, the sequence of steps in epoch $t + 1$ tends to be similar to the sequence in epoch t so the weight trajectory has a semi-periodic behavior. A danger is that the trajectory will converge to a limit cycle, as shown, and be unable to reach the minimum. One way to break the cycle is to change the pattern selection order. Reduction of the learning rate may also break the cycle or, if done gradually, may reduce the "diameter," allowing it to close in around the minimum. Circles show the weights at the start of each epoch and line segments show the single-pattern steps within each epoch.

It is common, therefore, to adjust the learning rate as training progresses. The simplest scheme is to start with an intermediate value, let the system train to approximate convergence, and then gradually reduce the learning rate to zero to allow the system to settle to the minimum. The learning rate can also be adjusted dynamically depending on conditions encountered during training. It is desirable to maintain a balance between stochastic search and efficient progress down the error gradient. The learning rate should not be so large that any single weight update (or likely sequence of updates) can move the weight state to a completely new area of the weight space, but it should not be so small that the system merely approximates gradient descent. If a large majority of single-pattern vectors have a common direction (positive projection on the average vector, the gradient) then the learning rate can probably be increased. If the single-pattern vectors have no apparent common direction then the learning rate should be reduced. This will occur near a minimum, where the gradient goes to zero because the single-pattern vectors cancel. It may also occur at the bottom of a "ravine" in the error surface, where the single-pattern vectors often group into two bundles pointing in opposite directions across the long axis of the ravine. In these cases, smaller learning rates would allow the system to settle to the minimum. Section 9.8 describes the "search then converge" algorithm, an adaptive learning method that controls the learning rate automatically.

A side note about terminology: The label "on-line learning" may be confusing because it implies that learning may occur in the field during normal operation and that it is not necessary to take the system off-line for training. But on-line learning, like batch-mode learning, is normally done off-line during a separate training phase with controlled data sets. The label "pattern-mode learning" is sometimes used instead.

5.4 Common Modifications

5.4.1 Momentum

A common modification of the basic weight update rule is the addition of a *momentum* term. The idea is to stabilize the weight trajectory by making the weight change a combination of the gradient-decreasing term in equation 5.23 plus a fraction of the previous weight change. The modified weight change formula is

$$\Delta \mathbf{w}(t) = -\eta \, \frac{\partial E}{\partial \mathbf{w}}(t) + \alpha \Delta \mathbf{w}(t-1). \tag{5.25}$$

That is, the weight change $\Delta \mathbf{w}(t)$ is a combination of a step down the negative gradient, $-\eta \frac{\partial E}{\partial \mathbf{w}}(t)$, plus a fraction $0 \le \alpha < 1$ of the previous weight change. Typical values are $0 \le \alpha < 0.9$.

This gives the system a certain amount of inertia since the weight vector will tend to continue moving in the same direction unless opposed by the gradient term. Effects of momentum are considered in more detail in section 6.2. Briefly, momentum tends to damp oscillations in the weight trajectory and accelerate learning in regions where $\partial E/\partial w$ is small.

5.4.2 Weight Decay

Another common modification of the weight update rule is the addition of a *weight decay* term. Weight decay is sometimes used to help adjust the complexity of the network to the difficulty of the problem. The idea is that if the network is overly complex, then it should be possible to delete many weights without increasing the error significantly. One way to do this is to give the weights a tendency to drift to zero by reducing their magnitudes slightly at each iteration. The update rule with weight decay is then

$$\Delta \mathbf{w}(t) = -\eta \frac{\partial E}{\partial \mathbf{w}}(t) - \rho \mathbf{w}(t). \tag{5.26}$$

where $0 \le \rho \ll 1$ is the weight decay parameter. If $\partial E/\partial w_i = 0$ for some weight w_i, then w_i will decay to zero exponentially. Otherwise, if the weight really is necessary then $\partial E/\partial w_i$ will be nonzero and the two terms will balance at some point, preventing the weight from decaying to zero. Weight decay is considered in more detail in sections 6.2.4 and 16.5 and chapter 13.

5.5 Pseudocode Examples

At present, most artificial neural networks exist only as simulations on serial computers. The following samples illustrate the basic steps of back-propagation in 'C' pseudocode. Note, the purpose of the code is only to illustrate the algorithm. Real code would have to include many distracting details!

Forward Propagation In the feedforward step, an input pattern is propagated through the network to obtain an output. In 'C' pseudocode, this might look like

```
void forward_propagate( double *input_pattern )
   {
   /* copy pattern to input nodes */
   for( i=0; i<number_of_inputs; i++ )
      node_output[i+1] = pattern[i];
   node_output[0] = 1;    /* set bias to 1 */
```

```
/* compute outputs of the remaining nodes */
for( i=first_hidden_index; i<number_of_nodes; i++ ) {
    double sum = 0;
    for( j=0; j<i; j++ )
        sum += weight[i][j] * node_output[j];
    node_output[i] = sigmoid( sum );
    }
}
```

When the function returns, the network outputs are available in the values of the output nodes. Because of the feedforward node indexing scheme, each `node_output[j]` is ready and available when it is needed as input to following nodes $i > j$. The bias node has index 0 and input nodes have indices from 1 to `number_of_inputs`. The rest of the nodes are indexed in feedforward order, with the output nodes last. The entire network can thus be evaluated in a single sweep through the nodes without extra bookkeeping to keep track of layers or short-cut connections.

For simplicity, the weight matrix is square with slots for all possible connections (including unallowed backward connections). Mathematically, weight w_{ij} can be treated as zero if there is no connection from node j to node i. In practice, of course, it would be more efficient to store connection information for each node so that only those weights that actually exist are examined. Similar details are ignored here for simplicity.

Backward Error Propagation   The derivatives of the error on the current pattern with respect to the weights are calculated in the back-propagation step. The following pseudocode shows how this might be implemented assuming the network response to the pattern has just been calculated by forward propagation. The `*targets` argument points to an array of target values. For simplicity, assume there is one array element per network node so the same index can be used to access nodes and their target values. A sigmoid node function is assumed.

```
void backprop_node_deltas( double *targets )
    {
    /* calculate node deltas for output nodes */
    for( i=last_output_node; i>=first_output_node; i-- ) {
        double err = targets[i] - node_value[i];
        delta[i] = err * node_value[i]*(1-node_value[i]);
                    /* (sigmoid slope term) */
        }
```

```
/* then calculate deltas for hidden nodes, working backwards */
for( i=last_hidden_node; i>=first_hidden_node; i-- ) {
    delta[i] = 0;
    for( k=i+1; k<=last_output_node; k++ )
        delta[i] += weight[k][i] * delta[k];
    delta[i] *= node_value[i]*(1-node_value[i]);
                /* (sigmoid slope term) */
    }
}
```

Batch-Mode Weight Update   The code just described would normally be included in a larger loop to add up the weight change contributions from each pattern. One epoch of batch-mode training could be done as follows.

```
void backprop_batch_one_epoch(void)
    {
    /* clear the dEdW accumulators */
    for( i=0; i<number_of_nodes; i++ )
        for( j=0; j<i; j++ )
            dEdW[i][j] = 0;

    /* add up dEdW contributions from each pattern */
    for( ip=0; ip<number_of_patterns; ip++ ) {
        forward_propagate( pattern[ip] );
        backprop_node_deltas( targets[ip] );
        for( i=0; i<number_of_nodes; i++ )
            for( j=0; j<i; j++ )
                if ( weight_really_exists(i,j) )
                    dEdW[i][j] += delta[i] * node_value[j];
        }

    /* change the weights */
    for( i=0; i<number_of_nodes; i++ )
        for( j=0; j<i; j++ )
            weights[i][j] += learning_rate * dEdW[i][j];
    }
```

On-Line Weight Update   On-line training is even simpler because there is no need to clear and accumulate the single-pattern derivative terms. One pass through the training set in on-line mode could be done as follows.

```
void backprop_online_one_epoch(void)
   {
   /* for each pattern... */
   for( ip=0; ip<number_of_patterns; ip++ ) {
      index = choose_one_randomly();
      forward_propagate( pattern[index] );
      backprop_node_deltas( targets[index] );

      /* change the weights */
      for( i=0; i<number_of_nodes; i++ )
         for( j=0; j<i; j++ )
            if ( weight_really_exists(i,j) )
               weights[i][j] += learning_rate * delta[i]*node_value[j];
   }
}
```

5.6   Remarks

To reiterate, back-propagation refers to (1) an efficient method to calculate derivatives of the training error with respect to the weights, and (2) a training algorithm that uses those derivatives to adjust the weights to minimize the error. Other optimization methods can be used to update the weights, so it is not uncommon to hear of a network trained by, say, the conjugate gradient method using back-propagation to calculate the gradient.

Confusion may arise because the term *back-propagation network* is sometimes used to refer to a standard multilayer network trained by back-propagation. Although most people understand the term, it is not strictly correct because (1) the same network could be trained by other methods and (2) back-propagation can be used to train other types of networks. Back-propagation is simply one method, albeit the most common, for training these types of networks.

Although the algorithm is usually derived for a fully connected layered network, it can be applied to networks with arbitrary feedforward structure. Any number of weights can be held constant. It is also possible for internal nodes to have targets. This may be useful when it is known that the network must compute some intermediate function in order to calculate the final desired output. In this case, the node delta is the sum of deltas obtained by considering it as both an output node and a hidden node. (Section 16.10 discusses the use of this sort of information as hint functions.)

The thing that makes back-propagation more than a simple application of the derivative chain-rule is the ordering of the calculations. A naive application of the chain-rule separately for each of the W weights in a network could result in an $O(W^2)$ time algorithm: $O(W)$ time to calculate $\partial E/\partial w$ for a single weight multiplied by the W weights in the network. Back-propagation, in contrast, is an $O(W)$ time algorithm. Bishop [44] likens the practical importance of this difference to that of the fast Fourier transform (FFT).

A side note: In this book we mainly discuss feedforward networks of sigmoidal units and a large part is devoted to back-propagation and its variations. Although back-propagation is one the most popular learning techniques for neural networks, it is a mistake to equate the entire field with back-propagation in layered perceptrons. Even considering only non-biological networks, there are many optimization methods besides back-propagation and there are many structures in addition to layered sigmoidal networks. Most of the properties that make artificial neural networks attractive (e.g., potential parallelism, fast response, fault tolerance, learning from examples, generalization, etc.) have nothing to do with back-propagation per se. The algorithm is simply one of many possible methods to select the network weights. Ideally, any optimization method minimizing the same error function would produce the same weights so the resulting properties are not attributable to back-propagation alone. Likewise, the neural networks field contains more than just layered perceptrons. Although back-propagation and layered networks are adequate for many applications, there are good reasons to explore alternatives. Back-propagation, for example, often requires very long training times so much research has been devoted to finding faster methods. Similarly, there are applications where it is useful to build more structure into the network rather than using a simple fully connected layered structure. In a sense, back-propagation in layered feedforward networks could be viewed as a local minimum and it is hoped that further research will discover better methods. In any case, biological networks are certainly not simple layered feedforward structures and it is very unlikely that they adapt by back-propagation so we may have more to learn.

5.7 Training Time

Although back-propagation has been used successfully on a wide range of problems, one of the common complaints is that it is slow. Even simple problems may take hundreds of iterations to converge and harder problems may take many thousands of iterations. Training times of days or even weeks are not unusual for large practical applications.

Much work, therefore, has been done in search of faster methods. Effects of the learning rate and momentum are considered in chapter 6. Methods of weight initialization are considered in chapter 7. Chapter 9 summarizes a number of variations of the back-propagation algorithm intended to reduce training times and chapter 10 reviews some classical optimization methods that have better theoretical convergence properties.

The size of the training set obviously affects training times because each pass through the data takes twice as long when the data set is twice as big. Additional patterns that contain no new information may simply make learning slower. This depends on the training method and cost function, among other things. In batch-mode, each pass is slower but with a SSE cost function the weight changes will be twice as large so learning may converge in half the number of epochs if it remains stable. In on-line mode, each pass is slower but twice as many weight updates are done in each pass so the overall time may not change. Less obviously, the additional patterns may supply new information that restrict possible solutions and make the problem harder so that more iterations are required or they may supply missing information that makes the problem easier.

5.7.1   Scaling of Training Time

Hinton [169, section 6.10] argues that a network with W weights typically requires $O(W^3)$ training time on a serial machine. $O(W)$ cycles are required for each forward and backward propagation of a single pattern, $O(W)$ training patterns are typically needed to achieve good generalization, and (perhaps) $O(W)$ weight updates are required for each pattern. Implementation on parallel hardware would reduce this only by a factor of W resulting in $O(W^2)$ training time.

Tesauro and Janssens [367] observed that training time for the parity problem increases approximately as 4^d where d is the number of inputs (the predicate order). Although some problems are easy, Judd [202, 203] has shown that the general problem is NP-complete. That is, the training time scales exponentially with the problem size in the worst case. Networks of hard-limiting linear threshold elements are considered, but the results seem applicable to networks of sigmoidal units.

This problem is not unique to back-propagation, of course. Optimization methods cannot be held responsible for the rapid growth of the search space with the size of the problem. It does suggest, though, that a simple algorithm like back-propagation alone will not be adequate to find solutions for hard problems. Indeed, when solutions to interesting problems are found, the critical factor is often external information supplied by the network designer in selecting a network architecture, collecting and editing *relevant* data, choosing input-output representations, selecting an error function, and so forth.

Some possible causes of slow training include:

• Overly restrictive convergence criteria. If the trained network will be used for classification purposes it usually isn't necessary to train every output to within 10^{-6} of the target value.

• "Paralysis" due to sigmoid saturation.

- Flat regions in the error surface where the gradient is small.

- Ill-conditioning of the Hessian matrix (the matrix of second derivatives of the error with respect to the weights).

- A poor choice of parameters such as learning rate and momentum.

- The simple-mindedness of gradient descent: more sophisticated algorithms may use available information more efficiently.

- The global nature of sigmoid functions. A change in one weight may alter the network response over the entire input space. This changes the derivatives fed back to every other weight and produces further weight changes whose effects reverberate throughout the network. It takes time for these interactions to settle.

- The size and distribution of the training set.

- Poor representations, irrelevant inputs.

- Delta attenuation in deep networks.

- Poor network architectures. The minimal-size network just adequate to represent the data may require a very specific set of weights that may be very hard to find. Larger networks may have more ways to fit the data and so may be easier to train with less chance of convergence to poor local minima.

Many of these factors are related of course. Sigmoid saturation may cause flat spots in the error surface, for example, which are reflected in a poorly conditioned Hessian, which, in turn, makes it difficult to choose a good learning rate. Some of these factors are due to weaknesses of back-propagation and might be avoided by algorithmic improvements while others are more fundamental.

One way to reduce training times is to increase the efficiency of the optimization procedure. Chapter 6 discusses the effects of the learning rate and momentum parameters and gives hints for selecting reasonable values. Chapter 9 summarizes variations of the back-propagation algorithm intended to improve training times; many are techniques for adaptively controlling the learning rate. Chapter 10 reviews more sophisticated optimization methods that are reputed to have better convergence properties than gradient descent.

Another way to improve training times is to give the network a headstart on a good solution. Chapter 7 discusses some network initialization techniques based on this idea.

Yet another way to reduce training times is to identify and fix the problems that cause slow convergence. The structure of the $E(\mathbf{w})$ landscape has a fundamental effect on training time; some common properties are discussed in chapter 8. Many of these are reflected in numerical properties of the Hessian matrix discussed in section 8.6. Delta-attenuation is described in section 6.1.8 in conjunction with learning-rate adjustment methods.

Finally, another way to speed things up is to change the problem. Part of the reason for slow learning is that the algorithm is limited to adjusting existing weights. If the network structure is poorly matched to the problem, this may be very difficult. Algorithms that are free to change the structure during learning are often able to learn much faster. Chapters 12 and 13 discuss constructive algorithms, which "grow" networks to fit the problem, and pruning algorithms, which reduce large networks to fit the problem.

Paralysis   In some cases, long learning times can be attributed to paralysis due to sigmoid saturation. That is, the sigmoid and related functions have nearly flat tails where the derivative is approximately zero for large inputs (positive or negative). Because δ_i is proportional to the slope f_i', this leads to small derivatives for weights feeding into the node and so on backward through the network. If many nodes are saturated, then weight derivatives may become very small and learning will be slow. In digital simulations, deltas may become so small that they are quantized to zero and learning stops (double precision arithmetic is sometimes recommended for this reason).

Large external inputs or large weights are a typical cause of saturation. Normalization of the inputs to a reasonable range and initialization with small random weights are standard remedies. The weight initialization range required to avoid saturation depends on the number of inputs to a node and their correlations so different ranges may be needed in different cases. Chapter 7 discusses some weight initialization techniques based on this idea. Gain-scaling (section 8.7) has also been suggested as a way to avoid and correct for saturation.

Regardless of how the network is initialized, the weights change during learning so saturation may become a problem at a later stage. Because paralysis can have such a strong affect on learning time, it is helpful to detect and correct it before it becomes serious. In software simulations, it is relatively easy to check for paralysis after each pattern presentation [382]. If a significant fraction (e.g., 1%) of nodes are near saturation (e.g., have absolute magnitude greater than 0.9 assuming tanh nodes), then steps can be taken to fix the problem (e.g., reduce the learning rate, reduce the sigmoid gain, or scale the weights). The computational cost of the test is insignificant so it can be done often to allow detection of imminent paralysis before it becomes a problem.

6 Learning Rate and Momentum

6.1 Learning Rate

Recalling (5.25), the back-propagation weight update with momentum is

$$\Delta \mathbf{w}(t) = -\eta \, \frac{\partial E}{\partial \mathbf{w}}(t) + \alpha \Delta \mathbf{w}(t-1).$$

The learning rate and momentum parameters η and α have an obvious direct effect on the training process so it is desirable to choose good values. Typical ranges are $0.05 \leq \eta \leq 0.75$ and $0 \leq \alpha \leq 0.9$ [330]. Many other factors also affect training, so these should be treated as reasonable guidelines rather than inviolable limits.

Although $\eta = 0.1$ is often suggested, this is basically an arbitrary constant, a "magic number,"—which *is not* appropriate for all problems or even at all times during training. It may work well for many problems, but much larger or smaller values may work better on particular problems. For one thing, the SSE error function is sensitive to the size of the training set. In the familiar two-input XOR problem, for example, there are four training patterns. If all training patterns are duplicated K times, the form of the target function is unchanged but E_{SSE} becomes K times as large, as do the partial derivatives and weight changes. If K is large, say 1000, the weights could become very large in a single step which would almost certainly drive the sigmoid nonlinearities into hard saturation and essentially halt learning. In effect, redundancy in the training set can amplify the effective learning rate to an unreasonably large value. This example is contrived, but similar things can happen when data is heavily clustered. If the clusters are well separated, each can be viewed as many repetitions of a single point with a small amount of noise.

One remedy for this problem would be to use the mean squared error

$$E_{MSE} = \frac{1}{M} \sum_{m=1}^{M} (t_m - y_m)^2$$

to normalize for the size M of the training set. This is reasonable, but it is common practice to use the unnormalized sum-of-squares error. An equivalent solution is to scale the learning rate by the size of the training set.

Unfortunately, there are other problems this does not fix. Redundant input or output nodes (e.g., multiple nodes with very similar training values) as well as internal redundancy (e.g., multiple hidden nodes computing similar functions) can have a similar amplifying effect. Less obvious redundancy in the form of linear dependencies also causes problems.

Other factors affecting the choice of learning rate include

- The distribution of the training data.

• Momentum. Momentum amplifies the effective learning rate to $\eta_{eff} = \eta/(1 - \alpha)$ so large momentum values call for smaller η values, in general.

• Weight magnitudes. If the weights are initialized to very small values, the calculated derivatives will be small and larger initial learning rates will be needed to achieve the same training speeds. But then as the weights grow during training, it may be necessary to reduce the learning rate to avoid instability and saturation.

• The shape of the error surface $E(\mathbf{w})$. The gradient $\partial E/\partial \mathbf{w}$ can change dramatically as $\mathbf{w}$ changes. Large learning rates are useful to traverse flat areas quickly, but small values may be needed to avoid instability in "hilly" areas. A single learning rate may not be optimal in all parts of the space.

• Stochastic training. In on-line training, where randomness of pattern selection acts as noise, it is usually necessary to gradually reduce η to zero in later learning stages to obtain convergence to stable weights.

• The difficulty of the problem. In vague terms, difficult problems seem to call for fine distinctions and small learning rates. Often this can be interpreted as ill-conditioning of the Hessian matrix.

Many of these factors are related, of course. The point is that, in general, it is not possible to calculate a best learning rate a priori.

The same learning rate may not even be appropriate in all parts of the network. The general fact that the error is more sensitive to changes in some weights than in others makes it useful to assign different learning rates to each weight. The problem of delta-attenuation (section 6.1.8), where input weight layers receive smaller back-propagated deltas and thus tend to learn much more slowly than output weight layers, makes it useful to use larger learning rates in the early layers. If a single global value must be used, compromises must be made.

Because poor training parameters can cause poor performance it is often necessary to do a mini-search for a good set of training parameters as part of the search for a good set of weights. This is a common criticism of back-propagation as an optimization algorithm. (Sometimes the algorithm is blamed for failure due to an unreasonable choice of parameters, however.)

The difficulty of choosing a good learning rate a priori is one of the reasons adaptive learning rate methods are useful and popular. A good adaptive algorithm will usually converge much faster than simple back-propagation with a poorly chosen fixed learning rate. The speed advantage may be small compared to training with an optimal constant learning rate, but even then adaptive methods relieve the user of the need to search for the optimal value. Most methods adapt the rate dynamically as appropriate for changing conditions and many assign different rates appropriate for different parts of the network. A few methods are summarized in chapter 9.

6.1.1   An Example

The following example is used to illustrate how different choices of learning rate and momentum affect the training process. The illustrations that follow do not show how to calculate good parameters, but they may help in recognizing when parameter changes are needed. It should be emphasized that the curves in the figures are unique to this example and different curves will be obtained from different networks, data sets, initialization conditions, and so forth. The example is intended to be representative in that most problems will show qualitative similarities, but quantitative differences should be expected. Similar illustrations can be found in [67, 194, 372].

Training Details   A 4/4/1 network was trained to learn the 4-bit parity problem using plain batch back-propagation. This problem was chosen because it is well understood and simple enough to repeat many times but not completely trivial. Input values were ± 1 and target values were ± 0.9. Tanh nonlinearities were used at the hidden and output nodes. Initial weights were uniformly distributed in $[-0.5, +0.5]$. A single nonadaptive learning rate was used for the entire network.

Note that *mean-squared-error* was used rather than sum-of-squares error. Use of MSE with learning rate η_o is equivalent to use of SSE with a learning rate η_o/M where M is the number of training patterns, $M = 16$ here. The difference is minor but affects the interpretation of the results.

A variety of learning rates from 0.001 to 10 (37 values) and momentums from 0 to 0.99 (14 values) were tested. One hundred trials were run for each parameter pair; 51,800 networks were trained in all, each with different random initial weights. Each network was allowed 5000 training epochs. Learning was considered successful (converged) if $E_{MSE} < 0.001$ or if every pattern was classified correctly with error less than 0.2. An attempt was made to detect stalled networks: if the change in E_{MSE} between epochs was less than 10^{-12} or if the magnitude of the gradient was less than 10^{-10}, the network was considered stuck and training was halted early. This saved training time but may have skewed the convergence probability estimates downward.

The average convergence time for each parameter pair was calculated as the sum of the times for the converged networks divided by the number of networks that converged

$$T_{avg} = \frac{\sum_i T_i}{N_{converged}}.$$

If no networks converged for a particular set of parameters, T_{avg} was set to 5000 for graphing purposes. The probability of convergence was estimated as the number of networks that converged divided by the number trained (100). Results are summarized in the following sections.

6.1.2 Training Time versus Learning Rate

Figure 6.1 shows typical plots of expected training time and probability of convergence versus learning rate η. The exact shape and scale of the curves will differ depending on details of the particular problem, but the shapes are characteristic. In general, the training time versus learning rate curve has a bathtub or "U" shape. At very small learning rates, training times are high simply because each weight change is so small; the convergence time is controlled mainly by the small step size and decreases as the learning rate increases. Beyond a certain critical value, however, the average training time increases sharply and the probability of convergence falls to zero. In the figure, the critical point shifts to lower learning rates as momentum increases.

The curves in figure 6.1 were obtained by averaging over many trials. Figure 6.1.2 shows the distribution of the data points behind the averages. At very high learning rates, most networks either do not converge or converge to poor solutions and become stuck. Of the networks that do converge, however, most do so very quickly. These probably depend on lucky initializations. Beyond the critical point, the average training time T_{avg} (excluding networks that do not converge) continues to decrease as learning rate increases but the probability of lucky initializations decreases faster. At some point the decreased likelihood of convergence outweighs training time improvements and the plotted training time increases sharply. ($T_{avg} = 5000$ was plotted when none of the 100 trials converged.)

A loose analogy can be made with driving a car. The time to reach your destination depends on situation-specific details such as the make of the car, weather and traffic conditions, and the general terrain along your route. For a given set of conditions, however, there is presumably an optimum speed with the lowest average travel time. The time depends directly on your driving speed but that also affects the probability of mishaps. At very low speeds, the risk of accident is negligible and you can almost always reduce travel time by driving faster. At increasing speeds, travel time decreases further but the risk of accident rises. At some point depending on particular conditions the probability of driving off the road and spending the morning at the repair shop approaches 1 and the expected travel time soars.

6.1.3 Interaction of Learning Rate and Momentum

Figure 6.1 illustrates that when the learning rate is small, large momentum values $\alpha \to 1$ generally increase the speed and probability of convergence. In the simulations, most cases

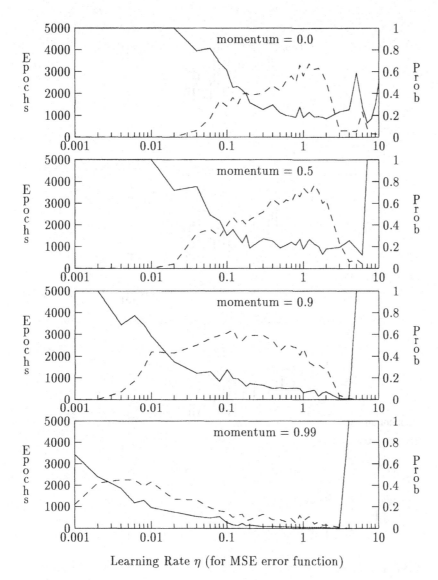

Figure 6.1
Average training time (solid) and convergence probability (dashed) versus learning rate for $\alpha = 0, 0.5, 0.9,$ 0.99. A 4/4/1 network was trained on the 4-bit parity problem with batch back-propagation and the MSE error function. Each point is the average of 100 runs with different random initial weights. Note: Use of the MSE error function rather than SSE normalizes the learning rate by the size of the training set. See section 6.1.1 for simulation details.

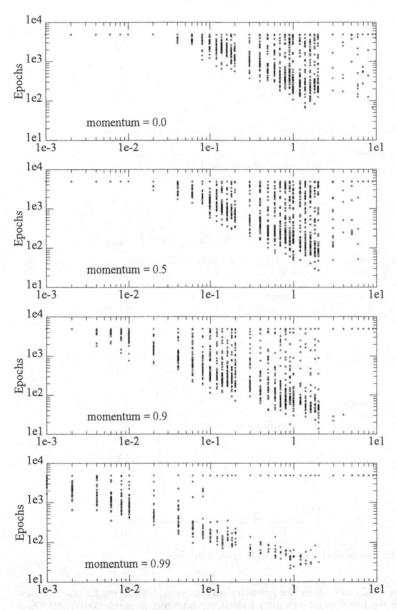

Learning rate η (for MSE error function)

with very small learning rates didn't converge within the allotted time unless α was large. (Of course, they might have converged eventually if more time were allowed.) In the figure, at $\eta = 0.01$ the highest probability of convergence was obtained for $\alpha = 0.99$. For large learning rates, the situation is reversed and very few cases converge unless the momentum is small. In terms of momentum, the figure shows the peak of the probability of convergence density function shifting to lower learning rates as α increases.

Section 6.2 shows that for small perturbations the *effective learning rate* with momentum is $\eta' = \eta/(1 - \alpha)$. That is, momentum has an amplifying effect on the learning rate. For $\alpha \to 1^-$, the denominator is small and the effective learning rate is large; at $\alpha = 0.99$, for example, $\eta' = 100\eta$. Figure 6.3 illustrates this, showing the expected training time and probability of convergence *vs. effective* learning rate for selected momentum values. Division by $1 - \alpha$ has the effect of sliding the curves horizontally so they overlay one another; there are random deviations, but the curves appear to follow the same basic trend.

The same effective learning rate can obtained from different combinations of η and α. The curves show that these yield roughly the same average training time but differ in the location of the critical point where convergence becomes unlikely. In this example it appears that higher effective learning rates can be obtained with small η and large α rather than vice versa. That is, convergence is obtained at $\eta' = 100$, for example, with $\alpha = 0.99$ but not with the lower momentum values.

6.1.4   Typical *E(t)* Curves

Batch Mode   Figures 6.4 and 6.5 show typical RMS error versus training time curves for various learning rates with constant momentum $\alpha = 0.5$. All curves were generated from the same initial weight vector. The training problem, network, and initialization parameters described in section 6.1.1 were used. Note that the learning rates in these figures are for the SSE error function; in Figures 6.1 through 6.3 the corresponding learning rates for the MSE function are 16 times larger.

Although the exact shape of the $E(t)$ curve is unique to each problem and choice of parameters (including the random starting point), several general things can be observed. At very low learning rates, the $E(t)$ curve is smooth, but training is very slow. The error almost always decreases with time, rarely if ever increasing, and there are long flat runs followed by relatively steep drop-offs. In this range, increased learning rates lead to faster

◄ **Figure 6.2**
Actual training times versus learning rate for various momentum values. At high learning rate and momentum, most networks either do not converge or converge to poor solutions and become stuck. Of the networks that do converge, however, most do so very quickly. Each vertical strip shows points for 100 networks initialized with different random weights. Note: Use of the MSE error function rather than SSE scales the learning rate by the size of the training set. See section 6.1.1 for details of the simulation.

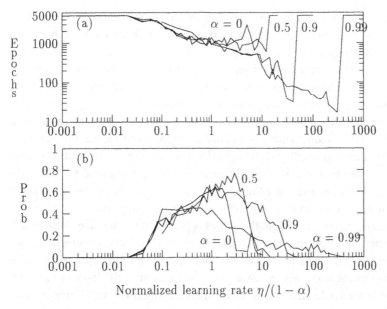

Figure 6.3
Average training time (a) and convergence probability (b) versus normalized learning rate for $\alpha = 0, 0.5, 0.9, 0.99$. With momentum, the effective learning rate is amplified to $\eta' = \eta/(1 - \alpha)$. The same effective learning rate can obtained from different combinations of η and α, which yield roughly the same average training time but differ in the location of the critical point where convergence becomes unlikely. In this example, it appears that small learning rates and large momentums are more stable. Note: Use of the MSE error function rather than SSE normalizes the learning rate by the size of the training set. Simulation details are described in section 6.1.1.

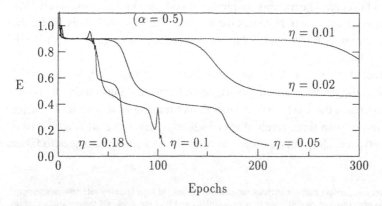

Figure 6.4
$E(t)$ curves for small SSE learning rates. At low learning rates, the $E(t)$ curves are smooth, but convergence is slow. As η increases, convergence time decreases but convergence is less reliable with occasional jumps in error. All networks were initialized with the same random weights.

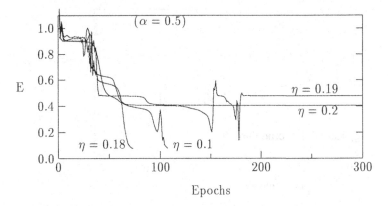

Figure 6.5
$E(t)$ curves for near-critical SSE learning rates. Below some critical learning rate, convergence time decreases as the learning rate η increases. At some point though the system becomes unstable and fails to converge. Note that the change is abrupt; at $\eta = 0.18$ it converges quickly but at $\eta = 0.19$ it overshoots the minimum and appears to get trapped on a plateau. The same network and initial weight vector were used in figure 6.4.

convergence. At the high end of the range, the system makes occasional "mistakes" leading to momentary jumps in error, but it usually recovers quickly.

Figure 6.1 showed that there is a critical learning rate above which convergence becomes very unlikely. Figure 6.4 shows $E(t)$ curves for near-critical learning rates. Just below the critical point, convergence becomes less reliable as η increases; mistakes become more common and the error may show transient chaotic oscillations. Finally, at even higher η values, the system becomes unstable and fails to converge. Note that the change is abrupt; at $\eta = 0.18$ the network converges quickly, at $\eta = 0.19$ it overshoots the minimum and appears to get trapped on a plateau, and at $\eta = 0.2$ it gets stuck sooner and never approaches the minimum. (The value $\eta = 0.2$ in this figure corresponds to $\eta = 3.2$ in figures 6.1 through 6.3.) In the analogy of a marble rolling down a hill, a similar abrupt change in outcomes may occur when a small change in the relative forces makes the difference between the marble rolling into one of two different valleys. In one case it has just enough energy to roll over a ridge and so ends up in valley A; in another case it just fails and rolls back down into valley B instead.

Overall, an aggressive (but subcritical) learning rate may produce faster learning even though it allows the error to increase occasionally. If the increases are mild and not too frequent, the benefits may outweigh the losses so the overall result is faster convergence. A small amount of chaos may also help the system explore more of the weight space. Beyond the critical value, however, the losses outweigh the benefits and the state either wanders aimlessly or gets stuck at high errors.

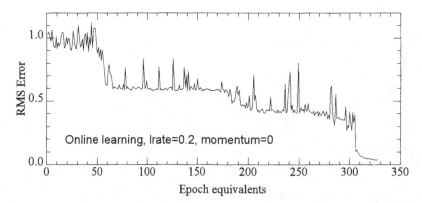

Figure 6.6
With on-line learning, patterns are chosen randomly and the weights are updated after each pattern presentation.
This introduces noise into the training process, leading to noisy $E(t)$ curves. In general, larger learning rates cause
higher noise levels.

On-Line Mode   With on-line learning, jitter in the $E(t)$ graph is normal. Figure 6.6 shows
a typical curve. Because weights are updated after each pattern presentation, there is a
tendency for the error to be lower on the most recently presented patterns. Presentation of
the patterns in random order avoids a bias toward patterns near the end of the training set,
but the randomness introduces noise that shows up in the $E(t)$ curves. When things work
well, the curve has a downward trend but is usually overlaid with noise whose amplitude
is related to the learning rate. If the noise level is high, the network may never settle to a
stable minimum so it is common to reduce the learning rate to zero gradually as training
progresses.

Because of this randomness, different on-line learning trials with identical initial weights
and training parameters will not follow the same trajectory. Figure 6.7 shows four different
training runs started with the same initial weights. One of the networks converges quickly
while the other three appear to get stuck in local minima. Cases (a) and (d) appear to follow
the same general path but the local deviations are different.

As in batch learning, there are interactions between the learning rate and momentum
in on-line learning. Momentum causes the same learning rate amplification effect when
learning rates are small. Figure 6.8 shows two on-line training trajectories for networks
with the same initial weights and learning rates but different momentum values. In the
figure the weight changes are small and convergence is slow for a small learning rate,
$\eta = 0.01$, and no momentum. With the same learning rate and $\alpha = 0.95$, the weight changes
are larger and this example converges quickly. The random properties of the trajectories
make it impossible to say that the $\alpha = 0.95$ case will always converge faster though.

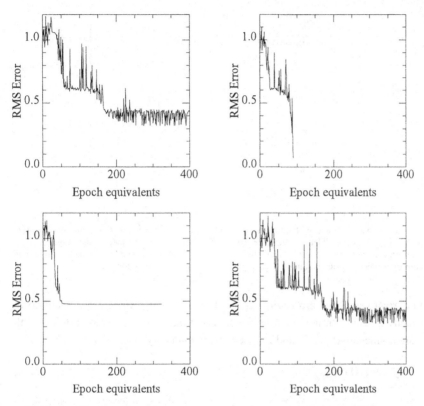

Figure 6.7
E(t) curves for on-line learning. On-line learning is stochastic so different runs with identical initial weights and training parameters will follow different trajectories. Shown are four different trials of on-line back-propagation applied to the 4-input parity problem with $\eta = 0.3$, $\alpha = 0$. All networks started with the same initial random weights. This learning rate appears high for this example—the noise level is high and three of the nets get stuck in a local minimum.

6.1.5   Learning Rate Selection

The preceding examples illustrate some effects of learning rate and momentum variations. In general, there is a trade-off between convergence speed and reliability of convergence. It should be clear that there is no fixed learning rate that is best for all problems.

6.1.6   Selection from Trace(H)

It is well-known that the optimal global learning rate for gradient descent on a linear problem is $\eta = 1/\lambda_{max}$ where λ_{max} is the largest positive eigenvalue of the Hessian matrix

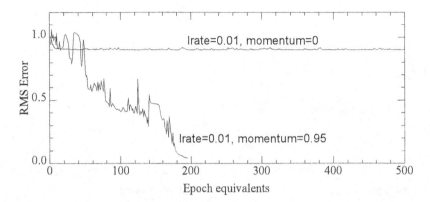

Figure 6.8
On-line learning $E(t)$ curves with and without momentum. Momentum also has a learning rate amplification effect in on-line learning. With a small learning rate, $\eta = 0.01$, (using SSE) and no momentum, the weight changes are small and convergence is slow. With the same learning rate and $\alpha = 0.95$, the weight changes are larger and this example converges quickly. Both examples were initialized with the same random weights.

$\mathbf{H}$ of second derivatives of the error with respect to the weights. Since λ_{max} is unknown unless $\mathbf{H}$ is analyzed, an estimate must be used. Assuming $\mathbf{H}$ is nonnegative-definite, all eigenvalues are nonnegative $\lambda_i \geq 0$ and λ_{max} can be bounded by

$$\lambda_{max} \leq \sum_i \lambda_i = \text{trace}(\mathbf{H}) \tag{6.1}$$

where $\text{trace}(\mathbf{H}) = \sum_i h_{ii}$. Estimates of the h_{ii} components can be obtained efficiently from the diagonal Hessian approximation (section 8.6.3). Of course, this overestimates λ_{max} so the resulting η value may be smaller than necessary but it is a reasonable starting point for an adaptive method.

A problem is that $\mathbf{H}$ will not be nonnegative-definite in general. At an arbitrary point on the $E(\mathbf{w})$ surface far from a minima, the matrix is likely to have both positive and negative eigenvalues since E curves up in some directions and down in others. There are, however, standard methods to make the approximation nonnegative.

6.1.7 Selection by On-Line Eigenvalue Estimation

LeCun, Simmard and Pearlmutter [94] describe a method for choosing the learning rate from an on-line estimate of the principal eigenvalue of the Hessian. The recipe is

1. Pick a random unit-length vector Ψ and two small positive constants α and γ, for example, $\alpha = 0.01$ and $\gamma = 0.01$.

2. Pick a training pattern X^p, do the forward and backward propagations and store the resulting gradient vector $G_1 = \nabla E^p(\mathbf{w})$.

3. Add a perturbation $\alpha \mathcal{N}(\Psi)$ to the current weight vector $\mathbf{w}$, where $\mathcal{N}(\cdot)$ denotes vector normalization: $\mathcal{N}(\mathbf{v}) = \mathbf{v}/\|\mathbf{v}\|$.

4. Perform a forward and backward propagation on the same training pattern using the perturbed weight vector and store the resulting gradient $G_2 = \nabla E^p(\mathbf{w} + \alpha \mathcal{N}(\Psi))$.

5. Update Ψ with the running average $\Psi \leftarrow (1 - \gamma)\Psi + \frac{\gamma}{\alpha}(G_2 - G_1)$.

6. Restore the weight vector to its original value.

7. Go to step 2 and repeat until $\|\Psi\|$ stabilizes.

8. Set the learning rate $\eta = \|\Psi\|^{-1}$ and continue with regular training.

The constant α controls the size of the perturbation; small values give better estimates but increase the chance of numerical errors. The constant γ smooths the estimate; small values give more accurate estimates but increase the convergence time. In [94] the authors recommend starting with a relatively large value, for example, $\gamma = 0.1$, and decreasing it until the fluctuations in $\|\Psi\|$ are less than about 10%. The point is to obtain an estimate of the proper order of magnitude for Ψ, not to calculate a precise value. Typically, $\|\Psi\|$ will converge in a few hundred iterations. This is an on-line estimate so each iteration has a cost comparable to two pattern evaluations and back-propagations. For large problems, the cost is small compared to the time needed to do a single training epoch.

The iteration is similar to the power method for calculating the largest positive eigenvalue of a matrix. A random vector Ψ can be expressed as a combination of the eigenvectors $\{\mathbf{v}_i\}$ of a given matrix (the Hessian $\mathbf{H}$ in this case)

$$\Psi = \sum_i a_i \mathbf{v}_i. \tag{6.2}$$

$\mathbf{H}$ is assumed to have full rank here. When Ψ is multiplied by $\mathbf{H}$, each eigenvector component grows by an amount proportional to its corresponding eigenvalue

$$\mathbf{H}\Psi = \sum_i a_i \lambda_i \mathbf{v}_i. \tag{6.3}$$

The component parallel to the principle eigenvector (call it $\mathbf{v}_1$) grows the most because its eigenvalue is largest. With iteration and renormalization

$$\Psi \leftarrow \mathbf{H}\mathcal{N}(\Psi),$$

the $\mathbf{v}_1$ component eventually dominates and Ψ approaches $\lambda_1 \mathbf{v}_1$, giving $\lambda_{max} \approx \|\Psi\|$. In the recipe just given, the product $\mathbf{H}\Psi$ is approximated by a finite-difference

$$\mathbf{H}\Psi = \frac{\nabla E(\mathbf{w} + \alpha\Psi) - \nabla E(\mathbf{w})}{\alpha} + O(\alpha^2). \qquad (6.4)$$

Exact calculation would require the equivalent of two training epochs—one for the original $\mathbf{w}$ and one for the perturbation. The preceding recipe is a further approximation using a running average of on-line estimates to approximate $E(\mathbf{w})$ and $E(\mathbf{w} + \Delta\mathbf{w})$.

Pearlmutter [297] describes an exact method for finding a product of $\mathbf{H}$ with a vector without evaluation of $\mathbf{H}$. This could be used instead of the finite difference approximation in equation 6.4.

6.1.8   Delta Attenuation in Layered Networks

It has been noted that the first layers of layered networks often learn very slowly because the error derivatives are attenuated as they propagate back from the output layer toward the input. For a node with value y, the sigmoid derivative is $y(1 - y)$ and takes values between 0 and 1/4; the tanh derivative is $1 - y^2$ and takes values between 0 and 1. Each node nonlinearity contributes a derivative factor that is normally less than 1, so the derivative may become very small after passing through several layers. This assumes the weights are $O(1)$ magnitude. When the weights are smaller, as they usually are just after random initialization, there is additional attenuation. The result is that $|\partial E/\partial w|$ tends to be very small for weights close to the inputs and so they change very slowly. Deep networks with many layers have been avoided for this reason because almost no learning occurs in the initial layers.

Because the partial derivatives are so small, larger learning rates may be appropriate for hidden units. Values as high as 10 can sometimes be used without causing instability [168]. If no other information is available it might be assumed that the node outputs y are uniformly distributed on $[0, 1]$ in which case the expected attenuation due to each sigmoid derivative is $E[y(1 - y)] = 1/6$. Rigler et al. [316] suggest rescaling the back-propagated derivatives by 6 to compensate. This would be equivalent to increasing the learning rate by 6 for weights into the last layer, by 36 for weights into the second-to-last layer, $6^3 = 216$ for weights 3 layers back from the output, and so on. These are only heuristics, however; it is not a necessary fact that partial derivatives are smaller for weights farther from the outputs. These are based on assumptions about the node nonlinearities and how the weights are initialized.

It seems reasonable to use larger learning rates in earlier layers to compensate for delta attenuation, but the values will depend on the particular training data and network used. The methods described attempt to rescale the learning rates relative to some global value so that each layer sees derivatives of roughly the same size, but they do not say how to control the global value. Without an automatic control algorithm it may be difficult to find a set of parameters that are both stable and efficient. A fixed learning rate is not necessarily appropriate anyway because conditions change as learning progresses. Adaptive learning rate techniques have the advantage of being able to adjust the rate dynamically to match current conditions. Rprop (section 9.6) seems to work better than some other methods in this case because the learning rate adjustments and weight updates depend only on the signs of the derivatives, not their magnitudes. Appropriate values can be found for each layer so early layers learn faster than they would otherwise and deep networks are not as difficult to train.

6.1.9   Learning Rate Fan-In Scaling

Scaling of the learning rate based on the number of inputs to each node was suggested by Plaut, Nowlan, and Hinton [299]. In [332], back-propagated δ values are scaled by the fan-in, which has the same effect. Some justification for this can be based on an eigenvalue analysis of the Hessian (see Appendix A.2).

   An intuitive explanation of why this might help is that immediately after initialization with small random weights all of the h hidden units compute approximately linear functions and their combined effect on the following layer is approximately that of a single linear "virtual" unit. If there is an optimum learning rate, say η^*, for the output weight of this virtual unit, then the learning rate for the output weights of the h actual units should be η^*/h so that they sum to η^*. This suggests relative values for learning rates in different layers, but it does not say how to choose η^*. Also, the same conditions may not hold later in learning.

   In [168], a separate learning rate is calculated for each hidden layer based on the number of weights into and out of each node. The initial value is then adapted based on the magnitudes of the back-propagated δ's.

   It is not clear if this heuristic has much effect unless there are large differences in layer sizes [9]. The heuristic of scaling the weight initialization range based on fan-in may achieve the same results without committing the system to a learning rate that may be inappropriate at later stages of learning. Algorithms that adjust a separate learning rate for each weight (e.g., Rprop) may be less troublesome; they generally achieve the same result in cases where this heuristic would help without causing problems in cases where it would not.

6.2   Momentum

Back-propagation with momentum can be viewed as gradient descent with smoothing. The idea is to stabilize the weight trajectory by making the weight change a combination of the

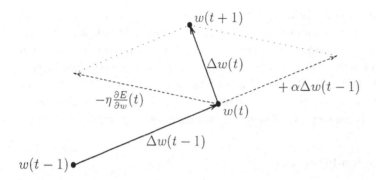

Figure 6.9
With momentum, the current weight change $\Delta \mathbf{w}(t)$ is a combination of a step down the negative gradient, $-\eta \frac{\partial E}{\partial \mathbf{w}}(t)$, plus a fraction $0 \leq \alpha < 1$ of the previous weight change. For $\alpha \approx 1$, opposing weight change components (horizontal) approximately cancel while complementary components (vertical) sum, producing a smoothing effect on the weight trajectory.

gradient-decreasing term in equation 5.23 plus a fraction of the previous weight change. The weight update rule is [330]

$$\Delta \mathbf{w}(t) = -\eta \frac{\partial E}{\partial \mathbf{w}}(t) + \alpha \Delta \mathbf{w}(t-1). \tag{6.5}$$

This is sometimes called the *generalized delta rule*. The weight change $\Delta \mathbf{w}(t)$ is a combination of a step down the negative gradient, $-\eta \frac{\partial E}{\partial \mathbf{w}}(t)$, plus a fraction $0 \leq \alpha < 1$ of the previous weight change (figure 6.9). For $\alpha \approx 1$, opposing weight change components approximately cancel while complementary components sum, leading to a smoothing effect on the weight trajectory. When successive gradients point in the same direction, the terms reinforce each other, leading to accelerated learning.

The smoothing effect of momentum can be illustrated by expansion of (6.5)

$$
\begin{aligned}
\Delta \mathbf{w}(t) &= -\eta \frac{\partial E}{\partial \mathbf{w}}(t) + \alpha \Delta \mathbf{w}(t-1) \\
&= -\eta \frac{\partial E}{\partial \mathbf{w}}(t) + \alpha \left(-\eta \frac{\partial E}{\partial \mathbf{w}}(t-1) + \alpha \Delta \mathbf{w}(t-2) \right) \\
&= -\eta \frac{\partial E}{\partial \mathbf{w}}(t) + \alpha \left(-\eta \frac{\partial E}{\partial \mathbf{w}}(t-1) + \alpha \left(-\eta \frac{\partial E}{\partial \mathbf{w}}(t-2) + \ldots \right) \right) \\
&= -\eta \sum_{k=0}^{\infty} \alpha^k \frac{\partial E}{\partial \mathbf{w}}(t-k). \tag{6.6}
\end{aligned}
$$

That is, with momentum the weight update is an exponential average of *all* the previous gradient terms rather than just the most recent term. Because $\alpha < 1$, the contribution from earlier derivative terms decays with each time step and the sum is dominated by the more recent terms. The time-constant of the system is controlled by α. For small α, the coefficients decay quickly as k increases so the system "forgets" earlier terms quickly. For large $\alpha \rightarrow 1^-$, however, the coefficients decay very slowly and the system has a long memory; the system will be stable but slow to react to changes in the error term.

The learning accelerating effect of momentum can be illustrated by considering the case where the derivative is constant, $\partial E / \partial \mathbf{w}(t) = J$. This is a reasonable approximation when η is very small so $\mathbf{w}$ does not change much with each step. It is also reasonable on flat areas of $E(\mathbf{w})$ where the gradient is small. Then

$$\Delta \mathbf{w}(t) = -\eta \sum_{k=0}^{\infty} \alpha^k \frac{\partial E}{\partial \mathbf{w}}(t - k)$$

$$= -\eta J \sum_{k=0}^{\infty} \alpha^k$$

$$= \frac{-\eta J}{1 - \alpha} \tag{6.7}$$

where the identity $\sum_{k=0}^{\infty} \alpha^k = 1/(1 - \alpha)$ (for $|\alpha| < 1$) is used in the last step. Without momentum, $\Delta \mathbf{w}(t)$ would be $-\eta J$. With momentum, however, $\Delta \mathbf{w}(t) = -\eta J/(1 - \alpha)$. Momentum thus has the effect of amplifying the learning rate from η to the effective value $\eta' = \eta/(1 - \alpha)$.

As $\alpha \rightarrow 1$, the effective learning rate can become very large, but the time constant also becomes large. Weight changes are affected by error information from many past cycles, which may make it difficult for the system to respond quickly to new conditions in the $E(w)$ surface. The weight trajectory may coast over a minimum but be unable to stop because of the continuing effects of earlier weight changes.

6.2.1 Effects of Momentum

As noted earlier, batch-mode back-propagation with a small learning rate is an approximation of gradient descent. Two problems with gradient descent are (1) when the learning rate is small, progress may be very slow (figure 6.10a) and (2) when the learning rate is too large and the error surface contains "ravines," the weight vector may oscillate wildly from one side of the valley to the other while creeping slowly along the length of the valley to the minimum, an effect sometimes called cross-stitching (figure 6.10b). Upon reaching the neighborhood of a minimum, it may overshoot many times before settling down.

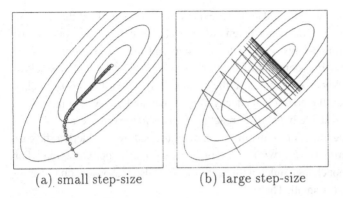

(a) small step-size   (b) large step-size

Figure 6.10
Gradient descent trajectories: (a) with a small step size (0.01), pure gradient descent follows a smooth trajectory, but progress may be very slow; (b) "cross-stitching"; When the step size is too big (0.1) and the error surface has "valleys," the trajectory may oscillate wildly from one side to the other while creeping slowly along the length of the valley to the minimum. Upon reaching the neighborhood of a minimum, it may overshoot many times before settling down.

Briefly, momentum has the following effects:

• It smooths weight changes by filtering out high frequency variations. When the learning rate is too high, momentum tends to suppress cross-stitching because consecutive opposing weight changes tend to cancel. The side to side oscillations across the valley damp out leaving only the components along the axis of the valley, which add up.

• When a long sequence of weight changes are all in the same direction, momentum tends to amplify the effective learning rate to $\eta' = \eta/(1 - \alpha)$, leading to faster convergence.

• Momentum may sometimes help the system escape small local minima by giving the state vector enough inertia to coast over small bumps in the error surface.

Cross-stitching is a problem for gradient descent when the learning rate is too large and error surface has steep-sided ravines that have a shallow slope along the axis. (This can be stated more technically in terms of the eigenvalues of the Hessian matrix, see section A.2.) Without momentum, the network has only the gradient information to guide its path. Because the gradient on one side of a steep valley points almost directly across the valley and has only a very small component along it, the weight vector tends to jump back and forth across the valley and progress along the axis of the valley is slow relative to the size of the weight changes. Also, upon reaching the neighborhood of a minimum, the weight vector may overshoot many times before settling down. With the momentum term, side to side oscillations tend to cancel but steps along the axis sum so progress along the

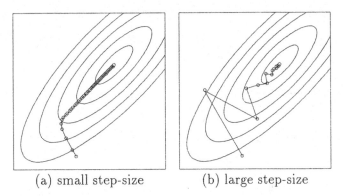

(a) small step-size   (b) large step-size

Figure 6.11
Gradient descent trajectories with momentum. With momentum, opposite (side to side) changes tend to cancel
while complementary changes (along the length of the valley) tend to sum. The overall effect is to stabilize the
oscillations and accelerate convergence. (a) When the step size is small, momentum acts to accelerate convergence
(step size 0.01 and momentum 0.99, cf. figure 6.10a). (b) Small amounts of momentum also help to damp
oscillations when the step size is too large (step size 0.1 and momentum 0.2, cf. figure 6.10b).

valley is faster. The network can follow the path of the ravine better, so the learning rate can
often be increased, leading to faster training times. Learning acceleration and oscillation
dampening effects of momentum can be seen in comparing Figures 6.10 and 6.11.

Too Much Momentum   With momentum, the state vector has a tendency to keep moving
in the same direction. Weight changes are affected by error information from many past
cycles—the larger the momentum, the stronger the lingering influence of previous changes.
In effect, momentum gives the weight state inertia, which "keeps the marble rolling,"
allowing it to coast over flat spots and perhaps out of small local minima.

A little inertia is useful for stabilization but too much may make the system sluggish; it
may overshoot good minima or be unable to follow a curved valley in the error surface. The
system may coast past minima and out onto high plateaus where it becomes stuck (section
6.2.2).

Interaction with Learning Rate   Many studies have claimed that momentum tends to
make choice of learning rate η less critical. When η is too small, successive weight updates
tend to be in the same direction and momentum effectively amplifies η to $\eta/(1 - \alpha)$. When
η is too large, successive updates tend to be in nearly opposite directions and momentum
causes them to cancel out, effectively reducing the learning rate. Some support is seen in
figure 6.1 where the probability of convergence density function is wider (on a logarithmic
scale) for $\alpha = 0.9$ than for $\alpha = 0$. On a linear scale, however, the width of the density

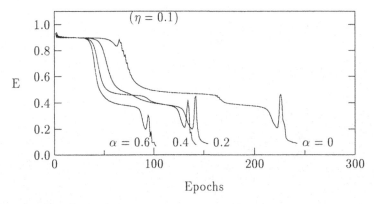

Figure 6.12
At the low end of the momentum range, α increases generally lead to faster convergence. Here the $E(t)$ curves are smooth. Occasional error spikes may occur but the system recovers quickly. All trajectories start from the same random weights.

function decreases in agreement with results that show that momentum reduces the stable range of learning rates for the LMS algorithm [343, 326].

6.2.2   Typical *E(t)* Curves with Momentum

Figures 6.12 and 6.13 show $E(t)$ curves for various momentum values and fixed learning rate. All curves were generated from the same initial weight vector as in figures 6.4 and 6.5. Simulation details are described in section 6.1.1.

At low momentum values, the $E(t)$ curves are smooth and larger values of α lead to faster convergence (assuming reasonable learning rates). Occasional spikes may occur but the system recovers quickly. The curves in figure 6.12 are all qualitatively similar so the increased convergence speed may be due mostly to amplification of the effective learning rate. That is, the system appears to be following the same basic trajectory at varying speeds.

As α increases past a certain point, however, convergence becomes unreliable (figure 6.13). At $\alpha = 0.6$ the system converges quickly, but at larger values it becomes stuck in a poor minimum. For $\alpha = 0.99$, $E(t)$ oscillates strongly and the system jumps from a poor minimum to a worse one at about $t = 100$.

6.2.3   Small-Signal Analysis, Momentum Only

The acceleration and smoothing effects of momentum can be explained in terms of small-signal analyses. The weight update equation with momentum is

$$\Delta w(t) = -\eta \frac{\partial E}{\partial w}(t) + \alpha \Delta w(t-1). \tag{6.8}$$

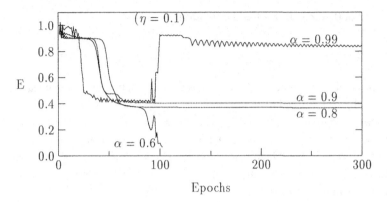

Figure 6.13
$E(t)$ curves for large momentum values. Convergence becomes unreliable when the momentum is too large for the learning rate η. This system converges quickly with $\alpha = 0.6$ but not with higher values. With $\alpha = 0.99$, $E(t)$ oscillates strongly and the system jumps from a poor minimum to a worse one at about $t = 100$. All trajectories start from the same random weights.

Convert this discrete-time iteration to a continuous-time system by the approximation $\dot{w} \equiv \frac{\partial w}{\partial t} \approx \frac{\Delta w}{\Delta t}$ and assume $\Delta t = 1$. Then

$$\dot{w}(t) = -\eta J + \alpha \dot{w}(t-1) \qquad (6.9)$$

where $J = \partial E / \partial w$. Another discrete-time to continuous-time approximation for the second derivative gives

$$\dot{w}(t) - \dot{w}(t-1) \approx \ddot{w}(t)\Delta t \qquad (6.10)$$

and

$$\alpha \ddot{w}(t) + (1-\alpha)\dot{w}(t) = -\eta J. \qquad (6.11)$$

This second-order differential equation is easily solved for certain special cases. Laplace transforms (e.g., [292]) are used in the following discussions.

Impulse Response   Assume J is an impulse at 0, that is, $J(t) = J_o \delta(t)$. This approximates the case of encountering a "cliff" in the $E(\mathbf{w})$ surface, where J is large, and then coasting on a flat plateau where $J \approx 0$. Taking Laplace transforms gives,

$$s^2 W + \frac{1-\alpha}{\alpha} s W = -\frac{\eta}{\alpha} J_o$$

$$W = -\frac{1}{s(s + \frac{1}{\tau})} \frac{\eta J_o}{\alpha} \qquad (6.12)$$

where $\tau = \alpha/(1-\alpha)$. For $0 < \alpha < 1$, this has the solution

$$w(t) = w(0) - \frac{\eta J_o}{1-\alpha}\left(1 - e^{-t/\tau}\right). \qquad (6.13)$$

For $\alpha \geq 1$, the solution is unstable. Otherwise $w(t)$ asymptotically approaches a final value $w(\infty) = w(0) - \eta J_o/(1-\alpha)$. Instead of taking a single step ηJ_o at $t = 0$, it takes many steps that asymptotically add up to a value $1/(1-\alpha)$ times as large.

Momentum thus has the effect of amplifying the learning rate from η to the effective value $\eta' = \eta/(1-\alpha)$. For $\alpha \to 1$, the effective learning rate can become very large, but the time constant τ also becomes large, which may make it difficult for the system to respond quickly to new conditions in the $E(w)$ surface.

Step Response Assume J is a step function at $t = 0$, that is, $J(t) = J_o u(t)$ where $u(t)$ is the unit step function

$$u(t) = \begin{cases} 0 & t < 0 \\ 1 & t \geq 0. \end{cases}$$

This is reasonable when η is small and the local error surface is nearly flat; the gradient changes very little in one iteration and can be approximated by a constant. Laplace transforms give

$$s^2 W + \frac{1-\alpha}{\alpha} s W = -\frac{\eta}{\alpha}\frac{J_o}{s} \qquad (6.14)$$

$$W = -\frac{1}{s^2(s + \frac{1}{\tau})}\frac{\eta J_o}{\alpha} \qquad (6.15)$$

where $\tau = \alpha/(1-\alpha)$ again. The solution is unstable for $\alpha \geq 1$. For $0 < \alpha < 1$, this has the solution

$$w(t) = w(0) - \frac{\eta J_o}{1-\alpha}t - \eta J_o\frac{\alpha}{(1-\alpha)^2}\left(1 - e^{-t/\tau}\right). \qquad (6.16)$$

This approximates a ramp function —a linear rise with t plus a transient term similar to (6.13). For $t \gg \tau$,

$$w(t) \approx w(0) - \frac{\eta J_o}{1-\alpha}\left(t - \frac{\alpha}{(1-\alpha)^2}\right) \qquad (6.17)$$

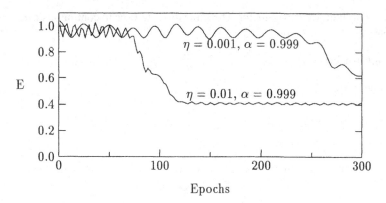

Figure 6.14
Oscillation in $E(t)$ due to momentum. With momentum, the weight vector has inertia, which allows it to "coast up hillsides" in the $E(w)$ surface. The larger the momentum and the smaller the learning rate, the farther it can rise and the longer it takes to stop. This, in combination with the $E(w)$ surface, can lead to oscillation. Mathematically, smaller η and larger α give the dynamic system a longer time-constant, visible here in a lower oscillation frequency. (These values were chosen to exaggerate the effect; they are not necessarily recommended.)

Frequency Response   The common term

$$W(s) \propto \frac{1}{s + \frac{1}{\tau}}$$

corresponds to a leaky integrator and has a low-pass frequency response. (A leaky integrator is an exponentially weighted averager.) This is another justification for the statement that momentum helps filter out high frequency oscillations in the weight changes. Recall that $\tau = \alpha/(1 - \alpha)$ becomes large as $\alpha \to 1$. The time-domain impulse response is

$$h(t) \propto e^{-t/\tau}.$$

Convolution of a signal $J(t)$ with $h(t)$ yields an exponentially weighted average $\overline{J(t)}$ which weights recent J values more heavily than older values.

Generally, smaller η and larger α values give the dynamic system a longer time-constant, visible in figure 6.14 as a lower frequency of oscillation.

6.2.4   Small-Signal Analysis, Momentum, and Weight Decay

It is relatively easy to extend these linear small-signal analyses to include weight decay terms. The new weight update equation is

$$\Delta w(t) = -\rho w(t) - \eta \frac{\partial E}{\partial w}(t) + \alpha \Delta w(t - 1) \tag{6.18}$$

where $0 \leq \rho \ll 1$ is the weight decay parameter. The same discrete-time to continuous-time approximations give

$$\dot{w}(t) = -\rho w(t) - \eta J + \alpha \dot{w}(t-1),$$

$$\dot{w}(t) - \dot{w}(t-1) \approx \ddot{w}(t)\Delta t,$$

and

$$\alpha \ddot{w}(t) + (1-\alpha)\dot{w}(t) + \rho w = -\eta J. \tag{6.19}$$

Impulse Response   When J is an impulse at 0, that is, $J(t) = J_o \delta(t)$, Laplace transforms give

$$W = -\frac{\eta}{\alpha} \frac{J_o}{(s^2 + \frac{1-\alpha}{\alpha}s + \frac{\rho}{\alpha})}. \tag{6.20}$$

The denominator has roots

$$s = \frac{1}{2\alpha}\left(-\beta \pm \sqrt{\beta^2 - 4\rho\alpha}\right) \tag{6.21}$$

where $\beta = 1 - \alpha$. For $\beta^2 - 4\rho\alpha > 0$, both roots are real. Critical damping occurs at

$$\rho_o = (1-\alpha)^2/(4\alpha). \tag{6.22}$$

This is a decreasing function of α. As $\alpha \to 1$, ρ must approach 0 to prevent oscillation. For $\rho < \rho_o$, both roots are real. For larger values, the roots are complex and the solution is an exponentially decaying sinusoid. Convergence of these types of systems is usually fastest when the system is slightly underdamped.

Step Response   When J is a step function at $t = 0$, that is, $J(t) = J_o u(t)$, Laplace transforms give

$$W = -\frac{\eta}{\alpha} \frac{J_o}{s(s^2 + \frac{1-\alpha}{\alpha}s + \frac{\rho}{\alpha})}. \tag{6.23}$$

Similar arguments are made by Bailey [15] using the damped oscillator equation

$$\ddot{w} + b\dot{w} + kw = 0. \tag{6.24}$$

Here $b = (1-\alpha)/\alpha$ and $k = \rho/\alpha$. They require $b < 1/N$ in order to average over all N patterns in the training set and choose $b = 1/(2N)$ as a reasonable value. This corresponds to $\alpha = 2N/(2N+1)$. Critical damping occurs when $k = (b/2)^2$, which corresponds to the value in equation 6.22.

6.3 Remarks

The preceding sections illustrate some effects that learning rate and momentum have on training and list some hints for recognizing when parameter changes are needed. It should be emphasized that the illustrations are based on a single small classification problem. The actual curves are unique to the example and different curves will be obtained from different networks with different training sets and initialization conditions. The examples are intended to be representative in that many problems will show qualitative similarities; quantitative differences should be expected however.

The main benefit of good parameters is faster training and the prevention of divergence to avoidable bad solutions. As in the more general case of tuning an optimization method, serious training difficulty may be an indication of problems more basic than optimization parameters. That is, if careful tuning of learning rate and momentum are needed to obtain good solutions, the effort might be better spent in reconsidering more fundamental things like the choice of representation or network architecture.

The difficulty of choosing a good learning rate *a priori* is one of the reasons adaptive learning rate methods are useful and popular. Most adapt parameters dynamically as appropriate for changing conditions and many assign different rates appropriate for different parts of the network. A few methods are summarized in chapter 9.

7 Weight-Initialization Techniques

The following sections summarize some techniques for initializing weights in sigmoidal networks. The basic motivation is to speed up learning by choosing better initial solutions. A survey and empirical comparison of a number of techniques is given by Thimm and Fiesler [368].

There are two clusters of methods. One consists of methods for choosing parameters controlling the distribution of random initial weights. The motivation here is to avoid sigmoid saturation problems that cause slow training. Most of these methods do not use domain-specific information. The other cluster consists of techniques for initializing the system from an approximate solution found by another modeling system; common choices include rule-based systems, decision trees, or nearest-neighbor classifiers. The motivation here is to reduce training times and probability of convergence to poor minima by starting the system near a good solution. An advantage of these methods, besides faster training, is that they provide ways to embed domain-dependent information in a network.

7.1 Random Initialization

The normal initialization procedure is to set weights to "small" random values. The randomness is intended to break symmetry while small weights are chosen to avoid immediate saturation.

Symmetry breaking is needed to make nodes compute different functions. If all nodes had identical weight vectors, then all nodes in a layer would respond identically and the layer would function as if it contained just one node. Likewise, each node would receive identical error information during back-propagation so weight changes would be identical and the weights would never have a chance to become different.

Small weights are needed to avoid immediate saturation because large weights could amplify a moderate input to produce an extremely large weighted sum at the inputs of the next layer. This would push the nodes well into the flat regions of their nonlinearities and learning would be very slow because of the small derivatives [241]. The weights should not be too small, however, because learning speed would then be limited by the small δ values back-propagated through the weights. Another factor is that the origin is a saddle point on many error surfaces.

Typically, weights are randomly selected from a range such as $(-A/\sqrt{N}, A/\sqrt{N})$, where N is the number of inputs (fan-in) to the node and A is a constant between 2 and 3. Division by the fan-in compensates for the increase in variance of the weighted-input sum with the number of inputs; without it, the sum could sometimes be large for large N

and the node would saturate often. The range $(-2.4/N, 2.4/N)$, where N is the number of node inputs, is another commonly cited choice [236].

Suppose the weights are selected from a range $[-w_o, +w_o]$. Many studies, for example [121, 235, 240, 393, 110, 241, 321, 368], have observed that an intermediate set of w_o values work best. Extreme values either do not converge or converge to poor solutions. Very small initial weights make it hard to escape from the $\mathbf{w} = \mathbf{0}$ weight vector, which is a poor local minimum or saddle point in many problems. With large w_o values, on the other hand, many nodes saturate, derivatives are small, and the net does not converge to a good solution in a reasonable amount of time. Within the range of values that work, the exact value is usually not critical. Thimm and Fiesler [368] suggest that it is better to choose too small a value rather than one that is too big because performance deteriorates very quickly once the upper threshold is crossed.

7.1.1   Calculation of the Initial Weight Range

One basis for selecting an initial weight distribution is to assume the inputs have some statistical distribution and select the initial weight distribution so that the probability of saturating the node nonlinearity is small.

Assume that the weights are independent of the inputs

$$E\left[w_i x_i\right] = E\left[w_i\right] E\left[x_i\right] \tag{7.1}$$

and that the weights are zero-mean, independent, and identically distributed

$$E\left[w_i\right] = 0 \quad \text{for all } i, \tag{7.2}$$

$$E\left[w_i w_j\right] = \sigma_w^2 \delta_{ij} \tag{7.3}$$

where $\delta_{ij} = 1$ if $i = j$ and 0 otherwise.

The weighted sum into a node with N inputs is

$$u = \sum_{i=1}^{N} w_i x_i \tag{7.4}$$

and by independence of w and x the expected value is

$$E\left[u\right] = \sum_{i=1}^{N} E\left[w_i\right] E\left[x_i\right] = 0. \tag{7.5}$$

Because the expected value is 0, the variance is then

$$E\left[u^2\right] = E\left[\left(\sum_{i=1}^{N} w_i x_i\right)^2\right]$$

$$= \sum_{i,j=1}^{N} E\left[w_i w_j x_i x_j\right]$$

$$= \sum_{i,j=1}^{N} E\left[w_i w_j\right] E\left[x_i x_j\right]$$

$$= \sum_{i,j=1}^{N} \sigma_w^2 \delta_{ij} E\left[x_i x_j\right]$$

$$= \sigma_w^2 \sum_{i=1}^{N} E\left[x_i^2\right].$$

Note that this does not require that the inputs be independent. Independence of w_i and w_j suppresses the effect of correlations between x_i and x_j on $E\left[u^2\right]$. If the inputs are zero-mean, identically distributed so $E\left[x_i^2\right] = \sigma_x^2$, then

$$\sigma_u^2 = N\sigma_w^2 \sigma_x^2 \qquad\qquad (7.6)$$

and

$$\sigma_u = \sigma_x \sigma_w \sqrt{N}. \qquad\qquad (7.7)$$

For $y = \tanh(u)$ nonlinearities, the input u needed to produce an output y is

$$u = \ln\frac{1+y}{1-y}. \qquad\qquad (7.8)$$

Let us say the node is saturated for $|y| > 0.9$ so $u_{sat} = \ln 19$. For sigmoid nodes, the constant is the same if saturation is taken to occur at $\mathrm{sigmoid}(u_{sat}) = 0.95$.

We want the probability that $u > u_{sat}$ to be small. This can be achieved by selecting the initial weight distribution so u_{sat} is several times σ_u. With, for example,

$$u_{sat} > 2\sigma_u \qquad\qquad (7.9)$$

the probability that a given node will be saturated will be about 5%. This assumes a Gaussian distribution for u, which is reasonable when N is large because of the central-limit theorem.

Uniform Weights   For weights initialized from a uniform distribution over the interval $[-w_o, +w_o]$,

$$\sigma_w = w_o/\sqrt{3} \tag{7.10}$$

$$\sigma_u = w_o\sqrt{N/3}\sigma_x \tag{7.11}$$

$$u_{sat} > 2w_o\sqrt{N/3}\sigma_x \tag{7.12}$$

$$w_o < \frac{u_{sat}}{2\sigma_x}\sqrt{\frac{3}{N}}. \tag{7.13}$$

For bipolar inputs $x_i \in \{-1, +1\}$ with equal probability for either value, $\sigma_x = 1$. Then, for $u_{sat} = \ln 19$

$$w_o < 2.55/\sqrt{N}. \tag{7.14}$$

For bipolar inputs with probability $P[x = 1] = p$, $\sigma_x = 2\sqrt{p(1-p)}$ and

$$w_o < 1.28/\sqrt{Np(1-p)}. \tag{7.15}$$

For binary inputs $x_i \in \{0, 1\}$ with probability $P[x = 1] = p$, $\sigma_x = \sqrt{p(1-p)}$ and

$$w_o < 2.55/\sqrt{Np(1-p)} \tag{7.16}$$

and

$$w_o < 5.1/\sqrt{N} \quad \text{(for } p = 1/2\text{)}. \tag{7.17}$$

For uniform inputs in the range $[-a, +a]$, $\sigma_x = a/\sqrt{3}$ and

$$w_o < 4.4/(a\sqrt{N}). \tag{7.18}$$

For Gaussian $N(0, \sigma_x)$ inputs,

$$w_o < 2.55/(\sigma_x\sqrt{N}). \tag{7.19}$$

Gaussian Weights   Similarly, for weights initialized from a Gaussian $N(0, \sigma_w)$ distribution,

$$\sigma_u = \sigma_w \sigma_x / \sqrt{N} \tag{7.20}$$

$$u_{sat} > 2\sigma_w \sigma_x / \sqrt{N} \tag{7.21}$$

$$\sigma_w < \frac{u_{sat}}{2\sigma_x \sqrt{N}}. \tag{7.22}$$

For $u_{sat} = \ln 19$,

$$\sigma_w < 1.47/(\sigma_x \sqrt{N}). \tag{7.23}$$

For bipolar inputs $x_i \in \{-1, +1\}$ with equal probability for either value, $\sigma_x = 1$ and

$$\sigma_w < 1.47/\sqrt{N}. \tag{7.24}$$

For bipolar inputs with probability $P\,[x = 1] = p$, $\sigma_x = 2\sqrt{p(1 - p)}$ and

$$\sigma_w < 0.74/\sqrt{Np(1 - p)}. \tag{7.25}$$

For binary inputs $x_i \in \{0, 1\}$ with probability $P\,[x = 1] = p$, $\sigma_x = \sqrt{p(1 - p)}$ and

$$\sigma_w < 1.47/\sqrt{Np(1 - p)} \tag{7.26}$$

and

$$\sigma_w < 2.94/\sqrt{N} \quad \text{(for } p = 1/2). \tag{7.27}$$

For uniform inputs in the range $[-a, +a]$, $\sigma_x = a/\sqrt{3}$ and

$$\sigma_w < 2.54/(a\sqrt{N}). \tag{7.28}$$

For multilayer networks, the inputs in the derivation above could actually be the outputs of a preceding layer. Because they have different statistical properties from the overall system inputs, each layer of weights will have a different ideal initialization range according to this approach. For large fan-ins, the weighted sum u into a node usually approaches a Gaussian distribution. If the initial weights into the node are chosen to avoid saturation, the distribution of the node outputs will also be approximately Gaussian but with a standard deviation multiplied by the slope s of the nonlinearity, $\sigma_{out} = s\sigma_u$. Similar adjustments are appropriate for nodes receiving weights from several different layers, as might happen in networks containing "leap-frog" weights.

It should be noted that the derivation depends on assumptions about the input distribution, which may not apply in a particular problem. In many problems, inputs will be

Table 7.1
Weight Initialization Parameters.

Input distribution	Weight distribution	
	Uniform$(-w_o, +w_o)$	Gaussian N$(0, \sigma_w)$
Bipolar $\{-1, 1\}$	$w_o < 1.28/\sqrt{Np(1-p)}$	$\sigma_w < 0.74/\sqrt{Np(1-p)}$
for $p = 1/2$	$w_o < 2.55/\sqrt{N}$	$\sigma_w < 1.47/\sqrt{N}$
Binary $\{0, 1\}$	$w_o < 2.55/\sqrt{Np(1-p)}$	$\sigma_w < 1.47/\sqrt{Np(1-p)}$
for $p = 1/2$	$w_o < 5.1/\sqrt{N}$	$\sigma_w < 2.94/\sqrt{N}$
Uniform$(-a, a)$	$w_o < 4.4/(a\sqrt{N})$	$\sigma_w < 2.54/(a\sqrt{N})$
Gaussian N$(0, \sigma_x)$	$w_o < 2.55/(\sigma_x\sqrt{N})$	$\sigma_w < 1.47/(\sigma_x\sqrt{N})$

clustered and the large fan-in assumption may not be valid for small networks. An alternative to relying on possibly invalid assumptions is to calculate an appropriate range numerically using the same basic procedure. The calculations are relatively simple and fast in most cases.

The objective of this initialization method is to minimize the probability that nodes will be saturated in the early stages of training. A potential problem, pointed out by Wessels and Barnard [393] (see section 7.1.4), is that this makes all nodes sensitive to all the training patterns so the decision boundaries of many nodes may move large distances before settling to a stable state. In some cases, hyperplanes may move completely out of the region occupied by the training data and produce stray nodes that contribute little useful information to the rest of the net. They suggest that occasional saturation helps to "pin the hyperplanes to the data." Because its derivatives are small when saturated, each node will be most sensitive to patterns near its hyperplane and relatively insensitive to more distant patterns. Initially at least, each node would be loosely specialized by sensitization to a different fraction of the data.

7.1.2   Initialization to Maximize BP Deltas

The derivation of section 7.1.1 provides criteria for selecting a weight initialization range for the input-to-hidden weights. The initialization range of the hidden-to-output weights can be selected in order to maximize the expected magnitude of the back-propagated deltas at the hidden nodes [321]. The expected magnitude of the back-propagated error is an increasing function of the weight range for small weight ranges. (If all the weights were zero, the back-propagated error would be zero.) But for large weight ranges, the output nodes saturate often so the back-propagated deltas are small. Rojas [321] reports that w_o values between 0.5 and 1.5 give similar results in empirical tests.

7.1.3   Initialization of Bias Weights

It was noted in section 3.1 that the distance d of a node's hyperplane from the origin is controlled by the bias weight

$$d = w_{bias}/\|\mathbf{w}\| \tag{7.29}$$

where $\mathbf{w}$ is the weight vector excluding the bias weight. When weights are initialized randomly, d will sometimes be large and the hyperplane may be far from the region containing the inputs. A remedy is to choose $w_{bias} < \|\mathbf{w}\|$ so the initial hyperplane always intersects the unit hypercube around the origin. This idea is mentioned in Palubinskas [294] among other places.

7.1.4   Constrained Random Initialization I

Some heuristics for setting the initial weights in order to decrease the chance of the network becoming trapped in a local minimum are discussed by Wessels and Barnard [393]. The following types of irregularities are defined:

Type 1.   Stray hidden nodes whose decision boundaries have drifted out of the region of the input space sampled by the examples. These nodes have nearly constant activation for all training inputs and contribute little useful information.

Type 2.   Hidden nodes duplicating function due to failure of symmetry breaking.

Type 3.   Hidden node configurations that result in all nodes being inactive in some regions of the input space, making the network insensitive to inputs there.

Type 1 and 2 errors are common with random initialization. As an alternative, initial weights can be chosen systematically so that the following occur [393]:

• The decision boundary of every hidden node crosses the region covered by the samples (to avoid type 1 errors).

• The decision boundaries have a wide range of different orientations (to avoid type 2 errors).

• The transition region of each hidden node covers about 20% of the input space (to avoid type 2 errors). When weights are initialized with small values, the nodes tend to compute nearly linear functions. Because the sum of two linear functions is also linear, the net might use two nodes to do what could be done by one. Initializing with weights large enough to make the node functions somewhat nonlinear helps to avoid this.

• Every part of the sampled region has at least one active hidden node (to avoid type 3 errors).

The initial hidden-to-output weights are set to the same small value, for example, 0.25. Random hidden-to-output weights are not required because symmetry is broken by the way the input-to-hidden weights are initialized. It might even be counterproductive if it masks the activities carefully set up in initializing the hidden node weights. Because the error back-propagated to a hidden node is proportional to its output weights, setting the weights equal makes each hidden node equally responsive to all the outputs. Very small values cause slow learning while values larger than 1 tend to cause saturation because large δ values are propagated back from the output nodes. The 0.25 value was based on empirical tests. Performance was said to be relatively insensitive to the exact value as long as it was not large enough to cause saturation (in which case performance dropped off drastically).

7.1.5 Constrained Random Initialization II

A similar method is described by Nguyen and Widrow [283]. Weight vectors are chosen with random directions, magnitudes are adjusted so each node is linear over a fraction of the input space with some overlap of linear regions between nodes with similar directions, and thresholds are set so the hyperplanes have random distances from the origin within the region occupied by the input data.

The following recipe gives similar results. Let $\mathbf{w}$ represent the weight vector excluding the bias and let θ denote the bias weight. The weighted sum into a node is $u = \mathbf{w}^T \mathbf{x} + \theta$.

1. First, set the weights so each vector has a random direction. A Gaussian or other spherically symmetric distribution should be used because this makes all directions equally likely; a uniform distribution tends to favor directions pointing to corners of the hypercube.

$$\mathbf{w} \sim N(0, 1)$$

2. Adjust the magnitude of $\mathbf{w}$ so the linear region covers a fraction of the input space. The best width for the linear region depends on the number of hidden nodes; with fewer hidden nodes, the linear region has to be wider so every point in the input space is covered by the linear region of some node.

The linear region of a sigmoid-like node roughly covers the region from ($-u_{sat}$ to $+u_{sat}$). For tanh nodes, $u_{sat} = \ln 19 = 2.94$. If the inputs lie in the interior of the unit hypersphere, the maximum weighted sum occurs when $\mathbf{x} = \mathbf{w}$

$$u_{max} = \|\mathbf{w}\|^2. \tag{7.30}$$

To make the linear region approximately 0.4 long (1/5 of the diameter of the input space), this should be about 5 times u_{sat}

$$u_{max} = 5u_{sat}. \tag{7.31}$$

Normalization of $\mathbf{w}$ to a magnitude $\|\mathbf{w}\| = \sqrt{5u_{sat}} = 3.84$ gives this result

$$\mathbf{w} \leftarrow 3.84 \frac{\mathbf{w}}{\|\mathbf{w}\|}.$$

3. Set the threshold so the distance of the hyperplane from the origin has a random distribution between 0 and 1 (again assuming inputs lie in the unit hypersphere). The distance of the hyperplane from the origin is $d = \theta/\|\mathbf{w}\|$ so choose

$$\theta = \|\mathbf{w}\|\tau \tag{7.32}$$

where τ is a random number between 0 and 1.

7.1.6   Remarks

• Many random weight initialization methods attempt to specify an appropriate range of initial weights. The equivalence between scaling weights by a constant factor and introducing a gain term in the sigmoid function means that similar results can be obtained by gain-scaling (section 8.7).

• There is some suggestion that on-line learning can tolerate saturation problems caused by large initial weights better than batch learning [241].

• In [368], no significant difference was found between uniform, normal, and unbalanced uniform distributions for initializing higher-order perceptrons. Empirical tests favored the method of section 7.1.4, but other methods gave similar results.

• The effects of initial weights on convergence time are examined by Kolen and Pollack [216, 217]. Plots of convergence time *vs.* initial weights (displayed as two-dimensional slices through the weight space) show fractal structure. Convergence regions are separated from nonconvergence regions by complex borders and certain mappings cannot be learned from initial weights in certain regions of the weight space.

7.2   Nonrandom Initialization

An alternative to random initialization is to base the initial state of the system on an approximate solution provided by another type of classifier or fitting system. The goal is to start the system at a reasonably good solution which can then be fine tuned by normal training methods. If things work as planned, the initial state will be in the basin of attraction of a good minimum so global search capability and convergence time are not critical issues and relatively simple training methods may therefore suffice. (However, techniques such as quasi-Newton methods or conjugate gradients may be preferred over back-propagation because final tuning is where they really outperform simpler methods.)

In many cases, the initialization time will be negligible compared to training times for randomly initialized networks. Even when the time is not negligible, it may be regained later because (1) the actual training time may be much shorter if the initial solution is good and (2) problems of convergence to poor local minima may be avoided because the system is already at an approximate solution when it starts. Often, only one fine-tuning run will be needed. With random initialization, in contrast, it is usually necessary to train a number of networks with different starting weights because of the possibility of poor local minima and the total training time for all networks should be considered when making comparisons.

Another reason for using nonrandom initializations is to embed domain-dependent information in a network. In many applications there is significant human knowledge that might be useful even though it might be incomplete or only partly reliable. Existing techniques may give reasonable but imperfect solutions or we may have partial knowledge about the form the solution should take. Pure training on examples in an unstructured network does not provide an efficient way to use this information. When training data are sparse, the external bias supplied by the initial solution may be a major factor in obtaining a solution that generalizes well.

7.2.1   Principal Components Initialization

Principal components analysis (PCA) attempts to identify the major axes of variation of a data set—the directions along which the data varies the most. The principal components of a data set are determined from the eigenvectors of the covariance matrix

$$\mathbf{R} = E\left[\mathbf{x}_k \mathbf{x}_k^T\right].$$

The eigenvalues measure the variance of the projection of the data onto the corresponding eigenvectors. The principal eigenvector (having the largest eigenvalue) indicates the direction along which the data varies the most; lesser eigenvectors (having smaller eigenvalues) indicate directions with lesser amounts of variation. PCA is discussed further in appendix B.

Going on the assumption that these are important directions for the function to be learned, one can initialize the input-to-hidden weight vectors along these directions. In a network with H hidden nodes, the H eigenvectors with the largest eigenvalues would be selected. A two-phase algorithm is described in [136]. In phase one, the input-to-hidden weights are fixed to the principal component directions while the output weights are trained. In the second phase, all weights are allowed to learn. The authors report a large drop in error after the first few iterations of the second phase and an overall speed up in learning times.

7.2.2   Discriminant Analysis Initialization

As an unsupervised method, principal components analysis ignores classification information when choosing its directions. Discriminant analysis, a related linear projection method,
uses class information and so may yield a better set of directions for classification purposes
(see section B.2).

7.2.3   Nearest Neighbor Classifier Initialization

A nearest neighbor classifier that performs well on a classification problem can be used to
initialize a layered network solution. The following method is described by Smyth [349].
Similar ideas are suggested by Raudys and Skurikhina [303] and others.

The process starts with a set of cluster centers for each class. The k-means algorithm, or a
similar method such as LVQ, may be used to select representatives. A bisecting hyperplane
is then created for every pair of centers with different class memberships. For n cluster
centers, there will be $n(n-1)/2$ hyperplanes; a culling algorithm selects the fraction of
these that actually separate adjacent centers. Each remaining hyperplane determines the
weight vector for a node in the hidden layer.

Next, the cluster centers are applied as inputs to calculate the hidden-to-output weights.
The hidden unit responses are treated as fixed in this phase so the hidden-to-output weights
can be found by solving a system of linear equations (e.g., by a pseudoinverse solution).
The response can then be fine tuned by normal back-propagation training.

It was noted that the method does not work for the XOR problem because of limitations
in the algorithm used to cull redundant hyperplanes [349]. This is a limitation in the specific
culling algorithm, however, not a fundamental problem.

The algorithm may allocate more hidden units than are actually needed because it
ignores the fact that hyperplanes can often be shared to separate more than one pair of
clusters. A post-training pruning step might address this problem.

Nearest neighbor initialization methods should work well if a nearest neighbor classifier
performs well on the classification problem. There is a question of how many cluster
centers to choose; the choice is presumably based on the performance of the nearest
neighbor classifier. It should be noted that simple unsupervised clustering procedures such
as the k-means algorithm use only the input patterns when selecting cluster centroids; the
output classifications are ignored. When the data are naturally clustered in the input space
and these clusters correspond to output classifications, unsupervised clustering methods
may select an adequate set of centroids. If not, then other centroid selection methods will
be required.

Also, nearest neighbor classifiers often require large data sets to achieve good accuracy
so random initialization may give better results when data are limited. In an empirical test,

randomly initialized nets generalized better in the sense that the difference between the training and test set errors was smaller. Because the nearest-neighbor initialization starts the network at reasonably good solution, it may be easier to overtrain.

7.2.4 Prototype Initialization

Another nearest-neighbor initialization is discussed by Denoeux and Lengellé [105]. There is one hidden node for each prototype. Input patterns are normalized so each input vector has unit length, $\|\mathbf{x}\| = 1$. This can be done without loss of information by increasing the input dimension by 1 to encode the (suitably scaled) magnitude. When the weight vectors are also unit length, $\|\mathbf{w}\| = 1$, then $\mathbf{w}^T\mathbf{x} = 2 - \|\mathbf{w} - \mathbf{x}\|^2$ and a sigmoid unit has properties similar to the Gaussian units normally used in radial basis functions. (The normalized inputs lie on surface of an n-dimensional sphere which is divided into two sections by the hyperplane defined by $\mathbf{w}$.) The hidden units thus have localized responses in the input space and can be viewed as recognizing prototype patterns.

When gains are high, the hidden layer response approximates a nearest neighbor selector. That is, for nonborderline cases, the hidden unit whose weight vector is closest to the input pattern will respond strongly while more distant hidden units respond weakly, if at all. The response at the hidden layer thus approximates a 1-of-N representation so hidden-to-output weights are independent and can be set directly from the value of the target function at the prototype location. If hidden unit j responds to the jth prototype p_j, for example, then hidden-to-output weight $w_j = f^{-1}(t_j)$ where f is the node nonlinearity function and t_j is the target value for the prototype. When prototype p_j is presented, hidden unit j outputs a 1, the other hidden unit outputs are approximately 0, and the output is $f(w_j) \approx t_j$.

Several methods are suggested for choosing prototypes. For continuous target functions, the best prototypes are at local extremes (peaks and dips) of the function. An algorithm producing prototypes at these locations is described.

When gains are relaxed, the network interpolates between the prototypes more smoothly so the method can be used for continuous regression problems. As in the method of section 7.2.3 there is a question of how many prototypes to choose.

Successful learning of the two-spirals problem (illustrated in figure 12.3) in about 1000 epochs was demonstrated in a 3/20/1 network. (The easy success may be attributable to the change in input representation, however, since the normalization provides a simple function of the radius r as an additional input. This makes the problem simple enough to be solved easily by a randomly initialized network.)

7.2.5 Initialization from a Decision Tree Classifier

Initialization from a decision tree is considered by Sethi [340]. A decision tree classifier performs a hierarchical series of tests on an input pattern to determine its classification.

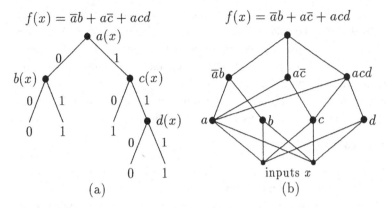

$$f(x) = \bar{a}b + a\bar{c} + acd \qquad\qquad f(x) = \bar{a}b + a\bar{c} + acd$$

(a)   (b)

Figure 7.1
Initialization from a decision tree. The function computed by the decision tree can be duplicated by a network of
linear threshold units [340]. The tree computes a Boolean function of the propositions evaluated at its decision
nodes so a two-hidden-layer network is sufficient if the tree's node decisions can be computed by linear threshold
elements. The network can be built by inspection of the tree. Training is not required; (a) is a decision tree and
(b) the equivalent network.

This can be represented as a tree (figure 7.1). Each node represents a test that can have one
of several outcomes. The result determines which outgoing path is taken and which test
is performed next. The path terminates in a leaf node when the result is an unambiguous
classification. For a given input pattern, evaluation starts at the root node and follows a path
to the leaf node with the appropriate classification.

Since a decision tree computes a Boolean function of the propositions evaluated at its
decision nodes, its function can be duplicated by a network of linear threshold units [340].
A two-hidden-layer network is sufficient if the tree's node decisions can be computed by
linear threshold elements. The network can be built by inspection of the given decision tree
(see [340] for details). Decision trees can usually be constructed quickly, so the overall
time needed to design a tree classifier, construct the equivalent network, and fine tune it by
training on examples may be much shorter than the time needed to train a network from
random weights.

7.2.6   Initialization from Symbolic Rule Systems

Another method of initialization constructs a network from a rule-based solution. In [342,
375] symbolic rules are embedded in the initial structure of a neural network by translating
the AND, OR, and NOT terms into corresponding network structures with appropriate
weights. (See figure 4.7 for implementation of AND and OR functions.) Note that this may
produce an irregular nonlayered network because the rules in the original system can have

arbitrary dependencies. Additional links with small random weights are provided to let the system add new terms that may be useful. Small values are used so the embedded rules dominate initially. The network is then trained from examples to improve its performance. Because the embedded symbolic rules are often classifications, the cross-entropy error function may be preferable to the mean-squared-error function [342]. The embedded rules represent the default knowledge of the system, so if weight-decay is used it may be desirable to let the weights decay to their initial values rather than zero.

7.2.7 Initialization from Fuzzy Rule Systems

For problems where the desired input-output relationship is well understood and express-ible by a small set of rules, initialization based on a fuzzy logic implementation has been suggested, e.g., [291]. This is similar to the method of section 7.2.6, but the original rules are fuzzy.

As a very simple example, if we know that the output should be large when two input variables, A and B, are large, we can prewire one of the hidden nodes to implement (A AND B) and connect it to the output node with a positive weight. (Simple logical functions such as AND, OR, and NOT are easy to implement in a single node by appropriate selection of the weights and thresholds. A AND B, for example, can be realized by connecting large positive weights from A and B and selecting the threshold so that the node is active only when both A and B are active.) The information in the rules initializes the network near a reasonably good solution which is then improved by further training on examples. Even when we don't have complete knowledge about the desired solution, we may have knowledge about certain aspects of it that can be "injected" into the network in this way.

7.2.8 Remarks

Bias   It should be noted that basing the initial state on a solution provided by another method introduces bias which may remain in the final network. Subsequent training may amount to mere second-order adjustments of the initial solution so a network initialized from a nearest-neighbor classifier, for example, may end up with classification properties similar to the nearest-neighbor classifier.

This is desirable in some cases because it provides some assurance that the network will behave properly in critical situations and it helps in understanding the trained network. When the initial solution is satisfactory, implementation as a neural network may be useful simply to gain properties such as parallel operation and some fault tolerance. In cases where the objective is simply to accelerate learning however, the bias may be a problem if the initial solution is only a poor guess.

Effect of the Optimization Procedure   The training procedure has some effect on how much of the initial bias will be retained in the final network. In cases where it is desirable to preserve the basic form of the initial solution, small learning rates are appropriate to avoid leaving the initial basin of attraction. Local search methods (such as gradient descent) are appropriate in this case rather than truly global search techniques which ignore the initial state. If the initial solution is good, more powerful gradient techniques such as quasi-Newton methods or conjugate gradient descent may be preferable to back-propagation since their convergence behavior in the neighborhood of a solution is much better.

8 The Error Surface

Because the network output is a function of its weights, the error is a function of **w**. In general, $E(\mathbf{w})$ is a multidimensional function and impossible to visualize. If it could be plotted as a function of **w**, however, E might look like a landscape with hills and valleys, high where E is high and low where E is low. Back-propagation, as an approximation to gradient descent, could then be viewed as placing a marble at some random point on the landscape and letting it roll downhill. If the surface were shaped like a smooth bowl, the marble (the weight state) would always roll to the lowest point; back-propagation would always find the best solution and local minima would never be a problem. Usually, of course, the surface is not so simple. Because the shape of the error surface has a fundamental effect on the learning process, it is useful to examine some of its properties. Many of the figures that follow are adapted from Hush, Horne, and Salas [183, 181].

8.1 Characteristic Features

Stair-Steps For classification problems the error surface often has a "stair-step" quality with flat regions separated by steep cliffs (figure 8.1a). The stair-step shape can arise because samples in finite training sets are sparse and because the classifier output changes sharply at a decision boundary in the input space. The decision boundary moves in the input space as the weights change but the error remains constant until the boundary crosses over a training sample and alters its classification. Either the reclassified sample is now classified correctly and the error drops a step, or the sample is now classified incorrectly and the error jumps a step. The $E(\mathbf{w})$ surface thus has flat areas where E doesn't change, separated by vertical steps where E changes discontinuously as the boundary crosses over a sample in the input space.

As the number of samples increases, the steps become more numerous and closer together (figure 8.1b); from a distance, the surface appears smoother. With continuous training data (samples available everywhere), many of the flat areas may disappear. The error can change continuously even if the node nonlinearity is a step function because the volume of positive and negative samples changes continuously as the boundary moves. Discontinuities may still occur though at points in the $E(\mathbf{w})$ space where the system decision boundary is parallel to and crosses a true boundary in the data.

The $E(\mathbf{w})$ surface also becomes smoother as the node nonlinearities of the classifier become smoother. With linear threshold units (step function nonlinearities) the plateaus of the error surface are truly flat and the steps between plateaus are truly discontinuous. When the step functions are replaced by smoother functions such as sigmoids, the steps are rounded and error surface is smoother. Figure 8.2 shows the smoothing effect of using a lower gain sigmoid. Indeed, one of the main reasons for using sigmoids rather than

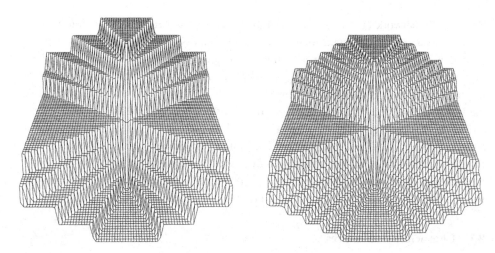

Figure 8.1
(a) The error surface of a classifier often has many flat plateaus separated by steep cliffs. (b) Increasing the number of samples creates more steps and moves them closer together (adapted from [181, 183]).

step functions is that the error surface becomes continuous so gradient based optimization methods can be used. Since gain scaling is equivalent to scaling all the node input weights by a constant factor (smaller weights correspond to smaller gains) this provides support for the heuristic of initializing with small weights.

The orientation and placement of a node hyperplane depends only on the ratio of its weights (section 3.1). As all weights are scaled equivalently, the location of the hyperplane stays fixed but the steepness of the sigmoid transition varies (increasing with the magnitude of the weight vector). For the system as a whole, the input-output transfer function is defined by cells bounded by the node hyperplanes; as all weights are scaled equivalently, the cell boundaries remain fixed but the steepness of the boundary transitions change. For small scale factors (small weights), the sigmoids have small slopes and the boundary transition regions may extend across entire cells, effectively smoothing over the stair steps. As the scale factor becomes large (large weights), the boundary transition regions shrink, the cell interiors flatten, and the steps become sharper.

Radial Features   For classification problems, the preceding means the $E(\mathbf{w})$ surface often has a radial or "star" topology because scaling all weights equivalently corresponds to moving along a radial line in weight space from the origin to infinity.

The surface is not truly "star-shaped" because the error can change nonmonotonically along a radial line in the region near the origin. Past a certain radius, however, the

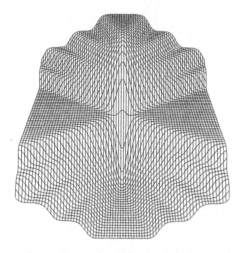

Figure 8.2
With a smaller tanh gain (0.1 in this case), the step transitions are smoother (cf. figure 8.1a). Gain scaling is equivalent to scaling all weights by a constant factor though so this does not change the basic shape of the error surface. In the figure, it corresponds to zooming in for a closer view of the origin.

classifications cease changing as the weights increase further. Once the scale factor is large enough, the classifications remain essentially constant and the error changes very little as the weight state moves along a line to infinity.

For {0, 1} training targets (or {−1, +1} targets for tanh node functions), the minimum error on the line often occurs at infinity because the target values are reachable only by making the weights approach infinity. (This is generally true for single layer networks and linearly separable data; there may be exceptions for multilayer networks, data sets which are not linearly separable, or data sets for which the optimal outputs are not 0 and 1 even though the target values are.) The error surface therefore often has rays or troughs extending radially from the origin with minima (or maxima) at infinity. Because the sigmoid slopes are extremely small in the saturation region, the slope along the bottom of the trough is also very small. Although it is not visible in figure 8.1a, there is a trough along the center of the lowest plateau.

Replacing the {0, 1} targets with {0.1, 0.9} values may move the minima in from infinity, but this may also introduce new minima in the form of small dips at the bottom of each cliff (figure 8.3); these are usually shallow and narrow, however. Consider how the error varies as a sigmoid is shifted sideways by varying the threshold. As the 0.9 part of the sigmoid passes over a 0.9 target, the error for that sample goes through zero. This creates

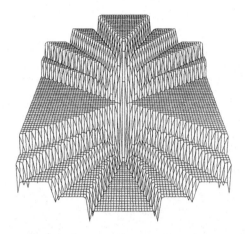

Figure 8.3
Replacing the $\{-1, 1\}$ targets with $\{-0.9, 0.9\}$ values produces a small dip at the bottom of each cliff. For illustration purposes, the tanh gain was reduced to $1/2$ to make the dip wider and smaller targets were used to make it deeper.

a local minimum (if other samples are sufficiently far away) because the error increases as the sigmoid is shifted to either side around this point. In the two-dimensional plots, this appears as a small gutter or trough along the bottom of each step. Similar effects can also occur at step tops in networks with hidden layers. One way to suppress the gutter is to change the error function so that outputs greater than 0.9 (for target values $t = 1$) and less than 0.1 (for $t = 0$ and sigmoid nodes) do not contribute to the error [181, 183]. (In section 8.5 this is called the LMS-threshold error function.) This could introduce truly flat plateau regions, however, causing problems for gradient-based training methods.

Troughs and Ridges   More significant troughs and ridges occur when the classifier cannot completely separate the training samples. Figure 8.4 shows the error surface for the two-weight classifier given a training set that is not linearly separable. The input data is one-dimensional (points on a line). As the threshold weight varies, the sigmoid shifts along the input axis and the error increases and then decreases again as the decision boundary crosses individual samples. This occurs for all values of the gain weight so the result is a trough in the error surface. A gradient based optimization method could easily get stuck in one of these troughs and so converge to a poor solution.

It is interesting to note that, in figure 8.4 at least, the troughs come together at the origin. This supports the idea of initializing with small weights, that is, near the origin, where all troughs (including the main basin) are reachable in just a few steps. Although true gradient following methods would not be able to escape from a poor trough, ap-

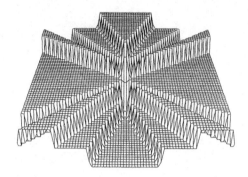

Figure 8.4
When the samples are not linearly separable, the error surface has radial troughs and ridges. A gradient based optimization method could easily get stuck in one of the troughs corresponding to a poor solution (adapted from [181, 183]).

proximations such as on-line or batch back-propagation with a noninfinitesimal step size would have an appreciable chance if better alternatives are sufficiently close. Of course, we should not jump to conclusions based on this one example; in many problems the origin is a local minimum and for these it may be better to initialize at some intermediate distance.

8.2   The Gradient is the Sum of Single-Pattern Gradients

With an SSE or MSE cost function, the $E(w)$ surface is the sum (or average) of the individual surfaces for each pattern and the total gradient is the sum (or average) of the single-pattern gradients. In other words, the error is shaped by the interaction of the weights with each of the individual training patterns. Figure 8.5 shows single-pattern gradients for a simple two-weight problem. These are the vectors that would be used for weight updates in on-line learning. On a "hillside" (a), most of the vectors point in a dominant direction. On a "ridge" (b) or at the bottom of a "valley" (c), there are often two bundles of vectors pointing in opposite directions across the valley. In on-line learning, the weights are updated from just one pattern and thus tend to oscillate across the valley. At a local minima (d) the vectors sum to zero; they may be large and distributed in all directions, or they may all go to zero. If they simply cancel without going to zero, the minimum will be unstable with on-line learning—the weight vector will move off the minimum if placed there. Point (e) shows a relatively "flat spot." These examples aren't universal since similar $E(w)$ features could be created in many ways, but they are common. Other cost functions may yield different behavior.

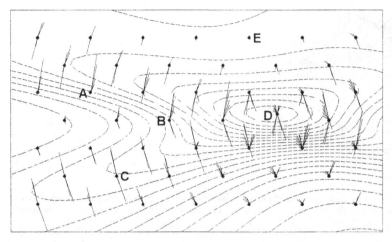

Figure 8.5
Single-pattern weight update vectors. With an SSE cost function, the $E(w)$ surface is the sum of individual
surfaces for each pattern and the total gradient is the sum of the single-pattern gradients. On a "hillside" (a),
most of the vectors point in a dominant direction. On a "ridge" (b) or at the bottom of a "valley" (c), there are
often two bundles of vectors pointing in opposite directions. At a local minima (d) the vectors sum to zero; they
may be large and evenly distributed in all directions, or they may all go to zero. Point (e) shows a relatively flat
spot.

8.3   Weight-Space Symmetries

Consider a network with two or more nodes in a hidden layer. The network output is
unchanged when all weights into and out of two hidden nodes, i and j, are swapped;
node i computes what node j used to and vice versa so the effect on the rest of the net
is unchanged. Equivalently, the node indexes could just be swapped or the locations in
the layer could be exchanged. There are $H!$ permutations for the position of H nodes in
a hidden layer, so this gives $H!$ different weight vectors that produce equivalent input-
output network functions. An immediate consequence of this is that the error surface will
not have a single global minimum (unless it is the zero vector); there will be many points
with equally small errors.

   Another symmetry results because the tanh function is odd, $f(-x) = -f(x)$. An equivalent response can be obtained by changing the sign of all the weights into and out of a
hidden node since changing the sign of the input weights simply changes the sign of the
node output and the effect on the following layer can be compensated by also changing the
sign of the output weights. Similar symmetries exist for networks of sigmoid nodes if the
biases of nodes in the following layer are adjusted when the signs are flipped because

$\mathrm{sigmoid}(x) = 1 - \mathrm{sigmoid}(-x)$.

Any combination of the hidden nodes may have their signs flipped, so there are 2^H possibilities.

Together, these give $M = 2^H H!$ different weight vectors that produce identical input-output functions. For every weight vector that produces a particular input-output function, there are at least $2^H H! - 1$ "twins" that produce equivalent responses. H does not have to be large for this to be a huge number, e.g., for $H = 10$, $M = 3.7$ billion.

For networks with more than one hidden layer, the number of symmetries is a product of similar terms for each layer [78]

$$M = \prod_\ell 2^{H_\ell} H_\ell! \qquad (8.1)$$

where ℓ indexes the hidden layers and H_ℓ is the number of nodes in layer ℓ.

Hecht-Nielsen [162] asked whether these symmetries exhaust the possibilities. Sussmann [362] showed that, aside from these symmetries, the weights of a feedforward single-hidden-layer network with tanh nodes are uniquely determined by the input-output map, provided that the network is irreducible (i.e., that no nodes can be removed without affecting the output). The results have been extended to reducible networks with more general node nonlinearities [232].

Hecht-Neilsen [163] showed that these symmetries give the weight space a structure of cone or wedge-shaped regions that differ only by symmetry. The cones are otherwise identical so each contains weight vectors for every input-output function the network can implement. In principle, a training system could restrict search to a single cone and still cover all possible input-output functions. Because M can be very large, this could reduce the size of the search space by a huge amount. Unfortunately, the remaining space is still huge. There might be some benefit for nonlocal methods such as the genetic algorithm as this would limit redundancy in the search. (An empirical test using a simulated annealing method on the 2-input XOR problem showed a reduction of search time by about 1/2 [198].) For local search (e.g., gradient) techniques, however, there is no good reason to stay inside a single cone because, after all, the cones are identical. It might also seem counterproductive because the introduction of the cone boundary as a hard constraint could give rise to additional poor local minima at the boundary. The cone boundaries are natural divisions, however, because of symmetry so pure gradient descent naturally stays in its starting cone [164] and there is no need for special measures to restrict the weight vector to a single cone.

8.4   Remarks

The efficiency of any optimization method depends on having a good fit between the basic
assumptions of the algorithm and the actual characteristics of the function being minimized. Many advanced optimization methods assume the error surface is locally quadratic,
for example, and may not do well on the "cliffs-and-plateaus" surface common in neural
network classifiers. In this case, the quadratic assumption is not reasonable on a large scale
so these optimizers may be no more efficient than simpler methods in finding a good approximate solution. The assumption, however, *is* usually reasonable near a minimum, in
which case these methods may be very efficient for final tuning of a near-solution found by
other methods.

For back-propagation, a large learning rate is needed to make progress across the large
flat regions. But near the "cliffs" where $\|\partial E / \partial \mathbf{w}\|$ is large, a small learning rate is necessary
to prevent huge weight changes in essentially random directions. If a fixed learning rate
is used, the value will have to be a compromise. One of the advantages of the common
technique of initializing with small random weights is that the system starts in the area
near the origin where the error surface is smoother and it has a better chance of finding the
right trough.

Before ending this discussion, it should be noted that the error surfaces illustrated in the
figures are for classification problems with small training sets. The error surfaces may be
very different for regression problems with large sample sizes. Based on figure 8.1, it is
reasonable to expect it to be smoother.

For regression problems where the target is a continuous function of its inputs, smooth
input-output functions are usually preferred. If there is sufficient data that the system cannot
fit every point exactly, then it must approximate multiple points by fitting a surface "close"
to them. For many cost functions, this surface can be thought of as the local average of
nearby points and will tend to be smooth because of the smoothing effects of averaging.
Because smoother functions generally correspond to smaller weights, the good minima
will usually be in the interior of the weight space rather than at infinity. Similarly, in
classification problems with many samples in overlapping clusters, it may be better to form
gradual transitions between classes in regions where they overlap. This again corresponds
to smaller weights and moves the minima in from infinity.

Of course, if there is so little data and the network is so powerful that it can fit every point
exactly, then there is no reason to expect it to form a smooth function, and minima at infinity
may survive. Even when a smooth function would be preferable, local minima at infinity
may survive corresponding to fitting a few of the points exactly while ignoring the rest;
these are likely to be shallow and narrow, however, and will probably be shadowed by better

minima closer to the origin. Although plateaus and cliffs will be apparent at large distances from the origin, this may be irrelevant because those regions will never be investigated by the learning algorithm.

The stair-step shape may survive in very underconstrained networks that can essentially classify each of the training points internally (e.g., by assigning a hidden "grandmother node" to each training sample). In this case, the global minima of the training set error would be at infinity and low generalization-error areas corresponding to smooth functions are unlikely to be minima.

8.5   Local Minima

Like all local search techniques, back-propagation may converge to a local minimum of the error rather than the global optimum. This is a fundamental characteristic of local search methods, not a defect of the implementation.

Random Restarts   One of the simplest ways to deal with local minima is to train many different networks with different initial weights. Training times can be long, so it may be useful to train a number of networks for a small number of iterations and then choose a fraction of the best for more extensive training. Although there are no guarantees, this tends to weed out bad starting points, favoring those already close to good solutions. Because many of the initial networks may converge toward equivalent solutions, a clustering procedure may be useful to choose a nonredundant subset.

If training is viewed as a dynamic process, each minimum (local or global) can be considered an attractor with a basin of attraction consisting of all the starting points that converge to it during training. With gradient descent, an initial weight vector will basically "roll downhill" until it reaches a minima; the minimum is the attractor and all points that flow into it form the basin of attraction. In figure 8.6, the dotted line separates basins of attraction of the local and global minima. Because the probability that a randomly selected starting point converges to a particular minimum is equal to the probability that it starts in its basin of attraction, the success of the random restart approach will depend on the relative sizes of the basins of attraction.

In theory, if we knew the relative sizes of the basins of attraction (and the distribution of the initial weights), we would be able to calculate how many random restarts would be needed to achieve a certain probability of landing in the basin of a global minima. Easy problems would have large global basins of attraction and hard problems would have small basins. In general, however, it is not practical to map the basins of attraction because evaluation of each point requires training a network to convergence. These ideas

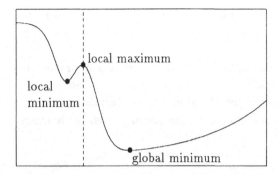

Figure 8.6
Local and global minima. A global minimum of a function can be defined as its lowest point, the input that gives
the lowest possible output. A local minimum is a point that is lower than all its neighbors, but higher than the
global minimum.

are, therefore, more useful as an explanation of why a problem is hard than as a tool to
improve training.

A further complication is that the basins of attraction depend on the weight-change
method as well as the static $E(\mathbf{w})$ function so different learning algorithms may have
different attractors for the same $E(\mathbf{w})$ function. With gradient descent, for example, several
local minima may have large regions of attraction. In principle, these shrink to infinitesimal
points with simulated annealing and almost all points belong to the basin of attraction
of the global minimum. Simple parameter changes in things like the learning rate and
momentum also affect the boundaries. In gradient descent with a small step size, the basins
are generally contiguous and have smooth boundaries. When the learning rate is too high,
however, the process can become chaotic and the basins of attraction may become disjoint
with very complex, possibly fractal, boundaries [216, 217].

With stochastic algorithms the discrete basins of attraction are replaced by probability
density functions. For every ending point z there is a density function over x measuring the
probability that starting point x ends at z. Loosely speaking, the regions of high probability
can be thought of as the basin of attraction of z.

The standard solution to the problem of local minima is to improve the optimization
algorithm. In the random restart approach, the optimization routine is augmented with
an outer loop searching over initial starting points —simple random search in this case.
This will not be effective if the global attractor basins are too small to find by random
sampling. It is possible to consider more sophisticated outer search techniques, but use of
such techniques is not widespread. Another approach is to use stochastic search methods
by introducing randomness at a lower algorithmic level. Simple examples include online

training, training with added input noise (jitter), or adding noise to the weights during up-dates. If these do not work, more sophisticated global search techniques such as simulated annealing or genetic algorithms may be needed.

Instead of improving the optimization algorithm, an alternative approach is to avoid creating local minima in the first place. If we knew more about their causes, we might be able to design networks and training algorithms without poor local minima. Unfortunately, relatively little is known. The following paragraphs outline a few results.

8.5.1   Single-Layer Nets Can Have Local Minima

Single-layer networks with linear outputs implement linear functions and minimum-MSE linear regression has a quadratic error surface with a single minimum so one might guess that single-layer networks do not have local minima. This ignores effects of the node nonlinearity.

Sontag and Sussmann [352, 353] (see also [408]) give conditions where this intuition is true. They show that if (1) the cost function does not penalize overclassification and (2) the data are linearly separable, then there are no local minima that are not global minima and gradient descent converges (to within a tolerance) globally from any starting point in a finite number of steps. Condition 1 means that the error is taken to be zero when the output "goes beyond what the target asks." With tanh nodes, for example, the error is taken to be zero when $y \geq 0.9$ for $t = 0.9$ or when $y \leq -0.9$ for $t = -0.9$, for target t and output y. Similar relations apply for sigmoids and other nonlinearities. This has been called the *LMS-threshold cost function*. Use of unobtainable targets, for example, 0 and 1 for the sigmoid, might be considered a special case.

There can be local minima when either of the two conditions fail. Dips like those in figure 8.3 can occur when condition 1 is not satisfied and troughs as in figure 8.4 may exist because the data is not linearly separable.

Auer, Herbster, and Warmuth [13] show that local minima can exist in a network consist-ing of a single neuron whenever the composition of the loss function (error function) with the node activation function is continuous and bounded. This result favors the entropic error function because the sigmoid and MSE error function meet the criterion and the sigmoid and entropic error function do not. Reference [13] also shows that artificial data sets can be constructed in which the number of minima grows exponentially with the input dimension.

It has been pointed out [58, 59] that one can find linearly separable data sets for which the MSE cost function has minima at weight vectors that do not separate all patterns correctly. The perceptron algorithm would classify these data correctly whereas back-propagation would not. This does not necessarily mean the MSE function has local minima though, it just shows that it differs from the function that counts the number of classification errors.

The results just discussed show that gradient descent will separate linearly separable data sets if condition 1 is satisfied (i.e., if overclassification is not penalized).

8.5.2   No Local Minima for Linearly Separable Data

Similar results for one-hidden-layer networks have been shown in [145, 127]. If the data are linearly separable, the network has a pyramidal structure after the inputs and a full-rank weight matrix, and the LMS-threshold cost function is used then no local minima exist and back-propagation will separate the data. A distinction is made between spurious local minima, which can be eliminated by the use of the LMS-threshold error function, and more serious structural local minima.

Together, these results show that there need not be local minima for linearly separable data sets. That is, there may be local minima in some set-ups, but steps can be taken to eliminate them. An important condition appears to be the use of the LMS-threshold error or the use of unobtainable targets, for example, 0 and 1 for the sigmoid, which eliminate the spurious local minima.

Of course, it is well-known that the perceptron learning algorithm will always find a set of weights that correctly classifies a linearly-separable data set. Optimal convergence of on-line back-propagation for linearly separable data, akin to the perceptron convergence property, is shown in [144] for a single-hidden-layer network using the LMS-threshold error function. The demonstration is similar to the perceptron convergence theorem. A side point of the paper is that on-line learning can be qualitatively different from batch-mode learning when the learning rate is not small and it is not necessarily a crude approximation of gradient descent.

These results are intriguing but, unfortunately, most interesting problems are not linearly separable. It is worth noting that a data set can sometimes be made linearly separable by changing the way variables are represented, but there are many other issues to consider.

Auer, Herbster, and Warmuth [13] show that a single-layer net has no poor local minima when the transfer function and loss function are monotonic and the data are realizable ($E(\mathbf{w}) = 0$ for some weights $\mathbf{w}$). This is not restricted to binary targets; linearly separable data sets with binary targets are realizable, but there are also realizable data sets with continuous targets.

8.5.3   Local Minima Really Do Exist

It has been suggested that (nearly) flat areas in error surface are sometimes mistaken for minima and that true local minima might be relatively rare. That is, the error may decrease so slowly as the weight vector creeps across a flat spot that it appears as if learning has stopped because the system has reached a minimum. Internally, it might be possible

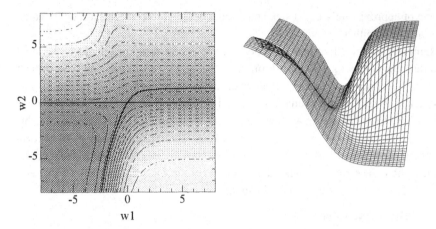

Figure 8.7
The error surface for a 1/1/1 network trained on the identity mapping illustrates that local minima do in fact exist. This surface has a good minima in the lower left quadrant, a poor minimum in the upper right quadrant, and a saddle point at the origin: (a) the contour plot, and (b) a view looking across the origin down the axis of the poor minimum.

to observe the weights moving in a consistent direction but from the outside it may be impossible to tell the difference. The fact that these are not minima is sometimes shown because the error resumes its decrease (sometimes sharply) if training is continued long enough for the system to cross the flat area. (Figures 6.4 and 6.12 show examples of this.)

Example It is easy to illustrate local minima in small networks. Figure 8.4 shows one case. An example of a very simple network having local minima is described by McClelland and Rumelhart [261]. The task is to do an identity mapping with a 1/1/1 network. The network has one input, one hidden unit, and one output. No bias weights are used so there are only two weights. The nonlinearities are sigmoids.

Given 0 or 1 as an input, the net should reproduce the value at the output. Figure 8.7 shows the error as a function of the weights w_1 and w_2. There is a global minimum in the lower left quadrant, a poor local minimum in the upper right quadrant, and a saddle point at the origin separating the two basins of attraction. The saddle point is visible in figure 8.7b. Although the poor minimum appears to be narrower in the contour plot, both have basins of attraction of approximately equal size and a random weight vector has a roughly equal chance of landing in either.

This example is contrived, of course. When adaptable bias weights are added, the local minimum disappears leaving two global minima separated by a saddle point. Use of tanh nodes and $\{-1, +1\}$ inputs would also remove the asymmetry causing the problem.

The existence of real local minima in nontrivial networks was demonstrated by McInerney et al. [263, 262]. (These are an abstract and an unpublished technical report. Hecht-Nielsen [162] reports some of the details.) After extensive simulations using closed-form expressions for the gradients and second derivatives, they were able to find a point on the error surface where the error was higher than at other points, where all gradients were zero, and where the Hessian was strongly positive-definite.

8.5.4 The Effect of Network Size

Aside from the fact that the architecture is poorly matched to the problem, the 1/1/1 network in the previous example is very small. The common wisdom is that if there are enough weights and/or hidden units then local minima do not exist or are not a major problem. Indeed, when bias weights are added to the simple network above, the local minimum disappears. McClelland and Rumelhart [261: 132] state, "[i]n problems with many hidden units, local minima seem quite rare." The extra degrees of freedom presumably provide more ways for potential local minima to flow into lower areas and eventually reach a global minimum. Of course, there are no guarantees as it is always possible to add extra degrees of freedom in ways that do not fix the problem.

A series of papers [301, 413, 150, 414, 415] have shown that if there are as many hidden nodes as there are training patterns then, with probability 1, there are no suboptimal local minima. According to Yu [413], a sufficient condition is that the network be able to fit every training pattern exactly, giving $E_{min} = 0$. Assuming consistent training data, this is always possible in a single-hidden-layer net when the number H of hidden nodes is as large as the number M of unique training patterns (actually $H \geq M - 1$ will do). Because most data sets contain regularities, fewer nodes will suffice in most cases; however, $M - 1$ hidden nodes in a single hidden layer will be *necessary* when the patterns are colinear with alternating target classes [280].

According to these results, the error surface will have no nonglobal minima if there are enough hidden nodes. This helps explain empirical observations that it is often easier to train larger networks than it is to train small ones. Larger networks seem to be less sensitive to parameters and less likely to become stuck during training. Of course, the requirement that the network be able to fit the data exactly allows it to "memorize" the data and conflicts with heuristic rules for obtaining good generalization so steps such as early stopping or pruning will be needed to avoid overfitting.

8.6   Properties of the Hessian Matrix

The Hessian, $\mathbf{H}$, of the error with respect to the weights is the matrix of second derivatives with elements

$$h_{ij} = \frac{\partial^2 E}{\partial w_i \, \partial w_j}.$$

Knowledge about the Hessian is useful for a number of reasons:

• The convergence of many optimization algorithms is governed by characteristics of the Hessian matrix. In second-order optimization methods, the matrix is used explicitly to calculate search directions. In other cases, it may have an implicit role. Slow convergence of gradient descent, for example, can often be explained as an effect of an ill-conditioned Hessian (see appendix A.2). The eigenvalues of $\mathbf{H}$ also determine how large the learning rate can be before learning becomes unstable. When $\mathbf{H}$ is known, an optimal rate can be chosen; in other cases, a more conservative choice must be made.

• Some pruning algorithms use Hessian information to decide which weights to remove. "Optimal brain damage" uses a diagonal approximation while "Optimal brain surgeon" uses the full approximation.

• The inverse Hessian can be used to calculate confidence intervals for the network outputs [44: 399].

• Hessian information can be used to calculate regularization parameters [44, section 10.4].

• Hessian information can be used for fast retraining of an existing network when additional training data becomes available [41].

• At a local minimum of the error function, the Hessian will be positive definite. This provides a way to determine if learning has stopped because the network reached a true minimum or because it "ran out of gas" on a flat spot.

Bishop [44, section 4.10] and Buntine and Weigend [62] provide summaries of a number of methods for calculation and approximation of the Hessian in neural networks. (The preceding list is partly drawn from [44, section 4.10].)

Sometimes the Hessian is required only as a means to obtain the product $\mathbf{H}\mathbf{v}$ for some vector $\mathbf{v}$. Pearlmutter [297] describes a fast method for finding this product which does not require evaluation of the Hessian.

8.6.1   Ill-Conditioning

An *ill-conditioned* matrix has a large ratio $|\lambda_{max}/\lambda_{min}|$, where λ_{max} is the largest eigenvalue and λ_{min} is the smallest (nonzero) eigenvalue. In the Hessian of the error with respect to the weights, this reflects the fact that the gradient changes slowly along one direction (determined by the eigenvector associated with λ_{min}) and changes rapidly along another direction (determined by the eigenvector associated with λ_{max}). The effect this has on gradient descent is discussed in section 10.5.1. Briefly, it requires that a small learning rate be used to avoid instability along the quickly changing direction, but then progress along the slowly changing direction will be slow and convergence times will be long. Appendix A.2 discusses the convergence rate of gradient descent in linear problems.

It appears that the Hessian is very often ill-conditioned in neural network training problems [37, 331, 92, 93] and it is common for many eigenvalues to be near-zero. Sigmoid saturation may cause effective loss of rank. Intuitively, small eigenvalues can be related to flat regions of the $E(\mathbf{w})$ surface where the error changes very slowly in most directions. It is worth noting that the outer-product approximation (see the following) will be rank-deficient when the number of weights exceeds the number of training patterns. This is not necessarily recommended, but not uncommon in neural networks.

An implication of ill-conditioning is that the expected efficiencies of higher order optimization methods may not be realized [331]. Ill-conditioning could lead to numerical instability or very large steps that take the system out of the region where the local approximation is valid. This is a well-known problem with Newton's method, for example, which is addressed by standard methods. The fix used in the Levenberg-Marquardt method is to choose the search direction based on a combination of the gradient and Newton directions.

Many of the techniques suggested for accelerating back-propagation are simple algorithmic modifications that optimize certain steps of the procedure without addressing the fundamental problem of ill-conditioning. A more basic way to decrease training time is to modify the problem so that the Hessian is better conditioned. The effectiveness of some common techniques can be explained in terms of their effect on the Hessian:

• normalization of inputs to zero-mean values with similar variances,

• use of bias nodes (which remove the mean internally),

• use of tanh nonlinearities rather than logistic sigmoids (because the outputs of tanh nodes tend to be zero-mean when their inputs are zero-mean whereas the outputs of sigmoid nodes always have a positive mean), and

• preprocessing (e.g., principal components analysis) to remove input redundancy.

8.6.2   Exact Calculation of the Hessian

Bishop, [41, 39] and [44, section 4.10.5], describes an $O(W^2)$ method for calculating the exact Hessian of a feedforward network. The procedure is somewhat involved for a general feedforward network so the simplified version [44, section 4.10.6] for single-hidden-layer networks is summarized here. For simplicity, the terms are given for a single pattern p; the complete expression is obtained by summing contributions from each pattern. Let indexes i and i' denote input nodes, j and j' denote hidden nodes, and k and k' denote output nodes. Each nondiagonal term of the Hessian involves two weights.

1. If both weights are in the second layer,

$$\frac{\partial^2 E_p}{\partial w_{kj} \, \partial w_{k'j'}} = z_j z_{j'} \delta_{kk'} H_{kk} \tag{8.2}$$

where z_j is the output of the jth node, $\delta_{kk'}$ is the Kronecker delta, and H_{kk} is defined at the end of the section.

2. If both weights are in the first layer,

$$\frac{\partial^2 E_p}{\partial w_{ji} \, \partial w_{j'i'}} = x_i x_{i'} f''(a_{j'}) \delta_{jj'} \sum_k w_{kj} \delta_k$$

$$+ \, x_i x_{i'} f'(a_{j'}) f'(a_j) \sum_k w_{kj'} w_{kj} H_{kk} \tag{8.3}$$

where x_i is the ith input, a_j is the weight sum into the jth hidden node, $f()$ is the node nonlinearity function, and $\delta_k = \partial E_p / \partial a_k$ is the delta term calculated by back-propagation.

3. If one weight is in each layer,

$$\frac{\partial^2 E_p}{\partial w_{ji} \, \partial w_{kj'}} = x_i f'(a_j) \left\{ \delta_k \delta_{jj'} + z_{j'} w_{kj} H_{kk} \right\}. \tag{8.4}$$

The term $H_{kk'}$

$$H_{kk'} = \frac{\partial^2 E_p}{\partial a_k \, \partial a_{k'}}$$

describes how errors in different output nodes interact to affect the overall error. For the sum-of-squares error function and *linear* output units, $H_{kk'} = \delta_{kk'}$.

8.6.3 Approximations

Second order optimization methods often require the Hessian matrix or an approximation. For mean-squared-error cost functions, the outer-product approximation is a common choice.

Outer-Product Approximation   For the mean-square error function, the Hessian can often be approximated reasonably well by the average of outer-products of the gradient vectors. This approximation is used by the Gauss-Newton optimization method (section 10.6.2).

The cost function E is the mean squared error between the desired output d and the actual output y which is a function of the weights w_k

$$E = \left\langle (d - y)^2 \right\rangle. \tag{8.5}$$

The $\langle\ \rangle$ brackets denote the average over the training set. For simplicity, assume y is a scalar. A single weight index (e.g., w_j) is used here since it is not necessary to identify the weight by the nodes it connects. The gradient $\mathbf{g}$ has components

$$g_j = \frac{\partial E}{\partial w_j} = 2 \left\langle (d - y) \frac{\partial y}{\partial w_j} \right\rangle \tag{8.6}$$

and the Hessian $\mathbf{H}$ has components

$$h_{ij} = \frac{\partial^2 E}{\partial w_i\, \partial w_j} = 2 \left\langle -\frac{\partial y}{\partial w_i} \frac{\partial y}{\partial w_j} + (d - y) \frac{\partial^2 y}{\partial w_i\, \partial w_j} \right\rangle. \tag{8.7}$$

This can be written

$$\mathbf{H} = 2(-\mathbf{P} + \mathbf{Q}) \tag{8.8}$$

where $\mathbf{P} = \left\langle \mathbf{gg}^T \right\rangle$ is the average outer-product of first-order gradient terms while $\mathbf{Q}$, $q_{ij} = \left\langle (d - y) \frac{\partial^2 y}{\partial w_i\, \partial w_j} \right\rangle$ contains second order terms. Because $\mathbf{P}$ is the sum of outer products of the gradient vector, it is real, symmetric, and thus nonnegative-definite ($\mathbf{w}^T \mathbf{P} \mathbf{w} \geq 0$ for all $\|\mathbf{w}\| \neq 0$). The number of training samples must be greater than the number of weights for it to have full rank.

The outer-product approximation is based on the assumption that first-order terms dominate higher order terms near a minimum. This is reasonable when the residual errors $(d - y)$ are zero-mean, independent, identically distributed values uncorrelated with the second derivatives $\partial^2 y / (\partial w_i\, \partial w_j)$. If this is true then, when the number of training points is large, $\mathbf{Q}$ should average to zero with a small variance and so can be ignored.

Of course, this assumption is not always valid. If there are too few training points, the variance of $\mathbf{Q}$ may be large. Also, if the network is too simple to fit the data, the errors may not be small or may be correlated with the second derivatives of y. (It can be argued that the errors and second derivatives will be correlated in many cases because an overly smooth network function will tend to "shave off the peaks" and "fill in the dips" of the target function. The function tends to peak where the target peaks and dip where it dips, but not quite enough, so at a peak of y the second derivatives are necessarily negative while the local errors $d - y$ tend to be positive.) A second caution is that the approximation may be valid only near points in the training set used to calculate the approximation. In practice, however, the approximation seems to work reasonably well especially when the larger algorithm does not rely too heavily on its accuracy.

The Diagonal Approximation   A further approximation is to assume that the Hessian is diagonal. This provides at least some of the Hessian information while avoiding the $O(W^2)$ storage and calculation costs demanded by the full approximation. In reality, **H** would be diagonal only if all weights affected the error independently, that is, only if there are no significant interactions between different weights. Most networks, however, have strong weight interactions so the Hessian usually has nonnegligible off-diagonal elements. The approximation therefore is not expected to be especially accurate; its main advantage is computational convenience. Effects of the approximation are discussed by Becker and LeCun [37]. A diagonal approximation is used in the "optimal brain damage" pruning method (section 13.2.3).

The second derivatives h_{kk} can be calculated by a modified back-propagation rule in about the same amount of time as a single back-propagation epoch. From [91], the diagonal elements are

$$h_{kk} = \frac{\partial^2 E}{\partial w_{ij}^2} = \frac{\partial^2 E}{\partial a_i^2} x_j^2 \qquad (8.9)$$

where a_i is the weighted sum into node i and $x_j = f(a_j)$ is the output of node j. Here the weights are indexed both by k and by the indexes i and j of the nodes they link. At the output nodes, the second derivatives are

$$\frac{\partial^2 E}{\partial a_i^2} = 2f'(a_i)^2 - 2(d_i - x_i)f''(a_i) \qquad (8.10)$$

(for all units i in the output layer). The second derivatives for internal nodes are obtained by a modified back-propagation rule

$$\frac{\partial^2 E}{\partial a_i^2} = f'(a_i)^2 \sum_\ell w_{\ell i}^2 \frac{\partial^2 E}{\partial a_\ell^2} - f''(a_i)\frac{\partial E}{\partial x_i}. \qquad (8.11)$$

The $f''(a_i)$ terms are sometimes ignored in the last two equations. This corresponds to using the diagonal of the outer-product approximation and gives guaranteed positive estimates of the second derivatives [91].

Finite-Difference Approximation   A finite-difference approximation of $\mathbf{H}$ is [44, pg. 154]

$$\frac{\partial^2 E}{\partial w_{ji} \, \partial w_{lk}} = \frac{1}{2\epsilon} \left\{ \frac{\partial E}{\partial w_{ji}}(w_{lk} + \epsilon) - \frac{\partial E}{\partial w_{ji}}(w_{lk} - \epsilon) \right\} + O(\epsilon^2). \tag{8.12}$$

Weight w_{lk} is perturbed first by $+\epsilon$ and then by $-\epsilon$. The first-order derivatives for all weights w_{ji} are calculated in each case and the second derivative is approximated by the difference between the two first-order derivatives, scaled by 2ϵ. There are W weights to perturb and each gradient calculation takes $O(W)$ time so the approximation take $O(W^2)$ time. The approximation errors are of size $O(\epsilon^2)$; small ϵ values are desirable for accuracy, but larger values are desirable to avoid numerical problems.

Because of its simplicity, the finite-difference approximation is useful during debugging to verify the correctness of other evaluation methods.

8.7   Gain Scaling

The typical node function can be written

$$a_i = \sum_j w_{ij} y_j$$

$$y_i = f(\beta_i a_i)$$

where $f()$ is the node nonlinearity and β_i is a gain parameter which controls the steepness of the function at 0. For sigmoid nonlinearities, $\frac{\partial y}{\partial a} = \beta y(1 - y)$ and at $a = 0$ the slope is $\beta/4$. Normally $\beta = 1$. Larger values increase the slope at 0 and narrow the width of the semilinear transition region. As $\beta \to \infty$, the response approaches a step function.

A number of studies, [196, 369] for example, have shown that every network with nonunity gains can be transformed into an equivalent network with unity gains by appropriate scaling of the weights (table 8.1). Further, if learning rates are also scaled appropriately, both networks will follow equivalent trajectories during training and produce equivalent outputs at the end of training.

Gain Control for Faster Learning   In many cases, the motivation for gain scaling is to accelerate the training process. Izui and Pentland [190] show that convergence time scales like $1/\beta$ without momentum and like $1/\sqrt{\beta}$ with momentum.

Lee and Bien [237] include parameters for the slope, magnitude, and vertical offset of the sigmoid function

Table 8.1
Relationship of Node Gain, Learning Rate, and Weight Magnitude (from [369]).

	with gain β	without gain
Node function	$\phi(\beta x)$	$\phi(x)$
Gain	β	1
Learning rate	η	$\beta^2 \eta$
Weights	$\mathbf{w}$	$\beta \mathbf{w}$

$$y_j = K/(1 + e^{-\beta a_j}) - L.$$

Here the gain is a fixed nonunity value. In empirical tests [9], the changes had weak effects. For $0.4 \leq \beta \leq 1.2$, learning speed and generalization increased with β, but for $\beta > 1.2$, learning became unstable "suddenly and severely" with few trials converging.

Several studies [354, 366, 312, 84] attempt to optimize the gain during training, most using gradient descent on the error. Most claim increased convergence speed and fewer problems with convergence to poor local minima. As noted, gain changes are equivalent to learning rate changes in a network without gains so optimization of gains has effects like an adaptive learning rate method. A gain change $\Delta\beta$ is equivalent to a learning rate change from $\beta^2 \eta$ to $(\beta + \Delta\beta)^2 \eta$ and a weight change from $\beta \mathbf{w}$ to $(\beta + \Delta\beta)\mathbf{w}$ [196, 369].

Gain Control to Prevent Sigmoid Saturation   Many weight initialization heuristics involve choosing an appropriate range for the initial random weights (see chapter 7). The equivalence between scaling the weights by a constant factor and introducing a gain term in the sigmoid function means that similar results can be obtained by gain scaling. In [240, 241] initial gains are chosen to avoid sigmoid saturation and its detrimental effects on learning time.

In [411], the gain is adjusted during training to prevent sigmoid saturation. If, during training, the errors are large but the back-propagated deltas are small then all the node gains are halved and the iteration repeated.

Gain Control for Improved Generalization   Gain scaling has been suggested as a way to improve generalization. In most cases, the idea is to start with small gains that increase gradually during training. This is said to be related to "continuation" or "homotopy" methods in numerical analysis. The intent is to force the system to fit large-scale features of the target function first by making it harder to fit small-scale details. The small initial gains make the network compute a smoother function than it otherwise would with the same weights and larger gains. Later, once large-scale features are learned, the gain is increased to let the system fit smaller features. The hope is that by forcing the system to start with a smooth fit and then gradually increasing its flexibility, this will increase the chance of convergence to the global minimum.

Kruschke [228, 229, 230] describes a pruning procedure based on gain-competition (section 13.4.2). Sperduti and Starita [354] describe a similar pruning method in conjunction with the use of gain scaling for faster training.

Gain Scaling to Train Networks of Hard-Limiters   In electronic circuit implementations, it is often desirable to use hard-limiting step functions for the node nonlinearity because they can be implemented with a simple switch. One way to train such networks is to gradually shift from a sigmoid to a step function during learning. (Training must be done in off-line simulations if the hardware can't implement the sigmoid.) A linear combination of the two functions

$$g(a) = \lambda f(a) + (1 - \lambda)h(a)$$

is used in [373]. Here a is the weighted-sum into the node, $f(a)$ is the sigmoid function, $h(a)$ is a step function, and λ changes from 1 to 0 linearly. A possible problem with this approach is that the $g(a)$ is still nondifferentiable at $a = 0$. Selection of the adjustment schedule for λ is another problem. Yu *et al.* [412] adjust the sigmoid gain instead, setting $\beta = 0.5e^{-SSE}$ where SSE is the sum-of-squares error. Initially, when the error is large, the gain is small; later the gain increases as the error decreases. Corwin, Logar, and Oldham [86] and Yu, Loh, and Miller [412] also use gain adjustment to train networks of hard-limiters.

9 Faster Variations of Back-Propagation

One of the common complaints about back-propagation is that it can be very slow. A typical training session may require thousands of iterations. Large networks with large training sets might take days or weeks to train. This chapter reviews a number of relatively simple variations of the basic algorithm that are intended to speed up learning.

It should be noted that things such as the network structure, the input-output representation, the choice of error function, and so on, often have much stronger effects on learning time (possibly orders of magnitude) than variations in the optimization method. At the time of training, however, these choices have already been made and the goal of the methods described next is to accelerate learning in a given network with the given data.

Many variations of the basic algorithm have been proposed and new ones continue to appear regularly. We will not attempt to summarize them all. Many methods are heuristic and somewhat ad hoc; others are founded on principled theory. Some are specialized to certain problem types, for example, classification, and do not always work well on other sorts of problems. Some draw on general optimization techniques specialized to neural network applications. To appreciate these, it is worth reviewing the classic optimization techniques (chapter 10).

Next, a few methods are listed that have stood up to testing and seem to work reasonably well on a wide range of problems. Also listed are some well-known methods that deserve mention if only to inform the reader who has heard of them and wonders what is involved.

9.1 Adaptive Learning Rate Methods

Many of the methods listed here are adaptive learning rate schemes. As noted in section 6.1, the often recommended learning rate of $\eta = 0.1$ is a somewhat arbitrary value that may be completely inappropriate for a given problem. For one thing, the magnitude of the gradient depends on how the targets are scaled; for example, the average error will tend to be higher in a network with linear output nodes and targets in a $(-1000, 1000)$ range than in a network with sigmoid output nodes and targets in $(0, 1)$. Also, when sum-of-squares error is used rather than mean squared error, the size of the error and thus the best learning rate may depend on the size of the training set [114]. The effective learning rate is amplified by redundancies such as near duplication of training patterns and correlation between different elements of the same pattern, and by internal redundancies such as correlations between hidden unit activities. The latter depend in part on the size and configuration of the network but change as the network learns so different learning rates may be appropriate in different parts of the network and the best values may change as learning progresses.

Given the difficulty of choosing a good learning rate a priori, it makes sense to start with a "safe" value (i.e., small) and adjust it depending on system behavior. Some methods adjust a single global learning rate while others assign different learning rates for each unit or each weight. Methods vary, but the general idea is to increase the step size when the error is decreasing consistently and decrease it when significant error increases occur (small increases may be tolerated).

In general, some care is needed to avoid instability. The best step size depends on the problem and local characteristics of the $E(\mathbf{w})$ surface (Chapter 8). Values that work well for some problems and some regions of the error space may not work well for others. It has been noted that neural networks often have error surfaces with many flat areas separated by steep cliffs. This is especially true for classification problems with small numbers of samples. As in driving a car, different speeds are reasonable in different conditions. A large step size is desirable to accelerate progress across the smooth, flat regions of the error surface while a small step size is necessary to avoid loss of control at the cliffs. If the step size is not reduced quickly when the system enters a sensitive region, the result could be a huge weight change that throws the network into a completely different region basically at random. Besides causing problems such as paralysis due to saturation of the sigmoid nonlinearities, this has the undesirable effect of essentially discarding previous learning and starting over somewhere else.

9.2 Vogl's Method (Bold Driver)

Vogl et al. [380] describe an adaptive learning rate method where the global learning rate $\eta(t)$ at time t is updated according to

$$\eta(t) = \begin{cases} \phi\eta(t-1) & \text{if } E(t) < E(t-1) \\ \beta\eta(t-1) & \text{if } E(t) > 1.05E(t-1) \\ \eta(t-1) & \text{otherwise} \end{cases} \tag{9.1}$$

where $\phi > 1$ and $\beta < 1$ are constants. Suggested values are $\phi = 1.05$ and $\beta = 0.7$. The name "bold driver" comes from Battiti [27]; there the value $\beta = 0.5$ is suggested based on the idea that an increase in E indicates a minimum has been overstepped and, on average it is reasonable to guess it is halfway between the current and previous weights.

In addition to decreasing the learning rate when the error increases significantly, the previous weight change is also retracted and the momentum parameter is reset $\alpha = 0$ for the next step. The justification for clearing α is that $\alpha > 0$ makes the current weight change similar to previous weight changes and the increase in the error indicates the need for a change in direction. Thus α is restored to its normal value after a successful step is taken.

In [380], learning speed increased by a factor of about 2.5 and 30 on two test problems. A similar method without momentum was unfavorably compared to conjugate gradient training on parity problems of various sizes in [27]. There it appears to give results similar to normal back-propagation with an optimally tuned fixed learning rate but without the need to search for the optimal learning rate.

The method was empirically compared to a number of other methods on a single test problem by Alpsan et al. [9]. In one case, learning was stopped as soon as all patterns were correctly classified (all outputs on all patterns correct within a tolerance 0.1 of the target values). With high momentum, it had about the same speed as optimally tuned back-propagation, but generalization was not as good. Generalization was better without momentum, but then learning was much slower than regular back-propagation. In a second case where convergence criteria required the outputs to essentially match the target values, the method converged whereas plain back-propagation did not, but it was not among the fastest methods. In an earlier test by the same authors, it was said to be somewhat unstable and no easier to tune than plain back-propagation.

9.3   Delta-Bar-Delta

Jacobs' delta-bar-delta algorithm [194] is one of the more often mentioned acceleration methods. Although some newer methods seem to perform better, it is well-known and many other methods are based on similar ideas. It is based on four heuristics:

1. Every parameter should have its own learning rate. It is not reasonable for every parameter to have the same learning rate because of differences in scaling, variance, and so on in different parts of the network.

2. Every learning rate should be allowed to vary over time because local properties of the error surface change as the weight vector moves over it. Learning rates that are appropriate in one area may not be appropriate in other areas.

3. The learning rate can be increased when the partial derivative of the error has the same sign over several steps. This tends to mean that the error surface has a small curvature and continues to slope in the same direction for some distance so it should be safe to increase the step size.

4. The learning rate should be decreased when the partial derivative changes sign several times in a row. This tends to mean that the weight vector is bouncing back and forth across a minimum and corresponds to high curvature in the error surface along that direction.

These heuristics lead to the following adjustment rule. Each weight w has its own learning rate $\eta(t)$, which is adjusted after each epoch according to

$$\Delta\eta(t) = \begin{cases} \kappa & \text{if } \bar{\delta}(t-1)\delta(t) > 0 \\ -\phi\eta(t) & \text{if } \bar{\delta}(t-1)\delta(t) < 0 \\ 0 & \text{otherwise} \end{cases} \quad (9.2)$$

where $\delta(t) = \frac{\partial E}{\partial w}$ at time t and $\bar{\delta}$ is the exponential average of past values of δ

$$\bar{\delta}(t) = (1-\theta)\delta(t) + \theta\bar{\delta}(t-1). \quad (9.3)$$

(Note, this δ is not the δ used in back-propagation.) The learning rate is incremented by a constant κ when δ and $\bar{\delta}$ have the same sign in consecutive iterations and it is decremented by a fraction of its current value when they have different signs. Note that the increase is linear while the decrease is exponential. The learning rate increases gradually when many consecutive steps all move in the same direction, but decreases quickly when conditions change.

As in normal back-propagation, the weight update is

$$w(t+1) = w(t) - \eta(t)\delta(t). \quad (9.4)$$

This is no longer equivalent to gradient descent on the error surface, however, because each weight has its own learning rate. In effect, the weights are updated based on partial derivatives plus estimates of curvature.

Typical parameter values are obtained from simulation results for several small problems reported by Jacobs [194]. Initial learning rates were $\eta_o = 0.8$ to 1. Typical parameter values were $\kappa = 0.03$ to 0.1 and $\phi = 0.1$ to 0.3 depending on the problem. Harder problems seem to require smaller values of κ and larger values of ϕ. This corresponds to a cautious policy: small increases in learning rate when things are going well and large decreases when things go badly. The averaging parameter $0 < \theta < 1$ does not seem to be critical, $\theta = 0.7$ was used in all cases. Larger values, approaching 1, give longer averaging times.

It is noted that these heuristics can fail in certain cases. For instance, the ideal situation would be to have separate learning rates for each direction identified by an eigenvector of the local Hessian matrix. Instead, it has separate learning rates for each of the coordinate directions in the $E(\mathbf{w})$ space. In the case of a ravine oriented 45° to two weight axes, for example, these heuristics cause the learning rates of both weights to decrease when the best option would be for them to increase *together*. Because the method is based on local computations only, the two weight changes cannot be coordinated. When changing one weight, the behavior of other weights is not considered.

In one empirical test [9], delta-bar-delta was among the fastest methods to learn to classify correctly (with all outputs within a loose tolerance of the desired values) but it was slow to reduce the error to very small values. In [239], it was slower than standard back-propagation with a carefully selected learning rate. The time difference was relatively small, however, and the adaptive method would probably be faster if the time spent in tuning the learning rate for standard back-propagation were included.

According to some reports, delta-bar-delta seems to be more sensitive to parameters than Rprop or quickprop. That is, the default values (κ, ϕ, θ) may work reasonably well on easy problems, but different parameters may be needed on hard problems and it may not be easy to find a good set.

Section 9.4 summarizes a similar method using multiplicative weight increases and momentum. Both are said to be implementations of heuristics proposed by Sutton [363]. Minai and Williams [266] describe an extended delta-bar-delta algorithm that adapts the momentum as well. There are more parameters to be tuned, however.

9.3.1 Justification

Justification for the seemingly *ad hoc* heuristic of basing the learning rate changes on the signs of successive partial derivatives $\frac{\partial E}{\partial w}(t)$ and $\frac{\partial E}{\partial w}(t-1)$ can be found in [194] and [160: 194]. Assuming a single output node y for simplicity, the mean squared error at epoch t is

$$E(t) = \frac{1}{2} \left\langle (d - y)^2 \right\rangle. \tag{9.5}$$

The brackets $\langle \rangle$ denote the mean over the training set and are dropped in what follows. The derivative of the error *with respect to the learning rate* η_{ij} can be written

$$\frac{\partial E}{\partial \eta_{ij}}(t) = \frac{\partial E}{\partial y_i}(t)\frac{\partial y_i}{\partial a_i}(t)\frac{\partial a_i}{\partial \eta_{ij}}(t) \tag{9.6}$$

where $a_i(t) = \sum_j w_{ij}(t)y_j(t)$ is the weighted-sum input to node i, $y_i(t) = f(a_i(t))$ is the node output, and f is the node nonlinearity, for example, the sigmoid function. Because

$$w_{ij}(t) = w_{ij}(t-1) - \eta_{ij}(t)\frac{\partial E}{\partial w_{ij}}(t-1) \tag{9.7}$$

we have

$$a_i(t) = \sum_j y_j(t) \left[w_{ij}(t-1) - \eta_{ij}(t)\frac{\partial E}{\partial w_{ij}}(t-1) \right]. \tag{9.8}$$

Differentiation with respect to $\eta_{ij}(t)$ gives

$$\frac{\partial a_i}{\partial \eta_{ij}}(t) = -y_j(t)\frac{\partial E}{\partial w_{ij}}(t-1). \tag{9.9}$$

From the back-propagation derivation, equation 5.10, we know

$$\delta_i = \frac{\partial E}{\partial y_i} \frac{\partial y_i}{\partial a_i} \tag{9.10}$$

and

$$\frac{\partial E}{\partial w_{ij}} = -\delta_i y_j. \tag{9.11}$$

Combining these results allows (9.6) to be rewritten

$$
\begin{aligned}
\frac{\partial E}{\partial \eta_{ij}}(t) &= \frac{\partial E}{\partial y_i}(t) \frac{\partial y_i}{\partial a_i}(t) \frac{\partial a_i}{\partial \eta_{ij}}(t) \\
&= \delta_i(t) \left(-y_j(t) \frac{\partial E}{\partial w_{ij}}(t-1) \right) \\
&= -\frac{\partial E}{\partial w_{ij}}(t) \frac{\partial E}{\partial w_{ij}}(t-1).
\end{aligned}
\tag{9.12}
$$

This says that the derivative of the error with respect to the learning rate η_{ij} is the negative of the product of the present and previous derivatives of the error with respect to the weight w_{ij}. Rather than being an ad hoc heuristic, this is actually a well-founded way of doing gradient descent on the error with respect to the learning rate. The delta-bar-delta update rule (9.2) modifies this slightly by smoothing $\frac{\partial E}{\partial w}(t-1)$.

9.4   Silva and Almeida

Delta-bar-delta is one of the more well-known adaptive learning rate methods. Silva and Almeida [346] proposed a variation using multiplicative weight increases and momentum. Both are said to be implementations of heuristics proposed by Sutton [363]. This is similar to the method of Vogl et al. with a separate learning rate for each weight.

The weight update rule is

$$w_{ij}(t) = w_{ij}(t-1) - \eta_{ij} \frac{\partial E}{\partial w_{ij}}(t) \tag{9.13}$$

where $\eta_{ij}(t)$ is the learning rate for weight w_{ij} at epoch t. The learning rate is adapted at each epoch according to

$$\eta_{ij}(n) = \begin{cases} u\eta_{ij}(n-1) & \text{if } \frac{\partial E}{\partial w_{ij}}(t)\frac{\partial E}{\partial w_{ij}}(t-1) > 0 \\ d\eta_{ij}(n-1) & \text{if } \frac{\partial E}{\partial w_{ij}}(t)\frac{\partial E}{\partial w_{ij}}(t-1) < 0 \\ \eta_{ij}(n-1) & \text{otherwise (no change)} \end{cases} \qquad (9.14)$$

where constants $u > 1$ and $0 < d < 1$ control the rate of increases and decreases. Typical values are $1.1 < u < 1.3$ and d slightly below $1/u$, for example, $d = 0.7$. This gives a slight preference to learning rate decreases, making the system more stable.

In contrast to Jacobs' delta-bar-delta method where the learning rate increases incrementally (additively), here both increases and decreases are multiplicative. This allows faster increases in the learning rate and, possibly, faster convergence, but it may sometimes lead to instability. If the learning rate becomes too large, the error may sometimes jump abruptly (e.g., when the system oversteps a minimum and "climbs up a cliff"). To avoid instability, the bad weight change is retracted and in most cases reapplication of the learning rate update rule (9.14) using the gradient evaluated at the rejected point will reduce the learning rate adequately to avoid the bad step in following iterations; if not, the learning rate may need to be decreased directly. In a benchmarking test [320], it is suggested that if the algorithm fails to find an error decrease after five consecutive iterations, all the learning rate parameters should be halved.

Because the learning rate can increase quickly, there is not a huge cost in selecting an initial rate that is too small. Ideally, the algorithm should be able to correct for an overly large initial learning rate, but sigmoid saturation and instability may cause problems so it is probably best to start with a small value and let the algorithm increase it if necessary.

Performance seems to deteriorate in obliquely oriented ravines in the error surface. In order to better handle these cases, a modified weight update rule was proposed

$$\Delta w_{ij}(t) = \eta_{ij} v_{ij}(t) \qquad (9.15)$$

where the 'smoothed gradient' is

$$v_{ij}(t) = \frac{\partial E}{\partial w_{ij}}(t) + \alpha v_{ij}(t-1) \qquad (9.16)$$

and $0 \le \alpha < 1$ functions like the momentum parameter.

It has been reported [9] that methods that increase the learning rate multiplicatively like this can be faster than methods that increase it additively, but they are less stable and parameter tuning may be difficult.

9.5 SuperSAB

SuperSAB [372] is another adaptive learning rate method based on the delta-bar-delta heuristics. It is based on an earlier method called SAB, which stands for "self-adapting back propagation." Like the method of Vogl et al. (section 9.4), the learning rate is both increased and decreased multiplicatively.

Parameters include the initial learning rate η_{start}, an increase factor $\eta^+ > 1$, and a decrease factor $0 < \eta^- < 1$. Each weight has its own learning rate $\eta_{ij}(t)$ which changes with time t. The algorithm is:

1. Initialize all learning rates $\eta_{ij}(0) = \eta_{start}$.

2. Do a back-propagation step with momentum.

3. For each weight w_{ij}

• if the sign of its derivative is unchanged then increase the learning rate, $\eta_{ij}(t+1) = \eta^+ \cdot \eta_{ij}(t)$;

• otherwise (the sign changed), retract the step $w_{ij}(t+1) = w_{ij}(t) - \Delta w_{ij}(t)$, decrease the learning rate $\eta_{ij}(t+1) = \eta^- \cdot \eta_{ij}(t)$, and set $\Delta w_{ij}(t+1) = 0$ so momentum has no effect in the next cycle.

4. Go to 2.

Typical suggested values are $\eta^+ = 1.2$ and $\eta^- = 0.5$. (There appear to be typographical errors in [372]. This is based on the explanation accompanying the formula.)

Reported results have been inconsistent. In some cases SuperSAB is among the fastest methods [9]; others have reported it to be very unstable [8]. The possibility of instability, especially when momentum is high, is noted in the original paper. This shows itself as a sudden large increase in the error. Sometimes the error will correct itself in subsequent steps; otherwise a restart may be necessary. Because η increases multiplicatively and can become large quickly, it is reasonable to set limiting values on both η and the maximum allowed weight magnitude. Because of the instability problems and because it does not appear to have major speed advantages, other methods may be preferable in general.

9.6 Rprop

Rprop [315, 314] stands for "resilient propagation." The main difference between it and most other heuristic back-propagation variations is that the learning rate adjustments and weight changes depend only on the signs of the gradient terms, not their magnitudes. It is argued that the gradient magnitude depends on scaling of the error function and can change greatly from one step to the next. On a complicated nonlinear error surface, the magnitude is basically unpredictable a priori and there is no reason why the step size should be proportional to the magnitude in general. In fact, it can be argued that the step size should be inversely proportional in order to take large steps where the gradient is small and to take small careful steps where the gradient is large [363].

Rprop is a batch update method; the weights and step sizes are changed once per epoch. Each weight w_{ij} has its own step size, or update-value, Δ_{ij}, which varies with time t according to

$$\Delta_{ij}(t) = \begin{cases} \eta^+ \cdot \Delta_{ij}(t-1), & \text{if } \frac{\partial E}{\partial w_{ij}}(t-1) \cdot \frac{\partial E}{\partial w_{ij}}(t) > 0 \\ \eta^- \cdot \Delta_{ij}(t-1), & \text{if } \frac{\partial E}{\partial w_{ij}}(t-1) \cdot \frac{\partial E}{\partial w_{ij}}(t) < 0 \\ \Delta_{ij}(t-1), & \text{otherwise} \end{cases} \tag{9.17}$$

where $0 < \eta^- < 1 < \eta^+$. A change in sign of the partial derivative corresponding to weight w_{ij} indicates that the last update was too big and the system has jumped over a minimum so the update value Δ_{ij} is decreased by a factor η^-. Consecutive derivatives with the same sign indicate that the system is moving steadily in one direction so the update value is increased slightly in order to accelerate convergence in shallow regions.

The weights are changed according to

$$\Delta w_{ij}(t) = \begin{cases} -\Delta_{ij}(t), & \text{if } \frac{\partial E}{\partial w_{ij}}(t) > 0 \\ +\Delta_{ij}(t), & \text{if } \frac{\partial E}{\partial w_{ij}}(t) < 0 \\ 0 & \text{otherwise} \end{cases} \tag{9.18}$$

Note that the change depends only on the sign of the partial derivative and is independent of its magnitude. If the derivative is positive, the weight is decremented by $\Delta_{ij}(t)$; if the derivative is negative, the weight is incremented by $\Delta_{ij}(t)$.

There is one exception. If the partial derivative changes sign (indicating that the previous step was too large and a minimum was missed), the previous weight-update is retracted

$$\Delta w_{ij}(t) = -\Delta w_{ij}(t-1) \quad \text{if } \frac{\partial E}{\partial w_{ij}}(t-1) \frac{\partial E}{\partial w_{ij}}(t) < 0 \tag{9.19}$$

Because this would cause another sign change on the next step, leading $\Delta_{ij}(t)$ to be decrease, the update-value is not adapted on the next step. In software, this can be achieved by storing $\frac{\partial E}{\partial w_{ij}}(t-1) = 0$, which prevents the change in the next step.

All update-values are initialized to a constant $\Delta_{ij} = \Delta_o$, which determines the size of the first weight change. A reasonable value is $\Delta_o = 0.1$. This is somewhat affected by the size of the initial weights, but does not seem to be critical for simple problems. It is probably better to err in favor of choosing too small a value because an overly large value could lead to immediate node saturation. In [314], $\Delta_o = 0.001$ was used for the two-spirals problem, but values between 10^{-5} and 0.01 gave similar results.

The range of update-values is limited to $\Delta_{min} = 10^{-6}$ and $\Delta_{max} = 50$ to avoid floating-point underflow-overflow problems. Limiting Δ_{max} to smaller values, for example, 1, may give smoother decreases in the error at the cost of slower convergence. In [314], $\Delta_{max} = 0.1$ was used for the two-spirals problem.

The value $\eta^- = 0.5$ was chosen based on the reasoning that when the system overshoots a minimum, the minimum will be halfway between the current and previous weights, on average, so the step size should be reduced to half its previous value.

The value $\eta^+ = 1.2$ is a compromise. It should be large enough to allow fast growth in flat regions of the error function, but not so large that the system has to immediately reduce the update-value in the next step. The value 1.2 seems to work well on many problems and usually is not critical.

These default values seem to work well for most problems. In most cases, no changes are needed. In [315], only $\Delta_{max} = 0.001$ was changed for the two-spirals problem in order to avoid early saturation of the sigmoids. In most cases, Δ_o is the only other parameter that needs to be changed and its value is not critical as long as it is not too large.

Although it is not mentioned in the derivation, momentum can be used with beneficial effects on many problems. As usual, very high values of momentum may lead to instability.

In empirical comparisons, Rprop seems to be one of the faster and more reliable heuristic methods for a wide range of problems. There are, of course, cases where other methods do better, but Rprop is often a good choice for initial tests. For certain classification problems where the error criteria are satisfied as soon as all outputs are within a tolerance (e.g., 0.1) of their target values, it can be faster than second-order gradient methods such as conjugate gradient or Levenberg-Marquardt. This is problem dependent, however.

The success of Rprop can be explained, in part, by two factors. First, one reason for the slow convergence of gradient descent is that the gradient vanishes at a minimum so the step size becomes smaller and smaller as it nears the minimum. The error tends to decrease exponentially: fast at first, but slower later on. With Rprop, the step size does not depend on the magnitude of the gradient so learning does not slow to a crawl in the final stages.

Second, another problem with back-propagation in layered networks is that the derivatives tend to be attenuated as they propagate back from the output layer toward the inputs (see section 6.1.8). Each layer inserts a sigmoid derivative factor that is less than 1 (≤ 0.25 for sigmoids, ≤ 1 for tanh nodes) with the result that $|\partial E/\partial w|$ tends to be very small for weights far from the outputs and learning is correspondingly slow. Deep networks with many layers have been avoided for this reason because almost no learning occurs in the initial layers. Heuristic methods for setting different learning rates for each layer have been investigated, but they are difficult to tune by hand and a fixed learning rate is not necessarily appropriate anyway. Rprop seems to work better than some other adaptive learning rate techniques in this case because the learning rate adjustments and weight updates depend only on the signs of the derivatives, not their magnitudes. Appropriate values can be found for each layer so early layers learn faster than they would otherwise and deep networks are not as difficult to train.

9.7 Quickprop

Fahlman's Quickprop [121] differs from most of the other methods mentioned here in that it is not an adaptive learning rate technique. Like back-propagation, it is a local method; each weight w is considered separately.

It is "based on 2 risky assumptions":

• that $E(w)$ for each weight can be approximated by a parabola that opens upward and

• that the change in slope of $E(w)$ for this weight is not affected by all the other weights that change at the same time.

The weight update rule is dominated by a quadratic term

$$\Delta w(t) = \frac{S(t)}{S(t-1) - S(t)} \Delta w(t-1) \tag{9.20}$$

where $S(t) = \frac{\partial E}{\partial w}(t)$. Call the $S(t)/(S(t-1) - S(t))$ term β. The numerator is the derivative of the error with respect to the weight and $(S(t-1) - S(t))/\Delta w(t-1)$ is a finite difference approximation of the second derivative. Together these approximate Newton's method for minimizing a one-dimensional function $f(x)$: $\Delta x = -f'(x)/f''(x)$. Sutton [363] suggested a similar update term.

Three cases occur:

1. If the current slope has the same sign but is somewhat smaller in magnitude than the previous one, then $\beta > 0$ and the weight will change again in the same direction. The size of the change will depend on how much the slope was reduced by the previous step.

2. If the current slope has a different sign from the previous slope, then the weight has crossed over the minimum and is now on the opposite side of the valley. Since $\beta < 0$, the next step will backtrack, landing somewhere between the current and previous positions.

3. The third case occurs when the current slope has the same sign as the previous slope, but is the same size or larger in magnitude. This indicates that the first "risky assumption"

was not met and could occur where the function is not well-approximated by a parabola or where the assumed parabola opens downward.

To avoid taking an infinite step or a backward uphill move in case 3, a "maximum growth factor" parameter μ is introduced. No weight change is allowed to be larger than μ times the previous weight change. A value of $\mu = 1.75$ is recommended. Chaotic behavior may result when it is too large,

For cases 1 and 3, an additional term $-\eta S(t)$ representing simple gradient descent is added to (9.20) to bootstrap the process when the previous change $\Delta w(t - 1) = 0$. It is ignored in case 2 when the current slope is nonzero and differs in sign from the previous one since the quadratic term handles this case well.

In addition to these weight update rules, several other heuristics are sometimes used.

• It is argued that one of the reasons for the slow convergence of back-propagation is that the derivatives become very small when sigmoid node nonlinearities saturate. The sigmoid-prime heuristic simply adds 0.1 to the derivative of the sigmoid function so that it is always nonzero. This may accelerate learning in flat regions, but it may also make it difficult to settle to a minimum.

• Since the quadratic term may cause some weights to get very big, leading to floating-point overflow errors, a small decay term is added to the slope $S(t)$ calculated for each weight. Note that this is different from normal weight-decay, which acts directly on the weights.

• Finally, in some cases, a hyperbolic arctangent error function is used. That is, when back-propagating the error, the true derivative of the error with respect to the activation y of an output unit

$$\frac{\partial E}{\partial y} = -(d - y)$$

is replaced by

$-\text{arctanh}(d - y)$.

Strictly speaking, this is not an error function, as it modifies the calculated derivative, rather than the error itself. This goes to $\pm\infty$ at ± 1 and greatly magnifies the error for output units that are far from their target values. It also tends to cancel the vanishing derivative for nodes that are saturated at the wrong value, but this case is already handled by the sigmoid-prime term. To avoid numerical problems, a value of 17 (-17) is used for inputs greater than 0.9999999 (less than -0.9999999). This assumes the errors are in $(-1, +1)$. Simple scale changes will be needed for tanh nonlinearities and other cases. This heuristic is somewhat nonstandard and is not used in most cases.

In empirical comparisons, quickprop is often one of the faster, more reliable methods and outperforms most other heuristic variations of back-propagation on a wide range of problems. Only Rprop seems to be consistently better; it is perhaps somewhat more reliable, has fewer parameters to tune, and seems to be less sensitive to their values.

Quickprop does have a fixed learning rate parameter η that needs to be chosen to suit the problem. It might be possible to use adaptive methods to control this, but no methods have been described.

9.8   Search Then Converge

Most of the other methods mentioned in this chapter are designed for batch-mode learning. The following describes an adaptive learning rate method for on-line learning.

As noted in section 5.3.2, the weight trajectory in on-line learning is stochastic and jitters around the error surface. This randomness helps search more of the weight space and makes the system more likely to find a good minimum, but it also keeps the weights from settling to a solution so the asymptotic error may be relatively high. The standard solution is to reduce the learning rate gradually as learning progresses.

The classic schedule used in stochastic approximation [318] is $\eta(t) = c/t$ where c is a constant. This guarantees asymptotic convergence and is optimal for c greater than some threshold c^*, which depends on the problem [97]. There are problems with this, however. Convergence is slow when c is small, but if c is increased too much then excessively large parameter changes may occur at small t.

Darken and Moody [97] proposed the "search then converge" schedule

$$\eta(t) = \frac{\eta_o}{1 + t/\tau}. \tag{9.21}$$

This avoids the unstable behavior at small t, yet still has the desired asymptotic behavior c/t for $t \gg \tau$. For $t \ll \tau$, $\eta(t) \approx \eta_o$ and the system behaves like normal on-line learning with a constant learning rate. It is hoped that by the time $t \approx \tau$ the system will converge to and then hover around a good minimum. At $t \approx \tau$, $\eta(t)$ begins decreasing to allow the weights to settle to the solution. For $t \gg \tau$, $\eta(t) \approx c/t$ where $c = \tau \eta_o$, and the learning rate approaches the optimum stochastic approximation schedule. The schedule [98]

$$\eta(t) = \eta_o \frac{1 + \frac{c}{\eta_o} \frac{t}{\tau}}{1 + \frac{c}{\eta_o} \frac{t}{\tau} + \tau \frac{t^2}{\tau^2}} \tag{9.22}$$

has similar behavior, but decreases $\eta(t)$ faster at intermediate values of t.

A defect of these schedules is that they require the user to choose the parameter c. The optimal value is $c^* \equiv 1/2\alpha$ where α is the smallest eigenvalue of the Hessian evaluated at the minimum [98]. c^* is usually unknown, however, because the minimum has not been found yet. In theory, the Hessian could be estimated and its eigenvalues calculated, but this is computationally intensive and may not be possible in an on-line learning situation. (The main advantages of on-line learning are its computational simplicity and small storage requirements).

Darken and Moody [98] propose a way to do an on-line estimate of whether $c < c^*$ by observing the trajectory of the weight vector. The idea is that when c is too small, successive weight update vectors will be highly correlated. Convergence is slow because the weight changes are small; the gradient changes little from one step to the next so successive weight updates tend to point in similar directions.

An estimate of the drift is

$$D(t) \equiv \sum_k d_k^2(t) \tag{9.23}$$

$$d_k(t) \equiv \sqrt{T}\, \frac{\langle \delta_k(t) \rangle_T}{\sqrt{\langle (\delta_k(t) - \langle \delta_k(t) \rangle_T)^2 \rangle_T}} \tag{9.24}$$

where $\delta_k(t)$ is the change in the kth component of the weight vector at time t, and the brackets $\langle \cdot \rangle_T$ indicate the average over T weight changes. In [98], $T = at$, $a \ll 1$. The numerator is the average parameter change. The denominator is the standard deviation of the weight changes and becomes small when weight updates are highly correlated over time. $D(t)$ grows like a power of t when c is too small but remains finite otherwise.

9.9   Fuzzy Control of Back-Propagation

Network training is a dynamic process and the algorithms described in this chapter can be viewed as control systems whose purpose is to accelerate learning while avoiding instability. Fuzzy logic is a convenient way to convert a set of heuristics into a working algorithm and has been used with success in many simple control applications.

The main difference between fuzzy logic and conventional Boolean logic is that fuzzy logic deals with propositions that can have varying degrees of membership between true and false. This is useful for control applications because it allows the behavior to be described by easily understood IF–THEN rules that are interpolated to give smooth transitions between regions where different rules are active. Mechanisms of fuzzy inferencing are described in many references, so the details will be omitted here.

Many papers have been written on applications of fuzzy logic to neural network training. Control of back-propagation using fuzzy logic has been proposed by Arabshahi et al. [10], Choi et al. [81], and others. Arabshahi et al. [10] controls a single global learning rate while Choi [81] extends control to include the momentum term. Comparisons are made with standard back-propagation and Jacobs' delta-bar-delta rule on the 3-bit parity problem.

The central idea is to establish a set of IF–THEN rules for parameter control that are implemented using fuzzy logic. In Arabshahi et al. [10], the rule antecedants (the IF parts) are expressions involving the error E and the change in error $CE = E_n - E_{n-1}$ from one iteration to the next while the THEN parts (the rule consequents) specify $\Delta\eta$, how the learning rate should change given the conditions described in the antecedent. One rule might say that when E is low, and CE is low then the learning rate should increase by a small amount, for example. If both E and CE were actually low then this rule would be satisfied and the consequent would be asserted strongly. For slightly different values of E or CE, however, for example, when E is "lowish, but not really low," the rule would be satisfied less well and its consequent would be asserted less strongly.

At any particular time, many different rules will be satisfied to varying degrees and conflicts between active rules suggesting different actions are resolved by methods of fuzzy inferencing to obtain a single overall output.

In simple applications like this, fuzzy logic is used for interpolation. That is, the designer specifies the desired response at selected points on a grid in the input space and relies on fuzzy inferencing to interpolate between the points in a reasonable way. The designer thereby avoids the sometimes difficult problem of finding a clever algorithm or function that generates the desired response from the given inputs. An advantage of fuzzy systems, and local interpolation methods in general, is that the effects of each rule are relatively localized; rules don't interact globally so it is relatively easy to tune individual rules to improve local performance without worry that this will cause problems in other areas.

A fuzzy implementation of a set of heuristics, for example, the delta-bar-delta heuristics, will usually have the same basic behavior as the heuristics implemented by other means, although there may be small-scale differences. That is, the final performance of the system is determined much more by the quality of the heuristics than by the mechanisms of how they are implemented. Factors such as which input variables are considered, how they are represented, and how they are presumed to interact in their effects on the response will have much stronger effects on performance than whether they are implemented by fuzzy logic or by some other means. Fuzzy logic does not substitute for understanding a problem, but it is a convenient way to convert understanding into a working algorithm.

9.10   Other Heuristics

9.10.1   Gradient Reuse

Hush and Salas [182] suggest stepping along the line of the computed gradient as long as the error continues to decrease. This is similar to Cauchy's method (section 10.5.2), but it does not search for the exact minimum on the line. It uses fixed size steps along the line rather than, say, bisection search. As in Cauchy's method, there is a savings since the gradient calculation is avoided for each successful step along the line. The step size is increased when the reuse rate is high (indicating that steps are too small) and it is decreased when it's low (because the step size it too large).

9.10.2   Gradient Correlation

Franzini [126], Chan and Fallside [67] and Schreibman and Norris [336] describe gradient correlation methods that monitor the angle between successive gradient vectors to control the learning rate. An advantage of this approach is that a major change in gradient direction can be detected and the learning rate reduced *before* taking a step, thus reducing the need to retract bad steps.

The gradient correlation measures the cosine of the angle between successive values of the gradient $\mathbf{g}(t)$

$$\cos(\theta) = \frac{\mathbf{g}(t-1)^T \mathbf{g}(t)}{\|\mathbf{g}(t-1)\| \, \|\mathbf{g}(t)\|}. \qquad (9.25)$$

When the vectors are nearly parallel, $\cos \theta \approx +1$ and the learning rate can probably be increased. When $\cos \theta < 0$, the gradient has doubled back on itself to some extent and the learning rate should be decreased.

In [126] the learning rate is adjusted according to

$$\eta(t) = \begin{cases} \eta(t-1)\beta^+ \cos(\theta) & \text{if } \cos(\theta) > 0 \\ \eta(t-1)\beta^- & \text{otherwise} \end{cases} \qquad (9.26)$$

where values of $\beta^+ = 1.005$ and $\beta^- = 0.8$ are suggested. This tends to keep η near the maximum value such that successive gradients are nearly parallel and eliminates the oscillatory cross-stitching behavior in ravines of the error surface. In the single-problem benchmark [9], this method was slightly slower than standard back-propagation to learn to classify the training set, but when used with momentum, it was the fastest method to reduce the error to near zero. Removal of the $\cos \theta$ term from the η adjustment rule was suggested.

In [336], the learning rate switches between high and low values based on the correlation. It is reduced to its minimum value (0.01) and momentum is set to 0 as soon as the correlation became negative. The momentum returns to its normal value (0.9) gradually. Modifications may be needed to apply the idea in practice. In [9] it was slow to learn to classify correctly and could not further reduce the error to small values in the given amount of time, but generalization was said to be good.

9.10.3 Pattern Weighting Heuristics

A number of heuristics attempt to focus attention on the patterns with the worst errors. Often, this can be viewed as a modification of the error function to one which gives more emphasis to larger errors. If attention is focused only on the pattern with the largest error, the ideal result is to minimize the maximum error. Cater [65] gives each pattern a different weighting. Basically, the method identifies the pattern with the worst error and roughly doubles its learning rate in the next epoch.

The heuristic of "learn only if misclassified," used in [329] and later work, says that the actual output values do not really matter for classification problems as long as the classification is unambiguous. A tolerance band is defined and the error is considered to be zero for all outputs within the band. If the target is 0 and the output is 0.06, for example, the classification is obvious and there is no need to adjust the weights for this pattern.

Many methods like this can be considered as modifications of the error function and will lead to different solutions from the mean-squared-error function, in general. This may be a drawback if you actually want to optimize the mean-squared-error, but this normally is not the case for classification problems.

9.11 Remarks

All the methods summarized in this chapter were proposed to accelerate learning. It should be remembered that there are other factors affecting learning time that have not been considered here. As noted earlier, things such as network structure, data representation, choice of error function, and so on may have much stronger effects on performance and training time than the optimization method. Standard practices like the use of momentum, the use of tanh rather than sigmoid nodes, centering and normalization of inputs and outputs, the use of on-line versus batch updates, and so on also affect training times. If training time is a concern, it is best to explore these options before looking for fast training methods. Still, it may be necessary to train candidate networks in the process of comparing these factors and adaptive learning rate algorithms are a reasonable compromise between speed and robustness.

Often, adaptive learning rate methods are not any faster than standard back-propagation with *optimally tuned* parameters [239]. Even so, they effectively automate the search for good parameters and so may be more reliable and much easier to use. When the time needed to select optimal parameters by hand is considered, adaptive methods may retain the speed advantage. In any case, they are usually much faster than back-propagation with poor parameter choices.

A potential problem with some adaptive methods is that they introduce additional parameters that need to be tuned. In the worst case, it may be no easier to find a good set of parameters than it is to find a good set of parameters for standard back-propagation. Another concern is that they may require storage of more information. Delta-bar-delta, for example, stores a separate learning rate and $\bar{\delta}$ for each weight. This is not a problem in small computerized simulations, but it may be a factor in applications using limited hardware (e.g., custom integrated circuits). Standard on-line back-propagation requires the least amount of storage.

Alpsan et al. [8] asked if modified back-propagation algorithms were worth the effort and concluded that many were not. They note that optimally tuned back-propagation is often as fast as any other method and that many of the adaptive methods are sensitive to parameters and no easier to tune than standard back-propagation. They considered delta-bar-delta, superSAB, and Vogl's method, among others, but not Rprop or quickprop.

At this point, Rprop and quickprop seem to be the favored methods. Rprop has fewer critical parameters and may be more reliable in general. Other methods will often do better on specific problems, however, so it may be worth experimenting.

When training time is very important, it is worth considering the standard optimization algorithms, some of which are reviewed in chapter 10. These may be much faster than simple variations of back-propagation in some cases. This is somewhat problem dependent, of course. The second order methods seem to be most helpful in the final stages of function approximation problems where it is necessary to reduce the error to very small values. Methods like conjugate gradient descent or Newton's method will converge very quickly *in the neighborhood* of a local minimum, but they are not necessarily any faster (and may be slower) than simpler first order methods in the initial search stages. For classification problems where training is stopped as soon as all outputs are correct within a tolerance, for example, 0.2, of the target values on all patterns, the methods of this chapter may be as fast or faster than conventional second-order optimization methods. If it is necessary to continue the search to locate the minimum very precisely, then it may be worth switching over to a more sophisticated second order method for the final tuning.

If training speed is extremely critical, it may also be worth considering a completely different sort of approximation system since back-propagation training of MLP networks is one of the slowest training methods for any approximation system [239]. Many other approximation methods can achieve similar error rates (on suitable problems) with much shorter training times. Nearest-neighbor methods, for example, require almost no training time (simply store the patterns) but have longer recall times. Decision trees and parametric classifiers can also be developed quickly when they are applicable. Within neural network models, alternatives include radial basis function networks, LVQ, and ART networks.

9.12   Other Notes

• The focus in this chapter has been on training speed. Generalization is a different issue and the fastest training method will not always give the best generalization. At best, speed of learning and quality of generalization are orthogonal issues—completely independent— and a fast training method would achieve the same generalization as another method except it would get there faster. In the best case, a fast training method will simply arrive sooner at the point where cross-validation says training should stop. Of course, if no specific steps are taken to ensure good generalization, then a fast method might generalize worse than a slower method as it may have more chance to overfit in the same amount of time.

There have been suggestions that some of the faster methods generalize worse than slower methods [8, 9], but this has not been studied much. There is some reason to expect techniques that take long steps (e.g., Newton's method) to generalize less well because they may go well past the point of overfitting before it can be detected by cross-validation on a test set. This does not have to occur, however, and it can be addressed by methods such as weight decay, pruning, and regularization penalty terms.

• Most of these methods are for batch mode training. Chen and Mars [76] describe an adaptive stepsize algorithm said to be suitable for on-line training. Modifications may be required, however, and tuning may be difficult [9].

10 Classical Optimization Techniques

Terms like training and learning are often used in an artificial neural network context to describe the process of adapting a set of parameters (the weights) to achieve a specific technical result (minimization of the error on a training set). As such, learning can be viewed as a general optimization problem that may be addressed by numerous techniques.

Back-propagation is by far the most commonly used method for training MLP neural networks. Batch-mode back-propagation with a small learning rate (and no momentum) is a specialization of gradient descent to MLPs while on-line back-propagation is related to stochastic gradient descent. Gradient descent is not highly regarded in the optimization community, however, mainly because of its slow rate of convergence. This is a particular problem when the Hessian matrix is poorly conditioned, that is, when the gradient changes quickly in some directions and slowly in others, as it does in so-called ravines of the error surface.

Optimization is a mature field and many algorithms, some quite sophisticated, have been developed over the years. In appropriate circumstances, they may be better alternatives to back-propagation. Many converge much faster than gradient descent in certain situations while others promise a higher probability of convergence to global minima. This chapter reviews some of the standard methods. Aside from performance improvements they might provide, familiarity with these techniques is useful to understand back-propagation and its variants, many of which draw on ideas from the standard methods.

10.1 The Objective Function

To treat network training as an optimization problem, an objective function (or cost function) must be defined that provides an unambiguous numerical rating of system performance. The cost function reduces all the various good and bad aspects of a possibly complex system down to a single number, a scalar value, which allows candidate solutions to be ranked and compared. In short, it provides the working definition of optimal for the search algorithm, telling it what kinds of solutions to look for. It is important, therefore, that the function faithfully represent our design goals. If we choose a poor error function and obtain unsatisfactory results, the fault is ours for badly specifying the goal of the search.

Selection of the objective function can be a problem in itself since it is not always easy to develop a function that measures exactly what we want when goals are vague. It is often necessary to compromise between what we want, what we can measure, and what we can optimize efficiently. A few basic functions are very commonly used. The mean squared error is popular for function approximation (regression) problems because of its convenience in mathematical analysis. The cross-entropy error function is often used for classification problems when outputs are interpreted as probabilities of membership in an indicated class. In real-world applications, it may be necessary to complicate the function with additional terms to balance conflicting subgoals or to introduce heuristics favoring preferred classes of solutions.

10.2   Factors Affecting the Choice of a Method

Once an objective function has been chosen, many optimization algorithms may be applied. A few well-known methods are mentioned in the following sections. The list is not exhaustive by any means. We attempt to describe the most popular algorithms broadly, including the main assumptions behind them and their main advantages and disadvantages for neural network training. We do not attempt to give full implementation details or to describe special cases which need to be considered in real applications. Details of classical algorithms can be found in many texts, for example [138, 311, 302].

A minor point: optimization can be viewed as maximizing utility or as minimizing cost. To simplify the discussion, we consider it as minimization.

Ideally, all optimization routines would yield the same result, the global minimum of the error function. In practice though, some methods tend to work better than others in particular situations. There is generally a trade-off between speed, robustness, and the probability of finding the global minimum. Specialized algorithms may be very fast in certain situations, but not robust in other situations. Many methods embody assumptions about the problem that allow efficiencies to be obtained when the conditions hold, but may lead the algorithm astray otherwise. Algorithms that promise to find a global minimum tend to be much slower than less ambitious methods; most are relatively robust, however, because they make few assumptions about the problem.

Selection of an appropriate algorithm depends on many factors. Some include:

Differentiability.   Continuous functions allow the use of efficient gradient methods. If the function is differentiable everywhere and the derivatives are easy to evaluate, conjugate gradient methods are often recommended if local minima are not an extreme problem.

If the function is not differentiable or derivatives are not available, then less efficient evaluation-only methods may be necessary. Gradient methods can be used with gradient estimates obtained by finite-differences. If the function is known to be smooth but derivatives are not available, the conjugate-directions method is often recommended. If the function is not smooth or has many local minima, then global search methods such as simulated annealing and genetic algorithms may be required.

Classification versus regression.   In classification problems, the exact numerical output is not important as long as the class is indicated unambiguously. In continuous function approximation problems, the numerical values are important and target values must be matched closely to obtain a small error.

The advantages of methods using second-order gradient information seem to show up mostly in the latter case. That is, they excel at homing in on the exact minimum once the general basin of attraction has been found, but they are not really much better at finding the basin than other, simpler methods when the function is very nonlinear.

Local minima.   If there are relatively few really poor local minima, then random restarts of a local search algorithm may be sufficient. If there are many poor local minima, consider a global search method such as simulated annealing. Stochastic algorithms like simulated annealing promise convergence to the global minimum with probability 1, but can be very slow.

Problem size.   Algorithms that scale poorly may be adequate for small problems but become impractical for large networks with large training sets. Second-order methods requiring exact evaluation of the Hessian are generally impractical for large networks. Storage and manipulation of large matrices may also be a problem even for methods that approximate the Hessian.

Robustness.   Does the algorithm work well when preconditions are not satisfied exactly and when parameters are not optimally tuned? In general, robust algorithms make fewer assumptions and so tend to be slower than more optimistic algorithms (which are suited to the given problem).

Meta-optimization.   Back-propagation, for example, has a learning rate that must be selected; if momentum is used, it also must be given a value. Other algorithms have their own parameters that must be selected. Tuning these parameters may be a meta-optimization problem in itself and algorithms that are overly sensitive to parameter choices will be difficult to use for general problems. Meta-optimization may not be feasible for large problems where each training session takes days or weeks.

Is the data noisy?   If the data is noisy and there are not enough examples to suppress noise by averaging, then the observed errors must be viewed as random estimates and precise minimization of the training error will not necessarily correspond to minimization of the true expected error.

This is a generalization problem. If the problem is addressed by adding regularization terms to the objective function, then precise minimization may have real benefits and second-order methods may have advantages. If the problem is not addressed at all, then back-propagation (and other simple gradient descent methods) may be better *because of* their relative inability to locate the precise minimum. If the problem is addressed by early stopping, then the search may never enter the precise-minimization phase where second-order methods excel.

Clustering. Is the data smoothly distributed or clustered? If the data falls in well-separated clusters that correspond to target classes, learning is usually easier because fine distinctions are not required. As long as the decision boundary falls in the open space between clusters, its exact location is not critical so more solutions are feasible. When the clusters are well separated, on-line methods may be faster than batch methods because of redundancy in the data; almost all the information is contained in the cluster centroids.

In general, optimization algorithms can be classified as deterministic or stochastic. Most deterministic optimization algorithms can be classed as evaluation-only methods or gradient-based methods. The advantage of evaluation-only methods is their simplicity; no gradient calculation is required. They are most useful where internal system details are not accessible, where the objective function is not differentiable, or in complex systems where derivatives are difficult to calculate correctly. Their main disadvantage is inefficiency. It is almost always worth using gradient information if it can be obtained because convergence is usually much faster; the gradient points in precisely the direction that increases the function the fastest, after all. Because the gradient is easily calculated (by the back-propagation step) in MLPs with differentiable node nonlinearities, most neural network training algorithms use it. Even more information is available in second-order derivatives so methods that use the Hessian matrix, or approximations to it, can be very efficient under certain conditions. They may be impractical for large problems, however, because of storage and computation requirements involved in dealing with large matrices.

A problem with deterministic algorithms is that they always converge to the same end-point given the same starting point. The system will converge either to a local minimum or to the global minimum depending on the starting point. When local minima are rare and the basin of attraction of the global minimum is large, a few repetitions of the algorithm with different starting points may be enough to find good solutions. In other cases, more powerful methods are needed. The advantage of stochastic methods is that every state has a nonzero chance of occurrence so, if the procedure runs long enough, the global minimum will be visited eventually. Under certain conditions, many stochastic algorithms can promise a high likelihood of convergence to the global minimum. The problem is that this may take a *very* long time and guarantees are lost if the algorithm is terminated early.

10.3   Line Search

In many methods, the choice of a search direction is treated separately from the problem of how far to move along that direction. A number of methods, in fact, are defined by the way they choose the search direction and the existence of a perfect line search is assumed. Line search routines are basically one-dimensional optimization methods to find the minimum in a given interval. In general, they are a subcomponent of a larger overall algorithm, which applies them to find the minimum along a given line in a higher dimensional space.

The efficiency of the line search routine can be critical since, in many cases, the calculations needed to compute the search direction are relatively minor and most of the computation time will be spent in the line search. In general, there is a trade-off between the efficiency of the algorithm (the number of function and gradient evaluations required) and the precision with which the minimum can be located; more precision calls for more evaluations. General multidimensional algorithms that can tolerate some inexactness in the line search routine are preferred for this reason. If a lot is known about the function then evaluation at just a few points may be enough to locate the minimum exactly; for example, 3 points may be sufficient for a quadratic function. This is unusual, however, because functions are usually not so simple. In a typical case, a line search may require 10 to 20 function (and/or gradient) evaluations depending on the nonlinearity of the function and the precision demanded. In some cases, many more evaluations may be needed.

There are many different line search methods varying in efficiency and robustness. We will not describe them here since they are covered well in many optimization texts. As in the general case, there are specialized methods that may be very efficient in situations where they are appropriate, but may not work well in other cases. Methods using gradient information are usually more efficient than evaluation-only methods if the gradient calculation is inexpensive (as it is in neural network simulations). Whether the gradient calculation is worth the savings in function evaluations can be problem-dependent, however. If gradient information is used in the line search routine, it certainly pays to also use it in the computation of the search direction.

In most methods, the first task is to find an interval that brackets a minimum. This calls for three points where the interior point is lower than either end point and, unless you are lucky, will usually require more than three function evaluations to find. Given a bounding interval, the next task is to locate the minimum. One approach is to iteratively subdivide the interval until the uncertainty is tolerable; each step reduces the uncertainty by roughly half on average. The other main approach is to approximate the function on the interval (e.g., with a parabola) and then estimate the minimum location analytically. The first method is generally more robust, but the second method can be much faster. Some practical algorithms start with the first method and then switch to the second. Brent's method [302] is a common choice.

10.4   Evaluation-Only Methods

Evaluation-only methods search for minima by comparing values of the objective function at different points. In particular, they do not use gradient information. The basic idea is to evaluate the function at points around the current search point, looking for lower values. Algorithms differ in how test points are generated.

Simplicity is the main advantage of evaluation-only methods. Inefficiency is their main disadvantage; for smooth functions it usually pays to use gradient information if it is available. For MLPs with continuous node nonlinearities, the gradient is easily calculated in the back-propagation step. In computer simulations, the incremental cost (in time and complexity) is approximately the same as the cost of a forward evaluation.

Evaluation-only methods are most useful where internal system details are inaccessible (as in some integrated circuit implementations), where the transfer function of the system is not differentiable, or in complex systems where derivatives are difficult to calculate correctly. In spite of their inefficiency, some evaluation-only methods do have global convergence properties lacking in gradient-based methods.

10.4.1   Hooke-Jeeves Pattern Search

One of the simplest search methods is to take small steps along each coordinate direction separately, varying one parameter at a time and checking if the error decreases. If a step in one direction increases the error, then a step in the opposite direction should decrease it (if the step size is small enough). After N steps, each of the N coordinate directions will have been tested. If none of the steps decrease the error, the step size may be too big relative to the curvature of the error surface and the step size should be reduced.

Although this is simple to implement, it is very inefficient in high-dimensional spaces. For a neural network, each step would require evaluation of all the training patterns but change only a single weight. There is also a small chance of getting stuck at the bottom of an obliquely oriented 'ravine' in the error surface since the error decreases along the axis of the ravine but is higher along each of the coordinate directions so no more steps will be taken. Usually, however, the point is slightly off-center so the step size will merely reduce to a very small value resulting in slow convergence.

The Hooke-Jeeves pattern search method [311] greatly accelerates convergence in this situation by remembering previous steps and attempting new steps in the same direction. An *exploratory move* consists of a step in each of the N coordinate directions ending up at the *base point* after N steps. A *pattern move* consists of a step along the line from the previous base point to the new one. This may be oblique, in general. This becomes a temporary base point for a new exploratory move. If the exploratory move results in a lower error than the previous base point, it becomes the new base point. If it does not decrease the error, then the temporary base point is discarded and an exploratory move is done around the current base point. If this exploratory search fails, the step size is reduced. The search is halted when the step size becomes sufficiently small.

There are many heuristic variations, but simplicity is the main advantage of the method and once it's lost, more sophisticated methods are preferable.

10.4.2   Nelder-Mead Simplex Search

Another direct search method is based on the idea of using a population of points to determine the local shape of the error surface. The basic steps are:

1. Create a simplex (a regular convex polytope) in N dimensions and evaluate the function at each of the $N + 1$ vertices.

2. Identify the vertex with the highest error.

3. Reflect the vertex across the centroid of the other vertices. This tends to be a step downhill but not parallel to the gradient, in general.

4. Evaluate the function at the new point. If the error is lower, go to 2. Otherwise, reject the new point and try reflecting less far across the centroid (i.e., move the reflected point in towards the centroid).

5. Go to 2.

There are additional rules to handle some special cases. Eventually, the points straddle a local minimum and the vertices converge to a single point as the size is reduced. One problem of the basic algorithm is that the simplex could become very small if it has to "squeeze through" a tight area; convergence would be very slow from then on. The Nelder-Mead variation introduces rules for expanding and contracting the simplex to accelerate convergence and close in on the final minimum.

This method is relatively simple to implement. It is said to be reasonably efficient and tolerant of noise in the objective function. (Powell's method may be more efficient for many problems, however, although it is not as easy to implement.) Like other evaluation-only methods, it can be used on nondifferentiable functions. It may not be suitable to large neural networks though because it requires storage of approximately N^2 values ($N + 1$ vertices each specified by a vector of N weights).

In a neural network training example [103], simplex search was slow at first, but eventually reduced the error to a lower value than back-propagation. Quasi-Newton and Levenberg-Marquardt methods achieved even lower errors, however.

10.4.3   Powell's Conjugate Direction Method

Powell's conjugate direction method, sometimes called the direction set method, uses information from previous steps in order to choose the next search direction. A quadratic error function $E = \mathbf{x}^T \mathbf{H} \mathbf{x}$ is assumed, where $\mathbf{x}$ are the parameters to be optimized.

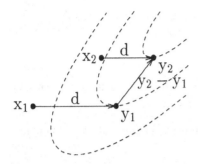

Figure 10.1
Conjugate directions. Powell's method uses the "parallel subspace property" of quadratic functions to find a set of conjugate directions without evaluating the Hessian. Given a quadratic function $\mathbf{x}^T\mathbf{H}\mathbf{x}$, a direction $\mathbf{d}$, and two points $\mathbf{x}_1$ and $\mathbf{x}_2$, if one does a line search from $\mathbf{x}_1$ along direction $\mathbf{d}$ to obtain a minimum $\mathbf{y}_1$ and another line search from $\mathbf{x}_2$ along direction $\mathbf{d}$ to obtain $\mathbf{y}_2$ then direction $(\mathbf{y}_2 - \mathbf{y}_1)$ is $\mathbf{H}$-conjugate to $\mathbf{d}$ [311].

A set of vectors $\mathbf{d}_1, \mathbf{d}_2, \ldots \mathbf{d}_r, r \leq N$, are mutually *conjugate* with respect to a symmetric $N \times N$ matrix $\mathbf{H}$ if they are linearly independent and [311]

$$\mathbf{d}_i^T \mathbf{H} \mathbf{d}_j = 0 \quad \text{for all } i \neq j. \tag{10.1}$$

Conjugate directions are useful because an N-dimensional quadratic function determined by $\mathbf{H}$ can be minimized by performing independent one-dimensional searches along any N mutually conjugate directions. The directions are uncoupled in the sense that minimizing along direction $\mathbf{d}_i$ does not undo any gains that were obtained by minimizing along previous directions. The reader is referred to an optimization text, for example, Reklaitis, Ravindras, and Ragsdell [311], for further details.

It would seem to be necessary to evaluate $\mathbf{H}$, the Hessian matrix of second derivatives, in order to find a set of conjugate directions, but in fact it is not. Powell's method exploits the parallel subspace property of quadratic functions, defined as follows, to find a set of conjugate directions without evaluating the Hessian. Given a quadratic function $\mathbf{x}^T\mathbf{H}\mathbf{x}$, a direction $\mathbf{d}$, and two points $\mathbf{x}_1$ and $\mathbf{x}_2$, if one does a line search from $\mathbf{x}_1$ along direction $\mathbf{d}$ to obtain a minimum $\mathbf{y}_1$ and another line search from $\mathbf{x}_2$ along direction $\mathbf{d}$ to obtain $\mathbf{y}_2$ then direction $(\mathbf{y}_2 - \mathbf{y}_1)$ is $\mathbf{H}$-conjugate to $\mathbf{d}$ [311] (see figure 10.1).

In N dimensions, Powell's method does N line searches to identify each conjugate direction using only function evaluations. If the error function actually is quadratic, it will find the minimum after N^2 (exact) line searches. Of course, more searches will usually be needed for general nonlinear functions and inexact calculations, but convergence is still quadratic. It is said to be as reliable as, and usually much more efficient than, other direct search methods.

For neural networks in which the gradient is easily obtained, the conjugate gradient method is preferred since it is much more efficient ($O(N)$ line searches for a quadratic function). In either case, for general nonlinear functions, the quadratic approximation is only reasonable near a minimum and other methods may be better to reach the general neighborhood in the first place.

10.5   First-Order Gradient Methods

The main disadvantage of evaluation-only methods is their relative inefficiency. When gradient information is available, it is almost always worth using because it tells exactly which parameter changes will minimize the error most at the current point. In digital simulations at least, it is easy to calculate the gradient for MLPs with differentiable node nonlinearities so most training methods are gradient based.

10.5.1   Gradient Descent

As noted, back-propagation is a variety of gradient descent. In gradient descent, new points are obtained by moving along the (negative) gradient direction. That is,

$$\mathbf{w}(t+1) = \mathbf{w}(t) - \eta \mathbf{g} \qquad\qquad (10.2)$$

where $\mathbf{g} = \frac{\partial E(\mathbf{w})}{\partial \mathbf{w}}$ is the gradient, $E(\mathbf{w})$ is the error function evaluated at $\mathbf{w}(t)$ and η is a step size or learning rate parameter. For a true approximation to gradient descent, $\eta \to 0$ should be very small (figure 10.2a), but larger values are often used in practice to speed-up convergence. Batch-mode back-propagation with a small learning rate is a specialization of gradient descent to MLPs where the back-propagation step is just a way of calculating the gradient by application of the derivative chain rule in the MLP structure. Back-propagation and its variations are discussed in chapters 5 and 9.

Gradient descent is not highly regarded in the optimization community mainly because of its slow rate of convergence. In theory, the asymptotic rate of convergence is linear. That is, the error is reduced by a constant factor at each step, $|e_{k+1}| \le C|e_k|$ where $C < 1$ is a constant. One problem is that the gradient never points to the global minimum except in the case where the error contours are spherical so many small steps are needed to arrive at the minimum. Another problem is that the gradient vanishes at a minimum so $\Delta\mathbf{w}$ approaches 0 and final convergence is very slow. Slow convergence is also a problem when the Hessian is poorly conditioned, that is, when the gradient changes rapidly in some directions but slowly in others. This is the case in so-called ravines of the error surface. When the step size is too large, the weight state may bounce from one side of the ravine to the other while making only slow progress along the ravine towards the true minimum (figure 10.2b),

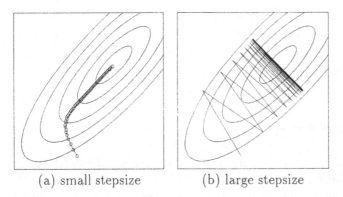

(a) small stepsize   (b) large stepsize

Figure 10.2
Gradient descent trajectories: (a) With a small step size (0.01), gradient descent follows a smooth trajectory, but progress may be very slow. (b) Cross-stitching: When the step size is too big (0.1) and the error surface has valleys, the trajectory may oscillate wildly from one side to the other while creeping slowly along the length of the valley to the minimum. Once it reaches the minimum, it may overshoot many times before settling.

an effect sometimes called cross-stitching. (Section A.2 discusses the convergence rate of gradient descent in linear problems.) The possibility of convergence to local minima is another common criticism applicable to all gradient-based methods.

The learning rate η is a parameter that must be selected. When it is too small, convergence will be very slow. When it is too large, the procedure may diverge (see figure 10.2). In practice, noninfinitesimal values of η are used in order to speed-up convergence and true gradient descent is only approximated. This is an unimportant detail in most cases. Stability requires that $0 < \eta < 2/\lambda_{max}$, where λ_{max} is the largest eigenvalue of the Hessian matrix. The optimum value is $\eta = 1/\lambda_{max}$ and with this choice, the convergence rate is governed by the slowest time constant $\frac{\lambda_{max}}{\lambda_{min}}$, where λ_{min} is the smallest nonzero eigenvalue (section A.2). When the Hessian is badly conditioned (i.e., nearly singular) the time constant can be large and convergence very slow. For nonlinear functions, the Hessian changes as the weight vector moves over the error surface. It is expensive to reevaluate the Hessian at each point so either a small learning rate is chosen arbitrarily or η is adjusted heuristically.

For best performance, different values of η are appropriate at different points on the error surface. Moderately large values are useful to reach the vicinity of a minimum quickly, but care has to be taken to avoid node saturation. Once a minimum has been located approximately, smaller step sizes are needed to avoid cross-stitching and allow the system to settle to a minimum. This is the situation where second-order methods usually outperform gradient descent. Effects of different learning rates on back-propagation are described in chapter 6. Variations of back-propagation that tune η dynamically are described in chapter 9.

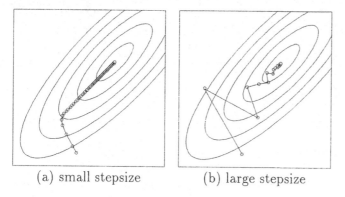

(a) small stepsize   (b) large stepsize

Figure 10.3
Gradient descent trajectories with momentum. With momentum, opposite (side-to-side) changes tend to cancel
while complementary changes (along the length of the valley) tend to sum. The overall effect is to stabilize the
oscillations and accelerate convergence: (a) When the step size is small, momentum acts to accelerate convergence
(step size 0.01 and momentum 0.99, cf. figure 10.2a); (b) small amounts of momentum also help to damp
oscillations when the step size is too large (step size 0.1 and momentum 0.2, cf. figure 10.2b).

The use of momentum is common in back-propagation. This can be thought of as gradient descent with smoothing controlled by the momentum parameter, $0 < \alpha < 1$. Briefly,
the weight update rule is

$$\Delta \mathbf{w}(t) = -\eta \mathbf{g} + \alpha \Delta \mathbf{w}(t-1) \tag{10.3}$$

where, as before, $\mathbf{g}$ is the gradient of the error evaluated at $\mathbf{w}(t)$ and η is the step size
or learning rate parameter. When the step size is too large, momentum helps to suppress
cross-stitching because consecutive opposing changes tend to cancel while complementary
changes sum. That is, for $\alpha \to 1^-$, the side to side oscillations across the valley effectively
cancel while the components along the axis of the ravine add up. When the step size is too
small, on the other hand, momentum helps accelerate learning by amplifying the effective
learning rate. When the gradient is constant, for example, the effective learning rate is
$\eta' = \eta/(1 - \alpha)$. Figure 10.3 illustrates these effects. Momentum is discussed in more detail
in section 6.2.

10.5.2 Best-Step Steepest Descent (Cauchy's Method)

Simple continuous gradient descent is the rule "wherever you are, evaluate the gradient
and take a step down it." When the step size is infinitesimal, this produces a curved path
that is orthogonal to the contours of the error surface at all points (figure 10.2a). This is
slightly different from optimal, or best-step, steepest descent. As the term is used in the
optimization community, this seems to mean Cauchy's method, for example [311], which

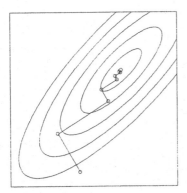

Figure 10.4
Cauchy's method uses the rule: wherever you are, evaluate the gradient and then move along that line until you
find a minimum. In each major iteration, it evaluates the gradient once and then does a line search to find the
minimum along that line.

uses the rule "wherever you are, evaluate the gradient and then move along that line until
you find a minimum." In each major iteration, it evaluates the gradient once and then does
a line search to find the minimum along that line (figure 10.4).

Although this may be useful in problems where the gradient calculation is expensive,
it doesn't seem to offer many benefits for (simulated MLP) neural networks in which the
gradient calculation has basically the same cost as a function evaluation. The minimum on
the line has no special significance and the calculations used in locating it precisely are
basically wasted. Few recommend the method, but it is often used for comparison to show
the benefits of more sophisticated methods. In neural network simulations, it is usually
slower than simple gradient descent.

10.5.3 Conjugate Gradient Descent

Conjugate gradient descent is one of the most often recommended optimization methods
for differentiable functions with many variables. Although it uses only first-order gradient
information, it is nearly as fast as full second-order methods. In addition, it is practical for
large problems because it avoids the need to store and manipulate the Hessian matrix by
assuming a locally quadratic function and using the property of conjugate directions.

As mentioned in section 10.4.3, A set of vectors $\mathbf{d}_1, \mathbf{d}_2, \ldots \mathbf{d}_r$, $r \leq N$, are mutually
conjugate with respect to a symmetric $N \times N$ matrix $\mathbf{H}$ if they are linearly independent
and [311]

$$\mathbf{d}_i^T \mathbf{H} \mathbf{d}_j = 0 \quad \text{for all } i \neq j. \tag{10.4}$$

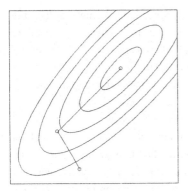

Figure 10.5
The conjugate gradient method converges in just N iterations (2 in this case) for an N-dimensional quadratic error function, but each iteration involves a line search that may require many evaluations of the error function.

This is useful because an N-dimensional quadratic function determined by $\mathbf{H}$ can be minimized by performing independent one-dimensional searches along any set of N mutually conjugate directions. The directions are uncoupled in the sense that minimizing along direction $\mathbf{d}_i$ doesn't undo gains that were obtained by minimizing along direction $\mathbf{d}_j$. Figure 10.5 illustrates the (two) steps taken for a two-dimensional quadratic error surface.

As in Powell's method, a set of conjugate search directions can be obtained without evaluating the Hessian matrix. In practice, the search direction $\mathbf{d}_k$ for step k is a combination of the current gradient $\mathbf{g}_k$ and the previous search direction $\mathbf{d}_{k-1}$

$$\mathbf{d}_k = -\mathbf{g}_k + \gamma \mathbf{d}_{k-1} \tag{10.5}$$

where the subscripts index time, not elements of the vectors. It has been noted that this could be thought of as back-propagation with the momentum parameter optimally adapted at each step. Parameter γ controls how much the next search direction is influenced by the previous search direction. There are a number of variations differing in how γ is chosen

$$\gamma = \frac{\|\mathbf{g}_k\|^2}{\|\mathbf{g}_{k-1}\|^2} \quad \text{(Fletcher-Reeves)} \tag{10.6}$$

$$\gamma = \frac{(\mathbf{g}_k - \mathbf{g}_{k-1})^T \mathbf{g}_k}{\|\mathbf{g}_{k-1}\|^2} \quad \text{(Polak-Ribiere)} \tag{10.7}$$

Although these are mathematically equivalent for quadratic functions, they give different results for general nonlinear functions, in which case the Polak-Ribiere form is preferred [302].

Minimization of a nonquadratic function will require more than N line searches but only N conjugate directions are available, so it is necessary to reinitialize the procedure periodically. There are various prescriptions for how and when to restart. The simplest is to reset the search direction to the gradient after N line searches.

Without restarts, later directions become linearly dependent and convergence is almost always linear [138]. With restarts, convergence is supralinear in theory, but in practice it is nearly always linear [138] because of round off errors, inexact line searches, the failure of the quadratic assumption, and so on. Still, it is usually much faster than simple gradient descent (which also converges linearly) because the scale factor may be much lower. Conjugate gradient and back-propagation were compared empirically on neural network N/2/N encoder problems in [360]; conjugate gradient was about an order of magnitude faster and back-propagation rarely converged for the harder (large N) problems, but it was estimated that both have roughly equal median time complexities. That is, training time scaled with N in approximately the same way.

The efficiency of the line search routine is critical because this is where most of the computation time is spent. Often, there are several parameters that must be tuned to obtain good performance. On simple problems, good line search routines may require as few as 3 to 4 function or gradient evaluations, but a typical search may require 10 to 20 evaluations, depending on parameter choices, nonlinearity of the function, and the precision required. It should be noted that some popular line search routines use parabolic approximations which may offer fast convergence for quadratic problems, but which may be slow or divergent for neural network error surfaces with stair-step shapes.

Scaled conjugate gradient descent [270] is a variation that eliminates the line search and all tunable parameters, but seems to have properties similar to the basic algorithm. It has been reported to be faster than the basic algorithm in some cases and slower in others. In [9], it was somewhat slower than other conjugate gradient methods.

Conjugate gradient descent has been compared with back-propagation in a number of studies [e.g., 26, 225, 27, 124, 197, 14, 19, 47, 69, 210, 75, 208, 360, 179, 296, 313, 383]. A detailed discussion and source code are provided in [258]. Most studies report an order of magnitude improvement in the number of iterations to convergence, an improved chance of convergence on hard problems, and smaller final errors. The reader should take care to note, however, if the iterations reported are the number of line searches or the total number of function (and/or gradient) evaluations. Where function evaluations or run-time are reported, it still appears to be faster, but the difference is not as great.

The results of performance comparisons with back-propagation seem to be task dependent [e.g., 377, 9]. In some cases, conjugate gradient is much faster; in others, it seems to have no advantage, or is slower. In [239] conjugate gradient worked well on simple problems, but simply converged (quickly) to a poor local minimum on a more difficult problem. Alpsan et al. [9] suggest that the difference depends on whether the problem is function approximation or classification. It is suggested that conjugate gradient (and other advanced methods) outperform back-propagation on function approximation problems where it is necessary to reduce the error to small values and that back-propagation generally does better on classification problems where training is stopped as soon as all patterns are correctly classified within a loose tolerance band. In [9], on a single network training problem, the time for conjugate gradient descent to correctly classify all patterns was similar to that of back-propagation without momentum and only half the speed of back-propagation with momentum. Generalization was poor.

An explanation for these results is that for very nonlinear functions, the quadratic approximation is not valid at a large scale so the conjugate gradient method has no advantage over simpler methods in initial stages of search (and its exact line searches may be superfluous). The quadratic approximation is usually valid, however, in a small region around an optimum, in which case conjugate gradient converges very quickly whereas gradient descent may actually slow down. For classification problems, the relaxed error criteria may be satisfied over a large region around a minimum so the search may end before the quadratic approximation becomes valid and the advantages of conjugate gradient come into play. For continuous regression problems, however, the region satisfying the error criteria is often much smaller so the search continues into a phase where conjugate gradient is by far superior.

Conjugate gradient descent was compared with (among other methods) back-propagation with an adaptive stepsize by Barnard and Holm [20]. The conjugate gradient method had lower errors and better generalization in early stages, but an adaptive algorithm achieved the same results after more iterations.

10.6 Second-Order Gradient Methods

Gradient methods using second-derivatives (the Hessian matrix) can be very efficient under certain conditions. Where first-order methods use a linear local approximation of the error surface, second-order methods use a quadratic approximation. If the function really is quadratic then a solution can be found very quickly (one step in Newton's method). The approximation is often good *in the vicinity of a minimum* in which case final convergence to the endpoint can be very fast. The approximation is often poor on a large-scale, however, so other methods may be better for initially finding the general neighborhood. The Levenberg-Marquardt method effectively switches from gradient descent to Newton's method as a minimum is approached.

10.6.1   Newton's Method

For smooth functions, Newton's method is the theoretical standard by which other optimization methods are judged. Because it uses all the first and second order derivative
information in its exact form, its local convergence properties are excellent. Unfortunately
though, it is often impractical because explicit calculation of the full Hessian matrix can be
very expensive in large problems. Many 'second-order' methods therefore use approximations built up from first order information. Some methods for calculating and approximating second derivatives in neural networks are reviewed by Buntine and Weigend [62].

Newton's method is based on a quadratic model of the error function

$$\hat{E}(\mathbf{w}) = E_o + \mathbf{g}^T \mathbf{w} + \frac{1}{2}\mathbf{w}^T \mathbf{H}\mathbf{w} \qquad (10.8)$$

where $\mathbf{g} = \frac{\partial E}{\partial \mathbf{w}}$ is the gradient vector, and $\mathbf{H}$ is the Hessian matrix of second derivatives with
elements $h_{ij} = \frac{\partial^2 E}{\partial w_i \, \partial w_j}$. $\mathbf{H}$ is assumed to be positive definite. This is simply a Taylor series
approximation truncated after the second order terms. Taking the derivative of $\hat{E}(\mathbf{w})$ with
respect to $\mathbf{w}$ and setting it equal to 0 gives

$$\mathbf{g} + \mathbf{H}\mathbf{w} = 0, \qquad (10.9)$$

which has solution $\mathbf{w}^* = -\mathbf{H}^{-1}\mathbf{g}$. If $\mathbf{H}$ is positive definite and $E(\mathbf{w})$ really is quadratic, the
solution could be obtained in a single step (figure 10.6). Usually, of course, E is not exactly
quadratic so iteration is necessary

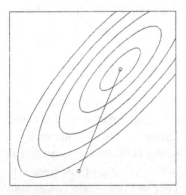

Figure 10.6
For quadratic error functions, Newton's method converges in a single step. For more general nonlinear functions,
Newton's method converges very quickly where the Hessian matrix is positive definite (e.g., in the vicinity of a
minimum) but may diverge elsewhere.

$$\mathbf{w}(t+1) = \mathbf{w}(t) - \eta \mathbf{H}^{-1}\mathbf{g} \qquad\qquad (10.10)$$

where η is a step-size parameter ($\eta = 1$ normally).

The advantage of Newton's method is that it converges very quickly in the vicinity of a minimum. Convergence is quadratic for quadratic error functions; that is, in the limit $|e_{k+1}| \le C|e_k|^2$ where $e = \mathbf{w} - \mathbf{w}^*$. Convergence requires that $\mathbf{H}$ be positive definite and $0 < \eta < 2/\lambda_{max}$ where λ_{max} is the largest eigenvalue of $\mathbf{H}$. In any case, η should be small enough to stay in the region where the quadratic approximation is valid.

A problem with the method is that it converges only where the Hessian is positive definite. (A symmetric matrix $\mathbf{H}$ is positive-definite if $\mathbf{x}^T\mathbf{H}\mathbf{x} > 0$ for all $\mathbf{x} \ne \mathbf{0}$. If the result is 0 for some $\mathbf{x} \ne \mathbf{0}$, $\mathbf{H}$ is positive-semi-definite. If the sign is positive or negative depending on $\mathbf{x}$, $\mathbf{H}$ is indefinite. All eigenvalues of a positive-definite matrix are nonzero and positive. Some eigenvalues of a positive-semi-definite matrix are zero. An indefinite matrix has eigenvalues of both signs.)

$\mathbf{H}$ could easily be indefinite in general nonlinear functions, especially far from a minimum, and it is common for it to be badly conditioned (nearly singular) in neural networks, especially if the number of training samples is smaller than the number of weights. Section 8.6 summarizes some properties of the Hessian in typical neural networks. When $\mathbf{H}$ has one or more negative eigenvalues, E has negative curvature in some directions, which would suggest that arbitrarily large steps would reduce the error by arbitrarily large amounts. These would likely move the system out of the region where its model is valid and, if really large, could lead to saturation of the sigmoid node functions. $\mathbf{H}$ might then be rank deficient if saturation makes enough second derivatives small relative to machine precision [28].

Modifications of the pure algorithm are necessary to prevent divergence in such cases. Ideas include limitations on the maximum step length, the use of line searches along the Newton direction when the step fails to decrease the error, and the use of matrix decompositions to solve (10.9).

Another problem, purely practical, is the need to evaluate, store, and invert the Hessian matrix at each iteration. In practice, dozens of iterations may be needed. Storage of the matrix requires $O(N^2)$ space and could become a problem on small computers and work stations as N exceeds 1000–2000. Exact evaluation of the matrix at a single point requires computations equivalent to approximately $O(N^2)$ epochs in a network with N weights. A simpler method might be able to make great gains with those N^2 function evaluations, possibly even solving the problem before Newton's method can take a single step. Finally, solution of (10.9) requires approximately $O(N^3)$ operations whether the matrix is actually inverted or not. (These are simple operations like addition and multiplication, however, rather than complex operations like evaluation of the network error function.) The N^2

evaluations will probably take more time for most neural networks when the training set is large because evaluation of each pattern will take $O(N)$ time and it can be argued that the number of training patterns should be at least $O(N)$ to ensure good generalization, in which case exact evaluation of the matrix could scale like $O(N^4)$.

The problem is illustrated in [38], where a modern nonlinear least squares optimization program (NL2SOL, ACM Algorithm 573) using the *exact* Hessian, generally achieved smaller errors than back-propagation, but training times were an order of magnitude longer (39 hours to do 50 iterations versus 2.2 hours to do 500,000 back-propagation iterations); the paper describes a hybrid quasi-Newton alternative.

10.6.2 Gauss-Newton

Calculation of the exact Hessian matrix can be expensive, so approximations are often used. The Gauss-Newton and Levenberg-Marquardt techniques take advantage of special structure in the Hessian for least squares problems and use the outer-product approximation of section 8.6.3. As noted in section 8.6.3, the Hessian can written as

$$\mathbf{H} = 2(-\mathbf{P} + \mathbf{Q}) \tag{10.11}$$

where $\mathbf{P} = \langle \mathbf{gg}^T \rangle$ is the average outer-product of first-order gradient terms while $\mathbf{Q}$, $q_{ij} = \left\langle (d - y)\frac{\partial^2 y}{\partial w_i \, \partial w_j} \right\rangle$ contains second order terms. Because $\mathbf{P}$ is the sum of outer products of the gradient vector, it is real, symmetric, and thus nonnegative-definite. Gauss-Newton is based on the assumption that the first-order terms dominate the second order terms near a solution. Of course, this assumption is not always valid, but the approximation seems to work reasonably well, especially when the larger algorithm does not depend too heavily on its accuracy.

The Gauss-Newton weight update is a solution of

$$\mathbf{g} = -\mathbf{P}\Delta\mathbf{w}. \tag{10.12}$$

This could be solved by inverting $\mathbf{P}$, although other methods have practical advantages. Convergence is eventually quadratic once $\mathbf{Q}$ vanishes leaving $\mathbf{P}$ as an accurate approximation of $\mathbf{H}$. This avoids the need for a costly exact evaluation of $\mathbf{H}$, but it still requires storage of the matrix and solution of a matrix equation.

10.6.3 The Levenberg-Marquardt Method

A problem with Newton's method is that it converges only where $\mathbf{H}$ is positive definite, but $\mathbf{H}$ could easily be indefinite for a general nonlinear function, especially far from a minimum. The Levenberg-Marquardt method (figure 10.7) is a compromise be-

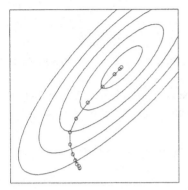

Figure 10.7
The Levenberg-Marquardt method is a compromise between Newton's method, which converges very quickly in the vicinity of a minimum but may diverge elsewhere, and gradient descent, which converges everywhere, albeit slowly. In general, the trajectory starts out like gradient descent but gradually approaches the Newton direction.

tween Newton's method, which converges quickly near a minimum but may diverge elsewhere, and gradient descent, which converges everywhere, though slowly. The search direction is a linear combination of the steepest descent direction $\mathbf{g}$ and the Newton direction $\mathbf{H}^{-1}\mathbf{g}$

$$\mathbf{w}_{k+1} = \mathbf{w}_k - (\mathbf{H} + \lambda\mathbf{I})^{-1}\,\mathbf{g}. \tag{10.13}$$

Parameter λ controls the compromise. This can be viewed as forcing $\mathbf{H} + \lambda\mathbf{I}$ to be positive definite by adding a scaled identity matrix. The minimum value of λ needed to achieve this depends on the eigenvalues of $\mathbf{H}$. The algorithm starts with λ large and adjusts it dynamically so that every step decreases the error. Generally it is held near the smallest value that causes the error to decrease. In the early stages when λ is large, the system effectively does gradient descent. In later stages, λ approaches 0, effectively switching to Newton's method for final convergence.

This avoids the divergence problem of Newton's method and the need for a line search, but still calls for storage and inversion of an $N \times N$ matrix. In the preceding description, $\mathbf{H}$ could be the true Hessian, but in practice the outer-product approximation of section 8.6.3 is usually used so Levenberg-Marquardt is commonly considered to be a first-order method applicable only to least squares problems.

The Levenberg-Marquardt method is compared to back-propagation and conjugate gradient descent by Hagan and Menhaj [148]. A variation combined with adaptive stepsize heuristics is described by Kollias and Anastassiou [218]. A detailed discussion and source code are provided in [258]. Results seem to be good on moderately sized problems.

10.6.4   Quasi-Newton Methods

Quasi-Newton methods, sometimes called variable metric methods, build an approximation of the inverse Hessian matrix iteratively using only first-order gradient information.
This removes the need to explicitly calculate and invert the Hessian, but not the need to
store the approximation. The two major variations are the Davidon-Fletcher-Powell (DFP)
and the Broyden-Fletcher-Goldfarb-Shanno (BFGS) methods. They differ in details, but
BFGS is generally recommended.

From [138], the BFGS update for the approximation $\mathbf{B}_k$ at step $k + 1$ is

$$\mathbf{B}_{k+1} = \mathbf{B}_k - \frac{1}{\mathbf{s}_k^T \mathbf{B} \mathbf{s}_k} \mathbf{B}_k \mathbf{s}_k \mathbf{s}_k^T \mathbf{B}_k + \frac{1}{\mathbf{y}_k^T \mathbf{s}_k} \mathbf{y}_k \mathbf{y}_k^T \qquad (10.14)$$

where $\mathbf{s}_k$ is the step taken and $\mathbf{g}_k$ is the gradient vector at iteration k, and $\mathbf{y}_k = \mathbf{g}_{k+1} - \mathbf{g}_k$.
When the search direction $\mathbf{p}_k$ is computed by solving

$$\mathbf{B}_k \mathbf{p}_k = \mathbf{g}_k \qquad (10.15)$$

and $\mathbf{s}_k = \alpha_k \mathbf{p}_k$ is the step taken after doing a line search along $\mathbf{p}_k$, this simplifies to

$$\mathbf{B}_{k+1} = \mathbf{B}_k + \frac{1}{\mathbf{g}_k^T \mathbf{p}_k} \mathbf{g}_k \mathbf{g}_k^T + \frac{1}{\alpha_k \mathbf{y}_k^T \mathbf{p}_k} \mathbf{y}_k \mathbf{y}_k^T. \qquad (10.16)$$

The initial approximation $\mathbf{B}_0$ is usually the identity matrix so the first step is an iteration of
best-step steepest-descent.

It is apparent that the formula preserves symmetry. For stability, it is critical that it also
preserve positive-definiteness. Some care must be taken in the implementation because loss
of positive-definiteness is possible due to limited-precision line searches and numerical
round-off errors. Exact line searches are not necessary for convergence, however, and
the method often converges faster (in terms of the number of function evaluations) using
inexact line searches.

Storage requirements may make the method impractical for large networks, but it may
be worth considering for small to moderate size networks. There do not seem to be major
performance advantages compared to conjugate gradient methods, however. In [19], BFGS
and conjugate gradient with restarts gave similar average errors on three neural network test
problems and had similar convergence speed. On a neural network function approximation
problem in [103], BFGS was able to achieve lower error than back-propagation, conjugate
gradient, and simplex search; only Levenberg-Marquardt achieved a lower error. In [146],
BFGS was the fastest and most reliable method in a comparison with conjugate gradient
and an adaptive stepsize version of back-propagation on a small problem. Quasi-Newton
training is specifically addressed in [2].

Although quasi-Newton methods have fast local convergence, this does not guarantee convergence to a good minimum. In [377], the DFP version converged to good solutions in only a third of 10,000 trials. In [9], DFP and BFGS gave basically the same results on a single real-world MLP training problem. Both located good minima in only half of the trials. In the other half they converged to local minima or suffered from numerical instability. Both were slower than standard back-propagation (with or without momentum) to learn the training set (classify correctly within error tolerances) and generalization was poor.

Limited Memory BFGS   One-step limited memory BFGS [138] is a variation that avoids the need to store a matrix. A quasi-Newton update formula is used, but $\mathbf{H}^{-1}$ is taken to be the identity matrix so only $O(N)$ storage is needed. In implementation, it is similar to conjugate gradients.

The search direction at step k is

$$\mathbf{d}_k = -\mathbf{g}_k + A_k\mathbf{p}_k + B_k\mathbf{y}_k \tag{10.17}$$

where A_k and B_k are scalar weighting factors

$$A_k = -\left(1 + \frac{\mathbf{y}_k \cdot \mathbf{y}_k}{\mathbf{p}_k \cdot \mathbf{y}_k}\right) \frac{\mathbf{p}_k \cdot \mathbf{g}_k}{\mathbf{p}_k \cdot \mathbf{y}_k} + \frac{\mathbf{y}_k \cdot \mathbf{g}_k}{\mathbf{p}_k \cdot \mathbf{y}_k} \tag{10.18}$$

$$B_k = \frac{\mathbf{p}_k \cdot \mathbf{g}_k}{\mathbf{p}_k \cdot \mathbf{y}_k} \tag{10.19}$$

and $\mathbf{g}_k$ is the gradient, $\mathbf{p}_k = \mathbf{w}_k - \mathbf{w}_{k-1}$, and $\mathbf{y}_k = \mathbf{g}_k - \mathbf{g}_{k-1}$.

An advantage of the method over conjugate gradients is its tolerance of inexact line searches, which allows significant computational savings. In an MLP training test for a real-world problem, computation time was reduced by a factor of eight relative to conjugate gradient with exact line searches even though four times as many inexact line searches were required [29] (as reported by Alpson et al. [9]). Formula (10.17) is used in [27], and a variation is described in [28].

10.7   Stochastic Evaluation-Only Methods

A problem with deterministic gradient-based methods is that they can get trapped in local minima. In some cases, a few repetitions of the algorithm with different starting points may be enough to find the global minimum, but in other cases, for example, when there are many poor local minima or the basin of attraction of the global minimum is small, more powerful methods may be needed.

The advantage of stochastic methods is that every state has a nonzero chance of occurrence so if the procedure runs long enough the global minimum is likely to be found eventually. (This in itself is not special; pure random search will also find the global minimum if given enough time, but no one recommends it.) Under certain conditions, methods like simulated annealing and genetic algorithms can guarantee convergence (in probability) to the global minimum. This may take a very long time, however, and the guarantee is lost if the search is terminated early.

As evaluation-only methods, both simulated annealing and the genetic algorithm have the advantage of being relatively easy to implement in the sense that the algorithm is uncomplicated and there are no complex matrix manipulations. They need very little problem-specific information. They do not require a gradient vector so they may be used on discontinuous functions or functions described empirically rather than analytically. Under certain conditions, they will tolerate a noisy evaluation function.

10.7.1 Simulated Annealing

Simulated annealing [211, 264] is a general optimization technique based on a physical analogy. A physical system will generally settle to the lowest accessible energy state, but random thermal agitation will sometimes excite it to higher energy states. This is undesirable if we want the system to settle to the lowest possible energy, but occasionally it helps by giving the system enough energy to overcome a barrier separating it from even lower states.

The example of a liquid freezing into a solid is often used for illustration. A liquid is a disordered system with high energy. As energy is withdrawn, the liquid cools and begins to freeze. If the liquid is cooled very quickly, it tends to freeze into a disordered mass of tiny crystals with many imperfections and dislocations between grain boundaries. These imperfections are sites of internal stress that have high energy. If the system is cooled very slowly on the other hand, it tends to form large well-ordered crystals with few imperfections and low internal energy.

By cooling the system slowly, we allow many opportunities for random thermal agitation to rearrange atoms into more stable low-energy configurations. Because these states are more stable, they tend to survive longer. Although the probability of entering a particular stable state by random chance may be low, the probability of leaving is even lower so the system as a whole thus tends to a more ordered, lower energy state.

According to the Boltzmann statistics for a system in thermal equilibrium at temperature T, the probability of a state s with energy E_s is

$$P_s = \frac{1}{Z}e^{-E_s/kT} \tag{10.20}$$

where Z is a normalization constant and k is Boltzmann's constant. At very high temperatures, the exponent is small and all states are almost equally likely. At intermediate temperatures, there is a strong bias toward lower energy states, but higher energy states still have significant probability. At very low temperatures, low energy states are much more likely than higher energy states.

For optimization, an analogy is made between the system energy and the error function; parameter vectors with low errors correspond to system states with low energy. New candidate vectors are generated by modifying the current vector by some random process, for example, by adding noise to the current search point; different noise distributions give different convergence properties. If the new point has a lower error (energy), it is accepted as the new search point. If the new point increases the error (energy) by an amount ΔE, it is accepted with probability

$$P = e^{-\Delta E/T}.$$

That is, there is a chance P that the higher-error vector will be accepted as the new search point and a chance $(1 - P)$ that it will be rejected, in which case new candidates will be generated from the original point. At high temperatures, the exponent is very small and almost all proposed changes are accepted. At low temperatures, the probability decreases very quickly as ΔE increases; changes that increase the error have very low probability of being accepted and the trajectory approaches gradient descent.

The advantage of stochastic algorithms like simulated annealing is that every state has a nonzero chance of occurrence so if the process continues long enough, every state, including the global minimum, will be visited eventually. A purely random search would immediately hop to another state after visiting the global minimum, but simulated annealing has a bias to lower energy states so it is likely to remain near or revisit the global minimum often.

The promise of the method is that if the system is cooled slowly enough, it will eventually converge to the global minimum (with probability 1). The catch is that this may take a very very long time and all guarantees are lost if the system is cooled too quickly (quenched) or stopped too soon. It has been shown that a temperature reduction schedule inversely proportional to the logarithm of time will guarantee convergence (in probability) to a global minimum [135]

$$T(t) = \frac{T_0}{\log(1 + t)}. \tag{10.21}$$

Because the logarithm increases slowly with t, this can take a very long time. In practice, this schedule takes too long and it is often more efficient to repeat the algorithm a number of times using a faster schedule (sacrificing claims of provable convergence in the process).

10.7.2 Genetic Algorithms

The genetic algorithm [173, 141] is a general optimization method based on an analogy to the evolution of species in nature. (Chapter 11 describes the algorithm in more detail; the following remarks outline the main points.) The idea is that individuals in a large population have varying traits which affect their reproductive success in the given environment. Successful individuals live long enough to mate and pass their traits to the next generation. Offspring inherit traits from successful parents so they also have a good chance of being successful. Over many generations, the population adapts to its environment; disadvantageous traits become rare and the average fitness tends to increase over time.

There are a number of evolutionary algorithms based on similar ideas. The genetic algorithm includes effects of mating—combination of traits from two successful parents to yield offspring that are similar to, but slightly different from, either parent. There is an element of randomness so it has stochastic properties similar to simulated annealing, but it acts on an entire population rather than a single individual.

For optimization purposes, individuals are represented by a bit-string that encodes the parameters of a particular solution and their fitness depends on the objective function. Offspring are generated from two parents by combining their bit-strings in various ways.

The principal advantage of the method is that it needs very little problem-specific information—just a function to evaluate parameter sets and assign fitness scores. In particular, it does not require gradient information and so may be used on discontinuous functions or functions that are described empirically rather than analytically. The mating selection and crossover operations are already somewhat random so, assuming appropriate parameters, the algorithm will tolerate moderate amounts of noise in the evaluation function. The crossover operation is nonlinear so the algorithm is not necessarily a hill-climbing method and is not particularly bothered by local maxima (minima). It is also easily parallelizable.

The principle disadvantage of the method is the amount of processing needed to evaluate a large population of candidates and converge to a solution over many generations. There are claims of convergence to a global maximum of the fitness function, but with small populations and aggressive culling of less successful solutions, convergence to a local maximum is possible. (This is similar to the case of cooling too quickly in simulated annealing.) Also, there are many parameters to be selected (population size, mutation rate, crossover method, fitness scaling, etc.) and it is not obvious how these affect the convergence properties. At this point, it is unclear if the algorithm is better than other methods such as simulated annealing.

A difficulty with the method for neural network optimization is the problem of incompatible genomes mentioned in section 11.3.1. The problem is that two successful individuals do not always yield a successful offspring when they mate; their bit-strings might represent points on two different local maxima and the combination might fall in a valley between them, for example. Peculiarities of the typical neural network structure aggravate this problem. Variations have been proposed to avoid the problem but they complicate the algorithm and detract from its advantage of simplicity.

10.8   Discussion

10.8.1   Are Assumptions Met?

When the objective function has special characteristics, specialized algorithms can often be developed to take advantage of them and perhaps obtain great efficiencies relative to more general algorithms. The problem is that although they may be very fast in the situations they were developed for, they may not be robust. That is, the assumptions they make may lead them astray and they may actually do worse than less specialized methods if their preconditions are not satisfied.

A number of methods such as conjugate gradient descent assume a quadratic function and exploit its special properties to achieve fast convergence. Unfortunately, neural network error surfaces may be highly nonlinear and are definitely not quadratic in the large scale. (Chapter 8 discusses properties of the $E(\mathbf{w})$ error surface that may cause problems—the existence of large flat areas separated by steep cliffs, for example.) Quoting from [302: 313]: "Quadratic convergence is of no particular advantage to a program which must slalom down the length of a valley floor that twists one way and another (and another, and another, . . . —there are N dimensions!). Along the long direction, a quadratically convergent method is trying to extrapolate to the minimum of a parabola which just isn't (yet) there; while the conjugacy of the $N - 1$ transverse directions keeps getting spoiled by the twists."

Another problem with methods based on a quadratic approximation is that the Hessian is often ill-conditioned in neural network training problems [37, 331] and so higher order methods may be no more efficient than simpler methods. When the number of weights exceeds the number of training samples, an outer-product Hessian approximation will be rank deficient. Sigmoid saturation may also lead to effective loss of rank. Ill-conditioning could lead to numerical instability or a large step that takes the system out of the region where the local approximation is valid. This is a well-known problem with Newton's method and there are standard fixes, but these add complications beyond the pure algorithm. The point is that a straight-forward implementation of a pure algorithm will not always work better than a simpler method unless these sorts of complications are addressed.

The quadratic approximation is usually valid in the neighborhood of a minimum though so it may be useful to use a more robust method for initial optimization, followed by a few iterations of a fast second-order method to tune the solution. Some theoretical justification is given in [394].

10.8.2 Back-Propagation Is Sometimes Good Enough

It has been said that "back-propagation is the second-best method for everything." That is, there are many algorithms which are faster and give better results in particular situations, but back-propagation and simple variants often do surprisingly well on a wide range of neural network training problems.

Standard optimization methods have been considered for neural network training in many studies. Most report faster training times, smaller errors, and better chance of convergence. This might leave the impression that they are uniformly better. There are cases, however, where back-propagation and its variations are faster or less prone to convergence to poor local minima than more sophisticated algorithms which should be better in theory. In [77], for example, several second-order methods are compared to back-propagation on a simple problem (seven weights plus an additional scaling parameter; the target is a sine function). All achieved smaller training errors, but all took more time. Alpsan et al. [9] evaluated approximately 25 different optimization techniques, including numerous variations of back-propagation, on a single real-world classification problem (classification of brainstem auditory evoked potentials). Quoting from the abstract [9]:

It was found that, comparatively, standard BP was sufficiently fast and provided good generalization when the task was to learn the training set within a given error tolerance. However, if the task was to find the global minimum [i.e., reduce the error to very small value], then standard BP failed to do so within 100000 iterations, but first order methods which adapt the stepsize were as fast as, if not faster than, conjugate gradient and quasi-Newton methods. Second order methods required the same amount of fine tuning of line search and restart parameters as did the first order methods of their parameters in order to achieve optimum performance.

In the same study, second-order methods showed a greater tendency to converge to local minima and the solutions found generalized worse than those found by first order methods. In other remarks, "None of the more sophisticated second order methods were able to learn [to classify] the training set faster than BP" [9]. Similar results have been reported elsewhere.

Part of the relative success of back-propagation may be due to its simple-mindedness; it makes very few assumptions. Part may also be due to special characteristics of the neural network training problem, for example, the shape of the typical error surface, that conflict with assumptions used by more sophisticated methods developed for other purposes. The remarks in section 10.5.3 about possible causes for the difference in performance on classification and continuous function approximation apply to most methods which assume a quadratic approximation. Basically, in classification, training is often stopped when all output errors are less than a certain value (e.g., 0.2) so the search may end before the quadratic approximation becomes valid and the advantages of the specialized algorithms don't have a chance to come into play. This may also be true to a lesser degree even for regression problems where the error tolerance is smaller. Early stopping based on cross-validation tests may also end the game before second-order methods become advantageous.

Part of back-propagation's success may also be due to network designers adapting to the algorithm. That is, it has been found that tricks such as input variable normalization, the use of tanh instead of sigmoid node functions, the use of $\{-0.9, 0.9\}$ targets instead of $\{0, 1\}$, the use of larger-than-necessary networks with early stopping and/or pruning, and so on seem to make learning easier and many of these have become standard practice. Some might view this as cheating because it changes the problem to fit the optimization method, but there is certainly no reason to intentionally design networks that are hard to train. Often, when such steps are taken, back-propagation or a simple variant may outperform more sophisticated methods. Some papers comparing conjugate gradients to back-propagation, for example, report on the order of 50,000 epochs to train a 4-4-1 network on the 4-input XOR problem. Back-propagation may actually take this long for the parameters used, but when simple fixes like those mentioned previously are taken, the problem becomes very easy and can generally be solved by back-propagation in a few hundred epochs. 40–50 epochs is typical for this problem with Rprop. On the simpler problem, conjugate gradient is not even as fast as back-propagation because it wastes evaluations in precise line searches.

Finally, aside from performance issues, there are sometimes good reasons for preferring simple algorithms.

• Simplicity may be important because computational resources are limited.

• Local algorithms are preferable for integrated-circuit implementation. Complicated matrix manipulations are not feasible on analog retina chips, for example. Simple methods like on-line back-propagation use information that is locally available at the weights being modified.

• Training time may not be a major consideration because it is usually a one-time procedure. The environment may change very slowly so frequent retraining is not necessary.

• In some studies, the algorithm is intended to be feasible in terms of what real neurons can do. The fact that more sophisticated algorithms exist is not relevant if they are not used by the system under study.

• Many sophisticated algorithms simply do not give better or faster solutions than simple variations of back-propagation on the problems considered.

• Some specialized algorithms are not robust. They do not work in all situations and break down if assumptions are not met. Simple implementations that ignore complications such as round-off error may not work well.

• More sophisticated algorithms often do not yield good generalization. Second-order methods can often achieve much smaller training set errors than back-propagation, but this may simply amount to overfitting when training data is limited.

10.8.3   Remarks

It is easy to get side-tracked into tinkering with optimization methods. It should be remembered that the optimization method is of secondary importance and factors such as representation, network structure, and choice of error function are more fundamental. If solutions are poor or training times are long, the problem could be more basic than the way the weights are tuned. A good optimization algorithm cannot fix problems introduced by a representation that hides needed information or an error function that does not measure the appropriate thing, after all. Sophisticated algorithms have their place, but they should generally be considered only other options have been exhausted.

Still, efficiency is important, especially for large networks with large data sets or in cases where many nets will be trained on similar data, so there are situations where it pays to "optimize the optimization method." If sophisticated algorithms are needed, consider using one of the highly efficient "canned" optimization programs that are available rather than writing from scratch. The best programs are already debugged, handle many special cases, and correctly deal with important implementation details that are seldom considered in simple descriptions of the pure algorithms. Some can switch between robust and specialized methods when appropriate. Most programs offer a selection of methods. Generally, it is necessary to understand something of the methods used by the program in order to fit the technique to the problem.

Other Notes

• Conjugate gradient descent and Levenberg-Marquardt are the classical methods most often mentioned for neural network training. Both are discussed in detail in this context in [258].

• Second order methods require the Hessian matrix or an approximation. Some possibilities are described in section 8.6.

• In several places above, inversion of the Hessian or other large matrixes is mentioned as a way of obtaining a solution. In practice, other methods that can handle rank-deficient and poorly conditioned cases are preferred. Techniques are discussed in numerical analysis texts.

• In optimization, it is usually desirable to find a solution as accurately as possible and overfitting is not considered directly. That is, the objective function is considered to be a completely accurate measure of what is sought; if generalization is one of the goals, it is assumed to be reflected in the objective function (e.g., via penalty terms). Similar considerations are encountered in the development of robust algorithms and the analysis of the sensitivity of the solutions obtained.

• It should be noted that if training is stopped when the error is less than a given tolerance, then it is usually the case that $E \neq 0$ and $\|\frac{\partial E}{\partial \mathbf{w}}\| \neq 0$ at the stopping point. This is contrary to the assumptions of some analyses. Some pruning algorithms, for example, assume $\|\frac{\partial E}{\partial \mathbf{w}}\| = 0$.

• There is nothing in these techniques that limits them to multilayer network structures. They can be applied to most other (continuous) neural network models as well.

• The optimization approach to training makes no claim of biological plausibility. Many of the methods are nonlocal, complex, and batch-oriented. The goal is simply to find a good set of weights for the problem at hand. Although back-propagation is not considered to be a particularly plausible model of learning in biological networks, it is at least driven by local computations.

• Neural networks are sometimes used as optimizing systems themselves, for example, the proposed use of Hopfield networks for solving the traveling salesman problem. The application of neural networks to problems normally cast as optimization or signal processing problems is considered in detail by Cichoki and Unbehaven [82].

• Shanno [341] discusses recent work in optimization methods in light of its utility to neural network training.

11 Genetic Algorithms and Neural Networks

One of the basic tasks in network design is to choose an architecture and weights appropriate for the given problem. The genetic algorithm (GA) [173, 141] is a general optimization method that has been applied to many problems including neural network training. It is appropriate for neural networks because it scales well to large nonlinear problems with multiple local minima.

As the name implies, the genetic algorithm is based on an analogy to natural evolutionary mechanisms. Many variations have been investigated, but the basic idea is competition between alternative solutions and "survival of the fittest." In this case, fitness is measured by a predefined objective function. Individuals in a large population have varying traits that affect their reproductive success in the given environment. Successful individuals live long enough to mate and pass their traits to their offspring. Offspring inherit traits from successful parents so they also have a good chance of being successful. Over many generations, the population adapts to its environment; disadvantageous traits become rare and the average fitness tends to increase over time.

One of the main advantages of the algorithm is that it requires very little problem-specific information. To apply the method to a specific problem, all that is needed is a fitness function that evaluates individual solutions and returns a rating of their quality, or "fitness." The algorithm itself operates on bit strings containing the "genetic code," that is, the parameters specifying a particular solution. Aside from the problem-specific evaluation function, all problems look the same to the algorithm, differing only in the length of the bit string and the number of units.

Because the algorithm needs so little problem-specific information, it is useful for complex problems that are difficult to analyze correctly. In particular, it does not need gradient information and so can be used on discontinuous functions and functions that are described empirically rather than analytically. It can also be used for temporal learning problems in which evaluation comes at the end of a long sequence of actions with no intermediate target values. It is not a simple hill-climbing method so it is not particularly bothered by local maxima. It will also tolerate a certain amount of noise in the evaluation function.

The algorithm has some of the flavor of simulated annealing in that many alternative solutions are examined and the search contains an element of randomness that helps prevent convergence to local maxima. It differs in that many candidate solutions are maintained rather than just one and elements of the better solutions are combined to generate new candidates. Like simulated annealing, it is a general optimization method that has applications beyond neural networks.

The main disadvantage of the method is the amount of computation needed to evaluate and store a large population of candidate solutions and converge to an optimum. Other techniques often converge faster when they can be used.

11.1   The Basic Algorithm

The basic operations are (1) selection based on fitness, (2) recombination of genetic mate-
rial by crossover, and (3) mutation. The algorithm operates on a population of many units.
Each unit has a bit string, its "genetic code," which encodes its solution to the given problem. The user supplies a problem-specific function that decodes the bit string, evaluates the
solution, and returns a value which is translated to a fitness score. The fitness score determines which units are selected for mating. High scoring solutions tend to be selected more
often than low scoring solutions and thus pass their characteristics to the next generation at
a higher rate.

   The basic algorithm starts with an initial population of N units with random parameters
encoded in a binary bit string. Larger population sizes generally increase the chance of
finding a good solution but, of course, require more processing time. The following steps
are repeated until a solution is found or patience is exhausted.

Evaluation.   Evaluate each unit and assign it a non-negative score (higher=better). Normalize by dividing by the sum of all scores to obtain fitness scores f_i in the range 0–1. If
any unit satisfies the goal criteria, discard the other units and stop.

Selection.   On N trials, select an individual i with probability f_i and copy it to the mating
population. Units can be selected with probability f_i by assigning each unit a segment of
the 0–1 interval proportional to its fitness and choosing a uniform random number; if the
number falls in the interval assigned to the kth unit then select unit k. In the case of three
units with fitness scores 0.1, 0.6, and 0.3, for example, the intervals would be 0–0.1, 0.1–
0.7, and 0.7–1.0. Figure 11.1 illustrates this by analogy to a roulette wheel where each unit
has a number of slots proportional to its fitness.

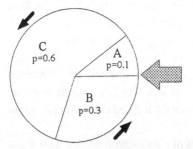

Figure 11.1
Selection. The genetic algorithm selects units for reproduction with probability proportional to their fitness. Units
with higher fitness (corresponding to more slots on the wheel) are more likely to be chosen than units with lower
fitness, but all units have some chance of being chosen.

Before crossover											
A	1	1	0	1	0	0	1	1	1	0	0	1
B	0	1	1	0	1	1	1	0	0	1	0	1

After crossover											
C	1	1	0	1	1	1	1	0	0	1	0	1
D	0	1	1	0	0	0	1	1	1	0	0	1

Figure 11.2
Crossover. Crossover mixes genetic codes inherited from two parents by crossing the bit strings at one or two random points. The bit strings encode characteristics of the parents so the offspring receives traits of both parents, but is not identical to either. The crossing point is random, so the mix of characteristics transferred varies with each mating.

Because of the element of chance, the number of times a unit reproduces will not be exactly proportional to its fitness, but, on average, if unit i has twice the fitness of unit j, then it will usually have about twice the offspring. Units with very low fitness ratings will rarely reproduce and face extinction.

Crossover.   Divide the mating population into pairs and mix their genetic information by crossing the bit strings at one or two random points. Figure 11.2 illustrates the operation. If units A and B have parameter strings 110100111001 and **011011100101**, for example , then they would produce offspring 011000111001 and **110111100101** if the crossing point is after position 4. The probability that crossover will occur is set by a parameter p_c. For $p_c < 1$, there is some chance that the parents simply survive in the next generation unaltered by crossover. This helps to preserve good solutions since some copies are likely to survive unchanged. Typical values are $p_c = 0.6$ to 0.9.

Mutation.   For each unit in the new set, flip each bit with some small probability; for example, $p_m \leq 0.001$. The number of mutations should be small to prevent deterioration of the algorithm into random search. The main purpose of mutation is to maintain population diversity. In general, p_m should be chosen so that mutations occur in only a small percentage of the population—in only one or two units for moderately sized populations.

Replacement.   Copy the newly created units to the working population. In some variations, new units replace their parents. In others, they replace the least fit units.

Many variations of the algorithm have been proposed. In the basic algorithm, all units have a chance to reproduce and large portions of parameter strings are exchanged during reproduction so it is possible for good solutions to be lost. One remedy is to allow only the most successful fraction of the population to mate, with their offspring replacing the less successful part of the population. Since the offspring do not replace their parents, this helps to preserve good solutions.

Other variations extend the biological analogy further by incorporating features such as paired chromosomes, dominance, inversion, and niche specialization. Some versions are Lamarckian, allowing adaptations made in the lifetime of a parent to be passed on to the offspring. Some vary the number of units that reproduce at each cycle. Some allow the population size to fluctuate and some maintain several subpopulations with only limited mixing. Goldberg [141] reviews many of these cases.

11.1.1   Effects of Crossover

By some accounts, crossover is responsible for most of the adaptive power of the algorithm. Crossover selects parameters from two good solutions and mixes them to create new combinations. The parent solutions were successful enough to be selected for reproduction so they presumably contain good parameter sets. Ideally, the offspring will inherit the best parameters from both parents and produce a new combination which is better than either.

Crossover is different from random search in that with crossover the offspring are in some sense intermediate between the two parents; they inherit some attributes from parent A and some from parent B but are identical to neither. This tends to confine the search to new combinations of parameters that have already proven useful. Random search, in contrast, is unguided and might create new units anywhere in the parameter space.

A *schemata* theory [141] has been developed to study how parameter strings evolve. A particular template of 1s, 0s and $*$s (don't cares) in a bit string, for example, $011***$ $*01***$, is called a *schema* (plural: schemata). Each bit in the string is simultaneously a component of many different schemata and each string simultaneously contains many overlapping schemata. Likewise, a single schema may be present in many strings in the population. The core idea is that a string containing a bit combination that is strongly correlated with good solutions is likely to be reproduced in the next generation. The *defining length* of a schema is the distance between its most separated defining bits. The distance between the leading 0 and the final 1 of $011***01***$, for example, is 8 bits. Schemata with long defining lengths contain widely separated significant bits and are more likely to be broken during crossover and thus less likely to survive than shorter schemata. Depending on how parameters are encoded in the bit string, this tends to make the algorithm favor low order, less complex, solutions over high order ones—usually a desirable feature for a learning algorithm.

11.1.2   Effects of Mutation

Mutation plays a rather small part in the standard algorithm. If the mutation rate is too large, the algorithm tends to degenerate into an inefficient random search. When all the units are very similar however, as in the final stages of convergence, crossover creates few new solutions and mutation becomes more important. Because all defining bits of a schema must survive mutation for the schema to survive, schemata with fewer defining bits are more likely to survive mutation than those with many defining bits. If simple solutions have representations in terms of small numbers of parameters (few bits), then this favors simpler and presumably more robust solutions. Overall, the combination of fitness selection, crossover, and mutation favors schemata with above average fitness, short defining length, and low order.

11.1.3 Fitness Scaling

Because the user-supplied evaluation function can be chosen arbitrarily, it is useful to scale the raw scores to obtain normalized fitness scores. If all units receive raw scores in the range from 1000 to 1005, for example, the best solutions would have very little advantage over the worst and the search would be essentially random. This might occur in late stages of the algorithm when most units are clustered around a good solution. Similarly, in early generations most units may have low raw scores and a unit that makes a significant (but not decisive) improvement may get a much higher score, allowing it to dominate the next generation and cause premature loss of population diversity. This effect is more important when populations are small.

Scaling of the raw scores helps prevent these problems. A linear transformation is often used to map the raw scores f to fitness values f'

$$f' = af + b.$$

In choosing a and b, it is desirable that $f_{avg} \rightarrow f'_{avg}$ so that one expects each average unit to produce one offspring. The number of offspring for the best unit is controlled by ensuring $f'_{max} = C_{mult} f_{avg}$, where C_{mult} is the desired number of offspring for the best unit. For small populations ($n = 50$ to 100), values of $C_{mult} = 1.2$ to 2 are suggested [141]. If this scaling results in negative scores, set them to 0. Other methods of fitness scaling are discussed by Goldberg [141].

11.2 Example

A very simple example illustrates the mechanics of the algorithm. Figure 11.3 shows the function

$$J(x) = 64 - (x - 7)^2.$$

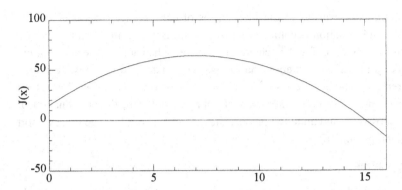

Figure 11.3
The function considered in the example.

for $0 \le x < 16$. Let the population consist of four units A, B, C, and D with solutions x encoded in 4-bit strings. (A simple function and small population were chosen to provide a clear example. Normal functions are not so simple and populations are larger.)

Units are initialized with random values for the first generation.

		Generation 1		
unit	x	bits	J	f_i
A	1	0 0 0 1	28	0.1854
B	9	1 0 0 1	60	0.3973
C	15	1 1 1 1	0	0
D	6	0 1 1 0	63	0.4742

After random selection weighted by fitness, the population is A, B, D, D. Unit C with fitness 0 has died and unit D, with the highest fitness, is selected twice.

	New Population
unit	
A	0 0 0 1
B	1 0 0 1
D	0 1 1 0
D	0 1 1 0

A mates to *D* and *B* mates to *D*, both with crossover after the 3rd bit.

Mating results

unit	
a	0 0 0 **0**
b	1 0 0 **0**
c	0 1 1 **1**
d	0 1 1 **1**

Mutation flips the 3rd bit in *a*.

Mutation results

unit	
a	0 0 **1** 0
b	1 0 0 0
c	0 1 1 1
d	0 1 1 1

The resulting population after one generation is

Generation 2

unit	x	bits	J	f_i
a	2	0 0 1 0	39	0.1696
b	8	1 0 0 0	63	0.2739
c	7	0 1 1 1	64	0.2782
d	7	0 1 1 1	64	0.2782

Units *c* and *d* have already reached the maximum of the function at $x = 7$ and the average score has increased from 37.75 to 57.75.

11.3   Application to Neural Network Design

The genetic algorithm is a general purpose optimization algorithm with applications beyond neural network design. It can be applied to network design in a number of ways—
from simply determining a few weights in a predetermined network to choosing the entire architecture: the number of layers and nodes, connections, weight values and node

functions. Because it does not need gradient information, it can be used on networks with binary units and/or quantized weights.

Several things should be considered in applying the algorithm to neural networks. One of the more important factors is the representation—how problem parameters are encoded in the bit string. Neural networks often have many weights so the parameter string may be long. Because crossover breaks the string, it is desirable to put related parameters near each other in the bit string as much possible. Network weights tend to be strongly interrelated, however, with values of weights in one layer depending on the values of many weights in other layers. This means that the useful schemata often have high order and are easily broken by mutation and crossover. This interdependence leads some [102] to eliminate the crossover operation; this is not typical however.

The following paragraphs describe some applications of the algorithm to neural network design.

Training and Evaluation   Some implementations [209] include a small amount of training in the fitness evaluation function. The idea is that one set of weights, A, might be worse that another set B, but set A might be much better than B after a small amount of training because of differences in the local terrain of the error space. In this case, unit A is closer to the solution than B even though it is initial performance is worse. Without training, the algorithm learns only the fitness of the initial point in the space. With training, each unit attempts to find the best spot reachable from its initial position; its fitness reflects the quality of a small area around the initial point so the algorithm searches more of the parameter space.

As in nature, the fitness of each unit is evaluated based on its performance after adaptation, but reproduction transmits the original parameters rather than the adapted parameters. The performance of a unit (in a sense) reflects the nearness of good solutions, and reproduction will tend to produce more offspring near good units, so the algorithm will tend to converge to good solutions.

Only a small amount of training is allowed, typically 5 to 10% of what would be required to train a random net to completion. If all units were trained to convergence, they could converge to the same or equivalent solutions and all units would have the same reproductive fitness regardless of the quality of their genes. In [209], it was found useful to allow each unit a different number of training cycles. Over a number of generations, this effectively measures the sensitivity of the gene to learning and rewards units which improve quickly with a small amounts of additional learning.

Subpopulations   In nature, isolation of subpopulations is one factor that contributes to the development of new species. The use of several subpopulations with limited mixing

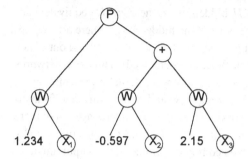

Figure 11.4
Representation of a neural network as a LISP expression. W represents a multiplication operation by an input weight and P represents a summation and the node nonlinearity.

allows aggressive optimization within each subpopulation while preserving diversity in the total population [398]. This is said to be more effective in preserving diversity than simply increasing the population size. One-at-a-time reproduction is used with fitness based on rank. The offspring do not replace their parents; they replace the worst units so good solutions are certain to survive.

GA Pruning of Neural Networks The genetic algorithm can also be used to prune neural networks [397]. Typically, the parameter string contains a bit for each weight in the original network; the bit is 1 if the connection is retained and 0 if it is pruned. The result of pruning is networks that are smaller, learn faster, and may generalize better.

Genetic Programming A related algorithm is *genetic programming* [221, 222, 223]. Koza and Rice [224] describe an algorithm to determine both the weights and connection architecture of a neural net. The network response function is encoded in a tree-structured LISP expression (figure 11.4) and the crossover operation exchanges subtrees between two parents. The major use of this representation has been outside of neural networks. It has been used for evolutionary adaptation of functions or programs whose statements have syntactic structure; it is useful because the subtree crossover operation preserves syntactic correctness.

11.3.1 Incompatible Genomes

A difficulty with application of the standard genetic algorithm to neural network optimization is the problem of incompatible genomes. In general, two successful individuals do not always yield a successful offspring when they mate; their bit-strings might represent points on two different local maxima and the combination might fall in a valley between them, for example. In a neural network with H hidden units, there are $H!$ equivalent solutions obtainable by shuffling the order of the units in the hidden layer. There are another 2^H equivalent solutions obtainable by changing the signs of all weights into and out of any combination of hidden units (which leaves their function unchanged). Thus, two networks might compute identical input-output functions using different internal representations in which case the network obtained by mixing their weights would be very different from either and probably a poor solution. Neural networks also tend to be underconstrained; there are often many different input-output functions that satisfy the objective function equally well so equally successful networks may not even compute a similar input-output function.

The effect is that little progress is made until a significant fraction of the population compute similar functions with similar internal representations. Once a cluster of compatible networks develops, they have a higher probability of mating successfully and may grow to dominate the population at the expense of possibly better isolated solutions. The system then does local hill-climbing and is unlikely to explore very different solutions. This produces a strong tendency to converge to local maxima since the particular solution that comes to dominate initially is a nearly random selection. In theory, this doesn't have to happen, but it's likely if parameters are chosen for fast convergence (e.g., small populations and aggressive culling). Variations have been proposed to avoid these problems but they complicate the algorithm.

11.4   Remarks

The genetic algorithm is a general stochastic search method that has been used successfully in a number of ways for neural network design [3, 4, 50, 52, 66, 68, 108, 109, 155, 156, 304, 319]. Its main advantages are that it requires very little problem-specific information and is relatively insensitive to local maxima (minima). The algorithm itself is relatively easy to implement. Unlike some other search techniques, it does not require detailed problem-specific knowledge in order to generate new search candidates. Gradients are not required so the algorithm can be applied to discontinuous functions or functions that are defined empirically rather than analytically. It is applicable to mixed problems containing both continuous and discrete variables.

Its main disadvantage is the amount of processing required to evaluate and store a large number of different network configurations. Although the actual bit manipulations take very little time, the user-supplied objective function must be evaluated many times and this can be very slow with large networks and large training sets. It is worth noting, however, that the candidate solutions can be evaluated independently so N parallel processors should give close to a factor of N reduction in computation time.

Another caveat is that although the algorithm itself needs little problem-specific information, the efficiency of the search and the quality of the results depend heavily on how parameters are represented in the bit string. This is quite problem dependent and use of the algorithm may involve experimenting with several different representations to find one that works well.

Although there are claims of convergence to global maxima of the fitness function, convergence to local maxima is possible with small populations and aggressive culling of less successful solutions. Also, there are many parameters to be selected (population size, mutation rate, crossover method, fitness scaling, etc.) and it is not obvious how these affect the convergence properties.

Because the main theoretical advantage of the algorithm is its global optimization property and its main disadvantage is its inefficiency, it may be useful to use the algorithm in conjunction with more efficient local search methods. For example, the genetic algorithm might be used to do a coarsely quantized search to find the region containing the global minimum and then more efficient methods used to fine tune the solution in this region.

12 Constructive Methods

One of the major tasks in the design of a network is the selection of an architecture and its configuration. How many layers should the network have, with how many nodes in each layer? Should every node in a layer connect to every node in the following layer? Obviously the best structure depends on the problem and performance may be poor if the structure is inappropriate. If there are too few units, the final error is likely to be large; training may not converge or may be very sensitive to initial conditions. If there are too many units, training times may be long and generalization may suffer.

Normally we just want to find a structure that works for the given problem. Although this is much easier than determining the theoretically optimum architecture, it may still be very difficult to decide a priori what architecture and size are appropriate for a problem. Some heuristics are available, but there are no dependable general rules for choosing a structure before training. A common ad hoc approach is to experiment with different configurations until one is found that works well. Unfortunately, this may be time consuming if many networks have to be tested before an adequate one is found.

Constructive methods attempt to adapt the size of the network to the problem by starting with a small network and adding layers and units as needed until a solution is found. The major advantage is that there is no need to make an a priori estimate of the correct network size. An unfortunate choice will not immediately condemn the network to failure and the trial-and-error search for a good size is avoided.

Theoretical Support There are good theoretical reasons for considering constructive algorithms. As noted in section 5.7, a common complaint about back-propagation is that it is too slow. The training time also appears to grow quickly as the problem size increases. Judd [204, 202] has shown that loading problem is NP-complete. That is, the training time scales exponentially with network size in the worst case. (The loading problem is the task of finding weight values such that the network imitates the training data, i.e., the task of "loading" the data into the network.) Baum and Rivest [35] showed that the problem is NP-complete even for networks containing as few as three neurons.

These results are an indication of the intrinsic difficulty of the computational problem, independent of the training algorithm. All algorithms, no matter how efficient, that deal with the task as it is posed face the same exponential scaling behavior and become impractical on very large problems. These results make it appear "unlikely that any algorithm which simply varies weights on a net of fixed size and topology can learn in polynomial time" [31: 201]. Baum [31], however, suggests that the difficulty is due to the constraint of a fixed network structure that only allows the algorithm to adjust existing weights. Algorithms with the freedom to add units and weights "can solve in polynomial time any learning problem that can be solved in polynomial time by any algorithm whatever. In this sense, neural nets are universal learners, capable of learning any learnable class of concepts" [31: 201].

A trivial example is an algorithm that simply allocates a node for every example in the training set to create a network that functions as a lookup table. Of course, more efficient solutions are generally preferred. Several types of non-MLP neural networks, for example, ART and radial basis function networks, can be thought of as adding new units when necessary to fit new data. Most learn much faster than MLPs trained by back-propagation.

Constructive Methods vs. Pruning Methods   Constructive methods complement pruning methods (chapter 13), which train a larger-than-necessary network and then remove unneeded elements. Both are means of adapting the network size to the problem at hand. Although pruning methods can be effective, they require an estimate of what size is "larger than necessary." Constructive methods can build a network without this estimate.

Because constructive methods sometimes add more nodes than necessary, it is often useful to follow with a pruning phase. In some algorithms the processes compete simultaneously, one attempting to add nodes while the other tries to remove them. At some point, the processes balance and the structure stabilizes.

When to Stop Adding Units   An issue that must be considered with constructive methods is when to stop adding new units. In general, the training-set error can be made as small as desired by adding more units, but the law of diminishing returns predicts that each additional unit will produce less and less benefit. The question is whether the incremental error reduction is worth the cost of the additional units in processing time, storage requirements, and hardware costs. For continuous problems, an infinite number of units might be needed to achieve zero error. One generally must declare some nonzero error to be acceptably small and stop when it is achieved.

Aside from the question of efficiency, there is the problem of overfitting and generalization. Chapter 14 discusses a number of factors affecting generalization. Briefly, the problem is that when training on sampled data (which may contain noise and have other imperfections), the error on the training set is only an estimate of the true error. The two error functions tend to be similar but slightly different so a change that reduces one will not always reduce the other. Usually, they have large-scale similarities with small-scale differences. As the network fits the large scale features of the training-set in the initial stages of training, both errors tend to decrease together as learning progresses. At some point, however, the network starts to fit small-scale features where the two functions differ and additional training starts to have a detrimental effect on the true error. Improvements in the training error no longer correspond to improvements in the generalization error and the network begins to overfit the data. Thus, for good generalization, it is often desirable to stop training before the training-set error reaches zero. Some implementations avoid the problem by passing it to the pruning algorithm; the constructive phase is allowed to continue well past the point of overfitting and then followed with pruning to satisfy generalization criteria.

Network Size versus Training Time   A secondary advantage of constructive algorithms is that overall training times may be shorter because useful learning occurs when the network is still small. That is, even if a small network cannot satisfy the error criteria, it may learn the dominant characteristics of the target function and thereby simplify learning in later stages. With nonconstructive methods, an inadequate network would be abandoned and anything it learned would have to be relearned by the next network tested. With constructive methods, the learning is retained and finer details are picked up as more nodes are added.

There seems to be a trade-off between training time and network size with fast algorithms tending to produce larger, less efficient networks. Many algorithms train the network until the error stops decreasing and then add more units and resume training, repeating until the error is acceptably small. The problem is that plateaus in the error versus time curve are common with back-propagation training of MLP networks. The $E(t)$ error curve often has long flat intervals followed by a sharp drop. In a flat region, it may be difficult to tell if the error has reached its final minimum or if it will decrease further if we let it train longer. A constructive algorithm that does not wait long enough may add unnecessary units; one that waits too long just wastes time. Thus, if one is impatient, the resulting network may be larger than necessary and may not generalize as well as possible. This is another reason for combining constructive and pruning methods.

There are, of course, more sophisticated methods of testing for (near) convergence than thresholding the $E(t)$ slope. Second derivative information in the form of the Hessian matrix (or at least its diagonal elements) may be useful, but will not entirely solve the problem because of the nonlinearity of the problem.

12.1   Dynamic Node Creation

For networks trained by back-propagation and similar methods, the most common procedure is to add new units when the error E reaches a (nonzero) plateau and stops decreasing, presumably because it's in a local minimum. The triggering condition used by Ash [11] (summarized in [277]) is

$$\frac{|E(t) - E(t - \delta)|}{E(t_o)} < \Delta_T \qquad (t \geq t_o + \delta) \tag{12.1}$$

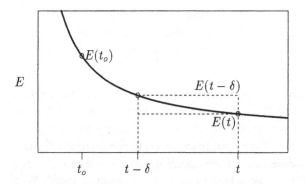

Figure 12.1
In many constructive algorithms, new units are added when the rate of improvement of the training error becomes small. Normalization by the magnitude of the error $E(t_o)$ obtained after the previous unit was added makes the triggering condition less dependent on the size of the error.

where t_o is the time at which the previous new node was added, δ is an interval over which the slope is measured, and Δ_T is the trigger value (figure 12.1). The requirement $(t \geq t_o + \delta)$ allows the network some time to adapt to the addition of the previous node before another is added.

The decision to stop is made by observing the size of the largest errors. The reasoning is that with cost functions like MSE, the error can often be reduced by making small improvements on many easy cases while ignoring large errors on a few difficult cases. As a result, the worst error may increase even as the average error decreases. Both errors tend to jump discontinuously when new units are added. The average error is normally small in later stages of learning so discontinuities in it might not be obvious, but the worst error is usually relatively large and often drops significantly when the critical number of units is reached. (This assumes that the data is consistent, however. If two training patterns with identical inputs have different targets, then no number of units will be able to reduce the worst error to zero.)

Hirose, Yamashita, and Hijiya [170] describe a similar method for adding nodes to a single-hidden-layer network when training stalls. The total error is evaluated periodically, for example, after every 100 weight updates. If it has not decreased significantly, for example, by at least 1%, then a new node is added. Note that these values probably depend on problem size and difficulty. For networks with many weights or problems with many training patterns, it may be necessary to wait longer before deciding that the network is stalled. An algorithm that does not wait long enough could add nodes continuously.

New nodes are added with small random initial weights. This perturbs the solution and usually causes the error to increase. The error normally decreases in subsequent training, however, which prevents the algorithm from immediately adding another new node in the next cycle. The perturbation could be avoided by initializing the new node with zero-valued weights, but zero-valued weights tend to remain near zero under back-propagation so $E(t)$ would remain flat and a new node would be added at the next opportunity, leading to a proliferation of redundant nodes with very small weights.

Since this procedure can only add nodes, the network may become very large. This is generally undesirable so the training phase is followed by a pruning phase which removes unnecessary nodes. Any reasonable pruning algorithm would probably work; the following method is used by Hirose, Yamashita, and Hijiya [170]. One node is removed at a time and the network is retrained; if it converges, then another hidden node is removed and so on. At some point, the network will not converge after removal of a node; the node is restored and the process halted. In the simulations described, the most recently added hidden nodes were removed first.

12.2 Cascade-Correlation

Fahlman and Lebiere [120] describe the cascade-correlation algorithm. New hidden units are added one at a time with each new unit receiving connections from the external inputs and *all* existing hidden units. Figure 12.2 shows the resulting (nonlayered) structure. Input

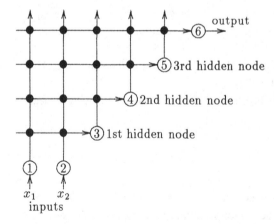

Figure 12.2
Cascade-correlation adds hidden units one at a time. Each new unit receives connections (shown as solid dots) from the external inputs and all existing hidden units. Its input weights are chosen to maximize the covariance of its response with the residual output error. Weights into existing hidden units remain unchanged. Then the weights from all the hidden units (new and old) to the output node are retrained to minimize the error. If the resulting error is acceptable, the network is complete; otherwise a new hidden unit is added and the process repeated.

weights to the new unit are chosen to maximize the correlation (covariance) of its response with the remaining output error. The unit is then added to the network and the weights from all the hidden units (new and old) to the output node are retrained to minimize the error. If the resulting error is acceptable, the network is complete; otherwise a new hidden unit is added and the process repeated.

The Algorithm   The algorithm begins with a network with no hidden units; inputs are connected directly to the outputs. The output nodes are usually sigmoidal, but linear nodes might be used for continuous mapping problems. The following steps are repeated until the error is acceptably small:

1. Train the weights of the output node(s) using any appropriate algorithm. Single-layer training rules such as the Widrow-Hoff delta rule or the perceptron learning algorithm may be used. There is no need to back-propagate errors through the hidden units since their input weights are frozen.

2. When no significant error improvement has occurred after a certain number of training cycles, evaluate the error. If it is small enough, stop.

3. Otherwise create a new unit with connections from the inputs and all pre-existing hidden units. Select its weights to maximize S, the magnitude of the covariance of the new unit's response V with the residual error

$$S = \sum_o \left| \sum_p (V_p - \overline{V})(E_{p,o} - \overline{E_o}) \right| \tag{12.2}$$

where o indexes the output units and p indexes the training patterns. The quantities $\overline{V}$ and $\overline{E_o}$ are the averages of V and E_o over all patterns.

   S can be maximized iteratively by gradient ascent. The derivative of S with respect to the ith weight is

$$\frac{\partial S}{\partial w_i} = \sum_{p,o} \sigma_o (E_{p,o} - \overline{E_o}) f'_p I_{i,p} \tag{12.3}$$

where σ_o is the sign of the correlation between the candidate's value and the output o, f'_p is the derivative of the candidate unit's activation function with respect to the sum of its inputs for pattern p, and $I_{i,p}$ is the input the unit receives from unit i for pattern p.

   When S stops improving, the new unit is added to the network and its input weights are frozen.

4. Go to step 1.

Only the magnitude of the new unit's correlation with the residual error is important, hence the absolute value in the formula for S. If the correlation is positive, a negative output weight can be chosen to decrease the error; if the correlation is negative, a positive output weight will do.

A variation of the algorithm is to allocate a pool of candidate units with random initial input weights. Let each maximize S individually and select the best for addition to the network. This decreases the possibility of adding a useless unit that got stuck during training and it explores more of the weight space simultaneously. Other types of units besides sigmoidal (e.g., radial Gaussian) may also be included in the candidate pool.

When the output weights are being trained, all other weights are frozen. Because the activations of the hidden units depend only on the input pattern and do not change when the output weights change, there is no need to recalculate their response to each input pattern. If sufficient memory is available, the hidden unit responses can be stored in an array for quick retrieval rather than recalculated with each pattern presentation. This can significantly speed up simulations of large networks.

Remarks

• There is no need to guess the best architecture before training. Cascade-correlation builds reasonable, but not optimal, networks automatically.

• Input weights for new hidden nodes are chosen to maximize S, the covariance of the node response with the remaining output error. This is not the same as minimizing the error and won't be optimal in general.

• The procedure generally doesn't find the smallest possible network for a problem and has a tendency to create deep networks so a final pruning phase may be desirable.

• Cascade-correlation learns quickly. Unlike back-propagation, training doesn't slow down dramatically as the number of hidden layers increases because only the output weights are retrained each time. For the problems studied, the learning time in epochs grows approximately as $N \log N$ where N is the number of hidden nodes finally needed to solve the problem [120]. On the two-spirals problem (figure 12.3), an average of just 1700 epochs was needed.

• Although cascade-correlation learns quickly, it can overfit the data [88]. Pruning or early-stopping based on cross-validation may be necessary to avoid overfitting; however, reasonably good generalization as measured by insensitivity to input noise was found in [149]. There, nets created by cascade-correlation tended to have saturated hidden nodes whose values change little when small amounts of noise are added to the inputs.

Figure 12.3
The two-spirals problem [233] is sometimes used as a benchmark for constructive algorithms because it requires careful coordination of many hidden nodes and is difficult to learn with simple back-propagation in a MLP network. (It is not representative of most real-world problems, however.) In a single-hidden-layer architecture, 40 or more hidden nodes are generally needed and training times are long. Most successful solutions use more than one hidden layer; some use short-cut connections.

• Hidden-unit input weights are frozen after the unit is added, so features detected by the unit will not be unlearned if the network is retrained with new data. This helps stabilize learning if the training data changes over time.

• "Divide and conquer," a similar method, is described in [322]. Unlike some other algorithms, it can create multiple hidden layers. Unlike cascade-correlation, it can create hidden layers with more than one node and it doesn't use a correlation measure. Like cascade-correlation, nodes are trained one-at-a-time with weights in other nodes held constant. As a result, back-propagation through hidden nodes is never necessary.

• A cascade-correlation architecture for recurrent networks is described by Fahlman [119]. A procedure similar to cascade-correlation, but using error minimization rather than co-variance maximization is described by Littmann and Ritter [248]; benchmarks of cascade-correlation are also included.

12.3 The Upstart Algorithm

Frean [128] describes the upstart algorithm for learning binary mappings with layered networks of linear threshold units. It will converge to zero error for any Boolean mapping, including problems that require hidden units. The networks that result are often smaller than those of the tiling algorithm (see later discussion).

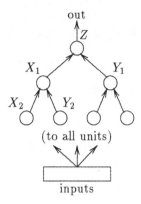

Figure 12.4
The upstart algorithm [128] starts with a single output unit Z. If errors remain after training, then daughter units X and Y are inserted to correct it. Ideally, X corrects Z when it is wrongly ON and Y corrects Z when it is wrongly OFF. If either X or Y cannot correct all the errors assigned to them, additional subunits are introduced to correct their errors and so on. The result is a tree structure for which there is an equivalent single-hidden-layer network.

The idea is that a unit Z can make two types of errors: "wrongly ON" and "wrongly OFF." A wrongly ON error can be corrected by adding a negative connection from a unit X, which is ON only when Z is wrongly ON. Likewise, a wrongly OFF error can be corrected by adding a strong positive connection from a unit Y which is ON only when Z is wrongly OFF.

The algorithm starts with a single output unit Z with weights chosen to separate as many of the training points as possible. If errors remain, daughter units X and Y are created to correct Z when it is wrong. Ideally, X corrects all the wrongly ON errors and Y corrects all the wrongly OFF errors. If either cannot correct all the errors assigned to them, additional subunits are introduced to correct their errors and so forth. Each new unit can always correct at least one error so the number of errors decreases at each step and the process eventually terminates when all patterns are classified correctly. The result is a tree structure (figure 12.4) for which there is an equivalent single-hidden-layer network.

The Algorithm The weights from the inputs to the output Z are trained to minimize the error and then frozen. Perceptron learning [325, 284] can be used, but will not converge to a stable solution if the patterns are not linearly separable. The "pocket" algorithm [133] can also be used. The following steps are then repeated recursively, first for Z, then for each of the daughter units X and Y, then for their daughters, and so on.

1. If Z makes any wrongly ON mistakes, create a new unit X. The targets for X are $\{o_z^\mu \wedge \neg t_z^\mu\}$ where o_z^μ and t_z^μ are the output and target for node Z on pattern μ. (The symbols

$\wedge$ and $\neg$ indicate the logical AND and NOT operations.) That is, X is designed to turn ON when Z is wrongly ON. When Z is ON and its target value is OFF, the target for X is ON; otherwise the target for X is OFF. The patterns for which both Z and the target are OFF can be eliminated from X's training set although this is not necessary.

Similarly, if Z makes any wrongly OFF mistakes, create a new unit Y with targets $\{\neg o_z^\mu \wedge t_z^\mu\}$. The patterns for which Z and the target are both ON can be eliminated from Y's training set.

2. Connect the outputs of X and Y to Z. The weight from X is large-negative and the weight from Y is large-positive. The size of the $X(Y)$ weight needs to exceed the sum of Z's positive (negative) input weights. These weights can be set explicitly, or by an appropriate training procedure.

3. Go to 1 and repeat recursively. That is, correct the errors of X and Y by generating two daughters for each.

The algorithm builds a binary tree of units from the output down to the inputs. The daughter nodes X and Y have an easier problem to solve than does Z. Each new unit can separate at least one of the incorrect patterns so they will always make fewer errors than their parent and will reduce the number of errors made by the parent if connected to it by appropriate weights. Daughter units are created only if the parent makes errors. The number of errors decreases with every branching, so at some stage none of the daughters will make any errors. This means their parents will not either and so on up to the top of the tree. As noted, some of the patterns for X and Y can be eliminated. This is not necessary, but speeds up training by a factor of about two [128].

Frean [128] shows that the resulting tree structure can be converted to an equivalent single-hidden-layer structure if the unnecessary patterns are not eliminated. The original Z unit and all the hidden units are placed in a single layer with the connections between them eliminated and a new output unit is created. The weights from the hidden units to the new output unit can be found by the perceptron algorithm, or by inspection of the tree structure.

12.4   The Tiling Algorithm

Mézard and Nadal [265] describe the tiling algorithm (figure 12.5) for constructing multi-layer networks of linear threshold units to solve binary mapping problems. It should also be suitable for mappings from continuous inputs to binary outputs.

Units are added a layer at a time from the inputs upward. The first unit in each hidden layer is called the master unit. It attempts to classify as many of the training patterns as possible based on the input from the previous layer. It is always possible to create a new master unit on the current layer that will make at least one less error than the master unit of

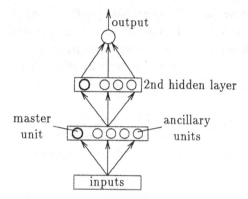

Figure 12.5
The tiling algorithm [265] adds a new hidden layer at each iteration. A master unit in each layer attempts to classify as many patterns as possible based on input from the preceding layer. If it cannot classify all patterns correctly, then 'ancillary' units are added until the layer produces a 'faithful' representation such that any two input patterns with different targets produce a different pattern of activity on the layer. This then serves as input for the next layer. It is always possible to create a master unit which makes fewer errors than the master unit in the previous layer so convergence is guaranteed if enough layers are added.

the preceding layer. Thus, if enough layers are created, the final master unit will not make any errors. Convergence is guaranteed because the number of layers required is limited by the number of patterns to be learned.

If the newly created master unit still makes some errors then additional "ancillary" units are added to the layer until it produces a "faithful representation" of the training patterns such that any two input patterns with distinct targets produce different patterns of activity on the layer.

The Algorithm

1. Create a master unit for the new hidden layer and train it to separate as many of the input patterns as possible.

2. If the new unit produces the correct responses for all patterns, then it is the final output unit. Stop.

3. Otherwise, add ancillary units to create a faithful representation on the current layer.

4. Go to 1.

These steps are explained in more detail in the following.

Generating the Master Unit   Assume there are p_o patterns to be learned and that the preceding layer $L - 1$ has been established. Layer $L = 0$ is taken to be the input layer. At layer L, let $\tau^\mu = (\tau_j^\mu)$, be the vector of activity patterns, or "prototypes," generated in the preceding layer. $\mu = 1, \ldots, p_{L-1}$ indexes activity patterns and $j = 0, \ldots, N_{L-1}$ indexes nodes in the previous layer ($j = 0$ is the index of a bias node and $j = 1$ is the index of the master unit in the preceding layer). A number V_μ of different input patterns may be represented by the same prototype τ^μ, $\sum_\mu V_\mu = p_o$. Let μ_o be the index of one of the patterns for which the master unit of the preceding layer makes an error, that is $\tau_1^{\mu_o} = -s^{\mu_o}$, where $s^{\mu_o} = \pm 1$ is the desired target.

The set of weights $w_1 = 1$ and $w_{j \neq 1} = \lambda s^{\mu_o} \tau_j^{\mu_o}$, $1/N_{L-1} < \lambda < 1/(N_{L-1} - 2)$ ensures that this master unit will make at least one less error than the master unit in the preceding layer. Let $\lambda = 1/(N_{L-1} - 1)$. When pattern μ_o is again presented, the unit output will be

$$m^{\mu_o} = \text{sgn}\left(\sum_{j=0}^{N_{L-1}} w_j \tau_j^{\mu_o}\right) \tag{12.4}$$

$$= \text{sgn}\left(\tau_1^{\mu_o} + s^{\mu_o} \lambda N_{L-1}\right)$$

$$= s^{\mu_o} \quad \text{if } \lambda > 1/N_{L-1}$$

so the pattern μ_o is stabilized. When another pattern μ is presented for which $\tau_1^\mu = s^\mu$ the unit output will be

$$m^\mu = \text{sgn}\left(\tau_1^\mu + s^{\mu_o} \lambda \sum_{j \neq 1, j=0}^{N_{L-1}} \tau_j^{\mu_o} \tau_j^\mu\right). \tag{12.5}$$

If $\mu \neq \mu_o$ then the sum is less than or equal $N_{L-1} - 2$ so if $\lambda < 1/(N_{L-1} - 2)$ then $m^\mu = \text{sgn}(\tau_1^\mu)$ and the classification of pattern μ is preserved. Thus, with this set of weights, the current layer will also stabilize prototype μ_o in addition to all the prototypes μ stabilized in layer $L - 1$,

If the unit is initialized with this set of weights and trained by the pocket algorithm [133] then the final set of weights will be at least as good. If training converges to zero error, then the new unit is the desired output. This happens when the targets are linearly separable in terms of the preceding layer activities. Otherwise ancillary units must be created.

Creating Ancillary Units   If the master unit still makes errors, then ancillary units must be created so that the layer generates a unique pattern of activity for all input patterns with different targets. Assume the preceding layer generates $p = p_{L-1}$ distinct prototypes $\tau^\mu = \tau_i^\mu$ where $i = 0, \ldots, N$ and $N = N_{L-1}$. The p prototypes are a faithful representation by construction. Each τ^μ is the prototype of one faithful class of the $(L-1)$th layer. The current layer must produce a mapping from these p patterns.

Suppose $1 + N'$ units have already been created and they produce p' distinct representations. In general, $p' < p$. If the p' patterns are not a faithful representation, then at least one activity pattern on this layer doesn't have a unique target. One of the unfaithful classes is selected and the next unit is trained to produce the mapping $\tau^\mu \to s^\mu$ for patterns μ belonging only to the unfaithful class. In the best case, the mapping will be learned perfectly and the unfaithful class will be broken into two faithful classes. Often, however, the mapping will not be linearly separable. In such cases it is possible to break the unfaithful class into two classes—one faithful and one unfaithful. In the worst case, the faithful class may consist of just one prototype.

This is repeated until the layer generates a faithful representation. In practice, if more than one unfaithful class exists, the smallest is selected first. If the new unit is able to separate this class successfully, then the next largest unfaithful class is also attempted with the same unit. As a result, each new unit breaks at least one class into two classes and at most p units are needed to create a faithful representation.

Other Notes

• For multiple output problems, a master unit can be created in each layer for each of the outputs.

• Results of simulations are described by Mézard and Nadal [265] for N-bit parity $N \leq 10$ and random Boolean functions $N \leq 8$. Random Boolean functions with $N = 8$ required an average of 7 hidden layers and about 55 hidden neurons. In comparison, a single-hidden-layer AND-OR network would require on the order of 2^8 hidden units to compute random functions. A typical function would require about 128 units.

• Simulations show that, in general, the number of units per layer decreases with each successive layer.

12.5   Marchand's Algorithm

Marchand, Golea, and Ruján [256] describe a method for constructing a one-hidden-layer network of linear threshold units to solve binary mapping problems (figure 12.6). It is always possible to classify N input patterns by creating N hidden nodes, each of which recognizes one of the patterns. The network would act like a look-up table and the number of nodes needed would grow linearly with the size of the problem. But this fails to capture correlations in the training data and the resulting network does not generalize well. Usually it is better if each hidden unit recognizes as many patterns as possible.

The algorithm described by Marchand, Golea, and Ruján adds hidden units sequentially. The weights of each new unit are chosen to split a group of patterns with like targets from

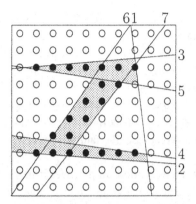

Figure 12.6
The algorithm of Marchand, Golea, and Ruján [256] creates a single-hidden-layer network of linear threshold units by adding hidden units sequentially. Each new unit slices off a group of training patterns that share the same target value. Filled and empty circles represent training points with positive and negative targets. Lines show the hidden unit decision surfaces; the numbers to the side indicate the order in which the hidden units were created. All points are classified correctly, although some are very close to the boundary.

the rest of the data. On one side of the hyperplane defined by the unit, all patterns have the same target value; on the other side, target values may be mixed. The separated patterns are then removed from the working set and the procedure repeated with additional hidden units. Each new hidden unit slices off another set of training patterns that share the same target. The procedure stops when all remaining patterns have the same target.

It is always possible to separate at least one pattern from the rest so in the worst case, no more than $N - 1$ nodes will be needed to recognize N patterns. In practice though, the patterns are often correlated because of regularities in the target function and clustering in the input distribution. Most slices can then remove more than one pattern so fewer than $N - 1$ nodes will be required in general.

The procedure sequentially creates h hidden units, which partition the input space into a number of regions, each containing one or more training patterns that share the same target. The resulting internal representation is linearly separable in that the desired target values can be generated from the hidden unit activities with no need for more hidden layers. The weight u_j from the jth hidden unit to the output unit can be found by the perceptron algorithm or it can be set as

$$u_j = 2^{h-j+1} \quad (\text{for } j = 1, \ldots, h) \tag{12.6}$$

$$u_o = \sum_{i=1}^{h} s_i u_i - s_h \qquad \text{bias weight} \tag{12.7}$$

where $-s_h$ is the target of the $(h + 1)$th cluster. These weights increase exponentially; the perceptron algorithm will generally find a different set.

Selection of Hidden Unit Weights   To obtain small networks, it is desirable for each hidden unit to slice off as many patterns as possible that share the same target. The following greedy procedure is simple, but not always optimal.

When adding hidden unit k, the working space has N^+ patterns with positive target $+1$ and N^- patterns with target -1. The procedure in [256] tries to find two weight vectors: one that excludes the largest number M^+ of positive patterns and one that excludes the largest number M^- of negative patterns. The vector with the largest ratio M^+/N^+ (or M^-/N^-) is then chosen.

To find the weight vector that maximizes M^+, a pattern ξ^μ with a positive target is chosen and weights are selected so that the unit has a $+1$ output for this pattern and a -1 output for all other patterns, $w_{kj} = \xi_j^\mu$, $j = 1, \ldots N_i$, with bias $w_{ko} = 1 - N_i$. At this point, all -1 patterns and pattern ξ^μ are correctly classified, but some of the other $+1$ patterns may be misclassified. One of the misclassified patterns is chosen and the perceptron rule is used to change the weights to also correctly classify the additional pattern without causing ξ^μ and the -1 patterns to be misclassified. If it succeeds, the change is accepted and the algorithm goes on to try another misclassified pattern. If it fails, another pattern is tried. After all the misclassified $+1$ patterns have been considered, the vector separates a certain number v_1 of the $+1$ patterns, but some are still misclassified (unless the patterns are linearly separable). This current weight vector is saved and all the properly classified $+1$ patterns are removed from the working set. The procedure is then repeated starting with another misclassified pattern to generate another weight vector. All $+1$ patterns, including the ones excluded by the first vector, are considered when computing the number v_2 excluded by the second vector. v_2 and v_1 are compared to choose the better weight vector. This is repeated until the best weight vector is found. A similar procedure maximizes M^-.

Remarks   Simulation results for the parity function, random binary functions, and the mirror symmetry problem are discussed by Marchand, Golea, and Ruján [256]. (The target in the symmetry problem is $+1$ if a vector of binary bits is symmetric about its center.) The net found for the symmetry problem was optimal; a similar solution could not be found by the tiling algorithm.

The search for hidden unit weight vectors may take a long time because it searches to find the one vector that excludes the largest number of patterns. The procedure starts with one pattern, say p_{start}, and scans all the other (positive) patterns to see if they are also separable with p_{start}. Then it increments p_{start} to the next pattern. This is a loop over all patterns inside another loop over all patterns so there are $O(M^2)$ steps (where M is the number of patterns), each of which calls the perceptron learning algorithm. For many problems, however, the running time seems reasonable compared to back-propagation.

12.6   Meiosis Networks

Hanson [153] describes meiosis networks, which work by splitting nodes. (In biology, meiosis refers to a process of cell division.) The algorithm varies the sizes of layers in a given network but does not add new layers. The description in [153] assumes a single-hidden-layer net, but other forms might also be used. In principle, the target function can be either continuous or discrete; the description in [153] presents results for several classification problems.

The optimization procedure is stochastic in that the network weights have noisy values, which change randomly from one instant to the next. The mean and variance for each weight are adjusted during training. The specificity or certainty of a node is estimated by the variance of its weights relative to their means. Nodes with high relative variances are candidates for splitting.

Weight values change randomly from one instant to the next according to a probability distribution such as

$$P\left[w_{ij} = w_{ij}^*\right] = \phi\left(\frac{w_{ij}^* - \mu_{ij}}{\sigma_{ij}}\right) \tag{12.8}$$

where $\phi()$ is an $N(0, 1)$ Gaussian density function. μ_{ij} and σ_{ij} are, respectively, the mean and standard deviation for the fluctuations of weight w_{ij}. Because of this variability, successive presentations of the same pattern can result in different outputs.

The initial network contains one hidden unit whose weights are initialized with random means and variances The mean is adjusted by gradient descent

$$\mu_{ij}(n + 1) = -\alpha \frac{\partial E}{\partial w_{ij}^*} + \mu_{ij}(n) \tag{12.9}$$

with a learning rate parameter α. The standard deviation changes depending on the magnitude of the gradient

$$\sigma_{ij}(n + 1) = \beta \left|\frac{\partial E}{\partial w_{ij}^*}\right| + \sigma_{ij}(n). \tag{12.10}$$

β is a learning rate parameter. Values $0.1 < \beta < 0.5$ are suggested in [153]. This update mechanism can only increase σ_{ij}. Decreases occur by a decay process

$$\sigma_{ij}(n+1) = \zeta\sigma_{ij}(n), \qquad (\zeta < 1). \tag{12.11}$$

As errors approach zero during training, the standard deviations decay to zero and the network becomes deterministic. Low values of ζ, for example, < 0.7, produce little node splitting; large values, for example, > 0.99, produce continual node splitting. A value of 0.98 was used in simulations.

The standard deviation of a weight is considered to be a measure of its certainty or prediction value; large variances tend to mean low prediction value. This process above tends to assign small variances to weights that converge quickly and high variances to weights that converge slowly. Presumably, quick convergence indicates that the weights are clearly necessary and adequate while slow convergence indicates a delicate balance between opposing forces that the net is unable to resolve quickly. That is, a high variance reflects uncertainty in the proper weight value.

Nodes with many uncertain weights are candidates for splitting. Nodes split when the standard deviation becomes large relative to the mean for both the input and output weight vectors

$$\frac{\sum_i \sigma_{ij}}{\sum_i \mu_{ij}} > 1 \tag{12.12}$$

and

$$\frac{\sum_k \sigma_{jk}}{\sum_k \mu_{jk}} > 1. \tag{12.13}$$

(It may be preferable to use the sum of absolute mean values here.) Child node weights are initialized with the same mean as the parent node and half the variance.

One problem with this splitting criterion is that nodes whose weights have small mean values are more likely to be split than other nodes. A completely unnecessary node whose mean weights are all zero would be split many times.

12.7   Principal Components Node Splitting

A method of node splitting based on detection of oscillation in the weight update directions is described by Wynne-Jones [410]. The idea is that when a network is too small, the weight vectors of hidden units may oscillate between several competing solutions. Oscillation may occur because there are two clusters of data within a class or because a decision boundary is pulled one way by one set of patterns and the other way by another set of patterns. Figure 8.5 illustrates clustering of the weight update directions that could lead to oscillation.

A large amount of weight oscillation is taken as a measure of insufficiency. Nodes whose weights oscillate the most are identified and split in two. The "child" nodes are initialized based on a principal components analysis of the oscillation in the parent node or by examination of the Hessian matrix of the network error with respect to the weights. The Hessian method has the advantage that it can also be applied to the input nodes to determine their relative importance.

This is usually better than initializing child nodes with random weights because it uses the information in the existing weights and usually causes less perturbation in the error. In high dimensional spaces, random weights are unlikely to be well-placed initially and considerable learning may be needed to move them to where they are useful.

Splitting   The network is allowed to train until it stops making progress. The weights are then frozen and the training set presented again to evaluate oscillation by computing the principal components of the covariance matrix of weight updates,

$$C = \sum_p \delta \mathbf{w}_p^T \delta \mathbf{w}_p. \tag{12.14}$$

C is the outer product of the weight updates $\delta \mathbf{w}_p = \partial E_p / \partial \mathbf{w}$ summed over the patterns p. The mean of $\delta \mathbf{w}$ is assumed to be zero. The largest eigenvalue and corresponding eigenvector of C give the magnitude of the oscillation and its direction. The node is split into two and the child nodes are initialized with weight vectors one standard deviation on either side of the parent vector along the direction of oscillation. This usually results in minimal perturbation of the existing solution but gives enough separation to break symmetry and allow the child nodes to converge to different solutions. Since computation of eigenvectors can be computationally expensive, more practical iterative techniques are mentioned by Wynne-Jones [410]. After splitting, the weights are unfrozen and training resumed.

Selecting Nodes for Splitting   The nodes most likely to benefit from splitting are those in which there are very pronounced directions of weight oscillation. Nodes can be compared on this basis by computing the ratio of the largest eigenvalue over the sum of the eigenvalues. This will be highest for nodes with a single dominant direction of oscillation. In high dimensional spaces, however, a node may have several directions with significant eigenvalues (in which case the node could be split along each direction). The ratio will be lower in this case so the ratio technique would not split these nodes until there are no other options. An alternative is to calculate the second derivative of the error with respect to a normalized parameter such as the node gating parameter α described by Mozer and Smolensky [275] (summarized in section 13.2.1). A high curvature of the error with respect to α_i indicates the error is sensitive to the weights of node i. The node is a good candidate for splitting if the curvature of the error in weight space has a dominant direction as indicated by eigen-values of the Hessian of $E(\mathbf{w})$. Nodes with a small second derivatives of the error with respect to α, on the other hand, have little differential effect on the error and are candidates for pruning. The same process can be used to estimate the sensitivity of the error to the presence or absence of input variables.

Backsliding   A potential problem with this method is that the child nodes often revert back to the position of the parent node because of the global properties of the sigmoid activations. That is, a node that makes a strong contribution to part of the global decision boundary may be influenced by training patterns that are far from the boundary. If the node is split, the child nodes may feel similar influences from the distant patterns and choose the same solution, leaving the global boundary unchanged. Node splitting may be more successful, therefore, in local networks such as radial basis functions than in MLP networks. In this case, oscillation in the Gaussian centers is detected.

12.8   Construction from a Voronoi Diagram

A constructive method based on Voronoi tessellation of the training data is described by Bose and others [55, 53, 54]. A similar method is described by Murphy [279].

   The Voronoi tessellation is related to the familiar nearest-neighbor-classifier partition. Figure 12.7 illustrates a two-dimensional example, but the principle applies in higher

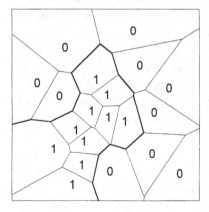

Figure 12.7
Constructive methods can be based on a Voronoi tessellation of the training points. The Voronoi diagram of a set of "base" points partitions the space into cells depending on which base point is closest. Each cell is a convex region bounded by hyperplanes. A layered network can be constructed which forms the same partition and generates the required outputs in each cell.

dimensions as well. Given a set of base points, the surrounding space is partitioned into regions, or cells, depending on which base point is closest. With a Euclidean metric, the resulting cells are convex regions bounded by hyperplanes. (Other tessellations using different metrics and different criteria are possible; this is the most common variation.) There are efficient algorithms for obtaining the partition in high dimensions. Most are based on its dual, the Delaunay tessellation.

Given a Voronoi diagram of the training points, a layered network can be generated to form the same partition and produce the required outputs in each cell. As noted in section 4.1, a network with two hidden layers would be sufficient. Nodes in the first hidden layer would implement the partition hyperplanes, nodes in the second hidden layer would combine these into the convex cell partitions, and the output node would combine these to generate the required output for each cell. It isn't necessary to implement every partition hyperplane, however, because many don't separate points with different labels.

The algorithm described by Bose and colleagues [55, 53, 54] automatically constructs a network to fit a given set of training data. It chooses the number of layers, number of nodes in each layer, and sets appropriate weights to realize the mapping. The layers are only partially connected in general. The process is completely automatic, so repetitive trial and error experiments with different structures and different training parameters are avoided, as well as long training times and uncertainties about convergence to local minima. The algorithm is rather involved, however, and will not be described here. Details can be found in [55, 53, 54].

Remarks   This method designs networks for classification problems with binary or discrete-class targets. Generalization issues are not addressed; with consistent data, the resulting network will classify every training point correctly.

Because the design is based on a nearest-neighbor classifier, the resulting network has properties like a nearest-neighbor classifier. That is, accuracy can be good when training data are abundant, but may be poor when data are sparse. Class boundaries may be rather jagged in some cases. Advantages over a naive nearest-neighbor classifier are economy (it does not store every training point) and evaluation speed (it does not slowly search through every training point to classify a new input).

In general, only hyperplanes that separate differently labeled cells need to be realized by hidden nodes. In some cases, a single hidden node can fill in for several hyperplanes of the Voronoi diagram so the resulting network can be relatively small. The network may not be minimal though because the algorithm is not always smart enough to see when a single hidden node could do the job of several partition hyperplanes. In figure 12.7, for example, there are 17 planes separating the 0s and 1s, but as few as three or four hidden nodes would probably be enough.

12.9   Other Algorithms

The preceding sections list only a few of the many algorithms that have been proposed. The list is not exhaustive by any means so we encourage the reader to explore further for a more complete survey. Genetic algorithms, for example, have been proposed to both generate the network structure and find the appropriate weights. Some of the weight initialization techniques mentioned in chapter 7 construct networks based on solutions provided by other method, for example, decision trees (section 7.2.5) or rule-based knowledge (section 7.2.6). A polynomial time algorithm using clustering and linear programming techniques to generate classifier networks is described in [276]. Projection pursuit regression [129, 185], a well-known statistical procedure, creates a system similar to a single-hidden-layer network with a linear output node. It is constructive in the sense that it adds projection directions (corresponding to hidden units) sequentially until the error is sufficiently small.

13 Pruning Algorithms

A rule of thumb for obtaining good generalization is to use the smallest system that will fit the data. Unfortunately, it usually is not obvious what size is best so a common approach is to train a series of networks of various sizes and choose the smallest one that will learn the data. The problem is that this can be time consuming if many networks must be trained before an acceptable one is found. Even if the optimum size were known in advance, the smallest network just complex enough to fit the data may be sensitive to initial conditions and learning parameters. It may be hard to tell if the network is too small to learn the data, if it is simply learning very slowly, or if it is stuck in a local minima due to an unfortunate set of initial conditions.

The idea behind pruning algorithms is to train an oversized network and then remove the unnecessary parts. The excess degrees of freedom of the large initial network allow it to learn reasonably quickly with less sensitivity to initial conditions while the reduced complexity of the trimmed system favors improved generalization. A side benefit is that the small resulting networks have other advantages such as economy and speed of operation. It may also be easier to interpret the logic behind their decisions as the network has less opportunity to spread functions over many nodes. (Some work has been done using pruning to help extract rules from a trained net, e.g., [374].)

The following sections summarize some pruning algorithms for feedforward networks like the multilayer perceptron, but the idea can also be applied to other systems such as associative networks [381] or tree structures [335].

Example   Figure 13.1 illustrates the benefit of pruning. Figure 13.1(a) shows the boundary formed by an intentionally overtrained 2/50/10/1 network (after about 1800 epochs of RProp training). There are 671 weights in the network, but only 31 data points, so the network is very underconstrained. Although the data are nearly linearly separable (with some overlap near the boundary), the classification boundary found by the network is very nonlinear and would probably not generalize well on additional data from the same function. Figure 13.1(b) shows the same network after pruning by a simple algorithm. 659 of the original 671 weights and 56 of the 64 original nodes are removed. The network is reduced to 2/2/2/1 with 12 weights and the boundary is much smoother. Fig. 13.1(c) shows the response after 500 more epochs of training. The tuning smooths the response further and rotates the decision surface so the second input is almost ignored. It would probably be pruned in additional iterations. The simple algorithm used here had no way to remove hidden layers. A more sophisticated method could reduce the network to a one-dimensional solution with just 2 weights. (This illustrates pruning as a method of feature selection. If certain inputs are irrelevant to the problem, the algorithm should remove their connections to the network.)

---

1. Substantial parts of this chapter were published as [308].

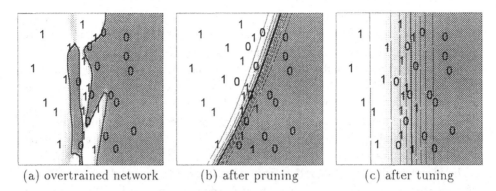

(a) overtrained network   (b) after pruning   (c) after tuning

Figure 13.1
Effect of pruning: (a) response of an overtrained 2/50/10/1 network, (b) response after pruning (659 of the 671 original weights and 56 of the 64 original nodes have been removed to produce a 2/2/2/1 network—8 nodes including the bias node), (c) response after further training.

13.1   Pruning Algorithms

A brute-force pruning method is: for every weight, set the weight to zero and evaluate the change in the error; if it increases too much then restore the weight, otherwise remove it. On a serial computer, each forward propagation takes $O(W)$ time, where W is the number of weights. This is repeated for each of the weights and each of M training patterns resulting in $O(MW^2)$ time for each pruning pass. A number of passes are usually required. An even more cautious method would evaluate the change in error for all weights and patterns and then delete just the one weight with the least effect. This would be repeated until the least change in error reaches some threshold and could take $O(MW^3)$ time. This would be very slow for large networks, so most of the methods described in the following take a less direct approach.

Many of the algorithms can be put into two broad groups. One group estimates the sensitivity of the error function to removal of elements and deletes those with the least effect. The other group adds terms to the objective function that penalize complex solutions. Most of these can be viewed as forms of regularization. Many penalize large connection weights and are similar to weight decay rules. A term proportional to the sum of all weight magnitudes, for example, favors solutions with small weights; those that are nearly zero are unlikely to influence the output much and can be eliminated. There is some overlap in these groups because the objective function could include sensitivity terms.

In general, the sensitivity methods operate on a trained network. That is, the network is trained, sensitivities are estimated, and then weights or nodes are removed. The penalty-term methods, on the other hand, modify the cost function so that minimization drives unnecessary weights to zero and, in effect, removes them during training. Even if the weights are not actually removed, the network acts like a smaller system.

13.2 Sensitivity Calculation Methods

13.2.1 Sensitivity Calculations I (Skeletonization)

Mozer and Smolensky [275] describe a method that estimates which units are least important and deletes them during training. A measure of the relevance, ρ, of a unit is the error when the unit is removed minus the error when it is left in place. Instead of calculating this directly for each and every unit, ρ is approximated by introducing a gating term α in the node function

$$o_i = f(\sum_j w_{ij}\alpha_j o_j), \qquad (13.1)$$

where o_j is the activity of unit j, w_{ij} is the weight to unit i from unit j, and f is the node nonlinearity. If $\alpha_j = 0$, unit j has no influence on the network and can be removed; if $\alpha = 1$, the unit behaves normally. The importance of a unit is then approximated by the derivative

$$\hat{\rho}_i = -\left.\frac{\partial E^\ell}{\partial \alpha_i}\right|_{\alpha_i=1}, \qquad (13.2)$$

which can be computed by back-propagation. This is evaluated at $\alpha = 1$ so α is merely a notational convenience rather than a parameter that must be implemented in the net. When $\hat{\rho}_i$ falls below a certain threshold, the unit can be deleted.

The usual sum of squared errors is used for training. To measure relevance, the function E^ℓ

$$E^\ell = \sum \left| t_{pj} - o_{pj} \right| \qquad (13.3)$$

is used rather than the sum of squared errors because it provides a better estimate of relevance when the error is small. Exponential averaging is used to suppress fluctuations

$$\hat{\rho}_i(t+1) = 0.8\hat{\rho}_i(t) + 0.2\frac{\partial E(t)}{\partial \alpha_i}. \qquad (13.4)$$

Segee and Carter [338] study the effect of this pruning method on the fault tolerance of the system. Interestingly, they found that the pruned system is not significantly more

sensitive to damage even though it has fewer parameters. When the increase in error is
plotted as a function of the magnitude of a weight deleted by a fault, the plots for the
pruned and unpruned networks are essentially the same. They report that the variance of
the weights into a node is a good predictor of the node's relevance and that the relevance of
a node is a good predictor of the increase in RMS error expected when the node's largest
weight is deleted.

13.2.2   Sensitivity Calculations II

Karnin [207] measures the sensitivity of the error function with respect to the removal of
each connection and prunes the weights with low sensitivity. The sensitivity of weight w_{ij}
is given as

$$S_{ij} = -\frac{E(w^f) - E(0)}{w^f - 0} w^f \tag{13.5}$$

where w^f is the final value of the weight after training, 0 is its value upon removal, and
$E(0)$ is the error when it is removed.

Rather than actually removing the weight and calculating $E(0)$ directly, they approximate S by monitoring the sum of all the changes experienced by the weight during training.
The estimated sensitivity is

$$\hat{S}_{ij} = -\sum_{n=0}^{N-1} \frac{\partial E}{\partial w_{ij}} \Delta w_{ij}(n) \frac{w_{ij}^f}{w_{ij}^f - w_{ij}^i} \tag{13.6}$$

where N is the number of training epochs and w^i is the initial weight. All of these terms are
available during training so the expression is easy to calculate and does away with the need
for a separate sensitivity calculation phase. When Δw is calculated by back-propagation,
this becomes

$$\hat{S}_{ij} = \sum_{n=0}^{N-1} [\Delta w_{ij}(n)]^2 \frac{w_{ij}^f}{\eta(w_{ij}^f - w_{ij}^i)}. \tag{13.7}$$

If momentum is used, the general expression in equation 13.6 should be used.

After training, each weight has an estimated sensitivity and the lowest sensitivity weights
can be deleted. Of course, if all output connections from a node are deleted, the node
itself can be removed. If all input weights to a node are deleted, the node output will be
constant so the node can be deleted after adjusting for its effect on the bias of following
nodes.

13.2.3   Sensitivity Calculations III (Optimal Brain Damage)

Le Cun, Denker, and Solla [91] describe the optimal brain damage (OBD) method in which the saliency of a weight is measured by estimating the second derivative of the error with respect to the weight. They also reduce network complexity significantly by constraining groups of weights to be equal.

When the weight vector $\mathbf{w}$ is perturbed by an amount $\delta\mathbf{w}$, the change in error is approximately

$$\delta E = \sum_i g_i \delta w_i + \frac{1}{2} \sum_i h_{ii} \delta w_i^2 + \frac{1}{2} \sum_{i \neq j} h_{ij} \delta w_i \delta w_j + O(\|\delta W\|^3) \tag{13.8}$$

where δw_i is the ith components of $\delta\mathbf{w}$, g_i is component i of the gradient of E with respect to $\mathbf{w}$, and the h_{ij} are elements of the Hessian matrix $\mathbf{H}$

$$g_i = \frac{\partial E}{\partial w_i}$$

$$h_{ij} = \frac{\partial^2 E}{\partial w_i \partial w_j}.$$

Because pruning is done on a well-trained network, the gradient is nearly zero and the first term in equation 13.8 can be ignored. When the perturbations are small, the last term will also be negligible. Because $\mathbf{H}$ may be a very large matrix, they make the simplifying assumption that the off-diagonal terms are zero. This leaves

$$\delta E \approx \frac{1}{2} \sum_i h_{ii} \delta w_i^2. \tag{13.9}$$

The second derivatives h_{kk} can be calculated by a modified back-propagation rule in about the same amount of time as one back-propagation epoch. The saliency of weight w_k is then

$$s_k = h_{kk} w_k^2 / 2. \tag{13.10}$$

Pruning is done iteratively, that is, train to a reasonable error level, compute saliencies, delete low saliency weights, and resume training. Application to pruning of tapped-delay networks is described in [365], in which the decision to stop pruning is based on the estimated generalization ability as determined by a modified AIC.

13.2.4   Sensitivity Calculations IV (Optimal Brain Surgeon)

For simplicity, the optimal brain damage method (section 13.2.3) assumes the Hessian is diagonal, but this is rarely true. In the optimal brain surgeon (OBS) method, Hassibi and Stork [157, 159, 158] use a linear approximation of the full Hessian to obtain better estimates of the saliencies.

When the weight vector $\mathbf{w}$ is perturbed by an amount $\delta\mathbf{w}$, the change in the error is approximately

$$\delta E = \left(\frac{\partial E}{\partial \mathbf{w}}\right)^T \cdot \delta\mathbf{w} + \frac{1}{2}\delta\mathbf{w}^T \cdot \mathbf{H} \cdot \delta\mathbf{w} + O(\|\delta\mathbf{w}\|^3) \qquad (13.11)$$

where $\mathbf{H} \equiv \partial^2 E/\partial \mathbf{w}^2$ is the Hessian matrix of second derivatives. Again, the first term is assumed to be near zero since E is at a minima.

For each weight w_q that could be set to zero, there is an associated adjustment of the remaining weights needed to reminimize the error. The algorithm combines these steps and seeks the weight adjustment vector $\delta\mathbf{w}$, which sets one weight w_q to zero and causes the least increase in the error. The constraint that $\delta\mathbf{w}$ sets element w_q to zero is expressed as $\mathbf{e}_q^T \cdot \delta\mathbf{w} + w_q = 0$ where $\mathbf{e}_q$ is the unit vector corresponding to weight w_q. The goal is to solve

$$\min_q \left\{ \min_{\delta\mathbf{w}} \left\{\frac{1}{2}\delta\mathbf{w}^T \cdot \mathbf{H} \cdot \delta\mathbf{w}\right\} \quad \text{such that } \mathbf{e}_q^T \cdot \delta\mathbf{w} + w_q = 0 \right\}. \qquad (13.12)$$

Using the Lagrangian

$$L = \frac{1}{2}\delta\mathbf{w}^T \cdot \mathbf{H} \cdot \delta\mathbf{w} + \lambda(\mathbf{e}_q^T \cdot \delta\mathbf{w} + w_q), \qquad (13.13)$$

the optimal adjustment vector and resulting change in error are

$$\delta\mathbf{w} = -\frac{w_q}{[\mathbf{H}^{-1}]_{qq}}\mathbf{H}^{-1}\mathbf{e}_q \qquad (13.14)$$

and

$$L_q = \frac{1}{2}\frac{w_q^2}{[\mathbf{H}^{-1}]_{qq}}. \qquad (13.15)$$

Starting with a trained network, the procedure is: calculate $\mathbf{H}^{-1}$ and find the q with the smallest saliency $L_q = w_q^2/(2[\mathbf{H}^{-1}]_{qq})$; if the change in error, L_q, is acceptable then delete weight q and adjust the remaining weights with $\delta\mathbf{w}$ (equation 13.14). Recalculate $\mathbf{H}^{-1}$ and repeat. Stop when L_q becomes too large and no more weights can be deleted without causing an unacceptable increase in error. Additional training may allow more weights to be deleted later.

The advantage of this method is that the remaining weights are readjusted automatically without the need for incremental retraining so the error introduced by eliminating the weight is generally lower. Unlike most other sensitivity methods, this method can account for correlated elements. Possible drawbacks are the time and memory needed to calculate and store $\mathbf{H}^{-1}$. Although the matrix inversion can be avoided by recursive calculations (using the assumption that $\frac{\partial E}{\partial \mathbf{w}} \approx 0$), the matrix may be large; $O(W^2)$ elements are needed for a network with W weights. The network of figure 14.5, for example, with 671 weights, would require 449,000 elements. In practice, some approximation of the Hessian is needed.

Some of the storage and computational objections are addressed in [158]. The recursive procedure for generating $\mathbf{H}^{-1}$ is generalized to any twice-differentiable error function and a dominant eigenspace decomposition of the inverse Hessian is described.

One possible objection to the optimal brain damage and optimal brain surgeon methods is that they are based on a Taylor series approximation, which is reasonable only for *small* perturbations. Complete removal of a weight is not necessarily a small perturbation, so the calculated saliency may be a poor predictor of the actual change in error. It is easy to generate plots which show that the error surface is usually not well-approximated by a quadratic at large scales.

A minor related problem is that the gradient is assumed to be zero because the network is at a minima, but this is true only if the network is trained to complete convergence. With algorithmic variations such as early stopping and weight clipping, this may not be true. (Weight clipping puts limits on the maximum allowed weight magnitudes.) Many of the networks described in this text were trained until certain error levels were reached (e.g., all outputs correct to within a tolerance band) and exact disappearance of the gradient was not achieved. This is a minor point, however, because it is easy to include the gradient term of equation 13.8 in the salience calculation. Another practical consequence of lack of convergence to a minimum is that the Hessian may not be positive definite.

These problems do not appear to be too serious for initial pruning of an underconstrained network. Figure 13.2 shows a plot of the actual change in error observed when a weight was deleted *vs.* the 'optimal brain damage' saliencies for a 10/3/10 network trained on the simple autoencoder problem (10 1-of-10 patterns). For this network, the small saliencies seem to be reasonably good predictors of the change in error. A similar pattern is observed on the 2/50/10/1 networks used elsewhere in these notes. After the network is partially pruned, however, the correspondence between saliency and change is error is not as good (even after retraining and recalculation of the saliencies) and it is possible to find small saliency weights which produce much larger increases in error than larger saliency weights (e.g., saliencies greater than about 0.1 in the figure).

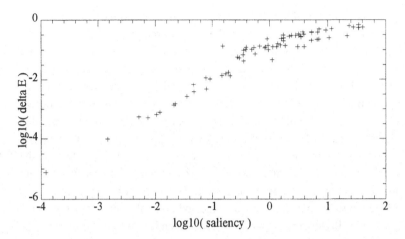

Figure 13.2
Pruning error versus weight saliency of optimal brain damage. Shown are the changes in error due to deletion of
a weight versus the OBD saliency for a 10/3/10 network trained on the simple autoencoder problem.

13.3   Penalty-Term Methods

The methods described so far attempt to identify nonessential elements by calculating the
sensitivity of the error to their removal. The methods described next modify the error
function so that error minimization effectively prunes the network by driving weights to
zero during training. The weights may be removed when they decrease below a certain
threshold; even if they are not actually removed, the network still acts somewhat like a
smaller system.

As an aside, it should be noted that the simple heuristic of deleting small weights is
just a heuristic. Obviously, if a weight is exactly zero, it can be deleted without affecting
the response. In many cases, it may also be safe to delete small weights because they are
unlikely to have a large effect on the output. This is not guaranteed, so some sort of check
should be done before actually removing the weight. Input weights may be small because
they're connected to an input with a large range; weights to output nodes may be small
because the targets have a small range. These objections are less important when inputs
and outputs are normalized to unit ranges, but there are cases where small weights may
be necessary; a small nonzero bias weight may be useful, for example, to put a boundary
near but not exactly at the origin. A more cautious heuristic would be to use the weight
magnitude to choose the order in which to evaluate weights for deletion.

Figure 13.3 shows the change in error due to deletion of a weight versus the weight
magnitude for a 10/3/10 network trained on the simple autoencoder problem (10 patterns
where 1 of 10 bits is set). The graph gives some support to the heuristic because the

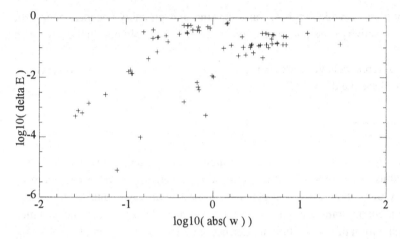

Figure 13.3
Pruning error versus weight magnitude. One of the simplest pruning heuristics is that small weights can be deleted since they are likely to have the least effect on the output. Shown are the errors due to deletion of a weight versus weight magnitude for a 10/3/10 network trained on the simple autoencoder problem. There are two separate, approximately linear trends. The upper group contains input-to-hidden weights while the lower group contains hidden-to-output weights.

smaller weights tend to give smaller changes in the error when the weight is deleted, but it also shows cases where smaller weights have more effect on the error than larger weights. The graph shows two separate approximately linear trends. The upper-left group contains mostly input-to-hidden weights, while the lower-right group contains mostly hidden-to-output weights. In many networks, weights close to the output may be larger than weights close to the input because the delta-attenuation effect of back-propagating through intermediate node nonlinearities causes input weights to grow slower.

13.3.1   Penalty Terms I

Chauvin [70], uses the cost function

$$C = \mu_{er} \sum_{j}^{P} \sum_{i}^{O} (d_{ij} - o_{ij})^2 + \mu_{en} \sum_{j}^{P} \sum_{i}^{H} e(o_{ij}^2) \tag{13.16}$$

where e is a positive monotonic function. The sums are over the set of output units O, the set of hidden units H, and the set of patterns P. The first term is the normal sum of squared errors, the second term measures the average "energy" expended by the hidden units. The parameters μ_{er} and μ_{en} balance the two terms. The energy expended by a unit—how much its activity varies over the training patterns—is taken as an indication of its importance.

If the unit activity has a wide range of variation, the unit probably encodes significant information; if the activity does not change much, the unit probably does not carry much information.

Qualitatively different behaviors are seen depending on the form of e. Various functions are examined that have the derivative

$$e' = \frac{\partial e(o^2)}{\partial o_i^2} = \frac{1}{(1+o^2)^n}$$

where n is an integer. For $n = 0$, e is linear so high and low energy units receive equal differential penalties. For $n = 1$, e is logarithmic so low energy units are penalized more than high energy units. For $n = 2$, the penalty approaches an asymptote as the energy increases so high energy units are not penalized much more than medium energy units. Other effects of the form of the function are discussed by Hanson and Pratt [154].

A magnitude-of-weights term may also be added to the cost function, giving

$$C = \mu_{er} \sum_j^P \sum_i^O (d_{ij} - o_{ij})^2 + \mu_{en} \sum_j^P \sum_i^H e(o_{ij}^2) + \mu_w \sum_{ij}^W w_{ij}^2. \tag{13.17}$$

Since the derivative of the third term with respect to w_{ij} is $2\mu_w w_{ij}$, this effectively introduces a weight decay term into the back-propagation equations. Weights that are not essential to the solution decay to zero and can be removed.

Simulations described in [72, 73] use the cost function

$$C = \mu_{er} \sum_{ip}^{OP} (t_{ip} - o_{ip})^2 + \mu_{en} \sum_{ip}^{HP} \frac{o_{ip}^2}{1+o_{ip}^2} + \mu_w \sum_{ij} \frac{w_{ij}^2}{1+w_{ij}^2}. \tag{13.18}$$

No overtraining effect was observed despite long training times (with $\mu_{er} = .1$, $\mu_{en} = .1$, $\mu_w = .001$). Analysis showed that the network was reduced to an optimal number of hidden units independent of the starting size.

13.3.2 Penalty Terms II (Weight Elimination)

Weigend, Rumelhart, and Huberman [386, 387, 388] minimize the following cost function

$$\sum_{k \in T} (t_k - o_k)^2 + \lambda \sum_{i \in C} \frac{w_i^2/w_o^2}{1 + w_i^2/w_o^2} \tag{13.19}$$

where T is the set of training patterns and C is the set of connection indices. The second term (plotted in figure 13.4) represents the complexity of the network as a function of the weight magnitudes relative to the constant w_o. At $|w_i| \ll w_o$, the term behaves like

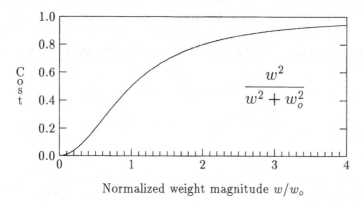

Normalized weight magnitude w/w_o

Figure 13.4
The normal weight-decay penalty term penalizes large weights heavily, which discourages their use even when they might be helpful. The weight-elimination penalty term in equation 13.19 saturates so large weights do not incur excess penalties once they grow past a certain value. This allows large weights when needed, while still encouraging the decay of small weights.

the normal weight decay term and weights are penalized in proportion to their squared magnitude. At $|w_i| \gg w_o$, however, the cost saturates so large weights do not incur extra penalties once they grow past a certain value. This allows large weights which have shown their value to survive while still encouraging the decay of small weights.

The value of λ requires some tuning and depends on the problem. If it is too small, it will not have any significant effect; if it is too large, all the weights will be driven to zero. Heuristics for modifying λ dynamically are described.

13.3.3   Penalty Terms III

Ji, Snapp, and Psaltis [195] modify the error function to minimize the number of hidden nodes and the magnitudes of the weights. They consider a single-hidden-layer network with one input and one *linear* output node. Beginning with a network having more hidden units than necessary, the output is

$$g(x; w, \theta) = \sum_{i=1}^{N} v_i f(u_i x - \theta_i) \tag{13.20}$$

where u_i and v_i are, respectively, the input and output weights of hidden unit i, θ_i is the threshold, and f is the sigmoid function.

The significance of a hidden unit is computed by a function of its input and output weights

$$S_i = \sigma(u_i)\sigma(v_i) \tag{13.21}$$

where $\sigma(w) = w^2/(1 + w^2)$. This is similar to terms in the methods previously described.

The error is defined as the sum of $\mathcal{E}_o$, the normal sum of squared errors, and $\mathcal{E}_1$, a term measuring node significances.

$$\mathcal{E}(w, \theta) = \eta \mathcal{E}_o(w, \theta) + \lambda \mathcal{E}_1(w) \tag{13.22}$$

$$= \eta \sum_{\pi=1}^{M} [g(x^\pi; w, \theta) - y^\pi]^2 + \lambda \sum_{i=1}^{N} \sum_{j=1}^{i-1} S_i S_j \tag{13.23}$$

where π indexes the training patterns, x^π and y^π are the input and desired output for pattern π, and η and λ are learning rate parameters. The $\mathcal{E}_1(w)$ term makes the algorithm favor solutions with fewer significant hidden units.

Conflict between the two error terms may cause local minima, so it is suggested the second term be added only after the network has learned the training set sufficiently well. Alternatively, λ can be made a function of $\mathcal{E}_o$ such as

$$\lambda = \lambda_o e^{-\beta \mathcal{E}_o}. \tag{13.24}$$

When $\mathcal{E}_o$ is large, λ will be small and vice versa.

A second modification to the weight update rule explicitly favors small weights

$$w_i^{n+1} = w_i^n - \eta \frac{\partial \mathcal{E}_o}{\partial w_i}(w^n, \theta^n) - \lambda \frac{\partial \mathcal{E}_1}{\partial w_i}(w^n) - \mu \tanh(w_i^n) \tag{13.25}$$

$$\theta_i^{n+1} = \theta_i^n - \eta \frac{\partial \mathcal{E}_o}{\partial w_i}(w^n, \theta^n) - \mu \tanh(\theta_i^n). \tag{13.26}$$

The new $\tanh(\cdot)$ term is modulated by μ:

$$\mu = \mu_o \left| \mathcal{E}_o(w^n, \theta^n) - \mathcal{E}_o(w^{n-1}, \theta^{n-1}) \right|. \tag{13.27}$$

This reduces μ gradually and makes it go to zero when the target-value component $\mathcal{E}_o$ of the error function ceases to change.

Once an acceptable level of performance is achieved, small magnitude weights can be removed and training resumed. It was noted that the modified error functions increase the training time.

13.3.4   Weight Decay

Many of the penalty-term methods include terms that effectively introduce weight decay into the learning process, although the weights don't always decay at a constant rate. The third term in equation 13.17, for example, adds a $-2\mu_w w_{ij}$ term to the update rule for w_{ij}. This is a simple way to obtain some of the benefits of pruning without complicating the learning algorithm much. A weight decay rule of this form was proposed by Plaut, Nowlan, and Hinton [299].

Ishikawa [187] proposed another simple cost function

$$C = \sum_{k \in T} (t_k - o_k)^2 + \lambda \sum_{i,j} |w_{ij}|. \tag{13.28}$$

The second term adds $-\lambda \, \mathrm{sgn}(w_{ij})$ to the weight update rule. Positive weights are decremented by λ and negative weights are incremented by λ.

A drawback of the $\sum_i w_i^2$ penalty term is that it tends to favor weight vectors with many small components over vectors with a single large component, even when this is an effective choice. The weight elimination term in equation 13.19 addresses this by making the penalty saturate past a certain value. Nowlan and Hinton [286] describe soft weight sharing, which uses a more complex penalty term modeling the prior probability distribution of the weights as a mixture of Gaussians. Unlikely sets of weights under this distribution have a higher cost, so the weights tend to conform to the distribution during training. If the distribution consists of two Gaussians, for example, one narrow and one broad, both centered at zero with approximately equal mixing proportions, then the narrow Gaussian exerts a strong force attracting the small weights to zero. Larger weights, however, are less influenced by the narrow Gaussian and so only feel the weaker force of the wider Gaussian. In practice, more than two Gaussians are used and their centers and spreads are also adapted to minimize the cost function [286].

Bias Weights   Some authors suggest that bias weights should not be subject to weight decay. In a linear regression $y = \mathbf{w}^T \mathbf{x} + \theta$, for example, the bias weight θ compensates for the difference between the mean value of the output target and the average weighted input. There is no reason to prefer small offsets, so θ should have exactly the value needed to remove the mean error.

In a sigmoidal node however, $y = f(\mathbf{w}^T \mathbf{x} + \theta)$, the bias θ has the effect of shifting the boundary sideways in the input space. If both the normal weights and the bias are scaled by the same factor λ, then the location of the boundary remains fixed while slope of the sigmoid transition varies. If the bias weight is not subject to equal decay, the boundary shifts as the weights change. The distance of the boundary from the origin is $\theta/\|\mathbf{w}\|$, where $\mathbf{w}$ excludes the bias weight; reduction of $\|\mathbf{w}\|$ by weight decay would shift the boundary away from the origin at the same time it reduces the slope. This suggests that bias weights should be subject to decay, at least for sigmoidal hidden nodes.

13.4   Other Methods

13.4.1   Interactive Pruning

Sietsma and Dow [345, 344] describe an interactive method in which the designer inspects a trained network and decides which nodes to remove. A network of linear threshold elements is considered. Several heuristics are used to identify noncontributing units:

• If a unit has a constant output over all training patterns, then it is not participating in the solution and can be removed. (Thresholds of units in following layers may need to be adjusted to compensate for its constant output.)

• If a number of units have highly correlated responses (e.g., identical or opposite), then they are redundant and can be combined into a single unit. All their output weights should be added together so the combined unit has the same effect on following units.

Units are unlikely to be exactly correlated (or have exactly constant output if sigmoid nodes are used), so application of the heuristics calls for some judgment.

A second stage of pruning removes nodes that are linearly independent of other nodes in the same layer, but which are not strictly necessary. The paper describes an example with four training patterns and a layer of three binary units. Two units are sufficient to encode the four binary patterns, so one of the three can be eliminated. It is possible for this to introduce linear inseparability (by requiring the following layer to do an XOR of the two units, for example), so a provision for adding hidden layers is included. This tends to convert short, wide networks to longer, narrower ones.

In a demonstration problem, the procedure was able to find relatively small networks that solved the test problem and generalized well. In comparison, randomly initialized networks of the same size (after pruning) were unable to learn the problem reliably. It was also observed that training with noise tends to produce networks which are harder to prune in the sense that fewer elements can be removed.

13.4.2   Local Bottlenecks

Kruschke [228, 230] describes a method in which hidden units "compete" to survive. The degree to which a unit participates in the function computed by the network is measured by the magnitude of its weight vector. This is treated as a separate parameter, the gain, and the weight vector is normalized to unit length. A unit with zero gain has a constant output; it contributes only a bias term to following units and doesn't back-propagate any error to preceding layers.

Units are redundant when their weight vectors are nearly parallel or antiparallel and they compete with others that have similar directions. The gains g are adjusted according to

$$\Delta g_i^s = -\gamma \sum_{j \neq i} \cos^2 \angle(w_i^s, w_j^s) \cdot g_j^s \qquad (13.29)$$

$$= -\gamma \sum_{j \neq i} \langle \hat{w}_i^s, \hat{w}_j^s \rangle^2 \cdot g_j^s, \qquad (13.30)$$

where γ is a small positive constant, $\hat{w}_i^s$ is the unit vector in the direction w_i^s, $\langle \cdot, \cdot \rangle$ denotes the inner product, and the superscript s indexes the pattern presentations. If node i has weights parallel to those of node j then the gain of each will decrease in proportion to the gain of the other and the one with the smaller gain will be driven to zero faster. The gains are always positive so this rule can only decrease them. (If equation 13.30 results in negative gains, they are set to 0.) Once a gain becomes zero, it will remain zero so the unit can be removed.

Gain competition is interleaved with back-propagation. Because back-propagation modifies the weights, the gains are updated and the weights renormalized after each training cycle.

This method effectively prunes nodes by driving their gains to zero. The parameter γ sets the relative importance of the gain competition and back-propagation. As usual, some tuning may be needed to balance error reduction and node removal. If γ is large, competition will dominate error reduction and too many nodes may be removed.

Sperduti and Starita [354] describe a similar pruning method in conjunction with the use of gain-scaling for faster training. As with weight decay, gain decay lets the gains of unneeded nodes to decrease to zero; the node outputs become effectively constant and can be removed after adjusting biases of nodes to which they send output weights.

13.4.3   Distributed Bottlenecks

Kruschke proposes another solution that puts constraints on the weights rather than pruning them [228, 229]. The network starts with a large hidden layer of random weights and the dimensionality of the weight matrix is reduced during training. The number of nodes and weights remains the same, but the dimension of the space spanned by the weight vectors is reduced so the network behaves somewhat like a smaller network. The dimensionality reduction has an effect similar to pruning, but preserves redundancy and fault tolerance.

The method operates by spreading apart vectors that are farther apart than average and bringing together vectors that are closer together than average. Let $d_{ij} = \|w_i - w_j\|$ be the distance between vectors w_i and w_j. The process starts with H vectors with a mean of zero and an initial mean separation of D. At each step, the mean distance is

$$\bar{d} = \frac{2}{H(H-1)} \sum_{i<j} d_{ij}. \qquad (13.31)$$

This calculation is nonlocal. The same paper describes a local method that works for the encoder problem but may not work for other problems.

After each back-propagation cycle, the weights are modified by

$$\Delta w_i = \beta \sum_{j \neq i} (d_{ij} - \overline{d})(w_i - w_j). \tag{13.32}$$

If $d_{ij} > \overline{d}$, then w_i is shifted away from w_j. If $d_{ij} < \overline{d}$, then w_i is shifted toward w_j. The vectors are then recentered and renormalized so that their mean is again zero and their mean separation is D, the initial mean distance. This is equivalent to doing gradient descent of the error function on the constraint surface.

In equation 13.32, β is a small positive constant that controls the relative importance of back-propagation and dimensional compression. If β is too large, all the vectors collapse into two antiparallel bundles—a single dimension—and effectively act like one node.

13.4.4 Principal Components Pruning

A similar idea is considered by Levin, Leen, and Moody [242]. Rather than actually eliminating links, the effective number of parameters is reduced by reducing the rank of the weight matrix for each layer.

The procedure starts with a trained network. For each layer starting with the first and proceeding to the output:

1. Calculate the correlation matrix Σ for the input vector to the layer

$$\Sigma = \frac{1}{N} \sum_k u(k) u^T(k). \tag{13.33}$$

where $u(k)$ is the column vector of outputs of the previous layer for pattern k.

2. Diagonalize $\Sigma = C^T D C$ to obtain C and D, the matrices of eigenvectors and eigenvalues of Σ. Rank the principal components in decreasing order.

3. Use a validation set to determine the effect of removing an eigennode. That is, set the least nonzero eigenvalue to zero and reevaluate the error. Keep the deletions that do not increase the validation error.

4. Project the weights onto the l dimensional subspace spanned by the remaining eigenvectors

$$W \rightarrow W C_l C_l^T$$

where the columns of C are the eigenvectors of the correlation matrix.

5. Continue with the next layer.

Advantages of the algorithm are that it is relatively easy to implement and reasonably fast. The dimensions of Σ are determined by the number of nodes in a layer rather than the number of nodes or weights in the entire network so the matrix sizes may be more reasonable. Retraining after pruning is not necessary.

This procedure falls between OBD (optimal brain damage) and OBS (optimal brain surgeon) in terms of its use of the Hessian information. OBS uses a linearized approximation of the full Hessian matrix that improves accuracy but makes it impractical for large networks. OBD uses a diagonal approximation of the Hessian that is fast but inaccurate; errors may be large and subsequent retraining may be necessary. This method effectively uses a linear block-diagonal approximation of the Hessian and has a computational cost intermediate between OBD and OBS.

13.4.5 Pruning by the Genetic Algorithm

In a different approach, Whitley and Bogart [397] describe the use of the genetic algorithm to prune a trained network. Each population member represents a pruned version of the original network. A binary representation can be used with bits set to 0 or 1 to indicate whether a weight in the reference network is pruned or not. After mating, the offspring (probably) represent differently pruned networks. They are retrained for a small number of cycles to allow them to fix any damage that may have occurred. As a reward for using fewer weights, heavily pruned networks are given more training cycles than lightly pruned networks. The networks are then evaluated on the error achieved after training. This favors small networks, but not if they reduce size at the cost of increasing error.

As described, each pruned net begins retraining with weights from the original unpruned network. They suggest that it might be better to inherit the weights from the parents so that more drastically pruned networks don't have to adapt to such a large step in a single generation.

They also allow direct short-cut connections from input to output—something perfectly valid for back-propagation, but sometimes not considered by experimenters—and suggest that this speeds up learning and makes it less likely to be trapped in local minima. This also allows removal of unnecessary hidden layers and could be applied to most of the other methods described. The simple example in figure 13.1, for instance, would benefit from this.

13.5 Discussion

Pruning algorithms have been proposed as a way to exploit the learning advantages of larger systems while avoiding overfitting problems. Many of the methods listed either calculate the sensitivity of the error to the removal of elements or add terms to the error function that favor smaller networks.

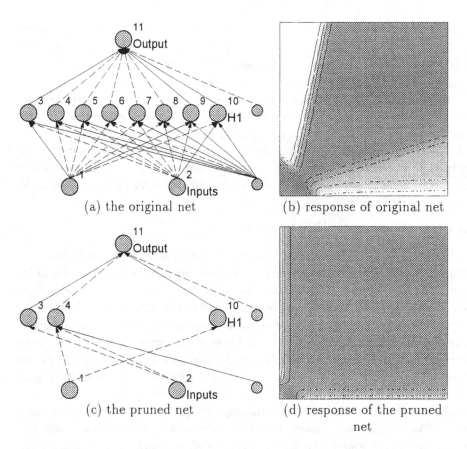

(a) the original net   (b) response of original net

(c) the pruned net   (d) response of the pruned net

Figure 13.5
A pruning problem. The original network is underconstrained for the 2-input XOR problem and chooses a correct but unexpected solution. (The training points are the four corners of the square.) A naive pruning algorithm is able to remove many redundant elements, but the resulting network is unlikely to generalize better than the original.

A disadvantage of most of the sensitivity methods is that they do not detect correlated elements. The sensitivities are estimated under the assumption that w_{ij} is the only weight to be deleted (or node i is the only node to be deleted). After the first element is removed, the remaining sensitivities are not necessarily valid for the smaller network. An extreme example is two nodes whose effects cancel at the output. As a pair they have no effect on the output, but each has a strong effect individually so neither will be removed. Partially correlated nodes are a less extreme but more common example. The optimal brain surgeon method, which uses the full Hessian, is better able to deal with correlated weights.

In the original problem, there is the question of when to stop training. With pruning algorithms, there is the similar question of when to stop pruning. If separate training and validation sets are available, the choice may be clear; if not, it may be somewhat arbitrary. Sensitivity methods delete elements with the smallest sensitivities first and there may be a natural stopping point where the sensitivity jumps suddenly. Penalty-term methods control the amount of pruning by balancing the scaling factors of the error terms. This choice may be tricky, however, if it must be made before training begins, so some methods control these parameters dynamically. A compensating advantage of the penalty-term methods is that training and pruning are effectively done in parallel so the network can adapt to minimize errors introduced by pruning.

Although pruning and penalty term methods may often be faster than searching for and training a minimum size network, they do not necessarily reduce training times because larger networks may take longer to train due to sheer size and pruning takes some time itself. The goal, however, is improved generalization rather than the training speed.

It should be noted that pruning alone is not a sufficient tool to guarantee good generalization. Figure 14.11, for example, illustrates near minimal networks that probably generalize differently. (Except for some possibly unneeded bias connections, the 2/2/1 networks are minimal for the 2-bit XOR problem unless short-cut connections are used.) No connections can be removed so pruning is not an option.

It should also be noted that there is no guarantee that pruning will always lead to a network that generalizes better. It may be that the larger network allows an internal representation that is unavailable to a smaller network and it may not be possible to change from one form to the other by simply removing elements. Overfitting might be so severe that it cannot be corrected by pruning alone. It may also turn out that pruning simply removes redundant elements but leaves the overall response essentially unchanged. That is, elements may be removed because they have little effect on the output; removing them does not change the basic solution and does not lead to better generalization. If the pruning algorithm removes elements without adjusting remaining weights, the response of the pruned network is unlikely to be smoother than the original—especially when small weights are more likely to be removed than large ones. Figure 13.5 illustrates a case where the pruned network is likely to generalize worse than the original.

14 Factors Influencing Generalization

14.1 Definitions

How is it possible to derive general rules from specific cases? Much of science is the search for simple rules to explain observed events. Generalization is an ancient philosophical problem that has been studied from many angles.

In the context of artificial neural networks and supervised learning, generalization is often viewed as an interpolation or approximation problem. That is, the examples are seen as points in a space and the goal is to find a function that interpolates between them in a reasonable way. If the data are noisy or uncertain, constraints may be relaxed to require only that the surface be 'near' the training points.

Other definitions of generalization are also possible. Generalization can be said to occur in associative memories or clustering systems that learn ideal class prototypes after training on specific instances of each class. (In some applications, this may be considered a defect because details of the individual patterns are forgotten.) The interpolation viewpoint also ignores the perhaps more realistic case of reinforcement learning where data occurs in the form of input-response-consequence triplets and there is no teacher or single-valued target function.

The following definition of generalization is used below. The training data consist of examples of the desired input-output relationship, $\{(\mathbf{x}_k, t_k)\}$, $k = 1, \ldots M$, where M is the number of training samples, $\mathbf{x}_k$ is the kth input pattern, and t_k is the corresponding desired output or target. Usually t_k is considered to be a value generated by some unknown target function $f^*(\mathbf{x}_k)$ or a sample drawn from an unknown joint distribution $p(t, \mathbf{x})$. For input $\mathbf{x}_k$ the network produces an output $y_k = y(\mathbf{x}_k)$ in response. Differences between the network output and desired target are measured by some error function E, often the mean squared error (MSE)

$$E^*_{MSE} = E\left[\|t_k - y_k\|^2 \right] \tag{14.1}$$

where $E[\cdot]$ denotes expectation. Usually, the true error cannot be measured exactly. When only samples are available, an approximation based on the training set error

$$\hat{E}_{MSE} = \frac{1}{M} \sum_{k=1}^{M} \|t_k - y_k\|^2 \tag{14.2}$$

is often used. Training consists of selecting a set of parameters that (hopefully) minimize the error on all future tests.

With no restrictions on the learning system, we can always find a function that fits any finite data set exactly. If nothing else, we can simply store the training patterns in a look-up table. The problem is that although the look-up table "learns" the training data perfectly, it cannot cope with novel patterns. What we really want is for the system to generalize from the training examples to the underlying target function so it produces correct (or at least reasonable) outputs in response to new patterns that have not been seen before. A system that learns the training data and also does well on new data is said to generalize well. It fails to generalize when it performs poorly on new data.

14.2   The Need for Additional Information

A fundamental reason for less than perfect generalization is that the problem is ill-posed because the samples alone do not uniquely determine an interpolating function (see figure 14.1). Any of an infinite number of functions passing through the sample points is equally valid according to the sample set error and other criteria are needed to choose among them. If nothing more is known about the target function, there is no basis for selecting one solution over another.

Additional information must be provided. This is often done by biasing the training procedure to favor certain types of solutions, thereby placing constraints on the sets of solutions considered. Different approximation methods can be viewed from this perspective in terms of the biases imposed and how they are implemented. Selection of a neural network rather than a polynomial approximation, decision tree, or some other fitting system already limits the set of solutions that will be considered; further selection of a particular structure, parameters, and training algorithm provides additional constraints. These choices may reflect unrecognized assumptions about the solution.

However they are implemented, the ability of the constraints to lead to good generalization depends on how well they reflect actual properties of the (unknown) target function

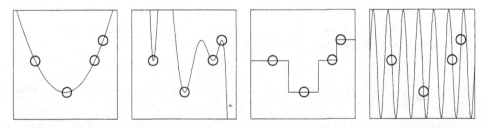

Figure 14.1
Samples alone do not provide enough information to uniquely determine an interpolating function. An infinite number of functions can be fit through the sample points; all are equally valid according to the sample set error and other criteria are needed to choose among them.

and is relatively independent of the optimization technique used to find a solution (assuming they are equally successful in satisfying the constraints).

14.3   Network Complexity versus Target Complexity

In order to generalize well, a system needs to be sufficiently powerful to approximate the target function. If it is too simple to fit even the training data then generalization to new data is also likely to be poor. (The true error may not be much worse than the training error, however, depending on how well the training data represents the target function.) If the network is powerful enough then good generalization is at least possible if not limited by other factors. In contrast to the rule of thumb that simpler is better, the larger network may generalize better since it is more powerful and better able to approximate the true target function. An overly complex system, however, may be able to approximate the data in many different ways that give similar errors and is unlikely to choose the one that will generalize best unless other constraints are imposed.

Figure 14.2 illustrates possible under- and overfitting. The fitting function is a linear combination of M evenly spaced Gaussian basis functions with width inversely proportional to M. At $M = 3$, the approximation is too simple and the error is large. At $M = 5$, the errors are smaller. At $M = 30$, the approximation may be overfitting the data.

Whether a given network overfits or underfits the data depends in part on the size of the training set. Figure 14.3 shows generalization error versus complexity curves for a slightly more complex function fitted by the same system of Gaussian basis functions. In general,

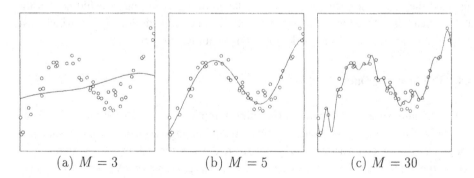

(a) $M = 3$ (b) $M = 5$ (c) $M = 30$

Figure 14.2
Underfitting and overfitting by a minimum-MSE approximation using M evenly spaced Gaussian basis functions with widths inversely proportional to M: (a) underfitting ($M = 3$), the approximation is too simple, (b) perhaps a reasonable fit ($M = 5$), and (c) possible overfitting ($M = 30$).

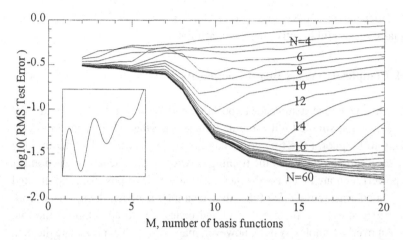

Figure 14.3
Generalization error versus network complexity for a minimum-MSE fit using M evenly spaced Gaussian basis functions for various sample sizes N. For intermediate sample sizes, the curve has a minimum at some intermediate value. (Each point is the average of 200 trials. Training samples are evenly spaced with some jitter but no additive noise. The target function is shown in the inset.)

the curve for a particular sample size N has a minimum at some intermediate complexity value M. Below a certain threshold, the approximation is too simple and all systems have large errors. At high values of M, the system begins to overfit and the error increases.

Unfortunately, if the target function is completely unknown, there is no way to determine a priori if the network is complex enough. Figure 14.2c may be overfitting if the data is noisy and the target function has a form similar to figure 14.2b, but it could be that the data are clean and the actual function is a complex deterministic function in which case figure 14.2b may be underfitting. Additional information is needed.

14.4 The Training Data

Ideally, the number and distribution of training samples should be such that minimizing the error on the samples gives results identical to minimizing the error on the true function. Poor generalization could arise due to problems in the way the training data is sampled. In general, the training set must be representative of the target function. A poor set of training data may contain misleading regularities not found in the underlying function although, when samples are randomly selected, this becomes less likely as the sample size grows.

For neural networks used as function approximators, generalization usually means interpolation. This does not imply an ability to extrapolate (figure 14.4).

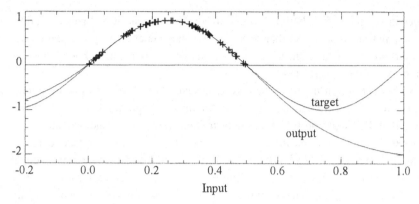

Figure 14.4
For neural networks used as function approximators, generalization usually means interpolation, not extrapolation. A 1/5/1 network with tanh hidden nodes and a linear output was trained on 50 points uniformly distributed in the first half cycle of $f(x) = \sin(2\pi x)$. The fit is good near the training data, but poor elsewhere.

14.4.1 Distribution of the Data

Systems are often developed under conditions slightly different from normal operating conditions and the resulting differences in training and test sample distributions could lead to poor generalization. Approximations using a mean squared error function are sensitive to the sampling density in the sense that the minimizer tends to focus on getting a good fit in densely sampled regions and may ignore large but rare errors in sparsely sampled regions. That is, when infinite numbers of samples were available everywhere, the mean squared error approaches the expected squared error

$$E = \int_{\mathbf{x}} (t(\mathbf{x}) - y(\mathbf{x}))^2 \, p(\mathbf{x}) \, d\mathbf{x}. \tag{14.3}$$

Errors are weighted by the sampling distribution $p(\mathbf{x})$ so the minimizer will be happy to let errors increase in regions where $p(\mathbf{x})$ is low if it can decrease errors in regions where $p(\mathbf{x})$ is high. Good generalization cannot be expected, therefore, if a network is trained on samples from one region but tested on samples from a completely different region. Most training methods assume training and test samples are drawn from the same distribution and modifications will be required if different distributions are used. Other error measures can be less sensitive to this factor than MSE.

When the target function has important features in low density regions, large sample sizes may be needed to obtain enough samples to adequately represent the function there. Large sample sizes will also be needed to obtain accurate estimates of the sampling density. Even if the training and test data share the same sampling function, a very small training set could give a misleading picture of the true density.

Differences in sampling distributions do not always have to cause bad generalization, however. A system trained on harder than average cases may generalize well even if it does only fair on the training data. Concentration on cases near classification boundaries has been useful in some problems [5, 184].

Differences in distribution may also be less important when other information is provided or the network is constrained appropriately. An image recognition system, for example, with a rotation invariant representation can be trained on images in one orientation and tested on images in another because the cases are effectively equivalent under the representation. Sampling differences may also be less important when the target function is simple enough that a fitting function that works well in the densely sampled regions also works in the sparsely sampled regions. That is, if there are so much data that the network is fully constrained everywhere, then small changes in the distribution of the data may have little effect on the solution chosen.

Finally, in some problems, there is the option of choosing the training samples, possibly while learning is in progress. The idea in [12] is to choose training samples that provide the most new information. This can be a useful strategy for any learning system, including people.

14.4.2   Number of Examples versus Target Complexity

Even when the training and test sampling densities match, generalization may suffer if the training set does not capture all significant features of the underlying target function. If the function is a bandlimited sum of sinusoids, for example, and samples are taken at less than the Nyquist rate, then essential features will be missed and the reconstruction will not generalize well.

Constraining knowledge about the generating function can reduce the number of samples needed to choose a hypothesis function. The knowledge that the function is a bandlimited sum of sinusoids, for example, allows a Nyquist rate to be set. (And further knowledge about the probabilities of likely functions may allow sampling at less than the Nyquist rate [327].)

In general, the number of examples required depends on the constraining knowledge. If the target function is known to be a polynomial of degree N or less, say, then $N + 1$ points are sufficient to determine which particular polynomial generated the data. If the target function is, in fact, an Nth order polynomial, then the chosen function should generalize perfectly. Of course, more complex function classes will generally require more samples and, in many cases, the number of samples required may be unreasonably large or unbounded, depending on the constraints. It may also be difficult to calculate the function even if it is known to exist. Finally, the constraining knowledge must be available in a form useful to the training procedure; it is not obvious how knowledge that the target is an Nth order polynomial could be made useful to a standard neural network training procedure, for example.

14.4.3   Number of Examples versus Network Complexity

In general, larger and more complex systems can compute more functions but need more examples to determine which function to choose (one aspect of the so-called curse of dimensionality). If the number of examples is small compared to the number of degrees of freedom of the network, then the network may be able to implement many functions consistent with the examples. Some of these may generalize better than others, but a learning algorithm guided only by errors on the samples has no way to tell and is unlikely to choose the one that generalizes best. As a rule, increasing the number of samples decreases the number of hypothesis functions consistent with the samples, but it will never reduce it to just one function unless the set of hypothesis functions is finite or there are other constraints.

If a network is underconstrained, that is, if it has more degrees of freedom (the number of weights, roughly) than the number of the training samples, then it may use the extra degrees of freedom to fit noise or spurious correlations in the data. Even though it may produce exactly the right output at each of the training points, it may be very inaccurate at other points. An example is a high-order polynomial fitted through a small number of points. Figure 14.5 shows an example of overfitting by an underconstrained network.

As with polynomial approximations, a rule of thumb is to use the smallest system that fits the data. If the system has only a limited number of degrees of freedom, it will usually use them to adapt to the largest regularities in the data and ignore the smaller, possibly

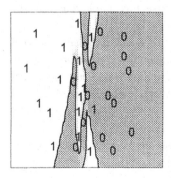

Figure 14.5
A 2/50/10/1 network with 671 weights trained on 31 points is very underconstrained. Although the points are nearly linearly separable, with some overlap, the decision surface is very nonlinear and is unlikely to generalize well. The solid line shows the network decision surface, the 0.5 contour. Other contours are omitted because the transitions are steep.

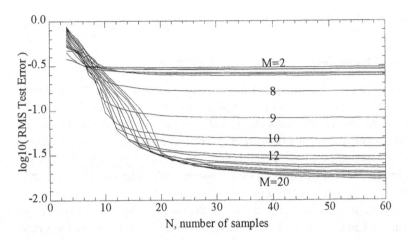

Figure 14.6
Generalization error versus sample size N for the Gaussian basis function approximation system of figure 14.3.

spurious, ones. (It should be noted that "degrees of freedom" is not a well-defined concept for nonlinear systems so it may be difficult to say how many samples are necessary to constrain a given network.)

Another general rule of thumb is that the number of samples should be several times larger than the number W of weights in the network. A simple perceptron (i.e., a linear threshold unit) with d inputs ($W = d + 1$) can always separate $N < d + 1$ arbitrarily labeled points and, if the points are randomly distributed, can separate almost all labelings of $2d$ or fewer points when d is large [87]. (This is discussed in section 3.3.) Thus, $O(3W)$ points may be needed to constrain even a simple perceptron. Of course, this simple rule of thumb may not hold for more complex functions and networks.

Figure 14.6 shows generalization error versus sample size N for the Gaussian basis function approximation system of figure 14.3. Higher complexity approximations (with more basis functions M in this case) yield smaller asymptotic errors, but need more samples before the error approaches the asymptotic value. With small sample sizes, lower complexity systems may generalize better. At $N = 15$, for example, the error of the $M = 20$ system is higher than that of the $M = 10$ system.

Figure 14.7 shows training and test set errors versus sample size N for selected M values. For small sample sizes, the training error is small but the test set error is high. As the sample size increases, the training error increases and the test set error decreases until both approach the same asymptotic value at large N. Note that the large M solutions have lower asymptotes, but the small M solutions approach their asymptotes faster. The

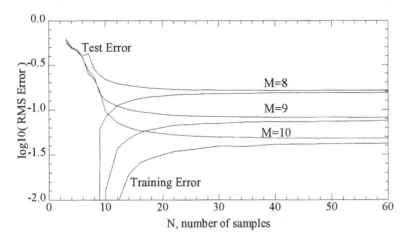

Figure 14.7
Training and test set errors versus sample size N for selected M values of the Gaussian basis function approximation system of figure 14.3. In general, the training set error is small for small sample sizes and rises as the
number of samples increases while the test set error is large for small sample sizes and decreases as the number
of samples increases. At large N, both approach the same asymptotic value.

figure gives some support to the heuristic that the sample size should be several times as
large as the number of free parameters since the knee of the $M = 10$ curve occurs near
$N = 10$.

14.4.4   Noise in the Samples

If the training data are noisy, the unknown target function can only be estimated. No
finite number of examples will uniquely determine a fitting function even if the number of
hypothesis functions is finite and the best that can be done is to choose among candidates
based on something like the mean-squared error or the probability of misclassification. If
one knows or assumes properties of the noise, then an optimal estimate can be made in
some cases.

In general, if the noise is independent and zero-mean, then errors can be reduced by
obtaining more samples since independent errors tend to cancel. (Systematic measurement
errors will not be reduced by simply averaging over more data, however.) More samples
will be needed to reduce the variance of the estimated error to an equivalent level when
noise levels are high.

With a static data set whose values are unchanging, there is no obvious indication that
the data are noisy. If noise is not considered and the system is allowed to fit the data exactly,
noise and all, then generalization may be poor.

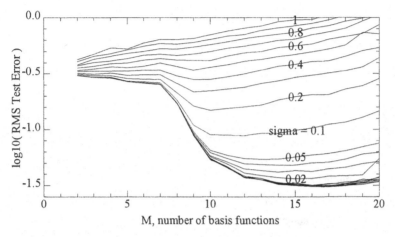

Figure 14.8
Generalization error versus M for various values of the additive noise variance σ. With a fixed sample size and increasing amounts of additive noise, minima of the generalization error curves occur at lower M values. The fitting function is the system of Gaussian basis functions used in figure 14.3. Training sample size $N = 20$. Each point is the average of 200 trials.

Increased amounts of noise may lead to overfitting at lower complexity levels. Figure 14.8 shows test set error *vs.* complexity curves for various levels σ of additive noise in the target values. The fitting function is the system of evenly spaced Gaussian functions system of figure 14.3 with training set size $N = 20$. With increasing amounts of additive noise, the minima of the error curves are higher and occur at lower M values.

14.4.5   Model Mismatch and Number of Examples

Ideally, the class of functions computable by the network would exactly equal the class of the generating function and the number of examples needed to constrain the network would be the same as the number of examples needed to determine the function by other means. This would be a parametric model. Usually however, the target function lies outside the class of functions computed by the network; no set of weights will yield a function that exactly matches the target everywhere so, at best, the network can only approximate the target. In this case, the number of examples needed to determine the best network may differ from the number of samples required to fit a parametric model. Although we need only $N + 1$ samples to fit a function we know to be an Nth order polynomial, this information is not available to the network and many more samples might be needed to train it. Because the network and target function classes differ, the network output will be an approximation and generalization will be imperfect even if the network fits an arbitrarily large number of data samples exactly.

14.5   The Learning Algorithm

14.5.1   Limitations of the Learning Algorithm

The size and structure of the network put an upper bound on its representational ability. Limitations of the learning algorithm, however, may prevent that potential from being realized. Some techniques predict generalization performance based on static network properties such as size and assume the learning algorithm will be powerful enough to find a solution if one exists. Of course, most learning algorithms are not perfect and may fail to find some solutions in any reasonable amount of time. Problems such as local minima and speed of convergence must be considered in practice.

14.5.2   Bias of the Learning Algorithm

All learning algorithms (except perhaps pure exhaustive search over an unlimited solution space) have biases. In many cases, bias is introduced in the form of heuristics that are not rigorously justifiable but which seem to help in practice. In any case, the bias helps generalization by favoring likely solutions over unlikely solutions. Of course, every heuristic can fail and if the bias is wrong, performance could suffer. Tailoring the bias to "agree with reality" is one of the most common ways of introducing external constraints necessary for good generalization. Many of the techniques discussed later are simply different ways of doing this.

It could be argued that part of the reason for the success of back-propagation on many problems is that it has a built-in bias for simple solutions. When initialized with small weights, the function computed by the network follows a path of increasing complexity from nearly constant functions to linear functions to more and more nonlinear functions as training continues. Because training is normally stopped as soon as some error criterion is satisfied, the algorithm is more likely to find a simple solution than to find a complex solution that gives the same result. As a result, a large network is not immediately saddled with a high complexity. Of course, back-propagation will not always stop with a simple solution if training continues.

14.5.3   Learning Dynamics: Overtraining/Overfitting

Generalization performance varies over time as the network adapts during training (see figure 14.9). A randomly selected initial configuration is likely to be completely inconsistent with the examples so both the training set and generalization errors are likely to be high before learning begins. During training, the network adapts to decrease the error on the training patterns. In the early stages of learning, the generalization error tends to decrease in step with the training error as the network captures the major features of the underlying

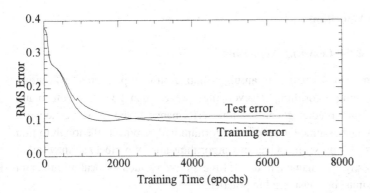

Figure 14.9
As training progresses, the generalization error may decrease to a minimum and then increase again as the network adapts to idiosyncrasies of the training data. Training and test errors are shown for an underconstrained network trained by back-propagation on 30 examples of the iris data and tested on the 120 remaining examples. (An underconstrained net and small learning rate were used to demonstrate overtraining. Smaller networks can learn the data in a much shorter time.)

function. If the training data are noisy or incomplete, however, they may contain misleading regularities. In addition to representing the general properties of the target function, it is likely to contain peculiarities unique to the particular data set and uncharacteristic of the target function. As these idiosyncrasies are exploited in later stages of learning, the improvement in generalization that comes from being right on the training examples is offset by errors (invisible to the learning algorithm) introduced elsewhere and the generalization error begins to increase again even though the training error continues to decrease. Chauvin [73] describes an example of this type of overtraining.

Thus, for a given underconstrained network, set of training data, and learning algorithm, there may be an optimal amount of training that gives the best generalization. Although further training might decrease the training-set error, it would increase the expected generalization error. The relationship between generalization and overtraining has been examined in many studies, for example [73, 74, 16].

Another way to view the situation is illustrated in figure 14.10. The training and test errors can be thought of as surfaces in the weight space. Neural networks are trained by adapting the weights to minimize the error on the training set. The training error surface is likely to be similar to the true error surface, but distorted somewhat depending on the training data. In particular, the minimum of the training error surface is likely to be displaced from the true minimum. Depending on how the network is initialized, the weight trajectory may pass by a true minimum on its way to the apparent (training error) minimum. The observed generalization error would then show an overall decreasing trend as the

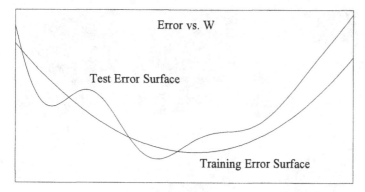

Figure 14.10
One explanation of overtraining is that the training error surface is similar to the true error surface but somewhat distorted so the apparent minimum is offset from the true minimum. The figure shows hypothetical error surfaces. Depending on how the network is initialized, the weight trajectory may pass over a true minimum on its way the apparent (training error) minimum.

network trajectory approaches both minima, followed by an increase as the network passes the true minimum and continues on to the false minimum.

Figure 14.10 also illustrates that whether or not overtraining is observed may depend on initial conditions [74] because a trajectory starting on the left side of the figure passes over the true minimum while one approaching from the right side does not. In other words, the fact that overtraining is not observed in one trial does not prove that the training data are adequate and that it will not occur in another trial with a different initialization. Also, since the training error surface may be distorted and offset in different ways depending on the training data, observation of overtraining may depend on peculiarities of different training sets even when the network is always initialized in the same state. The figure also shows that the generalization error may not decrease monotonically to a single minimum [16] and that local minima could confuse simple early-stopping schemes that halt when the validation error first bottoms out.

Example: Effect of Training Algorithms   Different training algorithms may give different generalization results depending on their built-in biases and ability to "exploit loopholes" in the training criteria. Figure 14.11 shows input-output responses of a 2/2/1 network trained by various algorithms on the 2-bit XOR problem. Inputs were coded as -1 and $+1$; targets were -0.9 and 0.9. Tanh nonlinearities were used. The corners of the squares correspond to the four training points. All the networks were trained to 100% correct response with an output considered correct if the error was less than or equal to 0.1. Batch and on-line learning, although not the fastest methods, give reasonably smooth and symmetric responses here; similar inputs would give similar outputs. The networks trained by

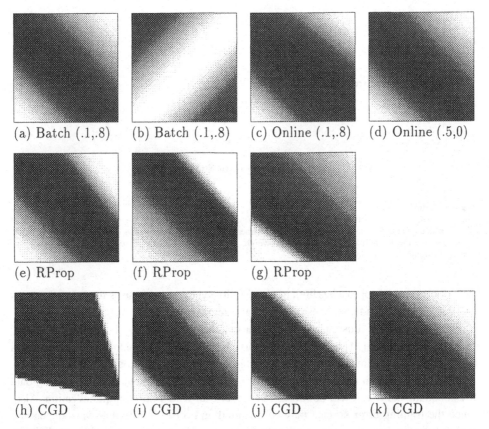

Figure 14.11
Different training algorithms may yield different generalization results. Shown are responses for a 2/2/1 net trained by various algorithms on the 2-bit XOR problem. Batch and "on-line" training appear to give reasonably smooth symmetric responses here (values in parentheses are the learning rate and momentum). RProp and conjugate gradient descent (CGD) appear to create less symmetric surfaces and allow sharp transitions near the training points at the corners. Networks (h), (j), and (k) appear sensitive to the training data and are unlikely to generalize well if the input values are changed slightly.

RProp [315] and conjugate gradient descent, faster methods, for example, show a tendency to asymmetric responses with sharp transitions close to the training points. This might be expected to lead to poor generalization on slightly different inputs; nets h, j, and k in particular would be sensitive to changes in the input data.

Although responses (a–d) might be preferred because they are symmetric and smooth, these were not among the training criteria. All the nets are equally good on the basis of training error. If smooth, symmetric responses are desired, this information has to be provided to the training procedure in some way.

The figure also illustrates that selection of a minimal network is not sufficient to guarantee good generalization. The 2/2/1 networks are nearly minimal (some of the bias connections may not be necessary) for the 2-bit XOR problem unless short-cut connections are allowed, but the instances will probably generalize differently.

14.6   Other Factors

Many other factors have strong effects on the difficulty of a learning task and thus on how well a system can be expected to generalize. The following lists a few items that involve higher-level decisions and generally fall outside the scope of designing a network to fit a given data set. Most are basic principles of good system design.

14.6.1   Choice of Error Function

It hardly needs to be said that the way in which errors are measured has a direct effect on the errors observed. It is generally assumed that identical measures are used for training and test errors, but it is common to choose an error function (e.g., mean squared error) because it is simple and convenient to use even though the real performance may be measured differently (misclassification rate, efficiency, etc.). Poor generalization due to training on one task and testing on another would not be surprising.

Poor performance might result because an inappropriate function is used to measure the error. From a Bayesian viewpoint, different error functions reflect different assumptions about the distribution of the model errors. The mean-squared-error function corresponds to selection of a maximum likelihood model under the assumption that the errors have a Gaussian distribution and is appropriate in ordinary linear regression where the errors are expected to cluster around zero with large errors less likely than small ones. For classification tasks with {0, 1} targets in which the network outputs are viewed as probabilities that the input belongs to a particular class, the cross-entropy error function is generally appropriate. Other error functions are appropriate under different assumptions about the error distribution.

14.6.2   Variable Selection

The selection of input and output variables (i.e., the choice of what information to provide, apart from how it is represented) is an extremely important factor in the difficulty of a learning problem. Certain pieces of information may make a problem very easy. The lack of crucial information may make a problem very difficult or impossible, or change it from a logical problem to a statistical problem. Of course, this is completely problem dependent and falls more in the realm of problem design than network training.

When the chosen variables do not supply needed information, identical inputs may have different targets due to differences in unsupplied variables. Noise in the input patterns can have a similar effect if it destroys necessary information and causes classes to overlap. In either case, the target is not a single-valued function and some error will always remain for any function the network chooses.

Even when the choice of variables does not introduce ambiguity, it still influences the complexity of the learning task and, when training data are limited, may determine if the data are sufficient to describe the target. If the target function is so complex when expressed in terms of the given variables that the available data are insufficient to describe it, then poor generalization could result. Another choice of variables might make the problem simple enough so that the data are adequate and good generalization is possible. The two-spirals problem [233] (illustrated in figure 12.3) is a hard benchmark problem for MLP networks in Cartesian coordinates, but easy in cylindrical coordinates.

It is also possible to confuse a network by supplying too much information in the form of redundant or irrelevant inputs. These increase the number of parameters in the system without supplying much usable information. Irrelevant inputs supply no useful information by definition, but when sample sizes are small the irrelevant inputs may have spurious correlations with the targets. More data will be required to demonstrate that they actually are irrelevant.

14.6.3   Variable Representation

The choice of how variables are represented to the network is also an important factor in learning difficulty. In cases where the network must interface with an external system, the choice may be fixed; in other cases, the representation is a free parameter. There is often a trade-off between economy of representation and decoding complexity. A one-dimensional variable could be coded by the activity on a single input unit; this is economical, but may make learning difficult if the function depends on it in a complex way. The use of a fine-grained "thermometer" code, on the other hand, might make learning easy, but cause generalization to suffer because the number of weights increases while the number of training samples stays fixed.

It is often desirable to choose representations that are invariant to certain irrelevant transformations; for example, invariance to shifts, scale, color, small rotations, and so on can be useful in character recognition. Of course, pre- or postprocessing may be needed to connect the network to the raw data and the cost has to be balanced against how much it simplifies the learning problem. Improvement in generalization due to the use of error-correcting output representations is suggested by Dietterich and Bakiri [107].

The choice of internal representation is also important and is determined in a broad way by the selection of the network structure. Local internal representations (as in radial basis functions, Kohonen maps, etc.) often make learning easy, but often do not generalize as well as global internal representations (e.g., sigmoidal hidden units). Most of these notes apply to any network architecture, but the focus here is on layered sigmoidal networks, so these differences in architecture will not be considered.

14.6.4 Modularity

Many practical problems can be partitioned into independent subproblems. If the system designer knows this, then the information should be incorporated in the network structure rather than requiring the network to learn it from the examples. Separate networks can then be trained independently for each subproblem and combined. The result is (1) shorter training times because each subnetwork is smaller, and (2) better generalization because each subnetwork is better constrained by the available examples. Say, for example, that a problem has two input variables, x_1 and x_2, and can be separated into two independent subproblems $y_1(x_1)$ and $y_2(x_2)$. If each input can take m values, then $O(m)$ examples describe each function adequately. To train a single network to solve both problems at once, $O(m^2)$ examples would be needed to describe the system adequately. If there are few examples and spurious correlations exist between y_2 and x_1, for example, the network is likely to take advantage of them and generalize poorly as a result.

14.7 Summary

Generalization is influenced by many factors. Items considered in this chapter include the following:

• The samples alone are insufficient to choose a good generalizer; more information must be provided. This is usually done by biasing the learning procedure in some way.

• The biases of the learning procedure must fit reality.

• The network must be powerful enough to fit the target.

• The data must be representative of the target function; there must be sufficient data to illustrate the target.

• The distribution of the training and test data should be similar.

• More data will generally be needed to achieve the same accuracy when the data are noisy.

• There must be enough data to constrain the net (or the net must be chosen so that it is constrained by the data and biases of the training procedure).

• Weaknesses of the learning procedure may lead to poor solutions.

• Dynamics of the learning procedure cause generalization to vary with training time; excessive training may lead to overfitting.

• The same error measure should be used for training and testing.

• Input variables should supply necessary information.

• An appropriate data representation should be chosen.

• Independent subproblems should be assigned to independent networks, rather than combined in a single system.

Remarks   The sections in this chapter list many factors that affect generalization and may give the impression that useful approximation is almost impossible because so many things could go wrong. However, the intent is to examine factors that need to be considered and might be encountered at one time or another in different problems. In most problems, many of these factors will not be critical.

Neural networks are often used to solve problems with hundreds of variables in spite of the curse of dimensionality that could make such problems very hard. Many problems turn out to be easier than expected. It is not clear why this happens. Some possible reasons are suggested in [79]:

• application studies use clever preprocessing or data encodings to simplify the learning task;

• many input variables are interdependent so the effective dimensionality is small;

• the high-dimensionality data has a nonuniform distribution or forms clusters that favor local representation methods; and

• getting the right bias (net structure, parameters, learning algorithm, etc.) may be much more important than learning from the data. An appropriate bias reduces the need for data.

15 Generalization Prediction and Assessment

The following sections outline some approaches to predicting and estimating generalization ability, either a priori from static parameters such as network size, or after observing training performance. The problem of estimating the true performance of a prediction system trained on a limited data set is a basic statistics problem so it is not surprising that many of these methods are direct applications of statistical techniques. Techniques mentioned here are covered in more depth in [44, 389, 317].

15.1 Cross-Validation

A rather direct way to estimate the generalization ability of a system is to measure the error on a separate data set that the network has not seen during training. In simple cross-validation, that is, the holdout method, the available data is divided into two subsets: a training set used to train the network and a test set used to estimate the true error rate. To avoid obvious bias, both sets should be random samples of the same population.

Ideally, both sets should be large because the larger the training set, the more accurate the approximation learned by the trained system, and the larger the test set, the more accurate the estimate of the true error rate. When data are limited, these goals conflict. As a compromise, sets of roughly equal size are usually chosen.

With large sample sizes the holdout method can be accurate, but it has limitations when sample sizes are small. The test samples are unavailable for training, so the network must be trained on less data with more risk of overtraining or overfitting. The validation set is used to guard against this, but, with just a small amount of validation data, the error estimate has a large variance and may be unreliable; an uncharacteristic test set could give a bad estimate of the error. If the training error surface is distorted because of sampling deficiencies, the validation error surface is likely to be similarly distorted when the data sets have similar sizes. In order for the validation set to be a better predictor of the true generalization error than the training set, it will usually have to be several times larger but this limits the amount of data that can be used for training.

Another problem is that, depending on the training algorithm, the solution could be indirectly biased toward the validation set so a third, completely different, data set is needed to form an unbiased estimate of the error. That is, it is common to train a number of networks and choose the one that performs best on the validation set. If thousands of networks were generated, a few might coincidentally have low errors on the validation set but still not generalize well. Because the validation set is used, albeit indirectly, as part of the training process, there is a danger of obtaining a biased solution.

Simple cross-validation as described here uses a single holdout set to estimate the generalization error. Resampling techniques such as leave-one-out, k-fold cross-validation, and bootstrapping [389, 115, 116] address limitations of the single holdout method by averaging over multiple holdout experiments using different partitions of the data into training and test sets. Once impractical, these sorts of methods have become feasible due to increasing computer processing power. Advantages are that the error estimates are generally more accurate, the network can be trained on almost all the data, and it can be tested on all of it. The drawback is an increased computational burden. It should be noted that these are nonparametric methods that do not make restrictive assumptions about data distributions and are not restricted to linear models.

Bootstrapping is one of the most accurate techniques, in general, but also one of the slowest. As noted, the estimate obtained from a single holdout set may have a large variance. Bootstrapping lowers the variance (at the expense of a slight increase in the bias) by averaging estimates obtained from many different partitions of the data [389]. It is common to use hundreds or thousands of subset estimates. If the method is used to obtain a more accurate one-time estimate of the generalization ability of a trained network, the computational burden may not be a critical factor because network training times are already long in most cases. This probably is not a practical way of comparing network architectures if each subset sample requires the training of a new network.

15.2 The Bayesian Approach

Bayesian methods provide ways to describe the effects of biases, sampling distributions, noise, and other uncertainties. The Bayesian approach incorporates external knowledge (or biases) about the target function in the form of prior probabilities of different hypothesis functions [251, 253]. The data set $D = \{(x_i, t_i), \ i = 1 \ldots m\}$, where x are the inputs and t the targets, is typically modeled as the sum of a deterministic function f and additive perturbations (noise) n representing prediction errors

$$t_i = f(x_i) + n_i. \tag{15.1}$$

Assuming the network output $y(x)$ is correct, the probability of the observed data is the probability that an error $t_i - y(x_i)$ is due entirely to the noise

$$P\left[t_i = f(x_i) + n_i \mid f = y\right] \quad = \quad P\left[n_i = t_i - y(x_i)\right]. \tag{15.2}$$

If the training cases are independent and the noise is independent and identically distributed, the probability of the entire training set given the assumption $f = y$ is

$$P\left[D \mid f = y\right] = \prod_{i=1}^{m} P\left[n_i = t_i - y(x_i)\right]. \tag{15.3}$$

If the noise is assumed to be Gaussian $N(0, \sigma)$, then

$$P\left[D \mid f = y\right] = \prod_{i=1}^{m} \frac{1}{\sqrt{2\pi}\,\sigma} \exp\left(-\frac{(t_i - y(x_i))^2}{2\sigma^2}\right) \qquad (15.4)$$

$$= \frac{1}{\sqrt{(2\pi)^m}\,\sigma^m} \exp\left(\frac{-E}{2\sigma^2}\right) \qquad (15.5)$$

where $E = \sum_{i=1}^{m}(t_i - y(x_i))^2$ is the usual sum of squared errors. Minimization of the mean-squared-error is thus equivalent to selection of a maximum likelihood model under the assumption that the errors are Gaussian. Other error functions are appropriate under different assumptions about the error distribution; a number are reviewed by Rumelhart et al. [328].

By Bayes' rule, the evidence for a model $y(x)$ given the data is

$$P\left[y \mid D\right] = \frac{P\left[D \mid f = y\right] P\left[f = y\right]}{P\left[D\right]}. \qquad (15.6)$$

External constraints (such as a bias toward smooth solutions) are reflected in the choice of model prior probabilities $P\left[f = y\right]$. The denominator $P\left[D\right]$ is the same for all models and can be ignored in comparing models.

Different model configurations can be compared by decomposing y into a choice of weights $\mathbf{w}$ and a network architecture H. (H specifies the number of layers, number of nodes, etc. and $\mathbf{w}$ specifies a set of weights in the given architecture.) The probability that a given set of weights is the correct choice given the data and the model H is

$$P\left[\mathbf{w} \mid D, H\right] = \frac{P\left[D \mid \mathbf{w}, H\right] P\left[\mathbf{w} \mid H\right]}{P\left[D \mid H\right]}. \qquad (15.7)$$

(Note: this is different from the probability that some learning algorithm will produce a particular set of weights.) For a given H, the prior $P\left[\mathbf{w} \mid H\right]$ can reflect a bias in favor of small weight values, for example. The probability of different models H_i is given by [251]

$$P\left[H_i \mid D\right] \propto P\left[D \mid H_i\right] P\left[H_i\right]. \qquad (15.8)$$

The priors $P\left[H_i\right]$ can reflect a bias in favor of models with small numbers of parameters, for example.

If all prior probabilities $P\left[H_i\right]$ are approximately equal, then the models can be compared based on the evidence [251]

$$P\left[D \mid H_i\right] = \int P\left[D \mid \mathbf{w}, H_i\right] P\left[\mathbf{w} \mid H_i\right]\, d\mathbf{w}. \qquad (15.9)$$

If **w** is k-dimensional and if the posterior distribution is approximately Gaussian, then [251, 253]

$$P\left[D \mid H_i\right] \approx P\left[D \mid \mathbf{w}_{mp}, H_i\right] P\left[\mathbf{w}_{mp} \mid H_i\right] (2\pi)^{k/2} \det^{-1/2} \mathbf{A} \qquad (15.10)$$

where $\mathbf{w}_{mp}$ is the maximum likelihood set of weights found by minimizing E and $\mathbf{A} = -\nabla\nabla \log P\left[\mathbf{w} \mid D, H_i\right]$ is the Hessian of E with respect to $\mathbf{w}$ evaluated at $\mathbf{w}_{mp}$. It has been argued [251, 253] that this approach has a built-in bias for simple models because the Occam factor $P\left[\mathbf{w}_{mp} \mid H_i\right] (2\pi)^{k/2} \det^{-1/2} \mathbf{A}$ is smaller for more complex models.

Remarks Perhaps in part because of its widespread success, criticisms of the Bayesian approach have been raised. From the viewpoint of the prediction system, approximation errors are random and unpredictable (otherwise it would be able to eliminate them) so errors are treated like noise and usually assumed to be independent and identically distributed. All network functions and most real target functions have structure, however, so errors may not be independent. The errors are often assumed to have some tractable distribution such as Gaussian (justified by the central limit theorem), but approximations are often made that hold only for large sample sizes. A common criticism of Bayesian approaches in general is that the prior probabilities may be subjective (i.e., biases rather than measured probabilities). This is not a major problem in cases where all the probabilities can be measured, or when the analysis is used for qualitative understanding, but may be a problem in quantitative predictions. Many of these criticisms are objections to the way the theory is applied, rather than defects of the theory itself.

15.3 Akaike's Final Prediction Error

A standard estimate of the test set error for a linear system is Akaike's final prediction error (FPE) [6, 7]:

$$\hat{E}_{test} = \frac{p + N}{p - N} E_{train} \qquad (15.11)$$

where p is the number of training samples and N is the number of parameters in the model.

A related estimate, Akaike's information criterion (AIC) [7], has been used to compare linear models with different numbers of parameters

$$AIC(\theta) = (-2) \log(\text{maximum likelihood}) + 2k \qquad (15.12)$$

where θ is a model with k parameters. If equation 15.5 is valid, then

$$AIC(\theta) = 2E + 2k \qquad (15.13)$$

where E is the usual mean-squared error. With this cost function, simple models are preferred over complex models if the increased cost of the additional parameters in the complex models do not result in corresponding decreases in the error. There are a number of similar criteria developed for linear systems.

The Effective Number of Parameters   A problem with these estimates is that they are asymptotic approximations valid only for linear systems with large sample sets. The assumptions are invalid for small sample sizes [61]. An extension to linear systems with finite sample sizes is considered by Hansen [152]. Some work has been done to extend this to nonlinear systems by estimating the *effective number of parameters* from derivatives of the error with respect to the weights [273]. One form, for a single-hidden-layer network, is [365]

$$\hat{E}_{test} = \frac{p + N_{eff}}{p - N_{eff}} E_{train} \tag{15.14}$$

where

$$N_{eff} = \sum_{ij}^{N_w} \left(\frac{\lambda_{ij}}{\lambda_{ij} + 2\alpha_w/p} \right)^2 + \sum_{j}^{N_W} \left(\frac{\Lambda_{ij}}{\Lambda_{ij} + 2\alpha_W/p} \right)^2 . \tag{15.15}$$

Here N_w and N_W are the number of weights (including thresholds) in the hidden and output units, respectively, and the λ's are second derivatives $\lambda_{ij} \equiv \partial^2 E_{train}/\partial w_{ij}^2$, $\Lambda_{ij} \equiv \partial^2 E_{train}/\partial W_{ij}^2$. This estimate is used to determine when to stop a pruning algorithm in [365].

15.4   PAC Learning and the VC Dimension

Valiant's PAC (probably approximately correct) learning model and the Vapnik-Chervonenkis (VC) dimension have been used to study the problem of learning binary valued functions from examples, for example, [376, 49, 1]. These relate the complexity of a learning system to the number of examples required for it to learn a particular function from a given class of functions. Briefly, if the number of examples is small relative to the complexity of the system, the generalization error is expected to be high.

Abu-Mostafa [1] provides a brief tutorial on which the following paragraphs are based. More complete descriptions can be found in several texts, [282] for example. A learning algorithm samples points $x \in X$, observes the target values $f(x)$, and tries to find a hypothesis function $g(x)$ that matches f everywhere. The examples are assumed to be drawn independently from some fixed distribution, which can be arbitrary as long as the same distribution is used for learning and testing. The hypothesis functions are drawn from a restricted class G. The algorithm chooses among hypothesis functions based on their performance on the samples. If the number of samples is too small, the estimated performance ν_g (the frequency of error on the test set) could differ significantly from the actual performance π_g and the algorithm could be fooled. A condition for uniform convergence [379] is

$$P\left[\sup_{g \in G} |\nu_g - \pi_g| > \epsilon\right] \le 4m(2N)\, e^{-\epsilon^2 N/8} \tag{15.16}$$

where m is a function which depends on G. For ν_g to approach π_g as the number of samples N becomes large, the righthand term must approach 0. The $e^{-\epsilon^2 N/8}$ term decays exponentially with N so convergence is possible if the function $m(2N)$ does not grow too fast. This is satisfied when $m(N)$ is polynomial in N, for example [1].

The growth function $m(N)$ measures the number of ways that G can label N arbitrary but independent points. The VC dimension d of class G measures the maximum number of points N for which a function in G can always be found that will fit the points no matter how they are labeled. For $N < d$, $m(N)$ grows exponentially with N (i.e. 2^N). For $N > d$, G cannot realize some labelings of the points and $m(N)$ ceases to grow exponentially. Thus $m(N) \le 2^d + 1$.

The importance of this to learning is that if the number of examples is large compared to the VC dimension of the target function class, then equation 15.16 promises uniform convergence. The estimated error rates will then be close to the actual rates and the learning algorithm has a reliable method to choose the best hypothesis.

The sample complexity $m(\epsilon, \delta)$ of a class G is the smallest sample size that guarantees uniform convergence for all target concepts in G and all sampling distributions. An upper bound is [49]

$$m(\epsilon, \delta) = \max\left\{\frac{4}{\epsilon}\log_2\frac{2}{\delta},\ \frac{8d}{\epsilon}\log_2\frac{13}{\epsilon}\right\}. \tag{15.17}$$

A lower bound is [117]

$$\Omega\left(\frac{1}{\epsilon}\ln\frac{1}{\delta} + \frac{d}{\epsilon}\right). \tag{15.18}$$

This is relevant to neural network training in that a network is capable of representing a certain class of concepts and so has some particular VC dimension (e.g., the VC dimension of a simple perceptron with k inputs is $k + 1$). If the network can be trained on a number

$m(\epsilon, \delta)$ of examples achieving an error no greater than ϵ on the training set, then, with probability $1 - \delta$, one expects that the true error is no greater than 2ϵ and similar average error can be expected on novel examples drawn from the same distribution.

By assuming a uniform sampling distribution, the VC dimension of a feedforward network with N nodes and W weights has been estimated as [33, 32, 34]

$$d_{VC} \leq 2W \log_2(eN). \tag{15.19}$$

This has been used to put an upper bound on the number of examples that might be needed to achieve a given generalization error rate. If the network can be trained with

$$m \geq O\left(\frac{W}{\epsilon} \log_2 \frac{N}{\epsilon}\right) \tag{15.20}$$

randomly selected training examples achieving an error rate of less than $\epsilon/2$, then a generalization error rate of at most ϵ can be expected for examples drawn from the same distribution (for $0 < \epsilon \leq 1/8$). This agrees with the rule of thumb that roughly $O(W/\epsilon)$ examples are needed to achieve a generalization error less than ϵ.

For a network with N inputs and one hidden layer of H units [33],

$$d_{VC} \geq 2\lfloor \frac{H}{2} \rfloor N. \tag{15.21}$$

This is approximately equal to the number of weights W for large H, also suggesting that $\Omega(W/\epsilon)$ examples are needed to achieve a generalization error less than ϵ.

Problems   Because the theory is very general, the estimated bounds are loose. Its main value to neural network design seems to be to indicate that if there are enough examples, then the training error should be a good predictor of the generalization error. This allows broad statements to be made about the appropriate size of a network given a particular amount of training data. These bounds, however, do not apply to networks with multiple continuous outputs and they do not say how to choose a suitable network given a particular set of examples to be learned. Other concerns are that the analysis is asymptotic, whereas data are often finite, and the bounds are worst-case (over any data distribution) and appear to be overly pessimistic; the number of examples required to satisfy PAC requirements is often very high. For practical problems, the average-case behavior may be more important. Numerical tests [85, 172] show that the average behavior can be better than the VC bounds in many cases.

The basic theory also ignores peculiarities of specific learning algorithms. Techniques such as pruning and regularization may add constraints that prevent full exploitation of the intrinsic network complexity. Large networks can realize complex functions, but they can also mimic simple (e.g., linear) functions. A network is usually initialized with small weights and the resulting input-output relationship is very smooth, almost linear. As the network is trained, the weights become larger and the transfer function more complex. The complexity of the transfer function thus depends on other factors in addition to network size. Some work has been done to estimate the *effective* number of parameters based on the network response function [378, 147]. Normally, the effective dimension cannot be calculated analytically but it may be estimated from network performance. This approach may be able to account for dynamic changes in network complexity as a result of training.

This is an active research area, however, and new results continue to appear. It is known, for example, that networks with continuous activation functions are more powerful than networks of threshold units. Recent work suggests that networks with continuous unit activations can have VC dimension at least as large W^2, where W is the number of weights [213]. This means that it may be very hard to constrain a network with reasonable numbers of examples.

16 Heuristics for Improving Generalization

Given that data are limited and may be sampled in nonrandom ways, and that little is known about the "complexity" of the target function, the problem is to produce a system that fits the data as accurately as possible. One of the first tasks is to choose a network architecture. Even when generalization is not explicitly mentioned, the intent is usually to find a network that is powerful enough to solve the problem but simple enough to train easily and generalize well. Generalization criteria usually favor choosing the smallest network that will do the job, but in small networks back-propagation, for example, may be more likely to become trapped by local minima and may be more sensitive to initial conditions. If the algorithm cannot find a solution that does well on the training set, the solution it does find is not likely to do well on the test set either and generalization will be poor. Given limitations in the learning algorithm, a network that learns the problem reliably may be more complex than absolutely necessary and may not generalize as well as possible. Thus, additional techniques are often needed to aid generalization.

The following sections discuss some specific techniques that have been suggested as ways to improve generalization. Some are based on theoretical principles while others are more heuristic. Purely numerical techniques are considered first, followed by techniques using domain-dependent prior information.

16.1 Early Stopping

Figure 14.9 shows that generalization performance can vary with time during training. When the network is underconstrained, the generalization error may reach a minimum but then increase as the network fits peculiarities of the training set that are not characteristic of the target function. One approach to avoid overfitting is to monitor the generalization error and stop training when the minimum is observed. The generalization error is commonly estimated by simple cross-validation with a holdout set although more sophisticated estimates may be used. In [243, 371, 337], the generalization ability of the network is estimated based on its pre- and post-training performance on previously unseen training data. Early-stopping is compared to a number of other nonconvergent training techniques by Finnoff, Hergert, and Zimmermann [123, 122]. A practical advantage of early stopping is that it is often faster than training to complete convergence followed by pruning.

Although early stopping can be effective, some care is needed in deciding when to stop. As noted in section 14.5.3, the validation error surface may have local minima that could fool simple algorithms into stopping too soon [16]. The generalization vs. time curve may also have long flat regions preceding a steep drop-off [16]. It should also be noted that figure 14.9 represents an idealized situation; the training curves are often noisy and may need to be filtered. A simple way to avoid many of these problems is to train until the network is clearly overfitting, retaining the best set of weights observed along the trajectory.

Although early stopping helps prevent overfitting, the results apply only to the chosen network. To achieve the best possible generalization, it is still necessary to test other network configurations and additional criteria will probably be needed to choose among them. The fact the overtraining is not observed in one training trial does not mean that it will not occur in another and is not proof that a suitable network size has been selected.

It can be argued that part of the reason for the relative success of back-propagation with early stopping is that it has a built-in bias for simple solutions because, when initialized with small weights, the network follows a path of increasing complexity from nearly constant functions to linear functions to increasingly nonlinear functions. Training is normally stopped as soon as some nonzero error criterion is met, so the algorithm is more likely to find a simple solution than a more complex solution that gives the same result. Cross-validation is a method for comparing solutions, but *stopping* when the validation error is minimum takes advantage of these special dynamics. It may be less effective for systems initialized with large weights or second-order algorithms that make large weight changes at each iteration.

16.2   Regularization

A problem is said to be *ill-posed* if small changes in the given information cause large changes in the solution. This instability with respect to the data makes solutions unreliable because small measurement errors or uncertainties in parameters may be greatly magnified and lead to wildly different responses. In contrast, a problem is *well-posed* if (*i*) it has a solution, (*ii*) the solution is unique, and (*iii*) the solution varies continuously with the given data. Violation of any of these conditions makes the problem ill-posed [370].

The idea behind regularization is to use supplementary information to restate an ill-posed problem in a stable form. The result will be a well-behaved, but approximate, solution of the original problem. Ideally, the bias introduced by the approximation will be more than offset by the gain in reliability. In general, domain-specific knowledge will be needed to stabilize a problem without changing it fundamentally.

Regularization has been studied extensively for linear systems. The book by Tikhonov and Arsenin [370] is a classic reference. In the context of learning from limited data, generalization is an unrealistic goal unless additional information is available beyond the training samples. One of the least restrictive assumptions is that the target function is smooth, that is, that small changes in the input do not cause large changes in the output. Given two functions that fit the data equally well, we tend to prefer the smoother one because it is somehow simpler or more efficient. This bias is embedded in the learning algorithm by adding terms to the cost function to penalize nonsmooth solutions. In addition to the usual term E_o measuring the approximation error, we add terms $\Omega(y)$ which measure how well the approximation function $y(\mathbf{x})$ conforms to our preferences

$$E = E_o + \lambda\Omega(y). \tag{16.1}$$

The regularizing parameter λ balances the trade-off between minimizing the approximation error and conforming to the external constraints. A regularizer favoring smooth functions is [300]

$$E = E_o + \lambda\|Py\|^2 \tag{16.2}$$

where the regularizer P is a differential operator. This rewards smooth functions (whose derivatives are small, on average) and penalizes nonsmooth functions (those with large derivatives).

Regularization can be fit into a Bayesian approach [274, 140]. Equation 16.2, for example, corresponds to a prior in equation 15.6

$$P\left[f = y\right] \propto \exp(-\lambda\|Py\|^2). \tag{16.3}$$

Approximation with radial basis functions (which are linear in their output weights) is equivalent to classical regularization under certain conditions [274, 140]. Radial basis functions, however, form mostly local internal representations and therefore usually do not generalize as well as sigmoid networks (e.g., [56]). Curvature-driven smoothing using second derivative information as a means of improving generalization in radial basis function nets is discussed by Bishop [42].

Regularization provides a way of biasing the learning algorithm, but its success depends on the choice of an appropriate value for the regularization parameter λ to determine how strong the bias should be. In many of the other proposed heuristics there is a similar parameter balancing the need to minimize training error with other constraints. The parameter has an important effect on the eventual solution and is usually determined by criteria such as cross-validation. Although not discussed here, it is often useful to change the parameter dynamically because overfitting usually is not a problem until the later stages of learning. In many cases, it helps to impose the constraints only after the network has made some progress in reducing the initial error. In difficult problems, for example, there may be long periods before the network makes any significant progress. If a strong weight decay rule were in force during this period, the network might never escape from the initial set of weights around $\mathbf{w} = 0$.

16.3   Pruning Methods

Pruning algorithms are surveyed in chapter 13. The following paragraphs outline a few main points. Because the target function is unknown, it is difficult to predict ahead of time what size network will learn the data without overtraining. Not knowing the optimum network configuration, one can train many networks and choose the smallest or least complex one that learns the data. Although simple, this approach can be inefficient if many networks must be trained before an acceptable one is found. Even if the optimum size is known, the smallest networks just complex enough to fit the data may (depending on the learning algorithm) be sensitive to initial conditions and learning parameters. It may be hard to tell if the network is too small to learn the data, if it is simply learning very slowly, or if it is stuck in a local minima due to an unfortunate set of initial conditions or parameters. Thus, even if one finds a small network that will reliably learn the data, there might be a still smaller network that would work but is very difficult to train.

The pruning approach is to train a network that is somewhat larger than necessary and then remove unnecessary elements. The large initial size allows the network to learn reasonably quickly with less sensitivity to initial conditions and local minima while the reduced complexity of the trimmed system favors improved generalization. In several studies, e.g., [345, 344], pruning techniques produced solutions for small networks that generalized well and were not reliably obtainable by training the reduced network with random weights.

Although pruning techniques provide a means to simplify a network, they must be guided by other criteria to decide how simple the network should be. That is, there is still a need for external information and theoretical criteria to decide when to stop pruning.

16.4   Constructive Methods

Pruning methods train a larger-than-necessary network and then remove unneeded elements. The opposite approach is to build a network incrementally, adding elements until a suitable configuration is found. The two approaches are complementary and often used together. Like pruning, constructive techniques are a means of adjusting the size of a network rather than a method for deciding what size is appropriate. Other criteria are still necessary to decide when to stop adding elements. A number of constructive methods are discussed in chapter 12. Cascade-correlation [120] is often cited as an example.

16.5   Weight Decay

One way to implement a bias for simple or smooth functions is to favor networks with small weights over those with large weights. Large weights tend to cause sharp transitions in the node functions and thus large changes in output for small changes in the inputs. A simple way to obtain some of the benefits of pruning without complicating the learning algorithm much is to add a decay term like $-\beta w$ to the weight update rule. Weights that are not essential to the solution decay to zero and can be removed. Even if they aren't removed, they have no effect on the output so the network acts like a smaller system. Weight decay rules have been used in many studies, for example, [299, 388, 387, 227]. Several methods are compared by Hergert, Finnoff, and Zimmermann [165].

Weight decay can be considered as a form of regularization (e.g., [227]). Adding a $\beta \sum_i w_i^2$ regularizing term to the cost function, for example, is equivalent to addition of a $-\beta w_i$ decay term to the weight update rule. A drawback of the $\sum_i w_i^2$ penalty term is that it tends to favor weight vectors with many small components over those with a few large components, even when this is an effective choice. An alternative [386, 387, 388] is

$$\lambda \sum_i \frac{w_i^2/w_o^2}{1 + w_i^2/w_o^2}. \tag{16.4}$$

When λ is large, this is similar to weight decay methods. For $|w_i| \ll w_o$, the cost is small but grows like w_i^2 while, for $|w_i| \gg w_o$, the cost of a weight saturates and approaches a constant λ. (The developers call this form 'weight elimination' to differentiate it from simple weight decay.)

Soft weight sharing [286, 285] is another method that allows large weights when they are needed by using a penalty term that models the prior likelihood of the weights as a mixture of Gaussians. In practice, a number of Gaussians are used and their centers and widths are adapted to minimize the cost function. This reduces the complexity of the network by increasing the correlation among weight values.

Hard weight sharing is commonly used in image processing networks where the same kernel is applied repeatedly at different positions in the input image. In a neural network, separate hidden nodes may be used to compute the kernel at different locations and the number of weights could be huge. Constraining nodes that compute the same kernel to have the same weights greatly reduces the network complexity [91].

Example   Figure 16.1 illustrates effects of weight decay. A 2/50/10/1 network was trained on 31 points using normal batch back-propagation (learning rate 0.01, momentum and weight decay 0). The network is very underconstrained. After 200 epochs the weight

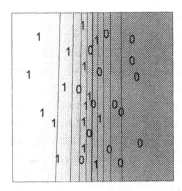

Figure 16.1
Effect of training with weight decay. A 2/50/10/1 network was trained using normal back-propagation for 200 epochs. Then weight decay was set to 1E-4 and training resumed for a total of 5000 epochs. Unlike figure 14.5, the decision surface is very simple and does not show obvious signs of overtraining.

decay was set to 1E-4 and training resumed for a total of 5000 epochs. Unlike figure 14.5 the decision surface is simple and smooth and doesn't show obvious signs of overtraining in spite of long training times. The response is basically that of a single sigmoid unit.

Figure 16.2 shows another example. Figure 16.2(a) shows the response of a network trained by normal batch back-propagation (learning rate 0.03, momentum and weight decay 0) until all patterns were correctly classified (error less than 0.1) at about 11,000 epochs. The network is underconstrained and the boundary is complex with steep transitions. Another net was trained with the same initial weights and learning rate but with weight decay increasing from 0 to 1E-5 at 1200 epochs, to 1E-4 at 2500 epochs, and to 1E-3 at 4000 epochs after which it was held constant. Figure 16.2(b) shows the response after 20,000 epochs. The surface is smoother and transitions are more gradual, but it could be argued that the data are still somewhat overfitted. Figure 16.2(c) shows the response after the learning rate was reduced to 0.01 and training resumed for another 1000 epochs. Further smoothing occurs because of the shift in balance between error minimization and weight decay.

In addition to showing the smoothing effects of weight decay, these examples show that the results may be hard to predict a priori. As in other regularization or penalty-term methods, there is a complex interaction between error minimization and constraint satisfaction. The particular value of the weight decay parameter (or regularization parameter in general) determines where equilibria occur, but it is difficult to predict ahead of time what value is needed to achieve desired results. The value 0.001 was chosen rather arbitrarily because it is a typically cited round number, but figure 16.2(b) is still perhaps somewhat overfitted.

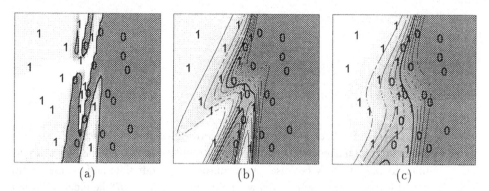

Figure 16.2
Effects of weight decay: (a) response of a 2/50/10/1 network trained by batch back-propagation until all patterns
were correctly classified at about 11,000 epochs; (b) response after 20,000 epochs of a network trained from the
same starting point with weight decay increasing to 0.001 at 4000 epochs; and (c) response of the network in (b)
after 1000 more epochs with the learning rate decreased to 0.01.

16.6   Information Minimization

A heuristic for improving generalization based on the idea of information minimization is
described by Kamimura, Takagi, and Nakanishi [205]. The uncertainty of a sigmoidal node
is taken to be maximum when its activation is 0.5. A pseudo-entropy of the network for a
particular set of patterns is defined as

$$H = -\sum_{k}^{K}\sum_{i}^{M}\left[v_i^k \log v_i^k + (1 - v_i^k)\log(1 - v_i^k)\right] \qquad (16.5)$$

where K is the number of input patterns, M is the number of hidden units, and v_i^k is the
activation of unit i for pattern k. The information in the network is given as

$$I = H_{max} - H$$
$$= KM \log 2 + H.$$

The entropy is used as a penalty function to minimize the information contained in the
network so the augmented error function is

$$E' = \beta E_o + \alpha H$$

where E_o is the standard sum of squared errors. Minimizing E' adds the term

$$\phi_i^k = v_i^k(1 - v_i^k)\log\frac{1 - v_i^k}{v_i^k}$$

to the weight adjustment rule, giving

$$\Delta w_{ij} = -\frac{\partial E}{\partial w_{ij}}$$

$$= \sum_k (\alpha \phi_i^k + \beta \delta_i^k)\, v_j^k.$$

Here, $\delta_i^k = \partial E_k / \partial a_i$ is the back-propagation delta term calculated in section 5.2. The use of H as a penalty term makes this an example of a regularization method. This also has effects similar to weight decay because (i) the entropy of a sigmoidal node is maximum when its output is 0.5, (ii) the output is 0.5 when the input is 0, and (iii) the input is 0 when the input weights are 0; that is, minimizing the weights would tend to minimize $-H$.

16.7   Replicated Networks

Another idea for improving generalization is to combine the outputs of several systems that differ in how they classify novel examples [245, 298, 189, 238, 63, 36, 111]. (Though not about neural networks per se [83] surveys many methods for combining forecasts.) The subsystems may differ due to variations in configuration, size, initialization, variations in the learning algorithm, differences in training data, and so on, or because they use completely different approximation models. The important factor is that they represent a variety of solutions to the same problem. There is no benefit in evaluating multiple models that all predict the same thing, after all.

With a mean-square error function, the best generalization would be expected when the system generates the expected value of all possible consistent functions, weighted by their probability of occurrence. That is

$$f^*(x) = \int f(x) p_f(f)\, df. \tag{16.6}$$

Averaging the output of different systems is a simple approximation to this expected value and tends to damp out extreme behaviors that might not be justified by the data. Additional advantages are improved fault-tolerance and the ability to retrain poorly performing subsystems using the ensemble average as the target.

Although more sophisticated combination methods are possible, a simple average may do as well as other methods in many cases [83]. A weighted average is often suggested

$$\sum_k c_k f_k(x). \tag{16.7}$$

The weighting factors c_k may be determined by a linear regression or depend on how well each subsystem performs on its training data; there are other possibilities. Because similar systems trained on similar data are likely to make similar predictions, colinearity of the $f_k(x)$ could make the linear regression ill-conditioned and result in a bad choice of c values. (This is one suggestion for why a simple average often does as well as more complicated methods.) Use of a convex linear combination in which $\sum_k c_k = 1$ is suggested in [60] for this reason.

Stacked-generalization [409] is a related method for improving generalization. Rather than simply averaging the outputs of several systems, the outputs are combined in more complex ways to maximize generalization.

The idea that replicating networks could help generalization might seem counterintuitive because N replicated networks would have N times as many weights and thus might need many more examples to constrain. The networks are trained independently, however, so the number of examples needed to train each does not change. If identical networks are trained on different subsets of the data (each net having a different holdout set used to control overfitting) and their outputs averaged to obtain the global output, this is similar to doing k-fold cross-validation or bootstrapping in parallel.

In general, a training set can contain regularities on many scales. Different subsystems with different biases, but trained with the same goals, are likely to agree about the large scale regularities that are obviously "supported by the data" while disagreeing mostly on smaller factors. An overtrained subsystem could choose a very idiosyncratic solution that is unlikely to match the real target function, but there are a huge number of ways to overfit the data and independent subsystems are likely to choose different ones. By averaging many responses, the total system expresses the consensus about obvious regularities recognized by most subsystems while avoiding extreme solutions in areas where there is disagreement.

A problem with this approach is that the number of systems that may need to be averaged in order to improve generalization significantly could be very large, particularly when the systems are complex; that is, the estimated mean in equation 16.6 could have a high variance. There is also still a need for external information to bias the learning algorithm to produce subnetworks that share the bias $p_f(f)$.

16.8   Training with Noisy Data

Many studies (e.g., [299, 118, 310, 387, 345, 246, 287, 267]) have noted that adding small amounts of input noise (jitter) to the training data often aids generalization and fault tolerance. Training with small amounts of added input noise embodies a smoothness assumption because we assume that slightly different inputs give approximately the same output. If the noise distribution is smooth, the network will interpolate among training points in relation to a smooth function of the distance to each training point.

With jitter, the effective target function is the result of convolution of the actual target with the noise density [307, 306]. This is typically a smoothing operation. Averaging the network output over the input noise gives rise to terms related to the magnitude of the gradient of the transfer function and thus approximates regularization [307, 306, 45].

Training with jitter helps prevent overfitting in large networks by providing additional constraints because the effective target function is a continuous function defined over the entire input space whereas the original target function is defined only at the specific training points. This constrains the network and forces it to use excess degrees of freedom to approximate the smoothed target function rather than forming an arbitrarily complex surface that just happens to fit the sampled training data. Even though the network may be large, it models a simpler system.

Training with noisy inputs also gives rise to effects similar to weight decay and gain scaling. Gain scaling [228, 171] is a heuristic that has been proposed as a way of improving generalization. (Something like gain scaling is also used in [252] to "moderate" the outputs of a classifier.) Effects similar to training with jitter (and thus similar to regularization) can be achieved in single-hidden-layer networks by scaling the sigmoid gains [305, 306]. This is usually much more efficient than tediously averaging over many noisy samples. The scaling operation is equivalent to

$$\mathbf{w} \to \frac{\mathbf{w}}{\sqrt{\|\mathbf{w}\|^2 \sigma^2 + 1}}$$

where σ^2 is the variance of the input noise. This has properties similar to weight decay. The development of weight decay terms as a result of training single-layer linear perceptrons with input noise is shown in [167]. Effects of training with input noise and its relation to target smoothing, regularization, gain scaling and weight decay are considered in more detail in chapter 17.

16.9 Use of Domain-Dependent Prior Information

The methods considered so far are mostly numerical techniques that make no use of problem-specific information. Another powerful way of favoring good generalization is through the use of domain-dependent prior information.

As noted earlier, samples alone are not enough to uniquely specify the target function in the absence of other constraints. In many applications where neural nets are considered, there is significant human knowledge that could be useful even though it is incomplete or only partially reliable. There may be existing techniques that give reasonable but imperfect solutions or we may know certain rules that should be satisfied by any correct solution. When the goal is to develop a working application, it makes sense to use as much of this information as possible.

The following sections review some ways of using domain-dependent prior information in a neural network. Some are based on the idea of adapting a good non-neural solution to provide the starting point for further fine tuning in a neural network structure. It should be noted that whether or not this leads to good generalization depends on many factors; in some cases it may merely accelerate learning by giving the network a good headstart, without really improving generalization.

16.10   Hint Functions

One way to provide additional constraints is through the use of "hints" [361, 416]. In addition to outputs for the function of interest, extra output nodes are added to the network and trained to learn certain hint functions. The hint functions should be related to the function of interest and are usually designed to be easier to learn. The extra functions may speed convergence by generating nonzero derivatives in regions where the original function has plateaued. They may also aid generalization by providing additional constraints and removing certain local minima of the original function. They discourage the choice of a solution that somehow matches the original function on the training samples but does not include intermediate concepts embedded in the hints. After training, the hint output nodes can be removed because they usually are not of interest in the overall system.

The term hints is usually used to refer to augmented outputs, but hint information can also be provided in the form of targets for the (normally) hidden nodes. Hints can also be provided by shaping the target function dynamically [193]. The initial target function is an easy to learn, coarse approximation of the desired function which is gradually made more similar to the desired function as the learner masters each stage. This is a standard technique in animal training.

16.11   Knowledge-Based Neural Nets

Rule-based systems, such as expert systems, have been used quite successfully in many applications. These systems use human information efficiently and there is interest in developing hybrid systems combining the high-level information processing abilities of symbolic systems with the adaptability of neural nets. A useful feature of expert systems which neural networks generally lack is the ability to explain the reasoning behind its conclusions.

One approach [342, 375] is to embed symbolic rules in the initial structure of a neural network by translating the AND, OR, and NOT terms into corresponding network structures with appropriate weights. (Simple variable-free propositional rules are easily translated to neural network structures.) Additional links with small random weights are provided to let the system add other terms that may be useful. The network is then trained from examples to improve its performance. Because the embedded symbolic rules are often classifications, the cross-entropy error function may work better than the mean-squared-error function [342].

Besides faster training due to a good initial solution, improved generalization has been observed in spite of imperfect embedded rules. This is attributed to "(1) focusing attention on relevant input features, and (2) indicating useful intermediate conclusions (which suggest a good network topology)" [342]. Given a sufficient number of examples, a standard network initialized with random weights should converge to the same asymptotic performance, but the knowledge-based networks generalize better when examples are sparse. Evidently "the initial knowledge is 'worth' some number of training examples" [342]. Some references for ways of using forms of prior knowledge other than symbolic rules are provided by Shavlik [342].

16.12 Physical Models to Generate Additional Data

When there is no theoretical understanding of the target function, training from examples is one of few options. In many cases, however, there may be a physical model that can provide useful information even if it is not completely accurate. Possibilities include

• a rough model exists that accounts for the main variables only and ignores small details;

• an accurate model exists, but is too cumbersome to use in practice; or

• an exact model exists, but it is difficult or expensive to measure all the variables needed by the model.

Models can be useful to generate artificial training data for cases where it is difficult to obtain real training data. In physical control systems, for example, it may not be practical to obtain data for unusual operating modes such as process faults. Use of a model to generate additional artificial data for unusual operating modes of a steel rolling mill is described by Röscheisen, Hofmann, and Tresp [323].

17 Effects of Training with Noisy Inputs

Noise is usually considered undesirable—something to be eliminated if possible, but many studies (e.g. [299, 118, 310, 387, 345, 246, 287, 339, 267]) have noted that adding small amounts of noise to input patterns during training often results in better generalization and fault tolerance.

A short explanation for these results is that the noise blurs the data. When random noise is added every time a pattern is presented, the network never sees exactly that same input twice, even when the same training pattern is selected, so it cannot simply "memorize" the training data. Averaging over the noise effectively smooths the target function and prevents the network from overfitting a limited set of training data. This turns out to be helpful for generalization because many of the functions that interest people tend to be smooth.

The following sections examine these ideas in more detail. The term jitter is used to refer to noise intentionally added to the inputs in contrast to undesired, uncontrolled noise from other sources.

17.1 Convolution Property of Training with Jitter

Consider a network trained with noisy input data, $\{\mathbf{x} + \mathbf{n}, t(\mathbf{x})\}$, where $\mathbf{n}$ is noise that varies with each presentation. During training, the network sees the clean target $t(\mathbf{x})$ in conjunction with the noisy input $\tilde{\mathbf{x}} = \mathbf{x} + \mathbf{n}$. The input $\tilde{\mathbf{x}}$ seen by the network may be produced by various combinations of inputs $\mathbf{x}$ and noises $\mathbf{n}$, while the target depends only on $\mathbf{x}$. Various targets may therefore be associated with the same noisy input $\tilde{\mathbf{x}}$. The network, however, can produce only a single output for any given input. For arbitrary noise and input sampling distributions, the effective target for a given input $\tilde{\mathbf{x}}$ is the expected value of the target given the noisy input

$$\langle t(\mathbf{x}) \mid \tilde{\mathbf{x}} \rangle = \frac{\int_n t(\tilde{\mathbf{x}} - \mathbf{n}) p_{\mathbf{x}}(\tilde{\mathbf{x}} - \mathbf{n}) p_{\mathbf{n}}(\mathbf{n}) \, d\mathbf{n}}{\int_\xi p_{\mathbf{x}}(\tilde{\mathbf{x}} - \xi) p_{\mathbf{n}}(\xi) \, d\xi}. \tag{17.1}$$

In the special case where the distribution $p_{\mathbf{x}}$ of the training inputs is uniform and the standard deviation of the noise is small relative to the extent of the input domain, the interaction between $p_{\mathbf{x}}$ and $p_{\mathbf{n}}$ will have little effect in the interior of the domain. In regions where these boundary effects can be ignored, the $p_{\mathbf{x}}$ terms cancel, the denominator integrates to one, and this simplifies to the approximation

$$\langle t(\tilde{\mathbf{x}} - \mathbf{n}) \mid \tilde{\mathbf{x}} \rangle \approx \int_{\mathbf{n}} t(\tilde{\mathbf{x}} - \mathbf{n}) p_{\mathbf{n}}(\mathbf{n}) \, d\mathbf{n}$$

$$\approx t(\tilde{\mathbf{x}}) * p_{\mathbf{n}}(\tilde{\mathbf{x}}). \tag{17.2}$$

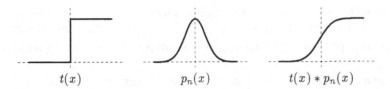

Figure 17.1
Convolution tends to be a smoothing operation. A step function, $t(\mathbf{x})$, convolved with a Gaussian, $p_\mathbf{n}(\mathbf{x})$, produces the Gaussian cumulative distribution. This resembles the original step function, but it is a smooth function similar to the sigmoid.

Thus, in this special case, the effective target when training with jittered input data is approximately equal to the convolution of the original target $t(\mathbf{x})$ and the noise density $p_\mathbf{n}(\mathbf{x})$.

Convolution tends to be a smoothing operation in general. If, for example, a step function, $t(\mathbf{x})$, is convolved with a Gaussian, $p_\mathbf{n}(\mathbf{x})$, the result is the Gaussian cumulative distribution which is a smoothed step function similar to the sigmoid (figure 17.1). This convolutional property resulting from jittered sampling is described by Marks [257].

Holmström and Koistinen [174, 214, 215] showed that training with jitter is consistent in that, under appropriate conditions, the resulting error function approaches the true error function as the number of training samples increases and the amount of added input noise decreases.

17.1.1   Effective Target for Sampled Data

The convolution property holds when training data are continuously and uniformly distributed over the entire input space and the magnitude of the noise is small. In practice, however, we usually have only a finite number of discrete samples $\{(\mathbf{x}_i, t_i)\}$ of the underlying function and the samples are not uniformly distributed in general. In this case, the distribution of $\tilde{\mathbf{x}} = \mathbf{x}_i + \mathbf{n}$ is not uniform and the optimum output function is modified.

Let the training set be $\{(\mathbf{x}_i, t_i) \mid i = 1 \ldots M\}$. During training, we randomly select one of the training pairs with equal probability, add noise to the input vector, and apply it to the network. Given that the training point is $\mathbf{x}_k$, a randomly selected point from the training set, the probability density of the noisy input $\tilde{\mathbf{x}}$ is

$$P\left[\mathbf{x} + \mathbf{n} = \tilde{\mathbf{x}} \mid \mathbf{x} = \mathbf{x}_k\right] = p_\mathbf{n}(\tilde{\mathbf{x}} - \mathbf{x}_k).$$

Training points are selected from the training set with equal probabilities $P\left[\mathbf{x} = \mathbf{x}_k\right] = 1/M$ so the probability density of the input seen by the network, $\tilde{\mathbf{x}}$, is

$$P\left[\tilde{\mathbf{x}}\right] \equiv P\left[\mathbf{x} + \mathbf{n} = \tilde{\mathbf{x}}\right] \tag{17.3}$$

$$= \sum_{k=1}^{M} P\left[\mathbf{x} + \mathbf{n} = \tilde{\mathbf{x}} \mid \mathbf{x} = \mathbf{x}_k\right] \, P\left[\mathbf{x} = \mathbf{x}_k\right]$$

$$= \frac{1}{M} \sum_{k=1}^{M} p_{\mathbf{n}}(\tilde{\mathbf{x}} - \mathbf{x}_k).$$

Given that a particular noisy input $\tilde{\mathbf{x}}$ is observed, the probability that it is generated by training data $\mathbf{x}_k$ plus noise is found by Bayes' rule

$$P\left[\mathbf{x} = \mathbf{x}_k \mid \mathbf{x} + \mathbf{n} = \tilde{\mathbf{x}}\right] = \frac{P\left[\mathbf{x} + \mathbf{n} = \tilde{\mathbf{x}} \mid \mathbf{x} = \mathbf{x}_k\right] P\left[\mathbf{x} = \mathbf{x}_k\right]}{P\left[\mathbf{x} + \mathbf{n} = \tilde{\mathbf{x}}\right]}$$

$$= \frac{p_{\mathbf{n}}(\tilde{\mathbf{x}} - \mathbf{x}_k)(1/M)}{(1/M) \sum_{j=1}^{M} p_{\mathbf{n}}(\tilde{\mathbf{x}} - \mathbf{x}_j)}$$

$$= \frac{p_{\mathbf{n}}(\tilde{\mathbf{x}} - \mathbf{x}_k)}{\sum_{j=1}^{M} p_{\mathbf{n}}(\tilde{\mathbf{x}} - \mathbf{x}_j)}. \tag{17.4}$$

Let P_k denote this probability.

The expected value of the training target, given the noisy training input $\tilde{\mathbf{x}}$, is then

$$\langle t_{\text{train}}(\tilde{\mathbf{x}} - \mathbf{n}) \mid \tilde{\mathbf{x}} \rangle = \sum_{i} t_i P_i$$

$$= \sum_{i} \frac{t_i \, p_{\mathbf{n}}(\tilde{\mathbf{x}} - \mathbf{x}_i)}{\sum_k p_{\mathbf{n}}(\tilde{\mathbf{x}} - \mathbf{x}_k)}. \tag{17.5}$$

This is the expected value of the training target given that the input is a noisy version of one of the training samples. As the number of samples approaches ∞, the distribution of the samples approaches $p_{\mathbf{x}}$ and equation 17.5 becomes a good approximation to equation 17.1.

Let $y(\tilde{\mathbf{x}})$ be the network output for the input $\tilde{\mathbf{x}}$. The expected value of the error while training, given this input, is

$$\tilde{\mathcal{E}} = \sum_{i=1}^{M} (t_i - y(\tilde{\mathbf{x}}))^2 P_i. \tag{17.6}$$

Abbreviate $y(\tilde{\mathbf{x}})$ with y. After expanding the square,

$$\tilde{\mathcal{E}} = (\Sigma t_i^2 P_i) - 2y(\Sigma t_i P_i) + y^2 \Sigma P_i$$

$$= (\Sigma t_i^2 P_i) - (\Sigma t_i P_i)^2 + \left[(\Sigma t_i P_i)^2 - 2y(\Sigma t_i P_i) + y^2 \Sigma P_i \right]$$

$$= (\Sigma t_i^2 P_i) - (\Sigma t_i P_i)^2 + \left[(\Sigma_i t_i P_i) - y \right]^2,$$

and

$$\frac{\partial \tilde{\mathcal{E}}}{\partial w} = -2 \left[(\Sigma_i t_i P_i) - y \right] \frac{\partial y}{\partial w}. \qquad (17.7)$$

In other words, under gradient descent, the system acts as if the target function is $\Sigma_i t_i P_i$, the expected value of the target in equation 17.5, given the conditions stated for P_i. This is a well-known result in optimal least squares estimation: the function that minimizes the sum-of-squares error is the expected value of the target given the input. From equation 17.7 the effective error function is

$$E_{eff} = \left[(\Sigma_i t_i P_i) - y \right]^2 \qquad (17.8)$$

in the sense that $\frac{\partial E_{eff}}{\partial w} = \frac{\partial \tilde{\mathcal{E}}}{\partial w}$. In contrast to conventional training where the target is defined only at the training points, the effective target when training with jittered inputs is a function defined for all inputs $\mathbf{x}$.

Figure 17.2 illustrates the point. Figure 17.2(a) shows the Voronoi map of a set of points in two dimensions, the basis for a nearest neighbor classifier. Figure 17.2(b) is expression

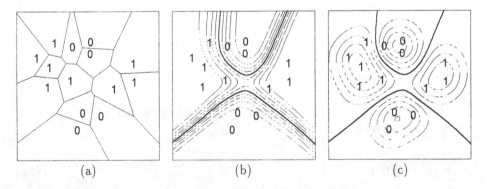

(a) (b) (c)

Figure 17.2
A nearest neighbor classification problem: (a) the Voronoi map for 14 points; and (b) the expected value of the classification given the noisy input as calculated in (17.5) for a Gaussian noise distribution with $\sigma = 0.1$. (c) The convolution of the training set with the same Gaussian noise. The zero contours of (b) and (c) coincide. (1s and 0s indicate classes; values 1 and -1 were actually used.)

(17.5) for the expected target given the noisy input. Figure 17.2(c) shows the convolution of the sampled target function with a Gaussian function; the convolution smooths the nearest neighbor decision surface and removes small features. Note that the zero contours in figures 17.2(b) and 17.2(c) coincide.

17.2   Error Regularization and Training with Jitter

Regularization is another method often used to improve generalization. In regularization, one often assumes that the target function is smooth and that small changes in the input do not cause large changes in the output. Poggio and Girosi [300], for example, suggest the cost function

$$\sum_i (y_i - t_i)^2 + \lambda \|Py\|^2 \tag{17.9}$$

where 'P is usually a differential operator' and λ balances the trade-off between smoothing and minimizing the error.

Jittering the inputs while keeping the target fixed embodies this smoothness assumption and results in a similar cost function. That is, we add small amounts of noise to the input data, assume that the target function does not change much, and minimize

$$\mathcal{E} = \{\langle [t(\mathbf{x}) - y(\mathbf{x} + \mathbf{n})]^2 \rangle\} \tag{17.10}$$

$$= \{t(\mathbf{x})^2 - 2t(\mathbf{x})\langle y(\mathbf{x} + \mathbf{n})\rangle + \langle y(\mathbf{x} + \mathbf{n})^2\rangle\} \tag{17.11}$$

where $\{u\}$ indicates the expected value of u over the training patterns and $\langle u \rangle$ indicates the expected value of u over the noise $\mathbf{n}$. For small magnitude noise, $\|\mathbf{n}\| \approx 0$, the network output can be approximated by the linear terms of a truncated Taylor series expansion

$$y(\mathbf{x} + \mathbf{n}) \approx y(\mathbf{x}) + \mathbf{g}^T \mathbf{n} \tag{17.12}$$

where $\mathbf{g} = \frac{\partial y}{\partial \mathbf{x}}$ is the gradient of the output with respect to the input. (A second-order approximation is given in appendix C.1.

Substitution into equation 17.11 and dropping the independent variable for brevity gives

$$\mathcal{E} \approx \left\{ \begin{array}{c} t^2 - 2ty - 2t\mathbf{g}^T \langle \mathbf{n} \rangle \\ +y^2 + 2y\mathbf{g}^T \langle \mathbf{n} \rangle + \mathbf{g}^T \langle \mathbf{n} \, \mathbf{n}^T \rangle \mathbf{g} \end{array} \right\}. \tag{17.13}$$

Assume zero-mean uncorrelated noise with equal variances, $\langle \mathbf{n} \rangle = 0$ and $\langle \mathbf{n} \, \mathbf{n}^T \rangle = \sigma^2 \mathbf{I}$. Then

$$\mathcal{E} \approx \left\{ t^2 - 2ty + y^2 + \sigma^2 \mathbf{g}^T \mathbf{g} \right\} \tag{17.14}$$

$$\approx \{(t - y)^2\} + \sigma^2 \left\{ \|\mathbf{g}\|^2 \right\}. \tag{17.15}$$

The term $\{(t - y)^2\} = E$ is the conventional unregularized error function and the term $\{\|\mathbf{g}\|^2\}$ is the squared magnitude of the gradient of $y(\mathbf{x})$ averaged over the training points.

$\mathcal{E}$ is an approximation to the regularized error function in equation 17.9. Like equation 17.9, it introduces a term which encourages smooth solutions [384, 42]. Comparison of equations 17.15 and 17.9 shows that σ^2 plays a role similar to λ in the regularization equation, balancing smoothness and error minimization. They differ in that training with jitter minimizes the gradient term at the training points whereas regularization usually seeks to minimize it for all $\mathbf{x}$.

Equation 17.15 shows that, when it can do so without increasing the conventional error, the system minimizes sensitivity to input noise by reducing the magnitude of the gradient of the transfer function at the training points. A similar result is derived in [260] and, by analogy with the ridge estimate method of linear regression, in [259]. A system that explicitly calculates and back-propagates similar terms in a multilayer perceptron is described by Ducker and Le Cun [112]. A more general approach using the Hessian information is described by Bishop [40, 42, 43]. A stronger result equating training with jitter and Tikhonov regularization is reported in [45].

Figure 17.3 illustrates the smoothing effect of training with input jitter. Figure 17.3(a) shows the decision boundary formed by an intentionally overtrained 2/50/10/1 feedforward

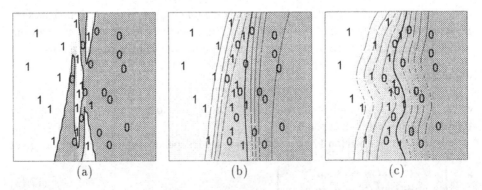

(a)   (b)   (c)

Figure 17.3
Smoothing effects of training with jitter: (a) an intentionally overtrained 2/50/10/1 feedforward network chooses an overly complex boundary and can be expected to generalize poorly; (b) the same network trained with Gaussian ($\sigma = 0.1$) input noise forms a much smoother boundary and better generalization can be expected; and (c) the expression in equation 17.5 for the expected value of the target function at an arbitrary point x.

network. With 671 weights, but only 31 training points, the network is very underconstrained and chooses a very nonlinear boundary. Training with jittered data discourages
sharp changes in the response near the training points and so discourages the network from
forming overly complex boundaries. Figure 17.3(b) shows the same network trained for the
same amount of time from the same initial conditions with additive Gaussian input noise
($\sigma = 0.1$). Despite very long training times, the response shows no effects of overtraining.
For reference, figure 17.3(c) shows the expected value of the target given the noisy input
as calculated in equation 17.5.

17.3   Training with Jitter and Sigmoid Scaling

A drawback of training with jitter is that it requires the use of a small learning rate and
many sample presentations in order to average over the noise. In certain special cases,
the expected response of a network driven by a jittered input can be approximated by
simply adjusting the sigmoid slopes. This is, of course, much faster than averaging over
the noise. This result provides justification for gain scaling as a heuristic for improving
generalization.

17.3.1   Linear Output Networks

Consider the function

$$y(\mathbf{x}) = \sum_k v_k \, h_k(\mathbf{x}) \tag{17.16}$$

where

$$h_k(\mathbf{x}) = g\left(w_k^T \mathbf{x} - \theta_k\right) \tag{17.17}$$

and $g(\cdot)$ is the node nonlinearity. This describes a single-hidden-layer network with a *linear*
output.

With jitter (and the approximations stated for equation 17.2), the expected output for a
fixed input $\mathbf{x}$ is

$$\langle y(\mathbf{x} + \mathbf{n}) \rangle \approx y(\mathbf{x}) \star p_{\mathbf{n}}(\mathbf{x})$$

$$\approx \sum_k v_k \, h_k(\mathbf{x}) \star p_{\mathbf{n}}(\mathbf{x})$$

$$\approx \sum_k v_k \left[h_k(\mathbf{x}) * p_{\mathbf{n}}(\mathbf{x})\right], \tag{17.18}$$

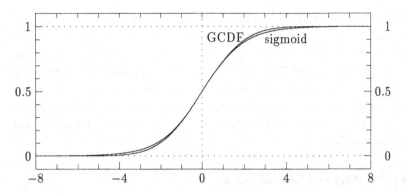

Figure 17.4
The conventional sigmoid $1/(1 + e^{-x})$ and the Gaussian cumulative distribution function (GCDF) (with $\sigma = 4/\sqrt{2\pi}$) have very similar shapes and give similar results when used as the node nonlinearities. The GCDF is useful in this analysis because it is shape invariant when convolved with a spherical Gaussian noise density.

that is, a linear sum of convolutions of the hidden unit responses with the noise density. The symbol $\star$ denotes correlation, $a(x) \star b(x) = \int_{-\infty}^{+\infty} a(\tau)b(\tau - x)\, d\tau$, which is different from convolution but the operations can be interchanged here if $p_\mathbf{n}(\mathbf{x})$ is symmetric.

In most neural network applications, the nonlinearity is the sigmoid $g(z) = 1/(1 + e^{-z})$. If, instead, we use the Gaussian cumulative distribution function (GCDF), which has a very similar shape (see figure 17.4), then the shape of the nonlinearity will be invariant to convolution with a Gaussian input noise density. That is, if we assume that the noise is zero-mean Gaussian and spherically distributed in N dimensions

$$p_\mathbf{n}(\mathbf{x}) = \frac{1}{\sigma_1^N (2\pi)^{N/2}} \exp\left(\frac{-\|\mathbf{x}\|^2}{2\sigma_1^2}\right) \tag{17.19}$$

(where $\|\mathbf{x}\|^2 = \mathbf{x}^T \mathbf{x}$) and the g nonlinearity is the Gaussian cumulative distribution function

$$g(z) = \int_{-\infty}^{z} \frac{1}{\sigma_2 \sqrt{2\pi}} \exp\left(\frac{-\tau^2}{2\sigma_2^2}\right)\, d\tau. \tag{17.20}$$

then the convolution in equation 17.18 can be replaced by a simple scaling operation

$$h_k(\mathbf{x}) * p_\mathbf{n}(\mathbf{x}) = g\left(a_k(\mathbf{w}_k^T \mathbf{x} - \theta_k)\right) \tag{17.21}$$

where a_k is a scaling constant defined below. A derivation is given in appendix C.2.

The significance of this is that when the equivalence (17.21) holds, the expected response of the network to input noise approximated by (17.18) can be computed exactly by simply scaling the hidden unit nonlinearities appropriately; we do not have to go through the time-consuming process of estimating the response by averaging over many noisy samples. That is,

$$\langle y(\mathbf{x} + \mathbf{n}) \rangle \approx \sum_k v_k g \left(a_k(\mathbf{w}_k^T \mathbf{x} - \theta_k) \right) \tag{17.22}$$

where the scaling constant a_k depends on the magnitude of the weight vector $\mathbf{w}_k$ and the noise variance

$$a_k = \frac{1}{\sqrt{\|\mathbf{w}_k\|^2 \sigma_1^2 + 1}}. \tag{17.23}$$

Note that the bias θ_k is not included in the weight vector and has no role in the computation of a_k. It is, however, scaled by a_k.

This does not say that we can train an arbitrary network without jitter and then simply scale the sigmoids to compute exactly the network that would result from training with jitter because it does not account for dynamics of training with random noise, but it does suggest similarities.

Example Figures 17.5(a) through (f) verify this scaling property. Figures 17.5(a) and (b) show the response of a network with two inputs, three GCDF hidden units, and a linear output unit. Figures 17.5(c) and (d) show the average response using spherically distributed Gaussian noise with $\sigma = 0.1$ and averaged over 2000 noisy samples per grid point. Figures 17.5(e) and (f) show the expected response computed by scaling the hidden units. The RMS error (on a 64×64 grid) between the averaged noisy response and the scaled expected response is 0.0145. The scaled expected response was computed in a few seconds; the average noisy response required hours on the same computer.

17.3.2   Relation to Weight Decay

The scaling operation is equivalent to

$$\mathbf{w} \to \frac{\mathbf{w}}{\sqrt{\|\mathbf{w}\|^2 \sigma_1^2 + 1}}.$$

Because the denominator is not less than 1, this always reduces the magnitude of $\mathbf{w}$ or leaves it unchanged. When $\sigma_1 = 0$ (no input noise), the weights are unchanged. When

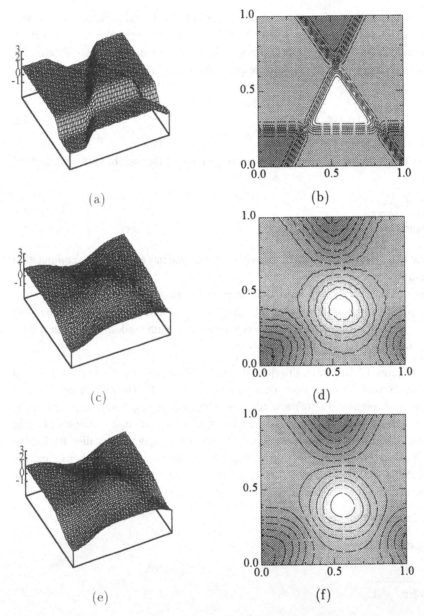

Figure 17.5
Equivalence of weight scaling and jitter averaging: (a) the transfer function of the original network and (b) its contour plot; (c) the average response with additive Gaussian input noise, $\sigma = 0.1$, averaged over 2000 noisy samples per grid point and (d) its contour plot; and (e) the expected response computed by scaling and (f) its contour plot.

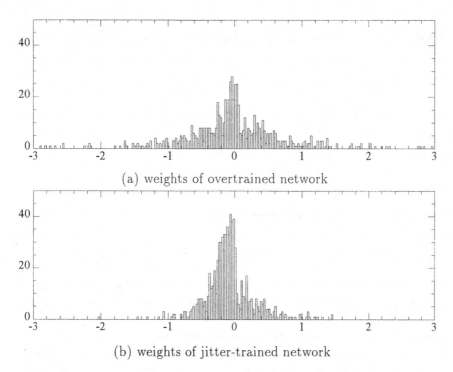

(a) weights of overtrained network

(b) weights of jitter-trained network

Figure 17.6
Weight-decay effects of training with jitter: (a) weights for the overtrained network of figure 17.3(a), $\sigma = 0.7262$; and (b) weights for the jitter-trained network of figure 17.3(b), $\sigma = 0.3841$.

$\sigma_1 \to \infty$, the weights approach zero. When $\|\mathbf{w}\|\sigma_1$ is small, the scaling has little effect. When $\|\mathbf{w}\|\sigma_1$ is large, the scaling is approximately

$$\mathbf{w} \to \frac{\mathbf{w}}{\|\mathbf{w}\|\sigma_1}$$

and the magnitude of $\mathbf{w}$ is reduced to approximately $1/\sigma_1$. This has some properties similar to weight decay [299, 388, 387, 308], another commonly used heuristic for improving generalization. The development of weight decay terms as a result of training single-layer linear perceptrons with input noise is shown in [167].

This is supported by figure 17.6, which shows histograms of the weights for the overtrained and jitter-trained networks of figure 17.3. Table 17.1 lists the standard deviations of the weights by layers. The jitter-trained network has smaller weight variance on all levels.

Table 17.1
Weight-decay Effects of Training with Jitter. Training with Jitter Tends to Produce Smaller Weights.

	Standard Deviations of Weights		
	overtrained network	jittered network	number of weights
In to H1 weights	1.1153	.5904	150
H1 to H2 weights	.5197	.2204	510
H2 to Out weights	1.6828	.4008	11
All weights	.7262	.3481	671

17.4   Extension to General Layered Neural Networks

The results previously discussed relating training with jittered data and regularization hold for any network. The analysis for gain scaling, however, is valid only for networks with a single hidden layer and a linear output node. More general feedforward networks have multiple layers and nonlinear output nodes. Even though the invariance property does not hold for these networks, these results lend justification to the idea of gain scaling [228, 171] and weight decay as heuristics for improving generalization.

The gain scaling analysis uses a GCDF nonlinearity in place of the usual sigmoid nonlinearity. Because these functions have similar shapes, this is not an important difference in terms of representation capability. (Differences might be observed in training dynamics, however, because the GCDF has flatter tails.) The precise form of the sigmoid is usually not important as long as it is monotonic nondecreasing; the usual sigmoid is widely used because its derivative is easily calculated.

The GCDF nonlinearity is used here because it has a convenient shape invariance property under convolution with a Gaussian input noise density. There may be other nonlinearities that, although not having this shape invariance property, are such that their expected response can still be calculated efficiently using a similar approach. If, for example, $g(x) * p_{\mathbf{n}}(x) = h(x)$, the function $h(x)$ may be different in form from $g(x)$, but still reasonably easy to calculate. As a specific example, if $g(x)$ is a step function and $p_{\mathbf{n}}(x)$ is uniform (both in one dimension), then $h(x)$ is a semilinear ramp function: 0 for $x < \alpha$, equal to x for $-\alpha \le x \le \alpha$, and 1 for $x > \alpha$. The expected network response can then be computed as a linear sum of $h(x)$ nonlinearities rather than a linear sum of $g(x)$ nonlinearities. Different nonlinearities must be used to calculate the normal and expected responses, but this is still much faster than averaging over many presentations of noisy samples.

The scaling results can also be applied to radial basis functions [271, 272, 300], which generally use Gaussian PDF hidden units and a linear output summation. The convolution of two spherical Gaussian PDFs with variances σ_1^2 and σ_2^2 produces a third Gaussian PDF with variance $\sigma_3^2 = \sigma_1^2 + \sigma_2^2$, so the expected response of these networks to noise is easily calculated using similar shape invariant scaling.

17.5   Remarks

Training with jitter, error regularization, gain scaling, and weight decay are all methods that have been proposed to improve generalization. Training with small amounts of jitter approaches the generalization problem directly by assuming that slightly different inputs give approximately the same output. If the noise distribution is smooth, the network will interpolate among training points in proportion to a smooth function of the distance to each training point.

With jitter, the effective target function is a smoothed version of the discrete training set. If the training set describes the target function well, the effective target approximates a smoothed version of the actual target function. The result is similar to training with a regularized objective function favoring smooth functions and the noise variance playing the role of the regularization parameter. Where regularization works by modifying the objective function, training with jitter achieves the same result by modifying the training data. In hindsight, the fact that training with noisy data approximates regularization is not surprising because this is the sort of thing regularization was developed to address.

Although large networks generally learn rapidly, they tend to generalize poorly because of insufficient constraints. Training with jitter helps to prevent overfitting by providing additional constraints. The effective target function is a continuous function defined over the entire input space whereas the original target function may be defined only at the specific training points. This constrains the network and forces it to use any excess degrees of freedom to approximate the smoothed target function rather than forming an arbitrarily complex boundary that just happens to fit the original training data (memorization). Even though the network may be large, it models a simpler system.

The expected effect of jitter can be calculated efficiently in some cases by a simple scaling of the node gains. This suggests the possibility of a post-training step to choose optimum gains based on cross-validation with a test set. This might make it possible to improve the generalization of large networks while retaining the advantage of fast learning.

The problem of choosing an appropriate noise variance has not been addressed here. Holmström and Koistinen suggest several methods based on cross-validation. Considerable research has been done on the problem of selecting an appropriate λ for regularization, especially for linear models. Because of the relationship between training with jitter and regularization, the regularization research may be helpful in selecting an appropriate noise level.

17.6 Further Examples

17.6.1 Static Noise

The use of dynamic jitter may interfere with some training algorithms because the measured error changes from moment to moment due to the jitter. Algorithms that adapt the learning rate depending on the change in error from one iteration to the next or algorithms that use information from previous iterations to choose the next search point could become unstable. It may also be inconvenient to add dynamic jitter to the data in closed simulation systems. In these cases it may be useful to use static noise, that is, to create a larger fixed training set by adding noisy versions of the original patterns.

Figure 17.7 illustrates the effect of training with a static noisy data set. Figure 17.7(a) shows the surface learned by a 2/50/10/1 network trained on the original 31 data points (724 epochs with RProp). The 31 points are almost linearly separable, but with 671 weights the network is very underconstrained and chooses a complex decision surface with sharp transitions. A static noisy data set of 930 points was generated by perturbing each of the original points with Gaussian noise ($\sigma = 0.1$) 30 times. (Thirty was chosen to give more training patterns than weights. Simulations using 5 and 10 noisy patterns per original point yielded complex boundaries.) The original points were not included in the new training set. Figure 17.7(b) shows the surface learned by a network initialized with the same weights

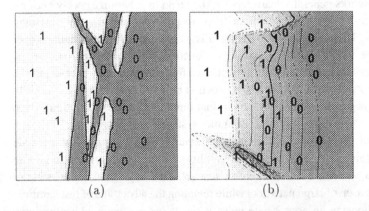

(a)   (b)

Figure 17.7
Training with static noise: (a) response of an underconstrained 2/50/10/1 net. The boundary is complex and transitions are steep, but the data is almost linearly separable. (b) Response of the same net trained on an enlarged data set obtained by replacing each original training point by 30 noisy points ($\sigma = 0.1$). The boundary is simpler and transitions are more gradual, but a few kinks remain. (1s and 0s denote the training points, the training values were 0.9 and -0.9.)

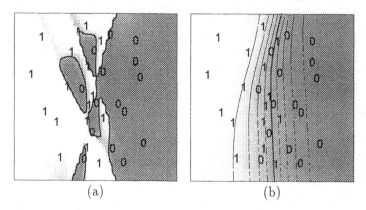

Figure 17.8
Cross-validation with jittered data. An artificial validation data set was created by generating 30 jittered points from each of the original 31 training points: (a) response of an underconstrained 2/50/10/1 net trained to convergence, and (b) response of the net with the best RMS error on the validation set (1s and 0s denote the training points, the training values were 0.9 and -0.9).

after 2500 epochs of RProp training. In most places, the decision surface is less complex and the transitions are more gradual, but a few kinks remain. Evidently the network was still able to exploit idiosyncrasies in the data so perhaps 930 points was not enough to constrain the network enough to prevent overtraining. (The second network was trained for a much longer time, however: 2,325,000 pattern presentations versus 22,444. The kinks might not have developed if the net were trained for an equivalent number of pattern presentations or an equivalent number of epochs, but this indicates that the augmented data by itself was not enough to prevent overtraining.)

17.6.2   Cross-Validation with Jittered Data

An artificial validation data set was created by generating 30 jittered points from each of the original 31 training points. Figure 17.8(a) shows the response of the network trained to convergence. Overfitting is obvious. Figure 17.8(b) shows the response of the network with the best validation error. Final convergence of the overtrained net occurred at 1365 epochs. The best validation was observed at 165 epochs.

More sophisticated versions of this approach are described by Musavi et al. [281] and Pados and Papantoni-Kazakos [293]. In both, the joint density $f(X, Y)$ is estimated by fitting Gaussians (not necessarily spherical) around each point. This is done by a radial basis function network in [293]. The resulting density estimate can then be used to estimate the generalization error of another network or, as in section 17.6.1, to generate a larger set of artificial training data.

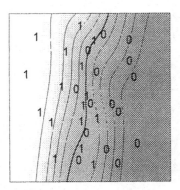

Figure 17.9
Smoothing an overtrained response. Given an overtrained net, a better estimate of the true function at a point **x** might be obtained by averaging a number of probes around **x** using a noisy input. The figure shows the expected response of the network in figure 17.7(a) to a noisy input ($\sigma = 0.1$) (1s and 0s denote the training points, the training values were 0.9 and -0.9).

17.6.3   Jitter Used to Discount an Overtrained Response

When system response time is not a critical consideration, averaging with jitter might be used to smooth the output of an overtrained network to obtain a more reliable response. That is, given an overtrained net, a better estimate of the true function at a point **x** might be obtained by averaging a number of probes around **x** using a noisy input

$$y' = \frac{1}{N} \sum_{k=1}^{N} y(\mathbf{x} + \mathbf{n}).$$

Figure 17.9 shows the expected response of the overtrained network in figure 17.7(a) to a noisy input ($\sigma = 0.1$). Unlike training with dynamic jitter, which slows training by requiring a small learning rate, or training with static jitter, which slows training by increasing the size of the training set, this allows fast training but mitigates the worst effects of overtraining at the expense of a slightly slower response during recall.

A Linear Regression

It is useful to review linear regression because the mathematics of single-layer perceptrons are very similar, because more general networks are often cascades of single-layer networks, and because linear analyses are often useful first-order approximations of nonlinear systems. Consider a linear system

$$y = \mathbf{x}^T \mathbf{w} \tag{A.1}$$

where $\mathbf{x}$ is an input vector and $\mathbf{w}$ is a weight vector to be determined. Let d be the desired output for the given input $\mathbf{x} \in \mathbf{R}^N$ and assume $\mathbf{x}$ and d have stationary statistics. The output y is one-dimensional here but the derivation is easily generalized to higher output dimensions. The single-sample error is $e = d - y$ and the squared error is

$$
\begin{aligned}
e^2 &= e^T e \\
&= (d - \mathbf{x}^T \mathbf{w})^T (d - \mathbf{x}^T \mathbf{w}) \\
&= d^2 - 2d\mathbf{x}^T \mathbf{w} + \mathbf{w}^T \mathbf{x}\mathbf{x}^T \mathbf{w}.
\end{aligned} \tag{A.2}
$$

Let the error function be $1/2$ the mean squared error (to suppress a factor of 2 later on)

$$
\begin{aligned}
2E &= E\left[e^2\right] \\
&= E\left[d^2\right] - 2E\left[d\mathbf{x}^T\right]\mathbf{w} + \mathbf{w}^T E\left[\mathbf{x}\mathbf{x}^T\right]\mathbf{w}.
\end{aligned} \tag{A.3}
$$

Note, E is the error function but $E[\cdot]$ denotes an expected value. Let $\mathbf{P} = E[d\mathbf{x}]$ and $\mathbf{R} = E\left[\mathbf{x}\mathbf{x}^T\right]$. $\mathbf{P}$ is the input-target correlation vector with elements $p_j = E\left[d x_j\right]$ and $\mathbf{R}$ is the input autocorrelation matrix with elements $r_{ij} = E\left[x_i x_j\right]$. Then (A.3) can be written

$$2E = E\left[d^2\right] - 2\mathbf{P}^T \mathbf{w} + \mathbf{w}^T \mathbf{R} \mathbf{w}, \tag{A.4}$$

which is a quadratic function of $\mathbf{w}$. $\mathbf{R}$ is a real symmetric matrix and thus positive-semi-definite, $\mathbf{w}^T \mathbf{R} \mathbf{w} \geq 0$, so E has a single global minimum. The derivative of E with respect to $\mathbf{w}$ is

$$\frac{\partial E}{\partial \mathbf{w}} = \mathbf{R}\mathbf{w} - \mathbf{P}. \tag{A.5}$$

Setting this to zero produces

$$\mathbf{R}\mathbf{w} = \mathbf{P}, \tag{A.6}$$

which can be solved to obtain the optimum weight vector $\mathbf{w}^*$

$$\mathbf{w}^* = \mathbf{R}^{-1}\mathbf{P}. \tag{A.7}$$

Numerical analysis texts suggest several ways to solve systems of linear equations that may be preferable to inversion when $\mathbf{R}$ is poorly conditioned.

Substitution into (A.4) and simplifying produces an expression for the minimum error obtained

$$2E_{min} = E\left[d_k^2\right] + \mathbf{w}^{*T}\mathbf{R}\mathbf{w}^* - 2\mathbf{P}^T\mathbf{w}^*$$

$$= E\left[d_k^2\right] - \mathbf{P}^T\mathbf{w}^*$$

$$E_{min} = \frac{1}{2}\left(\sigma_d^2 + \mu_d^2 - \mathbf{P}^T\mathbf{w}^*\right) \tag{A.8}$$

where μ_d and σ_d are the mean and standard deviation of the target. This may be smaller when $\mu_d = 0$, which is reasonable because (A.1) does not include an offset term.

It can be shown that the error is a quadratic function of the difference $\mathbf{w} - \mathbf{w}^*$

$$2E = 2E_{min} + (\mathbf{w} - \mathbf{w}^*)^T\mathbf{R}(\mathbf{w} - \mathbf{w}^*). \tag{A.9}$$

It is minimum at $\mathbf{w} = \mathbf{w}^*$ and increases quadratically with the difference $\mathbf{w} - \mathbf{w}^*$. At the optimum, the error is uncorrelated with the input

$$e = d - \mathbf{x}^T\mathbf{w}$$
$$e\mathbf{x} = d\mathbf{x} - \mathbf{x}\mathbf{x}^T\mathbf{w}$$
$$E\left[e\mathbf{x}\right] = \mathbf{P} - \mathbf{R}\mathbf{w}$$
$$= \mathbf{P} - \mathbf{R}\mathbf{R}^{-1}\mathbf{P}$$
$$= \mathbf{P} - \mathbf{P}$$
$$= 0.$$

This makes sense because correlation would indicate that the error contains remaining linearly predictable elements that could be reduced further by modifying $\mathbf{w}$.

A.1 Newton's Method

Let $\mathbf{g} = \frac{\partial E}{\partial \mathbf{w}} = \mathbf{R}\mathbf{w} - \mathbf{P}$. Then

$$\mathbf{R}^{-1}\mathbf{g} = \mathbf{w} - \mathbf{R}^{-1}\mathbf{P}$$
$$\mathbf{R}^{-1}\mathbf{g} = \mathbf{w} - \mathbf{w}^*$$

This gives the update rule

$$\mathbf{w}_{k+1} = \mathbf{w}_k - \eta \mathbf{R}^{-1} \mathbf{g}_k \qquad (A.10)$$

$$\Delta \mathbf{w}_{k+1} = \eta(\mathbf{w}^* - \mathbf{w}_k) \qquad (A.11)$$

(where the subscripts index time rather than vector elements). At each step, $\mathbf{w}$ is changed by a fraction η of the difference $(\mathbf{w}^* - \mathbf{w}_k)$. Because the error surface is quadratic, the solution could be obtained in a single step when $\eta = 1$. For nonlinear optimization tasks such as most neural network problems, however, the linear approximation is only locally valid and smaller step sizes are used to avoid straying too far from the region of validity; one-step convergence is not possible and iteration with a smaller step size is necessary. In the linear case, the eventual solution is the same however, $\mathbf{w}_\infty = \mathbf{w}^*$.

A.2   Gradient Descent

For large input dimensions (or small computers), storage and accurate inversion of $\mathbf{R}$ can be a problem so iterative procedures are often used. In simple gradient descent, $\mathbf{R}$ is replaced by $\mathbf{I}$ (actually, $\mathbf{R} = \mathbf{I}$ only for zero-mean, unit-variance, uncorrelated inputs) and the weight vector moves directly down the local gradient

$$\mathbf{w}_{k+1} = \mathbf{w}_k - \eta \mathbf{g}. \qquad (A.12)$$

The step size η controls how much $\mathbf{w}$ changes in each iteration. Although this will eventually converge to the optimal solution, the time required may be very long as the gradient, and thus the step size, approaches zero at the minimum.

Stability requires $0 < \eta < 2/\lambda_{max}$ where λ_{max} is the largest eigenvalue of $\mathbf{R}$ (see below). When $\eta > 2/\lambda_{max}$, the system will diverge. Because λ_{max} is usually unknown, a smaller than optimal step size must be used which may further slow convergence.

Convergence Rate of Gradient Descent   Assuming $\mathbf{R}$ is full rank with distinct eigenvalues, it can be decomposed into $\mathbf{R} = \mathbf{V} \mathbf{D} \mathbf{V}^T$ where $\mathbf{V}$ is the matrix whose columns are eigenvectors of $\mathbf{R}$ and $\mathbf{D}$ is the diagonal matrix whose entries are the corresponding eigenvalues. Because the eigenvectors are orthonormal, $\mathbf{V}$ is unitary, $\mathbf{V}^T = \mathbf{V}^{-1}$. After changing coordinates $\mathbf{z} = \mathbf{V}^T(\mathbf{w} - \mathbf{w}^*)$, equation A.9 can be written

$$2E = 2E_{min} + (\mathbf{w} - \mathbf{w}^*)^T \mathbf{R}(\mathbf{w} - \mathbf{w}^*)$$

$$= 2E_{min} + \mathbf{z}^T \mathbf{V}^T \mathbf{V} \mathbf{D} \mathbf{V}^T \mathbf{V} \mathbf{z} \qquad (A.13)$$

$$= 2E_{min} + \mathbf{z}^T \mathbf{D} \mathbf{z}. \qquad (A.14)$$

Because $\mathbf{D}$ is a diagonal matrix, E is now the sum of N uncoupled components

$$E = E_{min} + \frac{1}{2} \sum_{k=1}^{N} \lambda_k z_k^2 \qquad (A.15)$$

where z_k is the projection of $\mathbf{w} - \mathbf{w}^*$ on the kth eigenvector and λ_k is the corresponding eigenvalue. The gradient of E with respect to $\mathbf{z}$ becomes

$$\frac{\partial E}{\partial \mathbf{z}} = \mathbf{D}\mathbf{z}, \qquad (A.16)$$

which gives the gradient descent update rule

$$\mathbf{z}(t+1) = \mathbf{z}(t) - \eta\mathbf{D}\mathbf{z}(t). \qquad (A.17)$$

The components are decoupled, so we have N independent processes

$$z_k(t+1) = z_k(t) - \eta\lambda_k z_k(t)$$
$$= (1 - \eta\lambda_k)z_k(t) \qquad (A.18)$$

and after m time steps

$$z_k(t+m) = (1 - \eta\lambda_k)^m z_k(t).$$

For $z_k(t+m)$ to approach 0 as m becomes large, it is necessary that $|1 - \eta\lambda_k| < 1$, which requires $\lambda_k > 0$ and $0 < \eta < 2/\lambda_k$ for all k, that is,

$$0 < \eta < \frac{2}{\lambda_{max}}. \qquad (A.19)$$

with fastest convergence occurring at $\eta = 1/\lambda_{max}$. Le Cun, Simard, and Pearlmutter [94] describe an iterative method for estimating λ_{max} in a neural network; see section 6.1.7.

From equation A.18, we have

$$\Delta z_k = -\eta\lambda_k z_k.$$

The continuous-time approximation

$$\frac{dz_k}{dt} = -\eta\lambda_k z(t)$$

has solution

$$z_k(t) = e^{-\eta\lambda_k t} z_k(0), \qquad (A.20)$$

which shows the exponential nature of the convergence. The overall convergence is limited by the rate of convergence of the slowest component. Using the optimum $\eta = 1/\lambda_{max}$ gives

$$z_{slowest}(t) = \exp\left(-\frac{\lambda_{min}}{\lambda_{max}}t\right) z_k(0). \tag{A.21}$$

That is, the overall convergence is governed by the slowest time constant $\frac{\lambda_{max}}{\lambda_{min}}$, where λ_{min} is the smallest nonzero eigenvalue.

There may be a loophole here, however. Using (A.15), the overall error can then be expressed as

$$E = E_{min} + \frac{1}{2}\sum_{k=1}^{N} \lambda_k \exp\left(-2\frac{\lambda_k}{\lambda_{max}}t\right) z_k(0). \tag{A.22}$$

If we are satisfied when the error is small but nonzero, at 0.001 MSE say, then if $z_k(0)$ is small enough, the contribution of the kth component to the total error will be small and it will not be necessary to wait for these components to fully converge. Although small λ_k values cause slow convergence of the kth component, they also weight the contribution of the component to the total error.

An approximate expression for the distribution of eigenvalues in the case of random, uncorrelated inputs is given by Le Cun, Kanter, and Solla [92, 93] and leads to estimates of the learning time. The following points are made: Nonzero-mean inputs, correlations between inputs, and nonuniform input variances can all lead to increased spread between the minimum and maximum eigenvalues. For nonzero-mean inputs, there is an eigenvalue proportional to N so λ_{max} is much larger than in the zero-mean case and convergence time is slower. Subtracting the mean from the inputs suppresses the large eigenvalue and leads to faster training times. Nonuniform input variances can also lead to an increased spread in the eigenvalues which can be suppressed by rescaling the inputs. This result provides justification for centering and normalizing input variables.

For a multilayer network, the hidden layer outputs can be considered as inputs to the following layer. Because sigmoid outputs are always positive and therefore have a nonzero mean, while symmetric (odd) functions such as tanh are at least capable of a zero mean, this also provides justification for the empirical observation that use of tanh nonlinearities often produces faster training than sigmoid nodes. The result also provides justification for the suggestion of scaling the learning rate for each node by $1/M$, where M is the number of inputs into the node (see section 6.1.9).

A.3   The LMS Algorithm

The Widrow-Hoff learning rule [402], also called the LMS (least mean squares) algorithm or the delta rule is basically an iterative on-line implementation of linear regression. Like gradient descent, it avoids storing $\mathbf{R}$, but the LMS method reduces storage requirements even further. Gradient descent still requires $O(N)$ storage to accumulate error terms for the entire training set in order to approximate the true gradient before making a weight change. The LMS method avoids this may making weight changes as soon as errors occur. In the limit of very small learning rates, the result is the same. Like linear regression, it also minimizes the mean squared error of a linear fit so it shares many properties with linear regression and succeeds or fails in the same situations. An extensive summary of the LMS algorithm is provided by Widrow and Stearns [405].

As before, the half mean squared error is $E = \frac{1}{2} E \left[e^2 \right]$ and the gradient is $\mathbf{g} = \frac{\partial E}{\partial \mathbf{w}}$. The LMS algorithm does steepest descent using an estimate of the gradient *based only on the error on the current pattern*

$$\hat{\mathbf{g}} = \frac{1}{2} \frac{\partial e^2}{\partial \mathbf{w}} \tag{A.23}$$

$$= -e\mathbf{x}. \tag{A.24}$$

That is, it does on-line rather than batch learning. The update rule is then

$$\mathbf{w}_{k+1} = \mathbf{w}_k - \eta \hat{\mathbf{g}}_k \tag{A.25}$$

$$= \mathbf{w}_k + \eta e_k \mathbf{x}_k \tag{A.26}$$

where $0 < \eta < 2/\lambda_{max}$ for stability. Here, subscripts index pattern presentations rather than vector elements.

Because λ_{max} is unknown unless $\mathbf{R}$ is analyzed, an estimate must be used. $\mathbf{R}$ is nonnegative-definite, so all eigenvalues are nonnegative $\lambda_i \geq 0$ and λ_{max} can be bounded by

$$\lambda_{max} \leq \sum_i \lambda_i = \text{trace}(\mathbf{R}) \tag{A.27}$$

where $\text{trace}(\mathbf{R}) = \sum_i r_{ii} = \sum_i E \left[x_i^2 \right]$. Because this places a upper bound on λ_{max} that may too high, the resulting η value may be smaller than necessary. Adaptive learning rate methods, perhaps initialized this way, may be able to improve training speed by adjusting the rate based on observed training performance. As an aside, this provides justification for centering input variables because $E \left[x_i^2 \right] = \sigma_i^2 + \mu_i^2$ where σ_i^2 and μ_i are the variance and mean of input x_i; zero-mean inputs will produce lower estimates of λ_{max} and allow larger step sizes to be used.

B Principal Components Analysis

Suppose we have a set of zero-mean n-dimensional data vectors whose elements are correlated (figure B.1). If the data is not zero-mean, we can make it so by subtracting the average value beforehand. Because of the correlation, the data is partially redundant; knowledge of one variable gives us approximate information about the values of other variables.

It might be more natural to describe the data in terms of its variation along directions v_1 and v_2 (figure B.1). Most of the positional information is conveyed by the distance along v_1 with the distance along v_2 adding only a small correction. For highly correlated data, the contribution from v_2 will be small compared to that of v_1, so we might choose to ignore v_2 completely. This introduces some error but gives us a more compact description. Perfectly correlated data would lie along a line (or on a hyperplane, in general), so v_2 would be zero and we would lose nothing by describing the data entirely in terms of the distance along v_1.

Correlation can arise because a system has internal variables $v_1, v_2, \ldots v_n$ the effects of which are indirectly observed through intermediate variables $x_1, x_2, \ldots x_n$. Each observable variable is potentially affected by each internal variable. The observed variables may depend linearly on the internal variables, for example

$$x_1 = a_{11}v_1 + a_{12}v_2 + \ldots$$
$$x_2 = a_{21}v_1 + a_{22}v_2 + \ldots$$

$$\vdots$$

By observing correlations in the observed data, we may be able to identify the internal variables that control the system behavior. Knowing the correlations, we can then measure several observable variables and get good estimates of the internal state.

The purpose of principal components analysis (PCA) is to identify the important directions of variation of a data set. Singular value decomposition and the Karhunen-Loève transform have similar goals and are closely related techniques. The result may be a more natural coordinate system better aligned with the major axes of variation of the data. Sometimes these axes will correspond to natural features of the data.

Consider an arbitrary unit-length vector v. The projection x_v of a point x onto v is the point on v that is closest to x

$$x_v = (x^T v)v. \tag{B.1}$$

This is a vector with magnitude $(x^T v)$ extended along the unit vector v. Note that the residual component, $\epsilon = x - (x^T v)v$, is orthogonal to v, that is, $\epsilon^T v = x^T v - (x^T v)v^T v = x^T v - (x^T v) = 0$.

Obviously, the projected magnitude depends on the orientation of v. Given a set of vectors $\{x_i\}$, we can search for a unit vector v that maximizes the mean squared value of

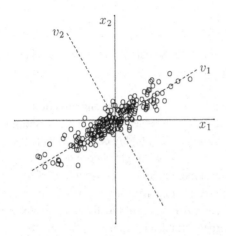

Figure B.1
Correlated data are partially redundant because knowledge of one variable gives approximate knowledge of the
other variables. In two dimensions, perfectly correlated data lie on a straight line; in n dimensions, they lie on a
lower dimensional subspace.

this projected distance. By definition, this yields the first principal component of the data
set. That is, the first principal component of a set of zero-mean vectors $\{\mathbf{x}_i\}$, $i = 1 \ldots m$,
$E\,[\mathbf{x}] = 0$, is the vector $\mathbf{v}_1$, which maximizes the variance of the projected magnitudes

$$E\left[(\mathbf{v}_1^T\mathbf{x})^2\right]. \tag{B.2}$$

After finding the first principal component, subtract the projection along that direction to
get an $(n-1)$-dimensional data set lying in a subspace orthogonal to $\mathbf{v}_1$. Then search
for a variance maximizing vector in this reduced space to obtain the second principal
component, $\mathbf{v}_2$. Further repetition yields the remaining components, $\mathbf{v}_3, \mathbf{v}_4, \ldots$. Because
the vectors $\mathbf{v}_i$ are unit-length and orthogonal, they form an orthonormal set

$$\mathbf{v}_i^T\mathbf{v}_j = \begin{cases} 1 & i = j \\ 0 & i \neq j \end{cases} \tag{B.3}$$

The vectors $\mathbf{v}_i$ can be calculated as follows. Let $y = \mathbf{x}^T\mathbf{v}$ be the projected distance of $\mathbf{x}$
along $\mathbf{v}$. Since $E\,[\mathbf{x}] = 0$, $E\left[y\right] = 0$. The variance of y is then

$$\sigma_y^2 = E\left[y^2\right] = E\left[y^Ty\right] = E\left[\mathbf{v}^T\mathbf{x}\mathbf{x}^T\mathbf{v}\right]$$

$$= \mathbf{v}^T E\left[\mathbf{x}\mathbf{x}^T\right]\mathbf{v}$$

$$= \mathbf{v}^T \mathbf{R}\mathbf{v} \tag{B.4}$$

where $\mathbf{R} = E\left[\mathbf{xx}^T\right]$ is the covariance matrix of the vectors $\mathbf{x}$. $\mathbf{R}$ is an $n \times n$ symmetric matrix so its eigenvalues are real. Because it is a covariance matrix, its eigenvalues are nonnegative. To maximize the variance subject to the condition that $\|\mathbf{v}\| = 1$ we can use the cost function

$$\mathbf{v}^T\mathbf{Rv} - \mu(\mathbf{v}^T\mathbf{v} - 1) \tag{B.5}$$

where μ is a Lagrange multiplier. Taking the derivative with respect to $\mathbf{v}$ and setting equal to zero gives

$$2\mathbf{Rv} - 2\mu\mathbf{v} = 0 \tag{B.6}$$
$$\mathbf{Rv} = \mu\mathbf{v}. \tag{B.7}$$

This is an eigenvalue problem. For a nonnull solution to exist, μ must be chosen to satisfy the characteristic equation

$$\det(\mathbf{R} - \mu\mathbf{I}) = 0. \tag{B.8}$$

That is, μ must be an eigenvalue of $\mathbf{R}$ and $\mathbf{v}$ must be the corresponding eigenvector. Taking λ as the eigenvalue and substituting into (B.4), we have

$$\sigma_y^2 = \mathbf{v}^T\mathbf{Rv} = \mathbf{v}^T(\lambda\mathbf{v}) = \lambda\|\mathbf{v}\|^2$$
$$= \lambda. \tag{B.9}$$

In summary, the direction vector that maximizes the variance of the projection is given by the principal eigenvector $\mathbf{v}_1$ of $\mathbf{R}$, and the corresponding eigenvalue λ_1 measures the variance of the projection along that direction. Similarly, eigenvector $\mathbf{v}_2$ maximizes the variance of the projection in the residual space orthogonal to $\mathbf{v}_1$ and so on. Assuming the eigenvalues are distinct, we can number them in order of decreasing magnitude

$$\lambda_1 > \lambda_2 > \ldots > \lambda_n \geq 0. \tag{B.10}$$

Assuming $\mathbf{R}$ has full rank, its eigenvectors form an alternate coordinate system with coordinate vectors numbered in order of their importance in explaining the variation of the data set. A vector $\mathbf{x}$ can be expressed as the sum of its projections along the orthogonal components $\mathbf{v}_i$

$$\mathbf{x} = \sum_{i=1}^{n} \alpha_i \mathbf{v}_i \tag{B.11}$$

where $\alpha_i = \mathbf{x}^T\mathbf{v}_i$ is the projection of $\mathbf{x}$ onto the ith coordinate vector. The vector $\alpha = (\alpha_1, \alpha_2, \ldots \alpha_n)$ is the representation of $\mathbf{x}$ in the new coordinate system. If $\mathbf{V}$ denotes the

$n \times n$ matrix containing eigenvector $\mathbf{v}_i$ in column i then in matrix notation

$$\mathbf{x} = \mathbf{V}\alpha. \tag{B.12}$$

The eigenvectors are orthonormal so $\mathbf{V}$ is unitary

$$\mathbf{V}^T\mathbf{V} = \mathbf{I}. \tag{B.13}$$

Note that $\|\mathbf{x}\|^2 = \mathbf{x}^T\mathbf{x} = \alpha^T\mathbf{V}^T\mathbf{V}\alpha = \alpha^T\alpha = \|\alpha\|^2$.

As noted, the principal component vectors of a data set form an orthogonal coordinate system with coordinate vectors numbered in order of their importance in explaining the variation of the data set. If $\mathbf{R}$ has rank $r < n$, it is singular and $n - r$ of its eigenvalues are zero. Some elements of $\mathbf{x}$ are exactly predicted by linear combinations of other elements so the data lies on an r-dimensional linear subspace embedded in the n-dimensional space. This provides an opportunity for data compression because the data can be described by fewer numbers in the new coordinate system. There is no variation along $n - r$ dimensions so we could omit those elements in the representation and obtain a more compact description without loss of information. Even if $\mathbf{R}$ has full rank, some of its eigenvalues may be small in which case the data has little variation along the corresponding dimensions. Element i contributes $\alpha_i\mathbf{v}_i$ to the position information. The mean squared error introduced by omitting element i is $\langle\alpha_i^2\rangle = \lambda_i$. Obviously, if we omit any component, it should be the one with the smallest eigenvalue since this incurs the smallest error. Likewise, if we omit m components, they should be the elements with the m smallest eigenvalues. In general, the rank r linear projection of a data set, $r < n$, with the lowest mean squared error is the projection onto the first r principal components of the data.

In practice, measurement noise and numerical errors complicate the process of calculating the eigenvectors. Some of the estimated eigenvalues may be very small but not identically zero so some judgment is required to decide if they should be set to zero or not. Numerical analysis texts suggest singular value decomposition as a preferable method for obtaining the projection directions since formation of the covariance matrix tends to square the numerical errors.

As a side note, figure B.2 illustrates the effect of not removing the mean vector. For the zero-mean data plotted in (a), the eigenvectors of the data correlation matrix accurately reflect the axes of data variation and the eigenvalues (0.9595 and 0.0417) estimate the variance along those directions. In (b), the same data is offset by $\mathbf{m} = (1, 2)$; the resulting eigenvectors are rotated and the eigenvalues (5.7016 and 0.2968) are larger. In this case, the first eigenvalue is dominated by the length of the offset vector, $\|\mathbf{m}\| = 5$. As noted in appendix A the maximum stable learning rate for gradient descent is inversely proportional to the maximum eigenvalue of the data correlation matrix so smaller learning rates must

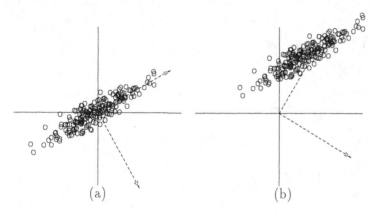

Figure B.2
Effect of nonzero-mean on the eigenvectors of the correlation matrix. (a) For zero-mean data, the eigenvectors of the correlation matrix indicate the main axes of data variation and the eigenvalues reflect the variance along each dimension. (b) For nonzero-mean data, the eigenvectors are rotated and the eigenvalues are influenced by the length of the offset vector.

be used to avoid stability problems and learning may take longer if the mean is not removed.

B.1   Autoencoder Networks and Principal Components

Consider a network with n inputs, $h < n$ *linear* hidden units, and n *linear* output units (figure B.3). What happens if we train the network to reproduce the input vector at its output? Given an input, the goal is to reproduce it at the output so the network acts as autoencoder, mapping an input pattern to itself.

This may seem pointless but note that $h < n$ so the hidden layer acts as a bottleneck that forces the network to form a compressed representation of the data. The hidden layer activities are a linear function of the inputs but the hidden layer is smaller than the input dimension so some information must necessarily be lost, in general. The best hidden layer representation will be one that preserves as much information about the input as possible. Ideally, it will ignore nonessential noise and reproduce only the most significant features of the input pattern.

Bourlard and Kamp [57] showed that the optimal (in a minimum mean squared error sense) hidden unit weights are determined by a set of vectors spanning the singular value decomposition of the input data. That is, the ideal representation formed at the hidden layer spans the same space as the h eigenvectors corresponding to the h largest eigenvalues of the covariance matrix of the training data. The network is linear so it can be collapsed

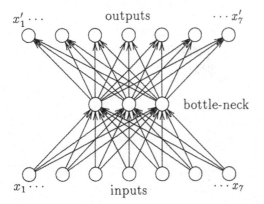

Figure B.3
An autoencoder network maps an input vector to itself. Given an input, the goal is to reproduce it at the output. A small hidden layer acts as a bottleneck and forces the network to find a compressed representation of the input pattern. With a linear network and a least squares error function, the ideal internal representation is related to the principal components of the training data.

into a single linear transformation $y = Fx$. The rank of F is limited in the preceding by h, the dimension of the hidden layer. From the principal components discussion, we know that the best rank h transformation is the projection onto the first h principal component directions. It turns out that linear hidden nodes are optimal in this case; nonlinear nodes cannot improve the approximation and only cause problems by introducing local minima that may confuse gradient descent optimizers. (If A is the hidden-to-output weight matrix and $\mathbf{h}(\mathbf{x})$ is the vector of hidden unit activities, the function to be minimized is $\langle \|\mathbf{x} - A\mathbf{h}\|^2 \rangle$. The output is a linear function of $\mathbf{h}$ so the optimal $\mathbf{h}(\mathbf{x})$ is a linear transform of the inputs $\mathbf{x}$.)

Baldi and Hornik [18] showed that the error function has a unique minimum at this solution. That is, for a linear network and a quadratic error function, the overall transformation F determined by the orthogonal projection onto the space spanned by the first h eigenvectors of $\mathbf{R}$ is a unique local and global minimum. Saddle points occur for solutions spanning other combinations of h or fewer eigenvectors of $\mathbf{R}$. In principle, this means the solution can be found by gradient descent methods such as back-propagation although conventional linear algebraic methods are generally more efficient.

In general, the solution obtained by training from random initial weights will not be identical to the principal components decomposition because it is only necessary that the hidden unit activities span the same space as the first h principal components. Let B and A be the optimal weight matrices determined by singular value decomposition. B is an $h \times n$ matrix of input-to-hidden weights and A is an $n \times h$ matrix of hidden-to-output weights. The hidden layer computes $h = Bx$ and the output computes $y = Ah = ABx$. Equivalent results can be obtained by the weights $B' = CB$ and $A' = AC^{-1}$ where C is any invertible $h \times h$ matrix. In general, C will depend on the random initial weights. The minimum identified by Baldi and Hornik [18] is unique in terms of the overall function F, which can be achieved by many different combinations of weight matrices A' and B'.

Because C can be a rotation matrix, there will not be a neat correspondence between the hidden units and the principal components projections. Principal components analysis separates the data into orthogonal components ranked in order of importance. Deletion of the first component will cause a larger error than deletion of the second and so forth. In a linear network trained by gradient descent from random initial weights, the contribution from each hidden unit tends to be more nearly equal. The autoencoder extracts the first h principal components but the matrix C typically spreads their functions approximately equally across the h hidden units [18]. The activities of the hidden units will not necessarily be uncorrelated. This may favor fault tolerance, but it is not necessarily helpful in data compression applications where it is useful to be able to pick components serially in terms of their importance. With PCA, we can do one decomposition and inspect the eigenvalues to see how many components are needed to achieve a desired approximation error. In a trained autoencoder, the functions are mixed among the h hidden units, so this is not possible. To find an approximation spanning the first $h - 1$ components, a completely new network with $h - 1$ hidden units must be trained from scratch.

Many papers have been written on the links between neural networks and principal components analysis. An entire book on subject is [106]. Oja and others [289, 290, 288, 71] have investigated Hebbian learning rules that extract principal components. Biological feasibility and local computation are interesting features of these algorithms. Many are on-line methods requiring no data storage. (However, on-line versions of conventional algorithms also exist.) Others have investigated data compression applications, for example, [334, 333]. More general results for linear networks, including but not limited to PCA, are surveyed in [17].

It is worth noting that, although neural networks are often very nonlinear, analysis of linear networks is informative because networks initialized with small weights tend to compute approximately linear functions in the early stages of training and only become significantly nonlinear after the weights grow to larger values. The initial training dynamics are often dominated by approximately linear interactions.

It should also be noted that a bottleneck structure does not automatically imply that the network must implement a principal components solution. The PCA solution is optimal only for linear networks or single-hidden-layer networks with linear outputs. With several nonlinear layers before and after the bottleneck, the bottleneck units are not linear functions of the input and cannot be interpreted in terms of principal components. In theory, anything could be transmitted through a bottleneck preceded by a sufficiently complex encoder and followed by a corresponding decoder. There are practical limits to this, of course.

B.2   Discriminant Analysis Projections

Although principal components is useful for data reduction, it does not always produce good directions for discriminating between output classes. As an unsupervised method, it sees only the input vectors and is blind to classification information. The problem is that large variations in the data do not always correspond to useful information; the variation could be due to noise or irrelevant signals from other processes. Ideally we would like to remove these sorts of irrelevant variations during preprocessing, but this is not always possible. Figure B.4 illustrates the problem. In figure B.4a, the main contribution to the variance of the input data comes from the separation between the class means so the directions found by PCA will be useful for discriminating between classes. In figure B.4b, however, the major axis of variation is along direction v_1 but the classes are separated along a minor direction v_2. If v_2 were removed for data compression, a system presented with the reduced data would not be able to separate the classes based only on the information in v_1.

Linear discriminant analysis (LDA), [130], for example, provides a way to reduce dimensionality in a supervised learning context. It has dimensionality reduction properties like principal components analysis, but also accounts for class information in forming the

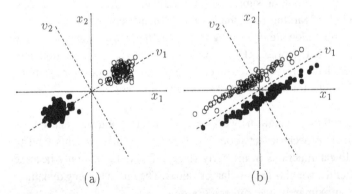

(a)   (b)

Figure B.4
Although principal components analysis sometimes produces directions useful for discriminating between classes, this is not always true. In (a) the main contribution to the variance of the input data comes from the separation between class means so the principal component directions are useful for discriminating between the classes. In (b) however, the major axis of variation is along direction v_1 but the classes are separated along the minor direction v_2.

projection. Given a set of Gaussian clusters corresponding to different target classes, the goal is to find a lower dimensional linear projection that maximizes the separation between class means and minimizes the spread of each cluster. Ideally, this minimizes overlap of the clusters in the projection and allows for unambiguous classification.

Following [130: chapter 10], suppose the data consists of m points $\mathbf{x}_i$, $i = 1 \ldots m$, grouped into K clusters which correspond to classes. Let $\mathbf{m}_k$, $k = 1 \ldots K$ be the mean vector of cluster k and $\mathbf{m}_o$ be the overall mean vector. The *within-class scatter matrix* $\mathbf{W}$ measures the covariance of the data points around the mean of their respective classes

$$\mathbf{W} = \sum_{k=1}^{K} P_k E \left[(\mathbf{x} - \mathbf{m}_k)(\mathbf{x} - \mathbf{m}_k)^T \mid \mathbf{x} \in \text{class } k \right]$$

$$= \sum_{k=1}^{K} P_k \Sigma_k \tag{B.14}$$

where P_k is the probability that a randomly selected point belongs class k. The *between-class scatter matrix* $\mathbf{B}$ measures the covariance of the class means around the overall mean

$$\mathbf{B} = \sum_{k=1}^{K} P_k (\mathbf{m}_k - \mathbf{m}_o)(\mathbf{m}_k - \mathbf{m}_o)^T \tag{B.15}$$

where $\mathbf{m}_o = E[\mathbf{x}] = \sum_{k=1}^{K} P_k \mathbf{m}_k$. The *mixture scatter matrix* is the overall covariance matrix of all points, regardless of their class

$$\mathbf{M} = E \left[(\mathbf{x} - \mathbf{m}_o)(\mathbf{x} - \mathbf{m}_o)^T \right] = \mathbf{W} + \mathbf{B}. \tag{B.16}$$

These matrices are chosen to be invariant to coordinate shifts.

We would like to find a projection that maximizes the separation between class means and minimizes the sizes of the projected clusters. The ideal projection would yield small, widely separated clusters with no overlap. A number of criteria can be used to measure cluster separability for optimization purposes. These include [130]

- $J_1 = \text{Tr}(S_2^{-1} S_1)$
- $J_2 = \ln|S_2^{-1} S_1| = \ln|S_1| - \ln|S_2|$
- $J_3 = \text{Tr}(S_1) - \mu(\text{Tr}(S_2) - c)$
- $J_4 = \text{Tr}(S_1)/\text{Tr}(S_2)$

where S_1 and S_2 are one of $\mathbf{B}$, $\mathbf{W}$, or $\mathbf{M}$. Possible combinations for $\{S_1, S_2\}$ include $\{\mathbf{B}, \mathbf{W}\}$, $\{\mathbf{B}, \mathbf{M}\}$, and $\{\mathbf{W}, \mathbf{M}\}$. Remarks on these choices can be found in [130].

Consider the matrix $\mathbf{W}^{-1}\mathbf{B}$ using $S_1 = \mathbf{B}$ and $S_2 = \mathbf{W}$. $\mathbf{B}$ and $\mathbf{W}$ are covariance matrices describing the variation between cluster means and within clusters, respectively. The principal eigenvectors of $\mathbf{B}$ maximize the spread of the projected class means. Similarly, the principal eigenvectors of $\mathbf{W}^{-1}$ minimize the average size of the projected clusters (because $1/\lambda$ is an eigenvalue of $\mathbf{W}^{-1}$ if λ is an eigenvalue of matrix $\mathbf{W}$). Intuitively at least, the matrix $\mathbf{W}^{-1}\mathbf{B}$ seems like a reasonable compromise to accomplish both purposes.

It turns out [130] that the linear projection maximizing J_1 consists of projection onto the principal eigenvectors of $S_2^{-1}S_1$. Although $S_2^{-1}S_1$ is not necessarily symmetric, it is the product of matrices with real nonnegative eigenvalues so its eigenvalues will be

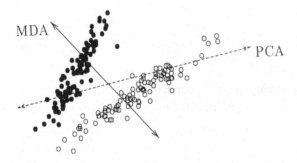

Figure B.5
The projection vectors found by discriminant analysis (MDA) and principal components analysis (PCA) for a simple data set.

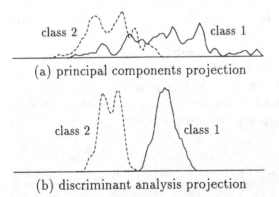

Figure B.6
Projection histograms for the MDA and PCA directions shown in figure B.5: (a) the principal components projection shows cluster overlap, and (b) the discriminant analysis projection separates the clusters well.

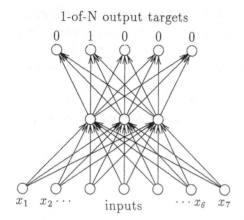

1-of-N output targets

0   1   0   0   0

x_1 $x_2 \cdots$ inputs $\cdots x_6$ x_7

Figure B.7
A single-hidden-layer *linear* network trained to perform classification with a 1-of-N target representation implements a form of discriminant analysis [385, 134].

nonnegative real and its eigenvectors orthogonal. A p-dimensional projection is obtained by extracting the p principal eigenvectors of the matrix. **B** has rank $K - 1$, where K is the number of clusters, because it is the covariance matrix of K class means so the dimension of the projection is limited by the number of clusters.

Figure B.5 illustrates the difference between the directions found by discriminant analysis and principal components analysis on a simple problem. Figure B.6 shows histograms of the resulting projections. In this example, the discriminant analysis projection separates the clusters well and the principal components projection shows cluster overlap.

Remarks A basic assumption in this analysis is that the clusters are roundish blobs described entirely by their mean and covariance structure, that is, Gaussian clouds. Optimal projections will not necessarily be found for more complex shapes. Sometimes a class consists of several distinct clusters; the compound cluster does not have the required structure so nonoptimal projections will probably result. One remedy is to present the algorithm with cluster labels instead of class labels, but this, of course, requires knowledge of the cluster structure.

Like PCA, discriminant analysis can be used to reduce the dimensionality of the data presented to a network. This reduces network size and may speed up training significantly if necessary information is not lost. Discriminant analysis is used for this purpose in [309].

Like PCA, discriminant analysis is a linear projection method so it can fail where nonlinear transformations are necessary. Neither will be able to separate classes that are not linearly separable, for example, but both techniques remain useful for neural network design in cases where the linear projection makes sense. Although discriminant analysis is a little more complex, it makes use of the class information and therefore gives better separation than principal components in certain cases. When the data have linear dependencies, both techniques can be useful for preprocessing.

Just as the linear autoencoder implements a form of PCA, it has been shown [385, 134] that a single-hidden-layer *linear* network trained to perform classification with a 1-of-N target representation implements a form of discriminant analysis (figure B.7).

C Jitter Calculations

The following calculations are used in chapter 17.

C.1 Jitter: Small–Perturbation Approximation

For small noise amplitudes, the network output $y(\mathbf{x} + \mathbf{n})$ can be approximated by

$$y(\mathbf{x} + \mathbf{n}) \approx y(\mathbf{x}) + \left(\frac{\partial y}{\partial \mathbf{x}}\right)^T \mathbf{n} + \frac{1}{2}\mathbf{n}^T \mathbf{H} \mathbf{n} \tag{C.1}$$

where $\mathbf{H}$ is the Hessian matrix with elements $h_{ij} = \partial^2 y/(\partial x_i \partial x_j)$. Assuming an even noise distribution so that $\langle n^k \rangle = 0$ for k odd, one can write

$$\mathcal{E} \approx \left\{ (t - y)^2 \right\} + \sigma^2 \left\{ \left\| \frac{\partial y}{\partial \mathbf{x}} \right\|^2 \right\}$$

$$+ \left\{ \sigma^2 (y - t)\mathrm{Tr}(\mathbf{H}) + \frac{\sigma^4}{4}\mathrm{Tr}(\mathbf{H})^2 + \frac{\sigma^4}{2}\mathrm{Tr}(\mathbf{H}^2) + \frac{m_4 - 3\sigma^4}{4}(\Sigma_i h_{ii}^2) \right\}$$

where m_4 is the fourth moment $\langle n^4 \rangle$. Dropping all terms higher than second order in σ gives

$$\mathcal{E} \approx \left\{ (t - y)^2 \right\} + \sigma^2 \left\{ (y - t)\mathrm{Tr}(\mathbf{H}) \right\} + \sigma^2 \left\{ \left\| \frac{\partial y}{\partial \mathbf{x}} \right\|^2 \right\} \tag{C.2}$$

and when $\mathbf{H}$ is assumed to be zero, this reduces to (17.15). The Laplacian term, $\mathrm{Tr}(\mathbf{H}) = \nabla^2 y$, omitted in (17.15), can be described as an approximate measure of the difference between the average surrounding values and the precise value of the field at a point [100]. The third term in (C.2) is the first order regularization term in (17.15).

Training with nonjittered data simply minimizes the error at the training points and puts no constraints on the function at other points. In contrast, training with jitter minimizes the error while also forcing the approximating function to have small derivatives and a local average that approaches the target in the vicinity of each training point.

C.2 Jitter: CDF–PDF Convolution in n Dimensions

The following shows that the convolution of an n–dimensional spherical Gaussian probability density function (PDF) and a Gaussian cumulative distribution function (CDF) results in another Gaussian CDF.

Let $f_1(\mathbf{x})$ be a spherical Gaussian PDF in n–dimensions

$$f_1(\mathbf{x}) = \frac{1}{\sigma_1^n (2\pi)^{n/2}} \exp\left(\frac{-\|\mathbf{x}\|^2}{2\sigma_1^2}\right) \tag{C.3}$$

and let $F_2(\mathbf{x})$ be a Gaussian CDF of the form

$$F_2(\mathbf{x}) = \int_{-\infty}^{w^T \mathbf{x}} \frac{1}{\sqrt{2\pi}} \exp\left(\frac{-\tau^2}{2}\right) d\tau. \tag{C.4}$$

This can be written as

$$F_2(\mathbf{x}) = \int_{-\infty}^{\hat{w}^T \mathbf{x}} \frac{1}{\sigma_2 \sqrt{2\pi}} \exp\left(\frac{-\tau^2}{2\sigma_2^2}\right) d\tau \tag{C.5}$$

where $\hat{w} = w/\|w\|$ and $\sigma_2 = 1/\|w\|$.

The convolution of F_2 and f_1 is the n–dimensional integral

$$F_2(\mathbf{x}) * f_1(\mathbf{x}) = \int_{\alpha} F_2(\alpha) f_1(\mathbf{x} - \alpha) \, d\alpha, \tag{C.6}$$

Separate $\mathbf{x}$ and α into components parallel and orthogonal to $\hat{w}$

$$\mathbf{x} = \ell \hat{w} + \gamma$$
$$\ell = \hat{w}^T \mathbf{x}$$
$$\hat{w}^T \gamma = 0$$
$$\alpha = k \hat{w} + \beta$$
$$k = \hat{w}^T \alpha$$
$$\hat{w}^T \beta = 0$$
$$\|\mathbf{x} - \alpha\|^2 = (\ell - k)^2 \|\hat{w}\| + 2(\ell - k)\hat{w}^T(\gamma - \beta) + \|\gamma - \beta\|^2$$
$$= (\ell - k)^2 + \|\gamma - \beta\|^2.$$

where ℓ and k are scalars and γ and β are n–dimensional vectors orthogonal to $\hat{w}$.

Then

$$F_2(\alpha) = \int_{-\infty}^{\hat{w}^T \alpha} \frac{1}{\sigma_2\sqrt{2\pi}} \exp\left(\frac{-\tau^2}{2\sigma_2^2}\right) d\tau$$

$$= \int_{-\infty}^{k} \frac{1}{\sigma_2\sqrt{2\pi}} \exp\left(\frac{-\tau^2}{2\sigma_2^2}\right) d\tau$$

$$f_1(\mathbf{x} - \alpha) = \frac{1}{\sigma_1^n (2\pi)^{n/2}} \exp\left(\frac{-\|\mathbf{x} - \alpha\|^2}{2\sigma_1^2}\right)$$

$$= \frac{1}{\sigma_1^n (2\pi)^{n/2}} \exp\left(\frac{-(\ell - k)^2}{2\sigma_1^2}\right) \exp\left(\frac{-\|\gamma - \beta\|^2}{2\sigma_1^2}\right)$$

$$= \frac{1}{\sigma_1\sqrt{2\pi}} \exp\left(\frac{-(\ell - k)^2}{2\sigma_1^2}\right) \cdot \frac{1}{\sigma_1^{n-1}(2\pi)^{(n-1)/2}} \exp\left(\frac{-\|\gamma - \beta\|^2}{2\sigma_1^2}\right)$$

$$\text{(C.7)}$$

and

$$F_2(\mathbf{x}) * f_1(\mathbf{x}) = \int_k \int_\beta \int_{-\infty}^{k} \frac{1}{\sigma_2\sqrt{2\pi}} e^{-\tau^2/(2\sigma_2^2)} d\tau \cdot \left(\frac{1}{\sigma_1\sqrt{2\pi}} e^{-(\ell-k)^2/(2\sigma_1^2)}\right)$$

$$\times \left(\frac{1}{\sigma_1^{n-1}(2\pi)^{(n-1)/2}} e^{-\|\gamma-\beta\|^2/(2\sigma_1^2)}\right) d\beta dk$$

$$= \int_k \int_{-\infty}^{k} \frac{1}{\sigma_2\sqrt{2\pi}} e^{-\tau^2/(2\sigma_2^2)} d\tau \cdot \left(\frac{1}{\sigma_1\sqrt{2\pi}} e^{-(\ell-k)^2/(2\sigma_1^2)}\right) dk$$

$$\times \int_\beta \frac{1}{\sigma_1^{n-1}(2\pi)^{(n-1)/2}} e^{-\|\gamma-\beta\|^2/(2\sigma_1^2)} d\beta$$

$$= \int_k \int_{-\infty}^{k} \frac{1}{\sigma_2\sqrt{2\pi}} e^{-\tau^2/(2\sigma_2^2)} d\tau \cdot \left(\frac{1}{\sigma_1\sqrt{2\pi}} e^{-(\ell-k)^2/(2\sigma_1^2)}\right) dk.$$

Thus $F_2(\mathbf{x}) * f_1(\mathbf{x})$ reduces to a one-dimensional convolution of a Gaussian CDF with standard deviation $\sigma_2 = 1/\|w\|$ and a Gaussian PDF with standard deviation σ_1. It can be shown (see section C.3) that this is a Gaussian CDF with variance $\sigma_3^2 = \sigma_1^2 + \sigma_2^2$.

Letting Z_a denote the Gaussian CDF function with standard deviation a,

$$F_2(\mathbf{x}) * f_1(\mathbf{x}) = Z_{\sigma_2}(\ell) * g(\ell)$$

$$= Z_{\sigma_3}(\ell)$$

$$= Z_1\left(\frac{\ell}{\sigma_3}\right)$$

$$= Z_1\left(\frac{\hat{w}^T\mathbf{x}}{\sqrt{\sigma_1^2 + (1/\|w\|)^2}}\right)$$

$$= Z_1\left(\frac{\|w\|\,\hat{w}^T\mathbf{x}}{\sqrt{\|w\|^2\sigma_1^2 + 1}}\right)$$

$$= Z_1\left(\frac{w^T\mathbf{x}}{\sqrt{\|w\|^2\sigma_1^2 + 1}}\right)$$

$$= F_2\left(\frac{\mathbf{x}}{\sqrt{\|w\|^2\sigma_1^2 + 1}}\right)$$

$$(C.8)$$

Thus, the convolution of a Gaussian CDF and a Gaussian PDF can be computed by a simple scaling of the original CDF.

C.3 Jitter: CDF–PDF Convolution in One Dimension

The following demonstrates that the convolution of Gaussian PDF with variance σ_1^2 and a Gaussian CDF with variance σ_2^2 results in a Gaussian CDF with variance $\sigma_3^2 = \sigma_1^2 + \sigma_2^2$. All the functions are one-dimensional.

Consider two independent random variables X_1 and X_2 with PDFs f_1 and f_2 and CDF's F_1 and F_2. The random variable $Y = X_1 + X_2$ has the PDF $f_1 * f_2$ and consequently its CDF is $F_1 * f_2 = f_1 * F_2$. Let X_1 and X_2 be zero mean Gaussian, $X_1 \sim N(0, \sigma_1^2)$ and $X_2 \sim N(0, \sigma_2^2)$, then, clearly, $Y \sim N(0, \sigma_1^2 + \sigma_2^2)$ has a Gaussian PDF with variance $\sigma_3^2 = \sigma_1^2 + \sigma_2^2$. Because Y has the CDF $f_1 * F_2$, $f_1 * F_2$ is a Gaussian CDF with zero mean and variance $\sigma_3^2 = \sigma_1^2 + \sigma_2^2$.

D Sigmoid-like Nonlinear Functions

In a large class of networks, each node computes a function $f(\mathbf{w}^T\mathbf{x})$ of its inputs $\mathbf{x}$. In most cases, $f(u)$ is chosen to be a bounded nondecreasing function of u; the sigmoid and tanh functions are common choices. Back-propagation and other gradient based training methods require that f be differentiable.

Table D.1 lists some functions commonly used for node nonlinearities. In general, scaled and translated functions $g(u) = af(ku) + b$, for constants a, b, and k, yield networks with equivalent representational properties. The tanh and sigmoid functions are related by $\tanh(u) = 2\,\text{sigmoid}(2u) + 1$, for example. There may be practical reasons however, for choosing one form over another.

Sigmoid The sigmoid, or logistic, function

$$y(u) = \frac{1}{1 + e^{-\lambda u}} \tag{D.1}$$

is a bounded, nondecreasing function of u. It approaches 0 for $u \to -\infty$, is 1/2 at $u = 0$, and approaches 1 for $u \to \infty$. It is approximately linear for small inputs ($u \approx 0$), but saturates for large positive or negative inputs. The name derives from this "s" shape. Other monotonic functions with similar shapes are often called sigmoidal. The optional parameter λ controls the slope in the linear region; with large values the response approximates a step function. Normally $\lambda = 1$ unless otherwise specified since equivalent results can be obtained by scaling the magnitude of the weight vector.

A useful property of the usual form (D.1) is that its derivative is easily calculated given the output

$$\frac{\partial y}{\partial u} = \frac{\lambda e^{-\lambda u}}{(1 + e^{-\lambda u})^2}$$
$$= \lambda y(1 - y). \tag{D.2}$$

The derivative is a bell shaped function, positive everywhere and largest at $u = 0$ where the slope is $\lambda/4$. For large positive and negative values of u, it approaches 0.

The inverse is

$$u = \frac{1}{\lambda} \ln \left(\frac{y}{1 - y} \right). \tag{D.3}$$

Tanh The tanh function is

$$y(u) = \tanh(\lambda u) \qquad = \frac{e^{\lambda u} - e^{-\lambda u}}{e^{\lambda u} + e^{-\lambda u}} \tag{D.4}$$

Table D.1
Common Node Nonlinearities

Name	Function $y(u)$	Derivative $\partial y/\partial u$
Sigmoid	$1/(1 + e^{-\lambda u})$	$\lambda y(1 - y)$
Tanh	$\tanh(\lambda u)$	$\lambda(1 - y^2)$
Step	$\begin{cases} 0 & u \leq 0 \\ 1 & u > 0 \end{cases}$	$\delta(u)$
Sign	$\begin{cases} -1 & u \leq 0 \\ 1 & u > 0 \end{cases}$	$2\delta(u)$
Clipped linear	$\begin{cases} -1 & u \leq -1/\lambda \\ \lambda u & -1/\lambda < u \leq 1/\lambda \\ 1 & u > 1/\lambda \end{cases}$	$\begin{cases} 0 & u \leq -1/\lambda \\ \lambda & -1/\lambda < u \leq 1/\lambda \\ 0 & u > 1/\lambda \end{cases}$
Inverse Abs	$u/(1 + |u|)$	$1/(1 + |u|)^2$

is a centered version of the sigmoid. It is -1 for $u = -\infty$, 0 for $u = 0$, and $+1$ for $u = +\infty$. The functions are related by $\tanh(u) = 2\text{sigmoid}(2u) + 1$. Its derivative, in terms of its output, is

$$\frac{\partial y}{\partial u} = \lambda(1 - y^2). \tag{D.5}$$

At $u = 0$, the slope is λ. Its inverse is

$$u = \frac{1}{2\lambda} \ln\left(\frac{1 + y}{1 - y}\right). \tag{D.6}$$

Step and Sign The unit step function is

$$y(u) = \begin{cases} 0 & u \le 0 \\ 1 & u > 0. \end{cases} \tag{D.7}$$

In engineering, this is sometimes called the 'Heaviside' step function. A node implementing $f(\mathbf{w}^T\mathbf{x})$ where f is a step function is also called a *linear threshold unit* (LTU). The derivative of the step function is the Dirac delta function $\delta(u)$, which is ∞ at $u = 0$ and zero everywhere else.

The sign function is the bipolar equivalent of the step function

$$y(u) = \begin{cases} -1 & u \le 0 \\ 1 & u > 0. \end{cases} \tag{D.8}$$

and has derivative $2\delta(u)$.

Clipped Linear The output of the clipped linear function is equal to its input for small inputs, but clips at large positive and negative values

$$y(u) = \begin{cases} -1 & u \le -1/\lambda \\ \lambda u & -1/\lambda < u \le 1/\lambda \\ 1 & u > 1/\lambda. \end{cases} \tag{D.9}$$

This may also be called a semilinear ramp function.

Its derivative is constant in the linear region and zero elsewhere

$$\frac{\partial y}{\partial u} = \begin{cases} 0 & u \le -1/\lambda \\ \lambda & -1/\lambda < u \le 1/\lambda \\ 0 & u > 1/\lambda. \end{cases} \tag{D.10}$$

Other Functions There are a number of alternative sigmoid-like functions occasionally used in special cases. One is

$$y(u) = \frac{u}{1 + |u|}. \tag{D.11}$$

In table D.1 this is called the Inverse Abs function, but it does not have a generally recognized name. The shape is similar to the tanh function, but convergence to the ± 1 asymptotes is slower. (The horizontal axis of the thumbnail figure in table D.1 spans $-10 < u < 10$.) Its derivative is

$$\frac{\partial y}{\partial u} = \frac{1}{(1 + |u|)^2}. \tag{D.12}$$

At $u = 0$, $\partial y / \partial u = 1$, but the derivative is more sharply peaked near 0 and has wider tails than the tanh function.

An advantage of this function is that it does not require transcendental functions that may be time consuming to calculate on some computers. This may be useful in digital implementations, but is not a particular advantage for analog electronic implementations because tanh functions are easily realized with differential amplifiers. The slower convergence to the asymptotes may help prevent paralysis during learning due to saturation of node nonlinearities.

References

[1] Abu-Mostafa, Y.S. The Vapnik-Chervonenkis dimension: Information versus complexity in learning. *Neural Computation* 1(3):312–317, 1989.

[2] Achenie, L.E.K. Computational experience with a quasi Newton based training of the feedforward neural network. In *World Congress on Neural Networks (San Diego)*, vol. 3, pp. 607–612. Lawrence Erlbaum, Hillsdale, NJ, 1994.

[3] Ackley, D. H. *A Connectionist Machine for Genetic Hillclimbing.* Kluwer, Boston, 1987.

[4] Ackley, D. H. and M. S. Littman. Learning from natural selection in an artificial environment. In *Proceedings of the International Joint Conference on Neural Networks (San Diego)*, vol. 1, p. 189, IEEE, New York, 1990.

[5] Ahmad, S., and G. Tesauro. Scaling and generalization in neural networks: a case study. In D. Touretzky, G. Hinton, and T. Sejnowski, editors, *Proceedings of the 1988 Connectionist Summer School*, pp. 3–10. Morgan Kaufmann, San Mateo, 1988.

[6] Akaike, H. Fitting autoregressive models for prediction. *Annals of the Institute of Statistical Mathematics* 21:243–247, 1969.

[7] Akaike, H. A new look at the statistical model identification. *IEEE Transactions on Automatic Control* AC-19(6):716–723, 1974.

[8] Alpsan, D., M. Towsey, O. Ozdamar, A. Tsoi, and D.N. Ghista. Are modified back-propagation algorithms worth the effort? In *IEEE International Conference on Neural Networks (Orlando)*, vol. 1, pp. 567–571. IEEE, New York, 1994.

[9] Alpsan, D., M. Towsey, O. Ozdamar, A.C. Tsoi, and D.N. Ghista. Efficacy of modified backpropagation and optimisation methods on a real-world medical problem. *Neural Networks* 8(6):945–962, 1995.

[10] Arabshahi, P., J.J. Choi, R.J. Marks, II, and T.P. Caudell. Fuzzy control of backpropagation. In *Proceedings of the First IEEE International Conference on Fuzzy Systems, (FUZZ-IEEE '92), San Diego*, pp. 967–972. IEEE, New York, 1992.

[11] Ash, T. Dynamic node creation in back-propagation networks. *Technical Report* 8901. Institute for Cognitive Science, UCSD, La Jolla, 1989.

[12] Atlas, L., D. Cohn, R. Ladner, M.A. El-Sharkawi, R.J. Marks II, M.E. Aggoune, and D.C. Park. Training connectionist networks with queries and selective sampling. In D.S. Touretzky, editor, *Advances in Neural Information Processing Systems (Denver)* (2), pp. 566–573, Morgan Kaufmann, San Mateo, 1990.

[13] Auer, P., M. Herbster, and M.K. Warmuth. Exponentially many local minima for single neurons. In D.S. Touretzky, M.C. Mozer, and M.E. Hasselmo, editors, *Advances in Neural Information Processing Systems* (8), pp. 316–322. MIT Press, Cambridge, 1996.

[14] Aylward, S., D.C. St. Clair, W. Bond, B. Flachsbart, and A.K. Rigler. One-dimensional search strategies for conjugate gradient training of backpropagation neural networks. In *Proceedings of the Artificial Neural Networks in Engineering (ANNIE'92) Conference, St. Louis*, vol. 2, pp. 192–202. IEEE, New York, 1992.

[15] Bailey, A.W. Automatic evolution of neural net architectures. In *Proceedings of the International Joint Conference on Neural Networks (Washington D.C.)*, vol. 1, pp. 589–592. IEEE, New York, 1990.

[16] Baldi, P., and Y. Chauvin. Temporal evolution of generalization during learning in linear networks. *Neural Computation* 3(4):598–603, 1991.

[17] Baldi, P., Y. Chauvin, and K. Hornik. Backpropagation and unsupervised learning in linear networks. In Y. Chauvin and D.E. Rumelhart, editors, *Backpropagation: Theory, Architectures, and Applications*, chapter 12, pp. 389–432. Erlbaum, Hillsdale, NJ, 1994.

[18] Baldi, P., and K. Hornik. Neural networks and principal component analysis: Learning from examples without local minima. *Neural Networks* 2(1):53–58, 1989.

[19] Barnard, E. Optimization for training neural nets. *IEEE Transactions on Neural Networks* 3(2):232–240, 1992.

[20] Barnard, E., and J.E.W. Holm. A comparative study of optimization techniques for backpropagation. *Neurocomputing* 6:19–30, 1994.

[21] Barron, A.R. Approximation bounds for superpositions of a sigmoidal function. In *Proceedings of the IEEE International Symposium on Information Theory*. IEEE Press, New York, 1991.

[22] Barron, A.R. Universal approximation bounds of a sigmoidal function. *Technical Report* 58. Statistics Department, University of Illinois, Urbana-Champaign, 1991.

[23] Barron, A.R. Universal approximation bounds for superposition of a sigmoidal function. *IEEE Transactions on Information Theory* 39(3):930–945, 1993.

[24] Barto, A.G. Reinforcement learning and adaptive critic methods. In D.A. White and D.A. Sofge, editors, *Handbook of Intelligent Control*, chapter 12. Van Nostrand Reinhold, New York, 1992.

[25] Barto, A.G., R.S. Sutton, and C.W. Anderson. Neuronlike adaptive elements that can solve difficult learning control problems. *IEEE Transactions on Systems, Man, and Cybernetics* SMC-13(5):834–846, 1983 (reprinted in J.A. Anderson and E. Rosenfeld, editors, *Neurocomputing*. 1988).

[26] Battiti, R. Accelerated backpropagation learning: Two optimization methods. *Complex Systems*, 3:331–342, 1989.

[27] Battiti, R. Optimization methods for back-propagation: Automatic parameter tuning and faster convergence. In *Proceedings of the International Joint Conference on Neural Networks (Washington D.C.)*, vol. 1, 593–596. IEEE, New York, 1990.

[28] Battiti, R. First- and second-order methods for learning: Between steepest descent and Newton's method. *Neural Computation* 4(2):141–166, 1992.

[29] Battiti, R., and G. Tecchiolli. Learning with first, second, and no derivatives: A case study in high energy physics. *Neurocomputing* 6:181–206, 1994.

[30] Baum, E.B. On the capabiliities of multilayer perceptrons. *Journal of Complexity* 4:193–215, 1988.

[31] Baum, E.B. A proposal for more powerful learning algorithms. *Neural Computation* 1(2):201–207, 1989.

[32] Baum, E.B. When are k-nearest neighbor and back propagation accurate for feasible sized sets of examples? In L.B. Almeida and C.J. Wellekens, editors, *Neural Networks, Proceedings EURASIP Workshop*, vol. 412 of *Lecture Notes in Computer Science*, pp. 2–25. Springer-Verlag, New York, February 1990.

[33] Baum, E.B., and D. Haussler. What size net gives valid generalization? In David S Touretzky, editor, *Advances in Neural Information Processing Systems* (1), pp. 81–90. Morgan Kaufmann, San Mateo, 1989.

[34] Baum, E.B., and D. Haussler. What size net gives valid generalization? *Neural Computation* 1:151–160, 1989.

[35] Baum, E.B., and R.L. Rivest. Training a 3-node neural network is NP-complete. In *Proceedings of the 1988 Workshop on Computational Learning Theory*, pp. 9–18. Morgan Kaufmann, San Mateo, 1988.

[36] Baxt, W.G. Improving the accuracy of an artificial neural network using multiple differently trained networks. *Neural Computation* 4(5):772–780, 1992.

[37] Becker, S., and Y. Le Cun. Improving the convergence of back-propagation learning with second order methods. In D. Touretzky, G. Hinton, and T. Sejnowski, editors, *Proceedings of the 1988 Connectionist Models Summer School*, pp. 29–37. Morgan Kaufmann, San Mateo, 1988.

[38] Bello, M.G. Enhanced training algorithms, and integrated training/architecture selection for multilayer perceptrons. *IEEE Transactions on Neural Networks*, 3(6):864–875, 1992.

[39] Bishop, C. Exact calculation of the Hessian matrix for the multilayer perceptron. *Neural Computation* 4(4):494–501, 1992.

[40] Bishop, C.M. Curvature-driven smoothing in backpropagation neural networks. *IEEE Transactions on Neural Networks* 4:882–884, 1993.

[41] Bishop, C.M. A fast procedure for retraining the multilayer perceptron. *International Journal of Neural Systems* 2(3):229–236, 1991.

[42] Bishop, C.M. Improving the generalization properties of radial basis function neural networks. *Neural Computation* 3(4):579–588, 1991.

[43] Bishop, C.M. Curvature-driven smoothing: A learning algorithm for feedforward networks. *IEEE Transactions on Neural Networks* 4(5):882–884, 1993.

[44] Bishop, C.M. *Neural Networks for Pattern Recognition*. Oxford University Press, Oxford, 1995.

[45] Bishop, C.M. Training with noise is equivalent to Tikhonov regularization. *Neural Computation*, 7(1):108–116, 1995.

[46] Block, H.D. The perceptron: A model for brain functioning. I. *Reviews of Modern Physics*, 34:123–135, 1962. (Reprinted in J.A. Anderson and E. Rosenfeld, editors, *Neurocomputing*. MIT Press, Cambridge, 1988).

[47] Blue, J. Training feed-forward neural networks using conjugate gradients. In *SPIE*, vol. 1661, p. 179. Society of Photo-Optical Instrumentation Engineers, Bellingham, WA, 1992.

[48] Blum, E.K., and L.K. Li. Approximation theory and feedforward networks. *Neural Networks* 4(4):511–515, 1991.

[49] Blumer, A., A. Ehrenfeucht, D. Haussler, and M. Warmuth. Learnability and the Vapnik-Chervonenkis dimension. *Journal of the Association for Computing Machinery* 36(4):929–965, 1989.

[50] Booker, L. Improving search in genetic algorithms. In L. Davis, editor, *Genetic Algorithms and Simulated Annealing*. Morgan Kaufmann, San Mateo, 1990.

[51] Booker, L. Using classifier systems to implement distributed representations. In *Proceedings of the International Joint Conference on Neural Networks (San Diego)*, vol. 1, p. 39. IEEE, New York, 1990.

[52] Booker, L.B., D.E. Goldberg, and J.H. Holland. Classifier systems and genetic algorithms. In J. Carbonell, editor, *Machine Learning: Paradigms and Methods*. MIT Press, Cambridge, 1990.

[53] Bose, N.K., and A.K. Garga. Neural network design using Voronoi diagrams: Preliminaries. In *Proceedings of the International Joint Conference on Neural Networks (Baltimore)*, vol. 3, pp. 127–132. IEEE Press, New York, 1992.

[54] Bose, N.K., and A.K. Garga. Neural network design using Voronoi diagrams. *IEEE Transactions on Neural Networks* 4(5):778–787, 1993.

[55] Bose, N.K., and P. Liang. *Neural Network Fundamentals with Graphs, Algorithms, and Applications*. McGraw-Hill, New York, 1996.

[56] Botros, S.H., and C.G. Atkeson. Generalization properties of radial basis functions. In R. P. Lippmann, J. E. Moody, and D. S. Touretzky, editors, *Advances in Neural Information Processing Systems* (3), pp. 707–713. Morgan Kaufmann, San Mateo, 1991.

[57] Boulard, H., and Y. Kamp. Auto-association by multilayer perceptrons and singular value decomposition. *Biological Cybernetics* 59:291–294, 1988.

[58] Brady, M.L., and R. Raghavan. Gradient descent fails to separate. In *Proceedings of the IEEE International Conference on Neural Networks (San Diego)*, vol. 1, pp. 649–656. IEEE, New York, 1988.

[59] Brady, M.L., R. Raghavan, and J. Slawny. Back propagation fails to separate where perceptrons succeed. *IEEE Transactions on Circuits and Systems* 36:665–674, 1989.

[60] Breiman, L. Current research. In D.H. Wolpert, editor, *The Mathematics of Generalization*, pp. 361–368. Addison-Wesley, Reading, MA, 1995.

[61] Breiman, L. Reflections after refereeing papers for NIPS. In D.H. Wolpert, editor, *The Mathematics of Generalization*, pp. 11–15. Addison-Wesley, Reading, MA, 1995.

[62] Buntine, W.L., and A.S. Weigend. Computing second derivatives in feed-forward networks: A review. *IEEE Transactions on Neural Networks* 5(3):480–488, 1994.

[63] Carpenter, G.A., S. Grossberg, N. Markuzon, J.H. Reynolds, and D.B. Rosen. Fuzzy ARTMAP: An adaptive resonance architecture for incremental learning of analog maps. In *Proceedings of the International Joint Conference on Neural Networks (Baltimore)*, vol. 3, pp. 309–314. IEEE, New York, 1992.

[64] Carroll, S.M., and B.W. Dickson. Construction of neural nets using the Radon transform. In *Proceedings of the International Joint Conference on Neural Networks (Washington D.C.)*, vol. 1, pp. 607–611. IEEE, New York, 1989.

[65] Cater, J.P. Successfully using peak learning rates of 10 (and greater) in back-propagation networks with the heuristic learning algorithm. In *Proceedings of the IEEE First International Conference on Neural Networks (San Diego)*. IEEE, New York, 1987.

[66] Caudill, M. Evolutionary neural networks. *AI Expert*, March 1991.

[67] Chan, L.-W., and F. Fallside. An adaptive training algorithm for back propagation networks. *Computer Speech and Language* 2:205–218, 1987.

[68] Chang, E. I., and R. P. Lippmann. Using genetic algorithms to improve pattern classification performance. In R.P. Lippmann, J.E. Moody, and D.S Touretzky, editors, *Advances in Neural Information Processing (Denver, 1990)* (3), pp. 797–803. Morgan Kaufmann, San Mateo, 1991.

[69] Charalambous, C. Conjugate gradient algorithm for efficient training of artificial neural networks. *IEE Proceedings* 139(3):301–310, 1992.

[70] Chauvin, Y. A back-propagation algorithm with optimal use of hidden units. In D.S. Touretzky, editor, *Advances in Neural Information Processing Systems (Denver, 1988)* (1), pp. 519–526. Morgan Kaufmann, San Mateo, 1989.

[71] Chauvin, Y. Principal component analysis by gradient descent on a constrained linear Hebbian cell. In *Proceedings of the International Joint Conference on Neural Networks (Washington, D.C.)*, vol. 1, pp. 373–380. IEEE, New York, 1989.

[72] Chauvin, Y. Dynamic behavior of constrained back-propagation networks. In D.S. Touretzky, editor, *Advances in Neural Information Processing Systems* (2), pp. 642–649. Morgan Kaufmann, San Mateo, 1990.

[73] Chauvin, Y. Generalization performance of overtrained back-propagation networks. In L.B. Almeida and C.J. Wellekens, editors, *Neural Networks, Proceedings EUROSIP Workshop*, vol. 412 of *Lecture Notes in Computer Science*, pp. 46–55. Springer-Verlag, New York, Feb. 1990.

[74] Chauvin, Y. Generalization dynamics in LMS trained linear networks. In R. Lippmann, J. Moody, and D. Touretzky, editors, *Advances in Neural Information Processing Systems* (3), pp. 890–896. Morgan Kaufmann, San Mateo, 1991.

[75] Chen, C.H., and H. Lai. A comparison study of the gradient descent and the conjugate gradient backpropagation neural networks. In *World Congress on Neural Networks (Portland)*, vol. 3, pp. 401–406. Erlbaum, Hillsdale, NJ, 1993.

[76] Chen, J.R., and P. Mars. Stepsize variation methods for accelerating the back propagation algorithm. In *Proceedings of the International Joint Conference on Neural Networks (Washington, D.C.)*, vol. 1, pp. 601–604. IEEE, New York, 1990.

[77] Chen, O.T.-C., and B.J. Sheu. Optimization schemes for neural network training. In *IEEE International Conference on Neural Networks (Orlando)*, vol. 2, pp. 817–822. IEEE, New York, 1994.

[78] Chen, S., S.A. Billings, and R. Hecht-Nielsen. On the geometry of feedforward neural network error surfaces. *Neural Computation* 5(6):910–927, 1993.

[79] Cherkassky, V., and F. Mulier. Statistical and neural network techniques for nonparametric regression. In *Selecting Models from Data*, Lecture Notes in Statistics 89, pp. 383–392. Springer Verlag, New York, 1994.

[80] Chester, D.L. Why two hidden layers are better than one. In *Proceedings of the International Joint Conference on Neural Networks (Washington D.C.)*, vol. 1, pp. 265–268. IEEE, New York, 1990.

[81] Choi, J. J., P. Arabshahi, R. J. Marks II, and T. P. Caudell. Fuzzy parameter adaptation in neural systems. In *Proceedings of the International Joint Conference on Neural Networks (Baltimore)*, vol. 1, pp. 232–235. IEEE, New York, 1992.

[82] Cichocki, A., and R. Unbehauen. *Neural Networks for Optimization and Signal Processing*. Wiley, 1993.

[83] Clemen, R.T. Combining forecasts: A review and annotated bibliography. *International Journal of Forecasting* 5(4):559–583, 1989.

[84] Codrington, C.W., and M.F. Tenorio. Adaptive gain networks. In *IEEE International Conference on Neural Networks (Orlando)*, vol. 1, pp. 339–344. IEEE, New York, 1994.

[85] Cohn, D., and G. Tesauro. Can neural-networks do better than the Vapnik–Chervonenkis bounds? In R.P. Lippmann, J.E. Moody, and D.S Touretzky, editors, *Advances in Neural Information Processing Systems (Denver, 1990)* (3), pp. 911–917. Morgan Kaufmann, San Mateo, 1991.

[86] Corwin, E.M., A.M. Logar, and W.J.B. Oldham. An iterative method for training multilayer networks with threshold functions. *IEEE Transactions on Neural Networks* 5(3):507–508, 1994.

[87] Cover, T. Geometrical and statistical properties of systems of linear inequalities with applications in pattern recognition. *IEEE Transactions on Electronic Computers*, 14:326–334, 1965.

[88] Crowder, III, R.S. Predicting the Mackey-Glass timeseries with cascade-correlation learning. In D.S. Touretzky, J.L. Elman, T.J. Sejnowski, G.E. Hinton, editors, *Connectionist Models: Proceedings of the 1990 Summer School*, pp. 117–123. Morgan Kaufmann, San Mateo, 1991.

[89] Le Cun, Y. Une procédure d'apprentissage pour réseau à seuil assymétrique. In *COGNITIVA 85: A la Frontière de l'Intelligence Artificielle des Science de la Connaissance des Neurosciences (Paris)*, pp. 599–604. CESTA, Paris, 1985.

[90] Le Cun, Y. Learning process in an asymmetric threshold network. In E. Bienenstock, F. Fogelman Soulié, and G. Weisbuch, editors, *Disordered Systems and Biological Organization*, pp. 233–240. Springer-Verlag, New York, 1986.

[91] Le Cun, Y., J.S. Denker, and S.A. Solla. Optimal brain damage. In D.S. Touretzky, editor, *Advances in Neural Information Processing Systems (Denver)* (2), pp. 598–605. Morgan Kaufmann, San Mateo, 1990.

[92] Le Cun, Y., I. Kanter, and S.A. Solla. Eigenvalues of covariance matrices: Application to neural-network learning. *Physical Review Letters* 66(18):2396–2399, 1991.

[93] Le Cun, Y., I. Kanter, and S.A. Solla. Second order properties of error surfaces: Learning time and generalization. In R.P. Lippmann, J.E. Moody, and D.S. Touretzky, editors, *Advances in Neural Information Processing Systems* (3), pp. 918–924. Morgan Kaufmann, San Mateo, 1991.

[94] Le Cun, Y., P.Y. Simard, and B. Pearlmutter. Automatic learning rate maximization by on-line estimation of the Hessian eigenvectors. In S.J. Hanson, J.D. Cowan, C.L. Giles, editors, *Advances in Neural Information Processing Systems* (5), pp. 156–163. Morgan Kaufmann, San Mateo, 1993.

[95] Cybenko, G. Approximation by superpositions of a sigmoidal function. *Technical Report 856*, Department of Electrical and Computer Engineering, University of Illinois, Urbana-Champaign, 1988.

[96] Cybenko, G. Approximation by superpositions of sigmoids. *Mathematics of Control, Signals, and Systems* 2:303–314, 1989.

[97] Darken, C., and J. Moody. Note on learning rate schedules for stochastic optimization. In R.P. Lippmann, J.E. Moody, and D.S. Touretzky, editors, *Advances in Neural Information Processing Systems* (3), pp. 832–838. Morgan Kaufmann, San Mateo, 1991.

[98] Darken, C., and J. Moody. Towards faster stochastic gradient search. In J.E. Moody, S.J. Hanson, and R.P. Lippmann, editors, *Advances in Neural Information Processing Systems* (4), pp. 1009–1016. Morgan Kaufmann, San Mateo, 1992.

[99] DasGupta, B., H.T. Siegelmann, and E. Sontag. On the intractability of loading neural networks. In V. Roychowdhury, K.-Y. Siu, and A. Orlitsky, editors, *Theoretical Advances in Neural Computation and Learning*, pp. 357–389. Kluwer, Boston, 1994.

[100] Davis, H.F., and A.D. Snider. *Introduction to Vector Analysis*, 4th edition. Allyn and Bacon, Boston, 1979.

[101] Davis, L. Mapping classifier systems into neural networks. In D.S. Touretzky, editor, *Advances in Neural Information Processing Systems* (1), pp. 49–56. Morgan Kaufmann, San Mateo, 1989.

[102] de Garis, H. Genetic programming: Modular neural evolution for Darwin machines. In *Proceedings of the International Joint Conference on Neural Networks (San Diego)*, vol. 1, p. 194. IEEE, New York, 1990.

[103] de Groot, C., and D. Wurtz. "Plain backpropagation" and advanced optimization algorithms: A comparative study. *Neurocomputing* 6:153–161, 1994.

[104] de Villiers, J., and E. Barnard. Backpropagation neural nets with one and two hidden layers. *IEEE Transactions on Neural Networks* 4(1):136–141, 1993.

[105] Denoeux, T., and R. Lengellé. Initializing back propagation networks with prototypes. *Neural Networks* 6(3):351–363, 1993.

[106] Diamantaras, K.I., and S.Y. Kung. *Principal Component Neural Networks, Theory and Applications.* John Wiley & Sons, New York, 1996.

[107] Dietterich, T., and G. Bakiri. Error-correcting output codes: A general method for improving multiclass inductive learning programs. In D.H. Wolpert, editor, *The Mathematics of Generalization*, pp. 395–407. Addison-Wesley, Reading, MA, 1995.

[108] Dodd, N. Optimisation of network structure using genetic techniques. In *Proceedings of the International Joint Conference on Neural Networks (Washington D.C.)*, vol. 1, pp. 965–970. IEEE, New York, 1990.

[109] Dominic, S., R. Das, D. Whitley, and C. Anderson. Genetic reinforcement learning for neural networks. In *Proceedings of the International Joint Conference on Neural Networks (Seattle)*, vol. 2, pp. 71–76. IEEE, New York, 1991.

[110] Drago, G.P., and S. Ridella. Statistically controlled activation weight initialization (SCAWI). *IEEE Transactions on Neural Networks* 3(4):627–631, 1992.

[111] Drucker, H., C. Cortes, L.D. Jackel, Y. LeCun, and V. Vapnik. Boosting and other ensemble methods. *Neural Computation* 6(6):1289–1301, 1994.

[112] Drucker, H., and Y. Le Cun. Double backpropagation and increasing generalization performance. In *Proceedings of the International Joint Conference on Neural Networks (Seattle)*, vol. 2, pp. 145–150. IEEE, New York, 1991.

[113] Duda, R.O., and P.E. Hart. *Pattern Classification and Scene Analysis.* Wiley, New York, 1973.

[114] Eaton, H.A.C., and T.L. Olivier. Learning coefficient dependence on training set size. *Neural Networks* 5(2):283–288, 1992.

[115] Efron, B. *The Jackknife, the Bootstrap and Other Resampling Plans.* SIAM, Philadelphia, 1982.

[116] Efron, B., and R.J. Tibshirani. *An Introduction to the Bootstrap.* Chapman & Hall, New York, 1993.

[117] Ehrenfeucht, A., D. Haussler, M. Kearns, and L. Valiant. A general lower bound on the number of examples needed for learning. In *Proceedings of the 1988 Workshop on Computational Learning Theory.* Morgan Kaufmann, San Mateo, 1988.

[118] Elman, J.L., and D. Zipser. Learning the hidden structure of speech. *Journal of the Acoustical Society of America* 83(4):1615–1626, 1988.

[119] Fahlman, S. E. The recurrent cascade-correlation architecture. In R.P. Lippmann, J.E. Moody, and D.S. Touretzky, editors, *Advances in Neural Information Processing Systems (Denver, 1990)* (3), pp. 190–196. Morgan Kaufmann, San Mateo, 1991.

[120] Fahlman, S. E., and C. Lebiere. The cascade-correlation learning architecture. In D.S. Touretzky, editor, *Advances in Neural Information Processing Systems (Denver, 1989)* (2), pp. 524–532. Morgan Kaufmann, San Mateo, 1990.

[121] Fahlman, S.E. Faster-learning variations of back-propagation: An empirical study. In D. Touretzky, G. Hinton, and T. Sejnowski, editors, *Proceedings of the 1988 Connectionist Models Summer School*, pp. 38–51. Morgan Kaufmann, San Mateo, 1988.

[122] Finnoff, W., F. Hergert, and H.G. Zimmermann. Extended regularization methods for nonconvergent model selection. In S.J. Hanson, J.D. Cowan, and C.L. Giles, editors, *Advances in Neural Information Processing Systems* (5), pp. 630–637. Morgan Kaufmann, San Mateo, 1993.

[123] Finnoff, W., F. Hergert, and H.G. Zimmermann. Improving model selection by nonconvergent methods. *Neural Networks* 6(6):771–783, 1993.

[124] Fitch, J.P., S.K. Lehman, and F.U. Dowla. Ship wake detection procedure using conjugate gradient trained artificial neural networks. *IEEE Transactions on Geoscience and Remote Sensing* 29(5):718, 1991.

[125] Flower, B., and M. Jabri. Summed weight neuron perturbation: An O(N) improvement over weight perturbation. In S.J. Hanson, J.D. Cowan, and C.L. Giles, editors, *Advances in Neural Information Processing Systems* (5), pp. 212–219. Morgan Kaufmann, San Mateo, 1993.

[126] Franzini, M.A. Speech recognition with back propagation. In *Proceedings of the Ninth Annual Conference of the IEEE Engineering in Medicine and Biology Society*, vol. 3, pp. 1702–1703. IEEE Press, IEEE, New York, 1987.

[127] Frasconi, P., M. Gori, and A. Tesi. Backpropagation for linearly-separable patterns: a detailed analysis. In *IEEE International Conference on Neural Networks (San Francisco)*, vol. 3, pp. 1818–1822. IEEE, New York, 1993.

[128] Frean, M. The upstart algorithm: A method for constructing and training feedforward neural networks. *Neural Computation* 2(2):198–209, 1990.

[129] Friedman, J. H., and W. Stuetzle. Projection pursuit regression. *Journal of the American Statistical Association* 76(376):817–823, 1981.

[130] Fukunaga, K. *Introduction to Statistical Pattern Recognition*. Academic Press, New York, 1972.

[131] Funahashi, K. On the approximate realization of continuous mappings by neural networks. *Neural Networks* 2(3):183–192, 1989.

[132] Gallant, A.R., and H. White. There exists a neural network that does not make avoidable mistakes. In *Proceedings of the IEEE International Conference on Neural Networks (San Diego)*, vol. 1, pp. 657–664. IEEE, New York, 1988 (reprinted in [395]).

[133] Gallant, S.I. Perceptron-based learning algorithms. *IEEE Transactions on Neural Networks* 1(2):179–191, June 1990.

[134] Gallinari, P., S. Thiria, F. Badran, and F. Fogelman-Soulie. On the relations between discriminant analysis and multilayer perceptrons. *Neural Networks* 4(3):349–360, 1991.

[135] Geman, S., and D. Geman. Stochastic relaxation, Gibbs distributions, and the Bayesian restoration of images. *IEEE Transactions on Pattern Analysis and Machine Intelligence* 6:721–741, 1984. (reprinted in J.A. Anderson and E. Rosenfeld, editors, *Neurocomputing*, MIT Press, Cambridge, 1988).

[136] Georgiou, G.M., and C. Koutsougeras. Embedding domain information in backpropagation. In *Proceedings of SPIE Conference on Adaptive and Learning Systems, Orlando, Fla.* Society of Photo-Optical Instrumentation Engineers, Bellingham, WA, 1992.

[137] Gibson, G.J., and C.F.N. Cowan. On the decision regions of multilayer perceptrons. *Proceedings of the IEEE* 78(10):1590–1594, Oct. 1990.

[138] Gill, P.E., W. Murray, and M.H. Wright. *Practical Optimization*. Academic Press, New York, 1981.

[139] Girosi, F., and T. Poggio. Representation properties of networks: Kolmogorov's theorem is irrelevant. *Neural Computation* 1(4):465–469, 1989.

[140] Girosi, F., and T. Poggio. Networks for learning. In P. Antognetti and V. Milutinović, editors, *Neural Networks: Concepts, Applications, and Implementations*, chapter 6. Prentice Hall, Englewood Cliffs, NJ, 1991.

[141] Goldberg, D. E. *Genetic Algorithms in Search, Optimization, & Machine Learning*. Addision-Wesley, Reading, MA, 1989.

[142] Goldman, M. Communication complexity and lower bounds for threshold circuits. In V. Roychowdhury, K.-Y. Siu, and A. Orlitsky, editors, *Theoretical Advances in Neural Computation and Learning*, pp. 85–125. Kluwer, Boston, 1994.

[143] Goldmann, M., J. Håstad, and A. Razborov. Majority gates vs. general weighted threshold gates. In *Proceedings of the 7th Annual Structure in Complexity Theory Conference*, pp. 2–13. IEEE Computer Society Press, Los Alamitos, CA, 1991.

[144] Gori, M., and M. Maggini. Optimal convergence of on-line backpropagation. *IEEE Transactions on Neural Networks* 7(1):251–254, 1996.

[145] Gori, M., and A. Tesi. On the problem of local minima in backpropagation. *IEEE Transactions on Pattern Analysis and Machine Intelligence* 14(1):76–86, 1992.

[146] Green, R.W., and C.M. DeAngelis. An empirical comparison of backpropagation training algorithms. In *World Congress on Neural Networks (Portland)*, vol. 4, pp. 401–406. Erlbaum, Hillsdale, NJ, 1993.

[147] Guyon, I., V. Vapnik, B. Boser, L. Bottou, and S.A. Solla. Structural risk minimization for character recognition. In J.E. Moody, S.J. Hanson, and R.P. Lippmann, editors, *Advances in Neural Information Processing Systems* (4), pp. 471–478. Morgan Kaufmann, San Mateo, 1992.

[148] Hagan, M., and M. Menhaj. Training feedforward networks with the Marquardt algorithm. *IEEE Transactions on Neural Networks* 5(6):989–993, 1994.

[149] Hamamoto, M., J. Kamruzzaman, and Y. Kumagai. Generalization ability of artificial neural network using Fahlman and Lebiere's learning algorithm. In *Proceedings of the International Joint Conference on Neural Networks (Baltimore)*, vol. 1, pp. 613–618. IEEE Press, New York, 1992.

[150] Hamey, L.G.C. Comments on "Can backpropagation error surface not have local minima." *IEEE Transactions on Neural Networks* 5(5):844–845, 1994.

[151] Hampson, S.E., and D.J. Volper. Linear function neurons: Structure and training. *Biological Cybernetics* 53:203–217, 1986.

[152] Hansen, L.K. Stochastic linear learning: Exact test and training set averages. *Neural Networks* 6(3):393–396, 1993.

[153] Hanson, S.J. Meiosis networks. In D.S. Touretzky, editor, *Advances in Neural Information Processing Systems (Denver, 1989)* (2), pp. 533–541. Morgan Kaufmann, San Mateo, 1990

[154] Hanson, S.J., and L.Y. Pratt. Comparing biases for minimal network construction with back-propagation. In D.S. Touretzky, editor, *Advances in Neural Information Processing Systems (Denver, 1988)* (1), pp. 177–185. Morgan Kaufmann, San Mateo, 1989.

[155] Harp, S. A., and T. Samad. Genetic optimization of self-organizing feature maps. In *Proceedings of the International Joint Conference on Neural Networks (Seattle)*, vol. 1, pp. 341–346, 1991.

[156] Harp, S. A., T. Samad, and A. Guha. Designing application-specific neural networks using the genetic algorithm. In D.S. Touretzky, editor, *Advances in Neural Information Processing Systems* (2), pp. 447–454. Morgan Kaufmann, San Mateo, 1989.

[157] Hassibi, B., and D.G. Stork. Optimal brain surgeon. In S.J. Hanson, J.D. Cowan, and C.L. Giles, editors, *Advances in Neural Information Processing Systems (Denver, 1992)* (5), pp. 164–171. Morgan Kaufmann, San Mateo, 1993.

[158] Hassibi, B., D.G. Stork, and G. Wolff. Optimal brain surgeon: Extensions and performance comparisons. In J.D. Cowan, G. Tesauro, and J. Alspector, editors, *Advances in Neural Information Processing Systems* (6), pp. 263–270. Morgan Kaufmann, San Mateo, 1994.

[159] Hassibi, B., D.G. Stork, and G.J. Wolff. Optimal brain surgeon and general network pruning. In *IEEE International Conference on Neural Networks (San Francisco)*, pp. 293–299. IEEE, New York, 1993.

[160] Haykin, S. *Neural Networks, A Comprehensive Foundation*. Macmillan, New York, 1993.

[161] Hecht-Nielsen, R. Kolmogorov's mapping neural network existence theorem. In *Proceedings of the IEEE First International Conference on Neural Networks (San Diego)*, vol. 3, pp. 11–13. IEEE, New York, 1987.

[162] Hecht-Nielsen, R. Theory of the backpropagation neural network. In *Proceedings of the International Joint Conference on Neural Networks (Washington D.C.)*, vol. 1, pp. 593–605. IEEE, New York, 1989.

[163] Hecht-Nielsen, R. On the algebraic structure of feedforward network weight spaces. In R. Eckmiller, editor, *Advanced Neural Computers*, pp. 129–135. Elsevier, New York, 1990.

[164] Hecht-Nielsen, R. The munificence of high dimensionality. In I. Aleksander and J. Taylor, editors, *Proceedings of the 1992 International Conference on Artificial Neural Networks (ICANN-92)*, vol. 2, pp. 1017–1030. Elsevier, 1992.

[165] Hergert, F., W. Finnoff, and H.G. Zimmermann. A comparison of weight elimination methods for reducing complexity in neural networks. In *Proceedings of the International Joint Conference on Neural Networks (Baltimore)*, vol. 3, pp. 980–987. IEEE, New York, 1992.

[166] Hertz, J., A. Krogh, and R.G. Palmer. *Introduction to the Theory of Neural Computation*. Addison-Wesley, Reading, MA, 1991.

[167] Hertz, J.A., and A. Krogh. Statistical dynamics of learning. In T. Kohonen, K. Mäkisara, O. Simula, and J. Kangas, editors, *Artificial Neural Networks (ICANN-91)*, vol. 1, pp. 125–131. Elsevier, New York, 1991.

[168] Higashino, J., B.L. de Greef, and E.H.J. Persoon. Numerical analysis and adaptation method for learning rate of back propagation. In *Proceedings of the International Joint Conference on Neural Networks (Washington D.C.)*, vol. 1, pp. 627–630. IEEE, New York, 1990.

[169] Hinton, G.E. Connectionist learning procedures. *Artificial Intelligence* 40(1):143–150, 1989.

[170] Hirose, Y., K. Yamashita, and S. Hijiya. Back-propagation algorithm which varies the number of hidden units. *Neural Networks* 4(1):61–66, 1991.

[171] Hoehfeld, M., and S.E. Fahlman. Learning with limited numerical precision using the cascade-correlation algorithm. *IEEE Transactions on Neural Networks* 3(4):602–611, 1992.

[172] Holden, S.B. How practical are VC dimension bounds. In *IEEE International Conference on Neural Networks (Orlando)*, pp. 327–332. IEEE, New York, 1994.

[173] Holland, J. H. *Adaptation in Natural and Artificial Systems*. University of Michigan Press, Ann Arbor, 1975.

[174] Holmström, L., and P. Koistinen. Using additive noise in back-propagation training. *IEEE Transactions on Neural Networks* 3(1):24–38, Jan. 1992.

[175] Hornik, K. Approximation capabilities of multilayer feedforward networks. *Neural Networks* 4(2):251–257, 1991.

[176] Hornik, K. Some new results on neural network approximation. *Neural Networks* 6(8):1069–1072, 1993.

[177] Hornik, K., M. Stinchcombe, and H. White. Multilayer feedforward networks are universal approximators. *Neural Networks* 2(5):359–366, 1989 (reprinted in [395]).

[178] Hosmer, D.W., and S. Lemeshow. *Applied Logistic Regression*. Wiley, New York, 1989.

[179] Hsiung, J.T., W. Suewatanakul, and D.M. Himmelblau. Should back propagation be replaced by more effective optimization algorithms? In *Proceedings of the International Joint Conference on Neural Networks (Seattle)*, vol. 1, pp. 353–356. IEEE, New York, 1991.

[180] Huang, W.Y., and R.P. Lippmann. Neural net and traditional classifiers. In D. Anderson, editor, *Neural Information Processing Systems (Denver 1987)*, pp. 387–396. American Institute of Physics, New York, 1988.

[181] Hush, D.R., B. Horne, and J.M. Salas. Error surfaces for multi-layer perceptrons. *IEEE Transactions on Systems, Man, and Cybernetics* 22(5):1152–1161, 1992.

[182] Hush, D.R., and J.M. Salas. Improving the learning rate of back-propagation with the gradient reuse algorithm. In *Proceedings of the IEEE International Conference on Neural Networks (San Diego)*, vol. 1, pp. 441–447. IEEE, New York, 1988.

[183] Hush, D.R., J.M. Salas, and B. Horne. Error surfaces for multi-layer perceptrons. In *Proceedings of the International Joint Conference on Neural Networks (Seattle)*, vol. 1, pp. 759–764. IEEE, New York, 1991.

[184] Hwang, J.-N., J.J. Choi, S. Oh, and R.J. Marks II. Query learning based on boundary search and gradient computation of trained multilayer perceptrons. In *Proceedings of the International Joint Conference on Neural Networks (San Diego)*, vol. 3, pp. 57–62. IEEE, New York, June 1990.

[185] Hwang, J.-N., S.-R. Lay, M. Maechler, D. Martin, and J. Schimert. Regression modeling in back-propagation and projection pursuit learning. *IEEE Transactions on Neural Networks* 5(3):342–353, 1994.

[186] Irie, B., and S. Miyake. Capabilities of three-layered perceptrons. In *Proceedings of the IEEE International Conference on Neural Networks (San Diego)*, vol. 1, pp. 641–648. IEEE, New York, 1988.

[187] Ishikawa, M. A structural learning algorithm with forgetting of link weights. *Technical Report* TR-90-7. Electrotechnical Laboratory, Tsukuba-City, Japan, 1990.

[188] Ito, Y. Representation of functions by superpositions of a step or sigmoid function and their applications to neural network theory. *Neural Networks* 4(3):385–394, 1991.

[189] Izui, Y., and A. Pentland. Analysis of networks with redundancy. *Neural Computation* 2(2):226–238, 1990.

[190] Izui, Y., and A. Pentland. Speeding up back propagation. In *Proceedings of the International Joint Conference on Neural Networks (Washington, D.C.)*, vol. 1, pp. 639–642. IEEE, New York, 1990.

[191] Jabri, M., and B. Flower. Weight perturbation: An optimal architecture and learning technique for analog VLSI feedforward and recurrent multilayer networks. *Neural Computation* 3(4):546–565, 1991.

[192] Jabri, M.A., and B. Flower. Weight perturbation: An optimal architecture and learning technique for analog VLSI feedforward and recurrent multilayer networks. *IEEE Transactions on Neural Networks* 3(1):154–157, 1992.

[193] Jacobs, R.A. Initial experiments on constructing domains of expertise and hierarchies in connectionist systems. In D. Touretzky, G. Hinton, and T. Sejnowski, editors, *Proceedings of the 1988 Connectionist Models Summer School*, pp. 144–1153. Morgan Kaufmann, San Mateo, 1988.

[194] Jacobs, R.A. Increased rates of convergence through learning rate adaptation. *Neural Networks* 1(4):295–307, 1988.

[195] Ji, C., R.R. Snapp, and D. Psaltis. Generalizing smoothness constraints from discrete samples. *Neural Computation* 2(2):188–197, 1990.

[196] Jia, Q., K. Hagiwara, N. Toda, and S.Usui. Equivalence relation between the backpropagation learning process of an FNN and that of an FNNG. *Neural Networks* 7(2):411, 1994.

[197] Johansson, E.M., F.U. Dowla, and D.M. Goodman. Backpropagation learning for multilayer feed-forward neural networks using the conjugate gradient method. *International Journal of Neural Systems* 2(4):291–301, 1991.

[198] Jordan, F., and G. Clement. Using the symmetries of a multi-layered network to reduce the weight space. In *Proceedings of the International Joint Conference on Neural Networks (Seattle)*, vol. 2, pp. 391–396. IEEE, New York, 1991.

[199] Jordan, M.I. Constrained supervised learning. *Journal of Mathematical Psychology* 36(3):396–425, 1992.

[200] Jordan, M.I., and R.A. Jacobs. Modularity, unsupervised learning, and supervised learning. In S. Davis, editor, *Connectionism: Theory and Practice*, pp. 21–29. Oxford University Press, Oxford, 1992.

[201] Jordan, M.I., and D.E. Rumelhart. Forward models: Supervised learning with a distal teacher. *Cognitive Science* 16(3):307–354, 1992.

[202] Judd, J.S., editor. *Neural Network Design and the Complexity of Learning*. MIT Press, Cambridge, 1990.

[203] Judd, S. Learning in neural networks. In D. Haussler and L. Pitt, editors, *Proceedings of the 1988 Workshop on Computational Learning Theory*, pp. 2–8. Morgan Kaufmann, San Mateo, 1988.

[204] Judd, S. On the complexity of loading shallow neural networks. *Journal of Complexity* 4(3):177–192, 1988.

[205] Kamimura, R., T. Takagi, and S. Nakanishi. Improving generalization performance by information minimization. In *IEEE International Conference on Neural Networks (Orlando)*, pp. 143–147. IEEE, New York, 1994.

[206] Kandel, E.R., and J.H. Schwartz, editors. *Principles of Neural Science*, 2nd edition. Elsevier, New York, 1985.

[207] Karnin, E.D. A simple procedure for pruning back-propagation trained neural networks. *IEEE Transactions on Neural Networks* 1(2):239–242, 1990.

[208] Kasparian, V., C. Batur, H. Zhang, and J. Padovan. Davidon least squares based learning algorithm for feedforward neural networks. *Neural Networks* 7(4):661–670, 1994.

[209] Keesing, R., and D. G. Stork. Evolution and learning in neural networks: The number and distribution of learning trials affect the rate of evolution. In R.P. Lippmann, J.E. Moody, and D.S Touretzky, editors, *Advances in Neural Information Processing (Denver)* (3), pp. 804–810. Morgan Kaufmann, San Mateo, 1991.

[210] Kinsella, J.A. Comparison and evaluation of variants of the conjugate gradient method for efficient learning in feed-forward neural networks with backward error propagation. *Network: Computation in Neural Systems* 3(1):27–35, 1992.

[211] Kirkpatrick, S., C.D. Gelatt Jr., and M.P. Vecchi. Optimization by simulated annealing. *Science* 220:671–680, 1983 (reprinted in J.A. Anderson and E. Rosenfeld, editors, *Neurocomputing*, MIT Press, Cambridge, 1988).

[212] Kohonen, T. *Self-Organization and Associative Memory*, vol. 8 of *Springer Series in Information Sciences*, 2nd edition. Springer-Verlag, Berlin, 1988.

[213] Koiran, P., and E.D. Sontag. Neural networks with quadratic VC dimension. In D.S. Touretsky, M.C. Mozer, and M.E. Hasselmo, editors, *Advances in Neural Information Processing Systems* (8), pp. 197–203. MIT Press, Cambridge, 1996.

[214] Koistinen, P., and L. Holmström. Kernel regression and backpropagation training with noise. In *Proceedings of the International Joint Conference on Neural Networks (Singapore)*, pp. 367–372. IEEE, New York, 1991.

[215] Koistinen, P., and L. Holmström. Kernel regression and backpropagation training with noise. In J.E. Moody, S.J. Hanson, and R.P. Lippmann, editors, *Advances in Neural Information Processing Systems* (4), pp. 1035–1039. Morgan Kaufmann, San Mateo, 1992.

[216] Kolen, J.F., and J.B. Pollack. Backpropagation is sensitive to initial conditions. *Complex Systems* 4(3):269–280, 1990.

[217] Kolen, J.F., and J.B. Pollack. Back propagation is sensitive to initial conditions. In *Advances in Neural Information Processing Systems* (3), pp. 860–867. Morgan Kaufmann, San Mateo, 1991.

[218] Kollias, S., and D. Anastassiou. An adaptive least squares algorithm for the efficient training of multilayered networks. *IEEE Transactions on Circuits and Systems* 36:1092–1101, 1989.

[219] Kolmogorov, A.N. On the representation of continuous functions of several variables by superpositions of continuous functions of one variable and addition. *Doklady Akademii Nauk SSSR* 114(5):953–956, 1957 (in Russian).

[220] Kolmogorov, A.N. On the representation of continuous functions of several variables by superpositions of continuous functions of one variable and addition. *American Mathematical Society Translations* 28:55–59, 1963.

[221] Koza, J. *Genetic Programming*. MIT Press, Cambridge, 1992.

[222] Koza, J.R. A genetic approach to the truck backer upper problem and the inter-twined spiral problem. In *Proceedings of the International Joint Conference on Neural Networks (Baltimore)*, vol. 4, pp. 310–318. IEEE, New York, 1992.

[223] Koza, J.R., and M.A. Keane. Cart centering and broom balancing by genetically breeding populations of control strategy programs. In *Proceedings of the International Joint Conference on Neural Networks (San Diego)*, vol. 1, p. 198. IEEE, New York, 1990.

[224] Koza, J.R., and J.P. Rice. Genetic generation of both the weights and architecture for a neural network. In *Proceedings of the International Joint Conference on Neural Networks (Seattle)*, vol. 2, p. 397. IEEE, New York, 1991.

[225] Kramer, A.H., and A. Sangiovanni-Vincentelli. Efficient parallel learning algorithms for neural networks. In *Advances in Neural Information Processing Systems* (1), pp. 40–48. Morgan Kaufmann, San Mateo, 1989.

[226] Kreinovich, V.Y. Arbitrary nonlinearity is sufficient to represent all functions by neural networks: A theorem. *Neural Networks* 4(3):381–383, 1991.

[227] Krogh, A., and J.A. Hertz. A simple weight decay can improve generalization. In J.E. Moody, S.J. Hanson, and R.P. Lippmann, editors, *Advances in Neural Information Processing Systems* (4), pp. 950–957. Morgan Kaufmann, San Mateo, 1992.

[228] Kruschke, J.K. Creating local and distributed bottlenecks in hidden layers of back-propagation networks. In D. Touretzky, G. Hinton, and T. Sejnowski, editors, *Proceedings of the 1988 Connectionist Models Summer School*, pp. 120–126, Morgan Kaufmann, San Mateo, 1989.

[229] Kruschke, J.K. Improving generalization in back-propagation networks with distributed bottlenecks. In *Proceedings of the International Joint Conference on Neural Networks (Washington, D.C.)*, vol. 1, pp. 443–447. IEEE, New York, 1989.

[230] Kruschke, J.K., and J.R. Movellan. Benefits of the gain: Speeded learning and minimal hidden layers in back-propagation networks. *IEEE Transactions on Systems, Man, and Cybernetics* 21(1):273–280, 1991.

[231] Kurkova, V. Kolmogorov's theorem and multilayer neural networks. *Neural Networks* 5(3):501–506, 1992.

[232] Kurkova, V., and P.C. Kainen. Functionally equivalent feedforward neural networks. *Neural Computation* 6(3):544–558, 1994.

[233] Lang, K.J., and M.J. Witbrock. Learning to tell two spirals apart. In D. Touretzky, G. Hinton, and T. Sejnowski, editors, *Proceedings of the 1988 Connectionist Models Summer School*, pp. 52–59. Morgan Kaufmann, San Mateo, 1989.

[234] Lapedes, A., and R. Farber. How neural nets work. In D. Anderson, editor, *Neural Information Processing Systems (Denver 1987)*, pp. 442–456. American Institute of Physics, New York, 1988.

[235] Lari-Najafi, H., M. Nasiruddin, and T. Samad. Effect of initial weights on back-propagation and its variations. In *IEEE International Conference on Systems, Man, and Cybernetics*, vol. 1, pp. 218–219. IEEE, New York, 1989.

[236] Le Cun, Y. Generalization and network design strategies. Technical Report CRG-TR-89-4, University of Toronto, Department of Computer Science, 1989.

[237] Lee, J., and Z. Bien. Improvement of function approximation capability of backpropagation neural networks. In *Proceedings of the International Joint Conference on Neural Networks (Singapore)*, vol. 2, pp. 1367–1372. IEEE, New York, 1991.

[238] Lee, J.S.-J., J.-N. Hwang, D.T. Davis, and A.C. Nelson. Integration of neural networks and decision tree classifiers for automated cytology screening. In *Proceedings of the International Joint Conference on Neural Networks (Seattle)*, vol. 1, pp. 257–262. IEEE, New York, 1991.

[239] Lee, Y., and R.P. Lippmann. Practical characteristics of neural network and conventional pattern classifiers on artificial and speech problems. In *Advances in Neural Information Processing Systems* (2), pp. 168–177. Morgan Kaufmann, San Mateo, 1990.

[240] Lee, Y., S.-H. Oh, and M.W. Kim. The effect of initial weights on premature saturation in back-propagation learning. In *Proceedings of the International Joint Conference on Neural Networks (Seattle)*, vol. 1, pp. 765–770. IEEE, New York, 1991.

[241] Lee, Y., S.-H. Oh, and M.W. Kim. An analysis of premature saturation in back propagation learning. *Neural Networks* 6(5):719–728, 1993.

[242] Levin, A.U., T.K. Leen, and J.E. Moody. Fast pruning using principal components. In J.D. Cowan, G. Tesauro, and J. Alspector, editors, *Advances in Neural Information Processing Systems* (6), pp. 35–42. Morgan Kaufmann, San Mateo, 1994.

[243] Levin, E., N. Tishby, and S.A. Solla. A statistical approach to learning and generalization in layered neural networks. *Proceedings of the IEEE* 78(10):1568–1574, Oct. 1990.

[244] Lin, J.-N., and R. Unbehauen. On the realization of a Kolmogorov network. *Neural Computation* 5(1):18–20, 1993.

[245] Lincoln, W.P., and J. Skrzypek. Synergy of clustering multiple backpropagation networks. In D.S. Touretzky, editor, *Advances in Neural Information Processing Systems (Denver, 1989)* (2), pp. 650–657. Morgan Kaufmann, San Mateo, 1990.

[246] Linden, A., and J. Kindermann. Inversion of multilayer nets. In *Proceedings of the International Joint Conference on Neural Networks (Washington D.C.)*, vol. 2, pp. 425–430. IEEE, New York, 1989.

[247] Lippmann, R.P. An introduction to computing with neural nets. *ASSP Magazine*, pp. 4–22. April 1987.

[248] Littmann, E., and H. Ritter. Cascade network architectures. In *Proceedings of the International Joint Conference on Neural Networks (Baltimore)*, pp. 398–404. IEEE, New York, 1992.

[249] Lui, H.C. Analysis of decision contour of neural network with sigmoidal nonlinearity. In *Proceedings of the International Joint Conference on Neural Networks (Washington, D.C.)*, pp. 655–658. IEEE, New York, 1990.

[250] Maass, W., G. Schnitger, and E.D. Sontag. On the computational power of sigmoid versus boolean threshold circuits. In *Proceedings of the 32nd Annual Symp. on Foundations of Computer Science*, pp. 767–776. IEEE Computer Society Press, Los Alamitos, CA, 1991.

[251] MacKay, D.J.C. Bayesian interpolation. *Neural Computation* 4(3):415–447, 1992.

[252] MacKay, D.J.C. The evidence framework applied to classification networks. *Neural Computation* 4(5):720–736, 1992.

[253] MacKay, D.J.C. A practical Bayesian framework for backpropagation networks. *Neural Computation* 4(3):448–472, 1992.

[254] Makhoul, J. Pattern recognition properties of neural networks. In B.H. Juang, S.Y. Kung, and C.A. Kamm, editors, *Neural Networks for Signal Processing: Proceedings of the 1991 IEEE Workshop*, pp. 173–187. IEEE Press, New York, 1991.

[255] Makhoul, J., A. El-Jaroudi, and R. Schwartz. Formation of disconnected decision regions with a single hidden layer. In *Proceedings of the International Joint Conference on Neural Networks (Washington D.C.)*, vol. 1, pp. 455–460. IEEE, New York, 1989.

[256] Marchand, M., M. Golea, and P. Ruján. A convergence theorem for sequential learning in two-layer perceptrons. *Europhysics Letters* 11(6):487–492, 1990.

[257] Marks, R.J., II. *Introduction to Shannon Sampling and Interpolation Theory*. Springer-Verlag, New York, 1991.

[258] Masters, T., editor. *Advanced Algorithms for Neural Networks, A C++ Sourcebook*. Wiley, New York, 1995.

[259] Matsuoka, K. An approach to generalization problem in back-propagation learning. In *International Neural Network Conference (Paris)*, 2:765–768, 1990.

[260] Matsuoka, K. Noise injection into inputs in back-propagation learning. *IEEE Transactions on Systems, Man, and Cybernetics* 22(3):436–440, 1992.

[261] McClelland, J.L., and D.E. Rumelhart. Training hidden units: The generalized delta rule. In *Explorations in Parallel Distributed Processing: A Handbook of Models, Programs, and Exercises*, pp. 121–160. MIT Press, Cambridge, 1988.

[262] McInerney, J.M., K.G. Haines, S. Biafore, and R. Hecht-Nielsen. Can back propagation error surfaces have non-global minima? Technical report, Department of Electrical and Computer Engineering, University of California at San Diego, August 1988.

[263] McInerney, J.M., K.G. Haines, S. Biafore, and R. Hecht-Nielsen. kack propagation error surfaces can have local minima. In *Proceedings of the International Joint Conference on Neural Networks (Washington, D.C.)*, vol. 3, pp. 627, 1989 (abstract).

[264] Metropolis, N., A.W. Rosenbluth, M.N. Rosenbluth, A.H. Teller, and E. Teller. Equations of state calculations by fast computing machines. *Journal of Chemistry and Physics* 21:1087–1091, 1953.

[265] Mézard, M., and J.-P. Nadal. Learning in feedforward layered networks: The tiling algorithm. *Journal of Physics A* 22:2191–2203, 1989.

[266] Minai, A.A., and R.D. Williams. Acceleration of back-propagation through learning rate and momentum adaptation. In *Proceedings of the International Joint Conference on Neural Networks (Washington, D.C.)*, vol. 1, pp. 676–679. IEEE, New York, 1990.

[267] Minnix, J.I. Fault tolerance of the backpropagation neural network trained on noisy inputs. In *Proceedings of the International Joint Conference on Neural Networks (Baltimore)*, vol. 1, pp. 847–852. IEEE, New York, 1992.

[268] Minsky, M., and S. Papert. *Perceptrons, Expanded Edition*. MIT Press, Cambridge, 1988.

[269] Mitchison, G.J., and R.M. Durbin. Bounds on the learning capacity of some multi-layer networks. *Biological Cybernetics* 60:345–356, 1989.

[270] Moller, M.F. A scaled conjugate gradient algorithm for fast supervised learning. *Neural Networks* 6(4):525–533, 1993.

[271] Moody, J., and C. Darken. Learning with localized receptive fields. In *Proceedings of the 1988 Connectionist Models Summer School*, pp. 133–143. Morgan Kaufmann, San Mateo, 1988.

[272] Moody, J., and C. Darken. Fast learning in networks of locally-tuned processing units. *Neural Computation* 1:281–294, 1989.

[273] Moody, J.E. The effective number of parameters: An analysis of generalization and regularization in nonlinear learning systems. In J.E. Moody, S.J. Hanson, and R.P. Lippmann, editors, *Advances in Neural Information Processing Systems* (4), pp. 847–854. Morgan Kaufmann, San Mateo, 1992.

[274] Moore, B. Theory of networks for learning. In *SPIE* Vol. 1294, *Applications of Artificial Neural Networks*, pp. 22–30. Society of Photo-Optical Instrumentation Engineers, Bellingham, WA, 1990.

[275] Mozer, M.C., and P. Smolensky. Skeletonization: A technique for trimming the fat from a network via relevance assessment. In D.S. Touretzky, editor, *Advances in Neural Information Processing Systems (Denver, 1988)* (1), pp. 107–115. Morgan Kaufmann, San Mateo, 1989.

[276] Mukhopadhyay, S., A. Roy, L.S. Kim, and S. Govil. A polynomial time algorithm for generating neural networks for pattern classification: Its stability properties and some test results. *Neural Computation* 5(2):317–330, 1993.

[277] Müller, B., and J. Reinhardt. *Neural Networks, An Introduction*. Springer-Verlag, Berlin, 1990.

[278] Muroga, S. *Threshold logic and its Applications*. Wiley, New York, 1971.

[279] Murphy, O.J. Nearest neighbor pattern classification perceptrons. *Proceedings of the IEEE* 78(10):1595–1598, 1990.

[280] Murphy, O.J. An information theoretic design and training algorithm for neural networks. *IEEE Transaction on Circuits and Systems* 38(12):1542–1547, 1991.

[281] Musavi, M.T., K.H. Chan, D.M. Hummels, and K. Kalantri. On the generalization ability of neural network classifiers. *IEEE Transactions on Pattern Analysis and Machine Intelligence* 16(6):659–663, 1994.

[282] Natarajan, B.K. *Machine Learning, A Theoretical Approach*. Morgan Kaufmann, San Mateo, 1991.

[283] Nguyen, D.H., and B. Widrow. Improving the learning speed of 2-layer neural networks by choosing initial values of the adaptive weights. In *Proceedings of the International Joint Conference on Neural Networks (San Diego)*, vol. 3, pp. 211–226. IEEE, New York, 1990.

[284] Nilsson, N.J. *The Mathematical Foundations of Learning Machines*. Morgan-Kaufmann, San Mateo, 1990 (reprint).

[285] Nowlan, S.J., and G.E. Hinton. Adaptive soft weight tying using Gaussian mixtures. In J.E. Moody, S.J. Hanson, and R.P. Lippmann, editors, *Advances in Neural Information Processing Systems* (4), pp. 993–1000. Morgan Kaufmann, San Mateo, 1992.

[286] Nowlan, S.J., and G.E. Hinton. Simplifying neural networks by soft weight-sharing. *Neural Computation* 4(4):473–493, 1992.

[287] Oh, S., R.J. Marks, II, and M.A. El-Sharkawi. Query based learning in a multilayered perceptron in the presence of data jitter. In M.A. El-Sharkawi and R.J. Marks, II, editors, *Applications of Neural Networks to Power Systems (Seattle)* pp. 72–75. IEEE Press, New York, 1991.

[288] Oja, E. Neural networks, principal components, and subspaces. *International Journal of Neural Systems* 1(1):61–68, 1089.

[289] Oja, E. A simplified neuron model as a principal component analyzer. *Journal of Mathematical Biology* 15:267–273, 1982.

[290] Oja, E., and J. Karhunen. On stochastic approximation of the eigenvectors and eigenvalues of the expectation of a random matrix. *Journal of Mathematical Analysis and Applications* 106:69–84, 1985.

[291] Okada, H., et al. Initializing multilayer neural networks with fuzzy logic. In *Proceedings of the International Joint Conference on Neural Networks (Baltimore)*, vol. 1, pp. 239–244. IEEE, New York, 1992.

[292] Oppenheim, A.V., A.S. Willsky, and I.T. Young. *Signals and Systems*. Prentice-Hall, Englewood Cliffs, NJ, 1983.

[293] Pados, D.A., and P. Papantoni-Kazakos. A note on the estimation of the generalization error and the prevention of overfitting. In *IEEE International Conference on Neural Networks (Orlando)*, vol. 1, pp. 321–325. IEEE, New York, 1994.

[294] Palubinskas, G. Data-driven weight initialization of back-propagation for pattern recognition. In *Proceedings of the International Conferance on Artificial Neural Networks (ICANN'94)*, pp. 851–854. Springer-Verlag, London, 1994.

[295] Parker, D.B. Learning logic. *Technical Report* TR-47. Center for Computational Research in Economics and Management Science, Massachusetts Institute of Technology, Cambridge, 1985.

[296] Parker, D.B. Optimal algorithms for adaptive networks: Second-order back propagation, second-order direct propagation, and second-order Hebbian learning. In *Proceedings of the IEEE First International Conference on Neural Networks (San Diego)*, vol. 2, pp. 593–600. IEEE, New York, 1987.

[297] Pearlmutter, B.A. Fast exact multiplication by the Hessian. *Neural Computation* 6(1):147–160, 1994.

[298] Pearlmutter, B.A., and R. Rosenfeld. Chaitin-Kolmogorov complexity and generalization in neural networks. In R. Lippmann, J. Moody, and D. Touretzky, editors, *Advances in Neural Information Processing Systems (3)*, pp. 925–931. Morgan Kaufmann, San Mateo, 1991.

[299] Plaut, D.C., S.J. Nowlan, and G.E. Hinton. Experiments on learning by back propagation. *Technical Report* CMU-CS-86-126, Carnegie-Mellon University, Pittsburgh, 1986.

[300] Poggio, T., and F. Girosi. Networks for approximation and learning. *Proceedings of the IEEE* 78(9):1481–1497, Sept. 1990.

[301] Poston, T., C.-N. Lee, Y. Choie, and Y. Kwon. Local minima and back propagtion. In *Proceedings of the International Joint Conference on Neural Networks (Seattle)*, vol. 2, pp. 173–176. IEEE, New York, 1991.

[302] Press, W.H., B.P. Flannery, S.A. Teukolsky, and W.T. Vetterling. *Numerical Recipes in C*. Cambridge University Press, Cambridge, 1988.

[303] Raudys, S., and M. Skurikhina. The role of the number of training samples on weight initialization of artificial neural net classifier. In *RNNS/IEEE Symposium on Neuroinformatics and Neurocomputing (Rostov-on-Don, Russia)*, pp. 343–353. IEEE Press, New York, 1992.

[304] Rechenberg, I. Artificial evolution and artificial intelligence. In R. Forsyth, editor, *Machine Learning, Principles and Techniques*, pp. 83–103. Chapman and Hall Computing, New York, 1989.

[305] Reed, R., R.J. Marks, II, and S. Oh. An equivalence between sigmoidal gain scaling and training with noisy (jittered) input data. In *RNNS/IEEE Symposium on Neuroinformatics and Neurocomputing (Rostov-on-Don, Russia)*, pp. 120–127. IEEE Press, New York, 1992.

[306] Reed, R., R.J. Marks, II, and S. Oh. Similarities of error regularization, sigmoid gain scaling, target smoothing, and training with jitter. *IEEE Transactions on Neural Networks* 6(3):529–538, May 1995.

[307] Reed, R., S. Oh, and R.J. Marks, II. Regularization using jittered training data. In *Proceedings of the International Joint Conference on Neural Networks (Baltimore)*, vol. 3, pp. 147–152. IEEE, New York, 1992.

[308] Reed, R.D. Pruning algorithms—a survey. *IEEE Transactions on Neural Networks*, 4(5):740–744, 1993.

[309] Reed, R.D., J.E. Sanders, and R.J. Marks, II. Neural network aided prosthetic alignment. In *1995 IEEE International Conference on Systems, Man, and Cybernetics, Vancouver, British Columbia, Oct. 1995*, vol. 1, pp. 505–508, IEEE, New York, 1995.

[310] Refregier, Ph. and J.-M. Vignolle. An improved version of the pseudo-inverse solution for classification and neural networks. *Europhysics Letters* 10(4):387–392, 1989.

[311] Reklaitis, G.V., A. Ravindran, and K.M. Ragsdell. *Engineering Optimization, Methods and Applications*. Wiley, 1983.

[312] Rezgui, A., and Nazif Tepedelenlioglu. The effect of the slope of the activation function on the back propagation algorithm. In *Proceedings of the International Joint Conference on Neural Networks (Washington D.C.)*, vol. 1, pp. 707–710. IEEE, New York, 1990.

[313] Ricotti, L.P., S. Ragazzini, and G. Martinelli. Learning of word stress in a sub-optimal second order back-propagation neural network. In *Proceedings of the IEEE International Conference on Neural Networks (San Diego)*, vol. 1, pp. 355–361. IEEE, New York, 1988.

[314] Riedmiller, M. Advanced supervised learning in multi-layer perceptrons—from backpropagation to adaptive learning algorithms. *Computer Standards & Interfaces* 16, 1994.

[315] Riedmiller, M., and H. Braun. A direct adaptive method for faster backpropagation learning: The RPROP algorithm. In *IEEE International Conference on Neural Networks (San Francisco)*, vol. 1, pp. 586–591. IEEE, New York, 1993.

[316] Rigler, A.K., J.M. Irvine, and T.P. Vogl. Rescaling of variables in back propagation learning. *Neural Networks* 4(2):225–229, 1991.

[317] Ripley, B.D. *Pattern Recognition and Neural Networks*. Cambridge University Press, Cambridge, 1996.

[318] Robbins, H., and S. Monro. A stochastic optimization method. *Annals of Mathematical Statistics*, 22:400–407, 1951.

[319] Rogers, D. Predicting weather using a genetic memory: a combination of Kanerva's sparse distributed memory with Holland's genetic algorithms. In D.S. Touretzky, editor, *Advances in Neural Information Processing Systems* (2), pp. 455–464. Morgan Kaufmann, San Mateo, 1989.

[320] Rohwer, R. Time trials on second-order and variable-learning-rate algorithms. In *Advances in Neural Information Processing Systems* (3), pp. 977–983. Morgan Kaufmann, San Mateo, 1991.

[321] Rojas, R. Optimal weight initialization for neural networks. In *Proceedings of the International Conference on Artificial Neural Networks (ICANN'94)*, pp. 577–580. Springer-Verlag, London, 1994.

[322] Romaniuk, S.G., and L.O. Hall. Dynamic neural networks with the use of divide and conquer. In *Proceedings of the International Joint Conference on Neural Networks (Baltimore)*, vol. 1, pp. 658–663. IEEE, New York, 1992.

[323] Röscheisen, M., R. Hofmann, and V. Tresp. Neural control for rolling mills: Incorporating domain theories to overcome data deficiency. In J.E. Moody, S.J. Hanson, and R.P. Lippmann, editors, *Advances in Neural Information Processing Systems* (4), pp. 659–666. Morgan Kaufmann, San Mateo, 1992.

[324] Rosenblatt, F. The perceptron: a probabilistic model for information storage and organization in the brain. *Psychological Review* 65:386–408, 1958 (reprinted in J.A. Anderson and E. Rosenfeld, editors, *Neurocomputing*. MIT Press, Cambridge, 1988).

[325] Rosenblatt, F., editor. *Principles of Neurodynamics*. Spartan Books, Washington, D.C., 1962.

[326] Roy, S., and J.J. Shynk. Analysis of the momentum LMS algorithm. *IEEE Transactions on Acoustics, Speech, and Signal Processsing* 38:2088–2098, 1990.

[327] Ruderman, D.L., and W. Bialek. Seeing beyond the Nyquist limit. *Neural Computation* 4(5):682–690, 1992.

[328] Rumelhart, D.E., R. Durbin, R. Golden, and Y. Chauvin. Backpropagation: The basic theory. In Y. Chauvin and D.E. Rumelhart, editors, *Backpropagation: Theory, Architectures, and Applications*, chapter 1. Erlbaum, Hillsdale, NJ, 1994.

[329] Rumelhart, D.E., G.E. Hinton, and R.J. Williams. Learning internal representations by back-propagating errors. *Nature* 323:533–536, 1986 (reprinted in J.A. Anderson and E. Rosenfeld, editors, *Neurocomputing*. MIT Press, Cambridge, 1988).

[330] Rumelhart, D.E., G.E. Hinton, and R.J. Williams. Learning internal representations by error propagation. In D.E. Rumelhart and J.L. McClelland, editors, *Parallel Distributed Processing*, Vol. I, chapter 8. MIT Press, Cambridge, 1986 (reprinted in J.A. Anderson and E. Rosenfeld, editors, *Neurocomputing*. MIT Press, Cambridge, 1988).

[331] Saarinen, S., R. Bramley, and G. Cybenko. Ill-conditioning in neural network training problems. *SIAM Journal of Scientific Computing* 14(3):693–714, 1993.

[332] Samad, T. Backpropagation improvements based on heuristic arguments. In *Proceedings of the International Joint Conference on Neural Networks (Washington D.C.)*, vol. 1, pp. 565–568. IEEE, New York, 1990.

[333] Sanger, T.D. Optimal unsupervised learning in a single-layer linear feedforward neural network. *Neural Networks* 2(6):459–473, 1989.

[334] Sanger, T.D. An optimality principle for unsupervised learning. In D.S. Touretzky, editor, *Advances in Neural Information Processing Systems* (1), pp. 11–19. Morgan Kaufmann, San Mateo, 1989.

[335] Sankar, A., and R.J. Mammone. Optimal pruning of neural tree networks for improved generalization. In *Proceedings of the International Joint Conference on Neural Networks (Seattle)*, vol. 2, pp. 219–224. IEEE, New York, 1991.

[336] Schreibman, D.V., and E.M. Norris. Speeding up back propagation by gradient correlation. In *Proceedings of the International Joint Conference on Neural Networks (Washington, D.C.)*, vol. 1, pp. 723–726. IEEE, New York, 1990.

[337] Schwartz, D.B., V.K. Samalan, S.A. Solla, and J.S. Denker. Exhaustive learning. *Neural Computation* 2(3):374–385, 1990.

[338] Segee, B.E., and M.J. Carter. Fault tolerance of pruned multilayer networks. In *Proceedings of the International Joint Conference on Neural Networks (Seattle)*, vol. 2, pp. 447–452. IEEE, New York, 1991.

[339] Séquin, C.H., and R.D. Clay. Fault tolerance in feed-forward artificial neural networks. In Paolo Antognetti and Veljko Milutinović, editors, *Neural Networks: Concepts, Applications, and Implementations*, vol. 4, pp. 111–141. Prentice–Hall, Englewood Cliffs, NJ, 1991.

[340] Sethi, I.K. Entropy nets: From decision trees to neural networks. *Proceedings of the IEEE* 78(10):1605–1613, Oct. 1990.

[341] Shanno, D.F. Recent advances in numerical techniques for large scale optimization. In W.T. Miller, III, R.S. Sutton, and P.J. Werbos, editors, *Neural Networks for Control*, pp. 171–178. MIT Press, Cambridge, 1990.

[342] Shavlik, J.W. A framework for combining symbolic and neural learning. In V. Honavar and L. Uhr, editors, *Artificial Intelligence and Neural Networks: Steps Toward Principled Integration*, pp. 561–580. Academic Press, New York, 1994.

[343] Shynk, J.J., and S. Roy. The LMS algorithm with momentum updating. In *Proceedings of the IEEE International Symposium on Circuits and Systems*, pp. 2651–2654. IEEE, New York, 1988.

[344] Sietsma, J., and R.J.F. Dow. Neural net pruning—why and how. In *Proceedings of the IEEE International Conference on Neural Networks (San Diego)*, vol. 1, pp. 325–333. IEEE, New York, 1988.

[345] Sietsma, J., and R.J.F. Dow. Creating artificial neural networks that generalize. *Neural Networks* 4(1):67–79, 1991.

[346] Silva, F.M., and L.B. Almeida. Acceleration techniques for the backpropagation algorithm. In L.B. Almeida and C.J. Wellekens, editors, *Neural Networks, Proceedings EURASIP Workshop*, vol. 412 of *Lecture Notes in Computer Science*, pp. 110–119. Springer-Verlag, New York, 1990.

[347] Siu, K.-Y., V. Roychowdhury, and T. Kailath. *Discrete Neural Computation, A Theoretical Foundation*. Prentice-Hall, Englewood Cliffs, NJ, 1995.

[348] Siu, K.-Y., V.P. Roychowdhury, and T. Kailath. Depth-size tradeoffs for neural computation. *IEEE Transactions on Computers* 40(12):1402–1412, 1991.

[349] Smyth, S.G. Designing multi layer perceptrons from nearest neighbor systems. *IEEE Transactions on Neural Networks* 3(2):329–333, 1992.

[350] Sontag, E.D. Feedback stabilization using two-hidden-layer nets. *Technical Report* SYCON-90-11, Rutgers Center for Systems and Control, Princeton, NJ, 1990.

[351] Sontag, E.D. Feedback stabilization using two-hidden-layer nets. *IEEE Transactions on Neural Networks* 3(6):981–990, 1992.

[352] Sontag, E.D., and H.J. Sussmann. Backpropagation can give rise to spurious local minima even for networks without hidden layers. *Complex Systems* 3:91–106, 1989.

[353] Sontag, E.D., and H.J. Sussmann. Backpropagation separates when perceptrons do. In *Proceedings of the International Joint Conference on Neural Networks (Washington, D.C.)*, vol. 1, pp. 639–642. IEEE Press, New York, 1989.

[354] Sperduti, A., and A. Starita. Speed up learning and network optimization with extended back propagation. *Neural Networks* 6(3):365–383, 1993.

[355] Sprecher, D.A. On the structure of continuous functions of several variables. *Transactions of the American Mathematical Society* 115(3):340–355, 1965.

[356] Sprecher, D.A. A universal mapping for Kolmogorov's superposition theorem. *Neural Networks* 6(8):1089–1094, 1993.

[357] Stevenson, M., R. Winter, and B. Widrow. Sensitivity of feedforward neural networks to weight errors. *IEEE Transactions on Neural Networks* 1(1):71–80, 1990.

[358] Stinchcombe, M., and H. White. Universal approximation using feedforward networks with non-sigmoid hidden layer activation functions. In *Proceedings of the International Joint Conference on Neural Networks (Washington D.C.)*, vol. 1, pp. 613–617. IEEE, New York, 1989 (reprinted in [395]).

[359] Stone, G.O. An analysis of the delta rule and the learning of statistical associations. In D.E. Rumelhart and J.L. McClelland, editors, *Parallel Distributed Processing*, vol. I, chapter 11. MIT Press, Cambridge, 1986.

[360] Stone, J.V., and R. Lister. On the relative time complexities of standard and conjugate gradient back propagation. In *IEEE International Conference on Neural Networks (Orlando)*, vol. 1, pp. 84–87. IEEE, New York, 1994.

[361] Suddarth, S.C. *The Symbolic-Neural Method For Creating Models and Control Behaviors From Examples*. Ph.D. thesis, University of Washington, Seattle, 1988.

[362] Sussmann, H.J. Uniqueness of the weights for minimal feedforward nets with a given input-output map. *Neural Networks* 5(4):589–593, 1992.

[363] Sutton, R.S. Two problems with backpropagation and other steepest-descent learning procedures for networks. In *Proceedings of the 8th Annual Conference of the Cognitive Science Society*, pp. 823–831. Erlbaum, Hillsdale, NJ, 1986.

[364] Sutton, R.S. Learning to predict by the methods of temporal differences. *Machine Learning* 3:9–44, 1988.

[365] Svarer, C., L.K. Hansen, and J. Larsen. On design and evaluation of tapped-delay neural network architectures. In *IEEE International Conference on Neural Networks (San Francisco)*, pp. 977–984. IEEE, New York, 1993.

[366] Tawel, R. Does the neuron "learn" like the synapse. In *Advances in Neural Information Processing Systems* (1), pp. 169–176. Morgan Kaufmann, San Mateo, 1989.

[367] Tesauro, G., and B. Janssens. Scaling relationships in back-propagation learning. *Complex Systems* 2:39–44, 1988.

[368] Thimm, G., and E. Fiesler. Neural network initialization. In *International Workshop on Artificial Neural Networks, Malaga-Torremolinos, Spain, June 1995*, pp. 535–542. Springer-Verlag, New York, 1995.

[369] Thimm, G., P. Moerland, and E. Fiesler. The interchangeability of learning rate and gain in backpropagation neural networks. *Neural Computation* 8(2):451–460, 1996.

[370] Tikhonov, A.N., and V.Y. Arsenin. *Solutions of Ill-Posed Problems*. V.H. Winston & Sons, Washington D.C., 1977.

[371] Tishby, N., E. Levin, and S.A. Solla. Consistent inference of probabilities in layered networks: Predictions and generalization. In *Proceedings of the International Joint Conference on Neural Networks (Washington, D.C.)*, vol. 2, p. 403. IEEE, New York, 1989.

[372] Tollenaere, T. SuperSAB: Fast adaptive back propagation with good scaling properties. *Neural Networks* 3(5):561–573, 1990.

[373] Toms, D.J. Training binary node feedforward neural networks by backpropagation of error. *IEE Electronic Letters* 26(21):1745–1746, 1990.

[374] Towell, G. G., and J.W. Shavlik. Interpretation of artificial neural networks: Mapping knowledge-based neural networks into rules. In J.E. Moody, S.J. Hanson, and R.P. Lippmann, editors, *Advances in Neural Information Processing Systems* (4), pp. 977–984. Morgan Kaufmann, San Mateo, 1992.

[375] Towell, G.G., and J.W. Shavlik. Using knowledge-based neural networks to refine roughly-correct information. In S.J. Hanson, T. Petsche, M. Kearns, and R.L. Rivest, editors, *Computational Learning Theory and Natural Learning Systems, Vol. 2, Intersections between Theory and Experiment*, pp. 65–80. MIT Press, Cambridge, 1994.

[376] Valiant, L.G. A theory of the learnable. *Communications of the ACM* 27(11):1134–1142, 1984.

[377] van der Smagt, P.P. Minimization methods for training feedforward neural networks. *Neural Networks* 7(1):1–11, 1994.

[378] Vapnik, V. Principles of risk minimization for learning theory. In J.E. Moody, S.J. Hanson, and R.P. Lippmann, editors, *Advances in Neural Information Processing Systems* (4), pp. 831–838. Morgan Kaufmann, San Mateo, 1992.

[379] Vapnik, V.N., and A. Chervonenkis. On the uniform convergence of relative frequencies of events to their probabilities. *Theory of Probability and Its Applications* 16:264–280, 1971.

[380] Vogl, T.P., J.K. Mangis, A.K. Rigler, W.T. Zink, and D.L. Alkon. Accelerating the convergence of the back-propagation method. *Biological Cybernetics* 59:257–263, 1988.

[381] Wang, J.H., T.F. Krile, and J.F. Walkup. Reduction of interconnection weights in higher order associative memory networks. In *Proceedings of the International Joint Conference on Neural Networks (Seattle)*, vol. 2, pp. 177–182. IEEE, New York, 1991.

[382] Wasserman, P.D. Experiments in translating chinese characters using backpropagation. In *Proceedings of IEEE Computer Society Conference*, pp. 399–402, February 1988.

[383] Watrous, R.L. Learning algorithms for connectionist networks: Applied gradient methods of nonlinear optimization. In *Proceedings of the IEEE First International Conference on Neural Networks (San Diego)*, vol. 2, pp. 619–627. IEEE, New York, 1987.

[384] Webb, A.R. Functional approximation by feed-forward networks: A least-squares approach to generalization. *R.S.R.E. Memorandum* 4453, R.S.R.E., Malvern, U.K., 1991.

[385] Webb, A.R., and D. Lowe. The optimized internal representation of multilayer classifier networks performs nonlinear discriminant analysis. *Neural Networks* 3(4):367–375, 1990.

[386] Weigend, A.S., D.E. Rumelhart, and B.A. Huberman. Back-propagation, weight-elimination and time series prediction. In D. Touretzky, J. Elman, T. Sejnowski, and G. Hinton, editors, *Proceedings of the 1990 Connectionist Models Summer School*, pp. 105–116. Morgan Kaufmann, San Mateo, 1991.

[387] Weigend, A.S., D.E. Rumelhart, and B.A. Huberman. Generalization by weight-elimination applied to currency exchange rate prediction. In *Proceedings of the International Joint Conference on Neural Networks (Seattle)*, vol. 1, pp. 837–841. IEEE, New York, 1991.

[388] Weigend, A.S., D.E. Rumelhart, and B.A. Huberman. Generalization by weight-elimination with application to forecasting. In R. Lippmann, J. Moody, and D. Touretzky, editors, *Advances in Neural Information Processing Systems* (3), pp. 875–882. Morgan Kaufmann, San Mateo, 1991.

[389] Weiss, S.M., and C.A. Kulikowski. *Computer Systems That Learn: Classification and Prediction Methods from Statistics, Neural Nets, Machine Learning, and Expert Systems*. Morgan Kaufmann, San Mateo, 1991.

[390] Werbos, P.J. *Beyond Regression: New Tools for Prediction and Analysis in the Behavioral Sciences*. Ph.D. dissertation, Harvard University, Cambridge, 1974 (published as *The Roots of Backpropagation*, Wiley, 1994).

[391] Werbos, P.J. Backpropagation: Past and future. In *Proceedings of the IEEE International Conference on Neural Networks (San Diego)*, vol. 1, pp. 343–353. IEEE, New York, 1988.

[392] Werbos, P.J. Backpropagation and neurocontrol: A review and prospectus. In *Proceedings of the International Joint Conference on Neural Networks (Washington D.C.)*, vol. 1, pp. 209–216. IEEE, New York, 1989.

[393] Wessels, L.F.A., and E. Barnard. Avoiding false local minima by proper initialization of connections. *IEEE Transactions on Neural Networks* 3(6):899–905, 1992.

[394] White, H. Some asymptotic results for learning in single hidden layer feedforward network models. *Journal of the American Statistical Association* 84:1008–1013, 1989.

[395] White, H. *Artificial Neural Networks, Approximation and Learning Theory*. Blackwell, Cambridge, MA, 1992.

[396] Whitley, D. The GENITOR algorithm and selection pressure: Why rank-based allocation of reproductive trials is best. In *Proceedings Third International Conference on Genetic Algorithms.* (Washington D.C.), June 1990.

[397] Whitley, D., and C. Bogart. The evolution of connectivity: Pruning neural networks using genetic algorithms. In *Proceedings of the International Joint Conference on Neural Networks (San Diego)*, vol. 1, p. 134. IEEE, New York, 1990.

[398] Whitley, D., and T. Starkweather. Optimizing small neural networks using a distributed genetic algorithm. In *Proceedings of the International Joint Conference on Neural Networks (San Diego)*, vol. 1, p. 206. IEEE, New York, 1990.

[399] Widrow, B. Generalization and information storage in networks of adaline "Neurons". In M. C. Yovitz, G. T. Jacobi, and G. D. Goldstein, editors, *Self Organizing Systems 1962*, pp. 435–461. Spartan Books, Washington, D.C., 1962.

[400] Widrow, B. Pattern recognition and adaptive control. In *1964 IRE WESCON Convention Record*, pp. 269–277. IRE, 1964.

[401] Widrow, B., G.F. Groner, M.J.C. Hu, F.W. Smith, D.F. Specht, and L.R. Talbert. Practical applications for adaptive data-processing systems. In *1963 IRE WESCON Convention Record*, pp. 1–14, 1963.

[402] Widrow, B., and M.E. Hoff. Adaptive switching circuits. In *1960 IRE WESCON Convention Record*, pp. 96–104. IRE, New York, 1960 (reprinted in J.A. Anderson and E. Rosenfeld, editors, *Neurocomputing*. MIT Press, Cambridge, 1988).

[403] Widrow, B., and M.A. Lehr. 30 years of adaptive neural networks: Perceptron, madaline, and backpropagation. *Proceedings of the IEEE* 78(9):1415–1442, Sept. 1990.

[404] Widrow, B., and F.W. Smith. Pattern-recognizing control systems. In *Computer and Information Sciences (COINS) Symposium Proceedings*, pp. 288–316. Spartan Books, Washington D.C., 1963.

[405] Widrow, B., and S.D. Stearns. *Adaptive Signal Processing*. Prentice-Hall, Englewood Cliffs, NJ, 1985.

[406] Widrow, B., and R. Winter. Neural nets for adaptive filtering and adaptive pattern recognition. *Computer*, pp. 25–39, March 1988.

[407] Wieland, A., and R. Leighton. Geometric analysis of neural network capabilities. In *Proceedings of the IEEE First International Conference on Neural Networks (San Diego)*, vol. 3, pp. 385–392. IEEE, New York, 1987.

[408] Wittner, B.S., and J.S. Denker. Strategies for teaching layered networks classification tasks. In D.Z. Anderson, editor, *Proceedings of the Conference on Neural Information Processing Systems (Denver 1987)*, pp. 850–859. American Institute of Physics, New York, 1988.

[409] Wolpert, D.H. Stacked generalization. *Neural Networks* 5(2):241–259, 1992.

[410] Wynne-Jones, M. Node splitting: A constructive algorithm for feed-forward neural networks. In J. E. Moody, S. J. Hanson, and R. P. Lippmann, editors, *Advances in Neural Information Processing Systems* (4), pp. 1072–1079. Morgan Kaufmann, San Mateo, 1992.

[411] Yamada, K., H. Kami, J. Tsukumo, and T. Temma. Handwritten numeral recognition by multi-layered neural network with improved learning algorithm. In *Proceedings of the International Joint Conference on Neural Networks (Washington D.C.)*, vol. 2, pp. 259–266. IEEE, New York, 1989.

[412] Yu, X., N.K. Loh, and W.C. Miller. Training hard-limiting neurons using backpropagation algorithm by updating steepness factors. In *IEEE International Conference on Neural Networks (Orlando)*, vol. 1, pp. 526–530. IEEE, New York, 1994.

[413] Yu, X.-H. Can backpropagation error surface not have local minima? *IEEE Transactions on Neural Networks* 3(6):1019–1021, 1992.

[414] Yu, X.-H., and G.-A. Chen. On the local minima free condition of backpropagation learning. *IEEE Transactions on Neural Networks* 6(5):1300–1303, 1995.

[415] Yu, X.-H., and G.-A. Chen. Corrections to "On the local minima free condition of backpropagation learning." *IEEE Transactions on Neural Networks* 7(1):256–257, 1996.

[416] Yu, Yeong-Ho, and R.F. Simmons. Extra output biased learning. In *Proceedings of the International Joint Conference on Neural Networks (San Diego)*, vol. 2, pp. 161–166. IEEE, New York, 1990.

Index

Printed in the United States
by Baker & Taylor Publisher Services